Buddha, J
and Muhar

Buddha, Jesus and Muhammad

A Comparative Study

Paul Gwynne

WILEY Blackwell

This edition first published 2014
© 2014 John Wiley & Sons, Ltd

Registered Office
John Wiley & Sons, Ltd, The Atrium, Southern Gate, Chichester, West Sussex, PO19 8SQ, UK

Editorial Offices
350 Main Street, Malden, MA 02148-5020, USA
9600 Garsington Road, Oxford, OX4 2DQ, UK
The Atrium, Southern Gate, Chichester, West Sussex, PO19 8SQ, UK

For details of our global editorial offices, for customer services, and for information about how to apply for permission to reuse the copyright material in this book please see our website at www.wiley.com/wiley-blackwell.

The right of Paul Gwynne to be identified as the author of this work has been asserted in accordance with the UK Copyright, Designs and Patents Act 1988.

Library of Congress Cataloging-in-Publication Data applied for
Hardback ISBN: 978-1-118-46551-6
Paperback ISBN: 978-1-118-46550-9

A catalogue record for this book is available from the British Library.

Cover image: Top L–R: buddha © naphat/ Shutterstock, Christ icon © tlegend / Shutterstock, name of prophet muhammad © numbeos/iStockphoto, Middle: oriental patterns © emirsimsek/iStockphoto, floral design set © paul_june/iStockphoto, religious cross collection © Negrot/iStockphoto, Bottom: Slovakia sunset mountains © Ventura / Shutterstock
Cover design by www.simonlevyassociates.co.uk

Set in 10/12.5 pt GalliardStd by Toppan Best-set Premedia Limited
Printed in Malaysia by Ho Printing (M) Sdn Bhd

1 2014

For Noel, Colin and their families.

CONTENTS

PREFACE

Toward the end of the popular 1971 musical *Jesus Christ Superstar*, there is a song in which Judas interrogates a condemned Jesus about his personal motives and self-understanding. In the second verse Judas asks:

> Tell me what you think about your friends at the top.
> Now who d'you think besides yourself was the pick of the crop?
> Buddha was he where it's at, is he where you are?
> Could Muhammad move a mountain or was that just PR?

Lyricist Tim Rice's choice of Buddha and Muhammad as peers of Jesus "at the top" is instructive. In the popular imagination, these three are commonly seen to be the most prominent figures in religious history, and this perception is not without reason or solid grounding. In terms of hard statistics, they stand at the head of three major religious traditions, which together boast approximately 3.5 billion adherents – approximately half of the entire human race today. Moreover, it is not only about sheer numbers but also about extent in space and time. Buddhism, Christianity and Islam have been missionary movements from the very beginning and, consequently, their membership is now spread across the continents and islands of the world. They are truly global religions, having penetrated and changed thousands of local and regional cultures. In addition, the influence of Buddha, Jesus and Muhammad stretches back centuries, indeed millennia, to the times in which they lived. Countless generations of human beings have found their inspiration, shaped their behavior, and oriented their lives according to the words and deeds of these three men. Their powerful and widespread influence cuts across both geography and history. There-fore, it is no coincidence that they are often also included in more general lists (covering all domains of human enterprise and activity) of the most influential persons who have ever lived.

This book is an attempt to look at these three crucial lives, not in splendid isola-tion, but in a comparative manner. Needless to say, there already exists an enormous volume of biographical studies on Buddha, Jesus and Muhammad, dating from the earliest times to the current day. In the past century alone, hundreds of attempts have been made to revisit, reexamine and reinterpret their stories, often inspired by fresh discoveries in the fields of archaeology and ancient history or new developments in philosophy and theology. The sheer number of these biographies makes genuinely original contributions more and more difficult. Yet somewhat surprisingly, there have been very few works of an explicitly comparative nature. While the individual stories of Buddha, Jesus and Muhammad have been told and retold innumerable times, on very few occasions have they been told side-by-side. When a comparative study of the founders has been produced, invariably it involves a comparison of Jesus with either Buddha or Muhammad but rarely all three.[1] Some focus on their teachings or spirituality rather than the full life story.[2] Others are tendentious in nature, intent on demonstrating the superiority of Christianity and its founder over the main rivals.[3] Exceptions to the twofold comparison are F.H. Hilliard's 1956 book entitled *The Buddha, the Prophet and the Christ*, and the more recent publication, *Rivers of Paradise*, which featured five key religious figures: Moses, Confucius, Buddha, Jesus and Muhammad.[4] While Hilliard explicitly acknowledged his Christian bias, the *Rivers of Paradise* project was more objective, involving multiple authors from respective religious traditions. However, it was inherently restricted by its highly specific theme: namely, the extent to which each of the five figures conformed to Max Weber's definition of a "prophet". Such a dearth of literature in this area suggests that there is a serious scholarly gap that needs to be filled.

In order to achieve our aim, we have adopted a threefold approach: phenomenological, comparative and thematic. First, a phenomenological methodology will be used. Although absolute impartiality is an unrealistic ideal in any discipline, nevertheless, it is possible to set aside ideological concerns and to strive for a reasonable level of objectivity. Consequently, this book is not primarily concerned with the veracity or credibility of the claims of each founder or their religious tradition. Nor is it aimed at demonstrating the ascendancy or preeminence of one vis-à-vis the others, as was often the case in earlier forms of comparative religion. In this sense, our study is more interested in observation and description than judgment and proof. While it certainly seeks to compare the three figures in a fruitful manner, it does not seek to compare one of them "favorably" against the others. For this reason, the book may disappoint some Buddhists, Christians and Muslims who are convinced that their religious hero stands indisputably head and shoulders above the other two, and that any comparison should bear this out.

Second, the book will unpack the elements of each story within a comparative framework. In other words, the three lives are set alongside each other and that juxtaposition, by its very nature, casts different shades of light on them. This is the peculiar contribution of the comparative method. It highlights aspects that are easily taken for granted or entirely missed otherwise. It reveals both common elements and truly distinctive features. Thus, as the comparison unveils areas of similarity and difference, it simultaneously places the subject more firmly within its proper context and reinforces its undeniable uniqueness. Hopefully, this comparison will uncover hitherto unsuspected or underestimated links between Buddha, Jesus and Muhammad, but at the same time identify what makes each of them stand alone as an incomparable individual. Thus, it is important to ensure that genuine likenesses and differences are protected. It must navigate its way between the Scylla of artificial similarity and the Charybdis of utter uniqueness. As a result, this book may disappoint those whose tenet is that all religious founders are essentially the same, as well as those whose tenet is that these three have nothing in common.

Third, in order to facilitate the comparative methodology, the chapters are structured according to a series of 10 common themes. The list of these themes is far from exhaustive, since there are many other possibilities that could have been included. However, in the author's opinion, these 10 themes emerge as the most salient features of the three stories and thus they serve as a useful framework for the comparative aim of the project. The effect is that each story gradually unfolds as in a traditional biography, but this occurs in thematic blocks that cut across the three stories each time, providing an interesting and revealing cross-section. A brief summary of the main similarities and differences concerning the theme in question is then provided at the end of each chapter.

Our exploration begins with a look at the literary sources for the traditional portraits of Buddha, Jesus and Muhammad. This is given greater complexity because they all lived in the ancient past and there is a considerable gap between their death and the emergence of written biographical documents. The second chapter turns to their historical contexts. It briefly describes and compares the geographical, social, political and religious settings in which they lived. Traditions concerning their conception, birth, youth and entry into adulthood are then compared and contrasted in Chapter 3. In the following two chapters, we examine the turning point that marked the commencement of their public religious careers and the essential message that they wished to communicate to their contemporaries. Chapter 6 looks at the miraculous element in their adult life stories, tracing not only the different types of wonder said to have occurred, but also the religious context and theological significance given to these events. Chapter 7 examines the earliest group of followers, comparing their membership, backgrounds and motives as well as the guidelines and lifestyle proposed by the founder for the ordering of community life. A related theme taken up in Chapter 8 is the founder's attitude toward women in general and the various relationships they had with women in particular, including family, friends and followers. Chapter 9 explores the political dimension of their message and actions, comparing their engagement or nonengagement in the political arena as well as the ramifications that followed in each case. The final chapter examines the timing and the manner of their death, as well as the consequences and the theological meanings attached to the event. It concludes with a brief consideration of the way in which each religious tradition has developed its own definitions of the identity and status of the founder.

Most of these themes are common elements in the stories of any important religious figure but not necessarily in the same manner and to the same degree in each case. Some themes will apply in very similar ways across all three figures, thus reinforcing the genuine commonality between them. For example, the preliminary issues of sources and context are equally relevant, as are the themes of message and identity. Yet other themes will be more pertinent for one founder than for others, thus reminding us of the fundamental uniqueness of each. For example, the traditional biographies devote much more time exploring the Buddha's journey to enlightenment, the amazing political career of Muhammad and the premature, violent death of Jesus. We need to keep an eye out for such spikes on the graph, since they act as important markers of individuality.

As a comparative study of the life stories of the three subjects, one of the first questions to ask is: which story? One on hand, there is no such thing as "the" story of Buddha, Jesus or Muhammad. There are only multiple versions: canonical and noncanonical; classical and modern; sentimentally devotional and hard-nosed historical; ultraconservative and liberal; ecumenical, sectarian and secular. Like all biographies, each version is inevitably shaped and colored by the presuppositions and mindset of the biographer, whether he or she is writing in the first century or the twenty-first century. The effect is most felt in Buddhism due to its lack of a single canon – a point emphatically made by Richard Cohen in the Rivers of Paradise project.[5] On the other hand, there is a widely accepted general outline of the main events and features of each life, and this constitutes the main material for this comparative study. This general outline can be gleaned and collated from the range of contemporary scholarly biographies, which themselves rest on scriptural and traditional sources. For example, despite Cohen's misgivings, he goes on to consider the story of Siddhattha Gotama within the framework of the Ten Deeds that a Buddha must perform before entering nirvana. Thus, this book may also disappoint those who seek the so-called historical Buddha, Jesus or Muhammad behind the strata of traditional interpretations and embellishments. Such a quest is noble and worthwhile, but it is not our primary purpose. What we are comparing are the widely accepted life stories of the three persons as presented within each faith tradition and filtered through the lens of contemporary scholarship.

It is also necessary to say a brief word about the term "founder", which is being used as the collective noun to describe and gather together the three subjects. The etymological source of the term is the forging of an object from raw metal as in a foundry. It is usually applied to a person who establishes an organization or institution, especially in the context of business and commerce. Hence, a religious founder is presumed to be the one who intentionally initiates a new form of spiritual organization with its own particular purpose and structure. The danger here is that the term may not accurately describe the relationship between Buddha, Jesus and Muhammad, and the complex religious communities that arose as a result of their lives and teachings. In fact, ascertaining the degree to which each of these men truly "founded" a religion, in the tight sense of the term, is part of the task of this study. However, the term can be used in a looser sense, namely as an acknowledgement of a basic connection between the person in question and the broad religious traditions that followed. It simply refers to the claim that Buddhism, Christianity and Islam all stemmed from a single human life.

A similar note should be made about the choice of the term "Buddha" in the title of this work. The proper name of the person in question is Siddhattha Gotama and one could argue that this should be the preferred term if the focus is on the story of the individual himself rather than on theological designations. After all, "the Buddha" is a word meaning "Enlightened One", a title that tells us something about the religious status and identity of Siddhattha Gotama, just as "the Christ" and "the Prophet" are titles that tell us something about the religious status and identity of Jesus of Nazareth and Muhammad ibn 'Abdullah, respectively. However, as borne out by Tim Rice's lyrics above, "Buddha" has become the preferred means by which this particular person is denoted in the popular forum. Hence, the choice is a totally practical one, and for this work, we will use "Siddhattha" for the period of his life prior to his Enlightenment and "the Buddha" thereafter.

The earlier discussion raises a final issue concerning the anticipated readers of this book. As noted earlier, this is not an attempt to investigate further the historical Buddha, Jesus or Muhammad. Rather it is a comparative exercise aimed at tracing the spectrum of similarities and differences between the three most important religious figures in human history. Consequently, the author hopes that it will be germane to those engaged in formal or informal interfaith dialogue. In an era of globalization, it is perhaps more imperative than ever to build bridges of mutual understanding and respect between the great religious traditions, which have been all too frequently divided by prejudice, suspicion and ignorance. Similarly, this study should prove useful for students in religious studies courses, especially those with a strong comparative dimension. Finally, the book has also been written for the educated lay person who is interested in discovering a little more about these three exceptional persons and the ways in which their individual life stories both intersect and diverge.

I would like to express my profound gratitude to those academic colleagues who kindly reviewed the draft chapters: John D'Arcy May (Trinity College Dublin), Mehmet Ozalp (Charles Sturt University), Douglas Pratt (University of Waikato), Gerard Hall (Australian Catholic University) and Riaz Hassan (Flinders University). I am also indebted to the staff of Wiley Blackwell – Karen Raith, Rebecca Harkin, Georgina Coleby, Ruth Swan and Rhea Padilla – for their invaluable assistance throughout the publishing process. Finally, I would like to thank my wife, Kim Host, for her constant support throughout this project, including proofreading the manuscript.

Notes

1   See F.E. Peters (2011) *Jesus & Muhammad. Parallel Tracks. Parallel Lives*; William E. Phipps (1999) *Muhammad and Jesus: A Comparison of the Prophets and Their Teachings*; Richard Henry Drummond (1995) *A Broader Vision: Perspectives on the Buddha and the Christ*.

2   See Roy Amore (1978) *Two Masters, One Message*; Denise & John Carmody (1996) *In the Path of the Masters: Understanding the Spirituality of Buddha, Confucius, Jesus, and Muhammad*; Joey Green ed. (2002) *Jesus and Muhammad: The Parallel Sayings*; Marcus Borg & Jack Kornfield (2004) *Jesus and Buddha. The Parallel Sayings*.

3   See Mark Gabriel (2004) *Jesus and Muhammad: Profound Differences and Surprising Similarities*.

4   F.H. Hilliard (1956) *The Buddha, the Prophet and the Christ*; David Freedman & Michael McClymond eds. (2000) *The Rivers of Paradise: Moses, Buddha, Confucius, Jesus, and Muhammad as Religious Founders*.

5   Cohen 126.

NOTES

The following versions of scriptural texts have been used with permission:

Tipitaka. The Pali Canon. Access to Insight: Readings in Theravada Buddhism, ed. John Bullitt. Available online at http://www.accesstoinsight.org/tipitaka/index .html.

The Holy Bible: New Revised Standard Version with Apocrypha. New York: Oxford University Press (1991). Copyright 1989, Division of Christian Education of the National Council of the Churches of Christ in the United States of America. Used by permission. All rights reserved. Available online at http://www.devotions.net/ bible/00bible.htm.

The Holy Koran, translated by Mohammed H. Shakir. New York: Tahrike Tarsile Qur'an Inc., 1983. Available online at http://quod.lib.umich.edu/k/koran/.

Maps by Sally Host.

Foreign Terms

Diacritical marks have been avoided. Rough and smooth breathings have been included for Arabic words.

The anglicized spelling of most transliterated terms has followed *The Oxford Dictionary of World Religions* (2000, edited by John Bowker).

The Pali (rather than Sanskrit) version has been used for most Buddhist terms. See *Buddhist Dictionary of Pali Proper Names* at http://www.palikanon.com/english/ pali_names/dic_idx.html.

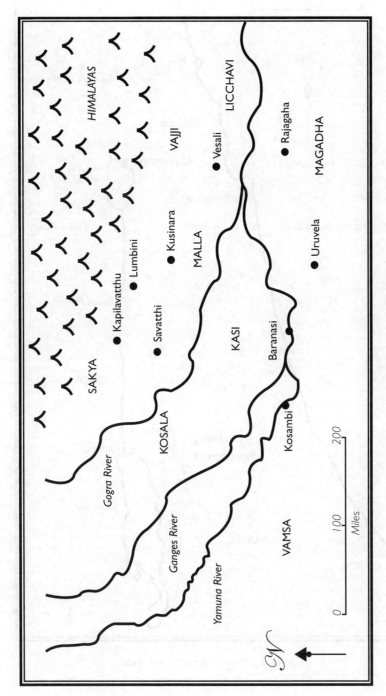

Map 1 Sixth-century BCE Northern India

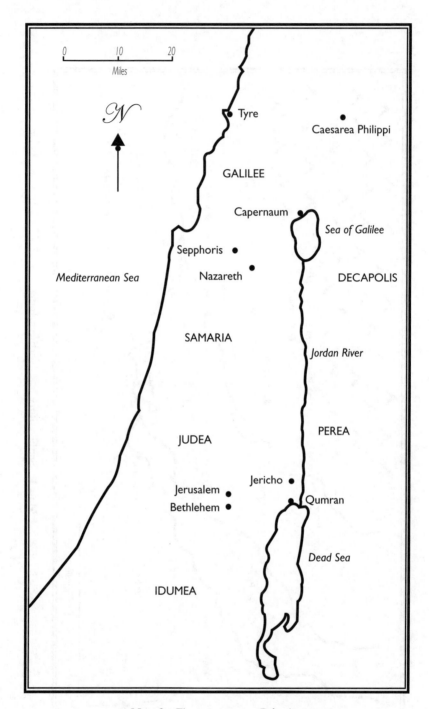

Map 2   First-century CE Palestine

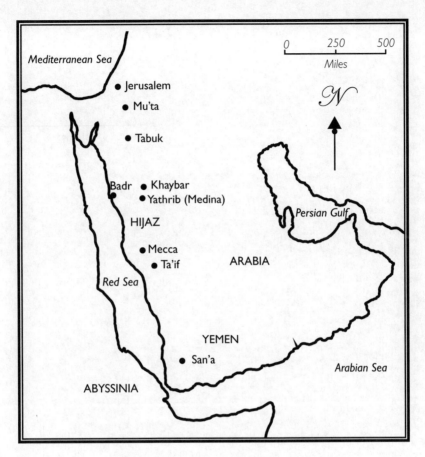

Map 3 Seventh-century CE Arabia

Chapter 1

SOURCES

We start our journey with an obvious fact, yet one that is far from trivial. It is simply this: all three founders lived and died long ago. It is approximately two and a half millennia since Siddhattha Gotama wandered the Ganges Plain and 2,000 years since Jesus first taught in Galilee, placing them both firmly in the period of classical antiquity. The most recent of the three, Muhammad, died in 632 CE, which puts him at the cusp of late antiquity and the early Middle Ages. Their lives and their worlds are separated from ours by a vast temporal gulf that renders them figures of ancient rather than modern history. There are many implications that arise from this fact but one of the most relevant is the question of information. A common problem for anyone studying ancient times is the frequent paucity of material, combined with its fragmentary nature and questions about its historical accuracy. Frequently, we just do not have much reliable data to go on, and this is the case for the three founders as well. This raises a series of initial questions. What are the key texts that have generated the standard versions of the lives of the Buddha, Jesus and Muhammad? When were they composed and by whom? To what degree are they consistent with each other? How do contemporary scholars – both inside and outside each religious tradition – assess their reliability and worth?

The Delay in Writing

The Buddha is said to have lived to be 80 years of age, and by the time of his death, his new spiritual movement had been established for over four decades, yet there is virtually no early information about him from nonreligious sources. The traditional story has been constructed almost entirely from Buddhist writings that, understandably, were written from a specifically religious viewpoint. That is not to say that these sources are bereft of historical information but the first point to acknowledge is that, for better or worse, the main sources for the life of the Buddha are texts authored

Buddha, Jesus and Muhammad: A Comparative Study, First Edition. Paul Gwynne.
© 2014 John Wiley & Sons, Ltd. Published 2014 by John Wiley & Sons, Ltd.

by persons who were his committed followers and viewed him through the lens of faith.

The second point that should be noted is the date of these texts. Even the earliest of them are separated from the Buddha by several centuries. If the first generations of Buddhists felt a strong compulsion to create a biography of the founder for posterity, then there is no convincing evidence that such a work ever existed.[1] One reason often proffered for the lack of an early written biography is the claim that the story of the Buddha is ultimately irrelevant. It is the message and not the man that matters. In fact, focusing on the man can easily distract one from the message. As the founder of the Lin-Chi tradition once summed up: "If you meet the Buddha, kill the Buddha".[2] In time, however, Buddhists began to feel the need to tell the story of the master as well as to pass on his eternal wisdom. It is as if his teaching about ultimate liberation could not be entirely divorced from his experience of seeking liberation. The Buddha's own arduous quest for escape from the enslaving wheel of rebirth was seen as a powerful demonstration of the truth of his message and a unique example of its practicality. To see the teacher was to see the teaching.[3]

Although precise dates are elusive, scholars have identified several broad phases in the gradual development of a complete written biography of the Buddha. The first of these is the oral phase. As far as we know, the Buddha and his earliest companions did not actually write anything. Theirs was a culture in which the master's doctrines were memorized and passed on orally. Accounts of the First Buddhist Council, which occurred soon after the Buddha's death, reflect the importance of this oral stage. Its main business was to establish an authentic collection of the Buddha's teachings and monastic guidelines, and it was the excellent memory of two monks that provided the material. The Buddha's cousin and personal assistant, Ananda, recited the sermons that he had witnessed firsthand, while Upali provided an account of the rules of community life that the Buddha had commended to his followers. For the next four centuries, that twofold collection of discourses and regulations was memorized and handed down from generation to generation within the monasteries of the new religious movement as it slowly expanded across Southern and Eastern Asia.

The second phase is marked by the emergence of written texts, in particular the Pali Canon, which dates back to the reign of the Sri Lankan regent Vattagamini during the first century BCE. Theravada Buddhism recognizes its contents as authoritative and definitive, thus ascribing it canonical status. These are its holiest scriptures. The Pali Canon consists of three subdivisions known as the Three Baskets (Tipitaka). The first of these is the Basket of Discipline (Vinaya Pitaka), which contains the Buddha's instructions concerning monastic life. It is believed that its many rules and regulations, which provide a comprehensive blueprint for monks and nuns, can be traced back to the contribution of Upali at the First Council. While it is primarily concerned with the ordering of the monastic community, the Vinaya Pitaka also contains snippets from the Buddha's life. Frequently, a rule or set of rules are preceded by a brief anecdote, which presents the original setting in which he delivered that particular teaching. In a similar fashion, the contents of the second basket, the Basket of Threads (Sutta Pitaka), are believed to be the sermons of the Buddha and other early disciples as recalled by Ananda at the First Council. Typically, each sermon is prefaced by Ananda's claim: "Thus on one occasion I heard the Buddha say. . ."

Like the first basket, the Sutta Pitaka focuses on doctrine rather than biography, but the sermons recorded here also contain fleeting references to episodes during the founder's life. In addition, it includes the Jataka Tales, which tell of the Buddha's previous reincarnations and his gradual spiritual progress over many lifetimes. The third basket, the Abhidhamma Pitaka (Basket of Higher Learning), is very different from the first two and is considered to be a later work. It consists of a more developed philosophical interpretation of time, mind and matter. As such, it has little or no information concerning the life of the historical Buddha.

As one of the oldest extant writings in Buddhism, the Pali Canon naturally enjoys pride of place among the many texts that provide information regarding the Buddha's story. Although scholars point out that later Chinese and Tibetan translations from older Sanskrit sources contain strands of material that possibly predate the Pali Canon, the Three Baskets remains "the single most useful source" for constructing the life of the Enlightened One.[4] However, there are still limitations concerning its biographical material. First, Pali was not the native tongue of the Buddha or his contemporaries, although it is a close cousin. Second, although the Canon claims to be the Buddha's own words, the texts often betray a typically Theravadan viewpoint.[5] Third, despite speculation about the possibility that some of the oral tradition behind the texts can be traced back to an early phase, the fact remains that the written texts are centuries removed from the Buddha. To a great extent, the best that we possess is how the Buddha's disciples viewed him 400 years after his death. Fourth, even if the original material is much older than the texts themselves, the nature of the bio-graphical information is very piecemeal. In this second phase, we may have written texts but we still do not yet have a complete and proper narrative. The bits and pieces of the Buddha's story are there as in a collage, but they primarily serve a didactic purpose, as the preface for a particular teaching or the context of a specific sermon.[6] There is no overall life story but only episodic fragments embedded in sermons to illustrate some practice.[7]

It is only in the third phase that a more complete picture of the Buddha's life is put into written form. Between the first century BCE and the second century CE, there appeared a number of important biographies, which reworked the fragmentary pieces from the oral and canonical phases into the standard story line. Eventually, Buddhism felt the need for more than just a disparate collection of the master's teachings. It required a new form of literature that traced the life journey of its founder more thoroughly, especially the key milestones along the way. One reason for this shift was the geographical expansion of the new religion across diverse national and cultural borders. The first "lives" of the Buddha were part of the overall missionary outreach, aimed at demonstrating the universal relevance of the man and his message. Another reason was the establishment of pilgrimage sites, each of which was said to be the location of an important episode in his life. The earliest three works that describe those great events in detail are the Mahavastu, the Lalitavistara and the Buddhacarita.

The Mahavastu is a product of the Lokottaravadan community, one of the earliest schools in Buddhism. Extant manuscripts are written in a hybrid form of Sanskrit and its oldest elements may stem from as early as the second century BCE. The Mahavastu is a lengthy collection of sayings and Jataka Tales, organized in a loose manner around a central biography of the Buddha. The title Mahavastu literally means "Great Event" and it refers to the birth of the Buddha in our time and space. The story is organized into three distinct stages. The first stage begins with his previous life as a bodhisattva in the age of Buddha Dipankara eons ago. The second stage begins with his penultimate reincarnation in Tusita Heaven where he meticulously plans the time, place and circumstances of his final rebirth. This section goes on to recount stories between his infancy and his Enlightenment. The third stage outlines his first seven weeks as the Buddha, the conversions of the earliest disciples and the successful visit to his hometown. Much of the material in this last section closely corresponds to the fragmentary versions found in the Pali Canon.

With the Mahavastu, Buddhism finally had a written text that focussed on the story of the founder, at least up to the institution of the monastic order. Yet invaluable as it is, the Mahavastu is not without its limitations. The work appears to lack a clear organizational structure, as if it was randomly thrown together. Furthermore, it unashamedly depicts the Buddha as a superhuman figure. He is conceived without intercourse, born painlessly and has minimal need of sleep, food or medicine. It is as if the Buddha lived on another plane of existence, scarcely affected by the suffering inherent in mundane human life. Such unabashed predilection for the miraculous naturally raises issues of plausibility in the mind of the modern reader.

A similar tendency is evident in the Lalitavistara, which consists of 27 chapters of composite literary styles. It contains a relatively continuous narrative in classical Sanskrit prose accompanied by numerous sections of verse in a more vernacular form of mixed Sanskrit. The original text was probably composed in an early Sarvastivadin environment but it has subsequently been overlaid and recast with Mahayanan material. It enjoys canonical status in the Mahayana tradition and has been widely influential across the centuries.[8] The composite nature of the work makes an estimation of its age difficult, but most contemporary scholars opt for the first century CE. The title literally means "an account of the sport (of the Buddha)". In other words, the final reincarnation of the Buddha is understood as the play (lalita) of a superior being, similar to the Hindu Puranas. The Lalitavistara begins with the splendid descent of the Buddha from Tusita Heaven into our world via his physical conception and birth. It finishes with the Buddha's first sermon to his five companions at Isipatana. Thus, its scope is very similar to the Mahavastu in that both texts terminate at the commencement of the teaching mission. They are more interested in the journey of the main subject from childhood to Buddhahood than the subsequent foundation of the monastic order and the dissemination of the message. The Lalitavistara also shares the Mahavastu's tendency to ascribe superhuman qualities to the main character.

The third of the earliest biographies is the Buddhacarita ("Acts of the Buddha") by Ashvaghosha.[9] Little is known of his personal life but it is thought that Ashvaghosha was a philosopher-poet and religious adviser in the court of Kanishka who reigned over the Kushan Empire from 127 to 151 CE. The original work was composed in Sanskrit and probably consisted of 28 cantos in which the life of the Buddha is described in some detail. Ashvaghosha's masterpiece is frequently preferred by scholars over the Mahavastu and the Lalitavistara for several reasons. First, it extends the narrative beyond the Enlightenment and first sermon, referring to a number of key events in the long missionary career of the Buddha, including his death. Second, the style of the Buddhacarita is not only elegant and lyrical, making it one of the finest examples of Buddhist literature, but it is also remarkably free of supernatural elements. In contrast to the authors of the Mahavastu and the Lalitavistara, Ashvaghosha exercised considerable restraint with regard to mythological embellishment. Third, the Buddhacarita displays greater organization of material and seems to be more faithful to the biographical fragments found in the Pali Canon. In time, a host of other biographies in various languages were produced across the full spectrum of Buddhist schools. Each is characterized by its own distinctive style and its own particular concerns. Yet there is a fundamental agreement on the general outline of the story, suggesting that most were derived from the original canonical fragments or the first generation of biographies described above.

Scientific scrutiny of the traditional sources commenced in the nineteenth century and scholars immediately faced a serious methodological difficulty.[10] The central figure of the early biographies is undoubtedly an impressive person, but on many occasions he seems hardly human. The story is so littered with miraculous occurrences that scholars understandably felt compelled to suspect, if not declare outright, that a healthy dose of legendary enhancement has been applied. The interval of several centuries between the Buddha's life and the written texts only served to reinforce the sense that the many unusual occurrences are subsequent additions by the pious authors. If many aspects are indeed later accretions, scholars began to ponder what constituted the original, historical core.

That question gave rise to two distinct approaches. The first, and most radical, approach was the claim that most, if not all, of the material in the traditional sources was mythological. Put simply, the Buddha never really existed, or if he did it was impossible to know anything about him.[11] The main proponents of this position were scholars who focused on comparative mythology, such as Rudolf Otto Franke, Emile Senart and Heinrich Kern.[12] In contrast, a second group of scholars was more hopeful that the Buddha had indeed existed and that it was possible to know something about him even though the truth lay hidden beneath many layers of fictional enhancement. The most famous academics in this group were Hermann Oldenberg and Thomas William Rhys Davids. With them the quest for the historical Buddha commenced, mirroring the same contemporary search for the historical Jesus among biblical scholars.[13] The goal of uncovering the man behind the myth sounded legitimate, but it quickly became apparent that the subjectivity of the scholars themselves had been underestimated. Personal presuppositions and prejudices were not easily put aside and the result was not the expected consensus but a frustrating variety of "historical Buddhas", each reflecting the deeper concerns and values of the historian. For example, the Buddha was variously portrayed as the founder of a rationalistic ethic, the discoverer of a scientific system of meditation, a social reformer who fought against the evils of Hinduism, a pioneer of democracy, a radical egalitarian and even an ideal Victorian gentleman.[14]

Today, Buddhist scholarship leans toward the second approach despite its problems. Most accept that the Buddha is not a totally fictional creation, arguing that a real historical person stands at the head of the Buddhist religion, which would be inexplicable otherwise.[15] Moreover, there is a growing confidence that the ancient texts, so replete with mythological elements, also contain genuine first-hand memories

of sixth-century BCE northern India. Yet most admit that the proliferation of miraculous elements in the traditional sources makes it almost impossible to reconstruct a
detailed account of the Buddha's life that would satisfy the demands of modern
history. To a real extent, the figure of the Buddha remains concealed behind the mists
of time. Perhaps nothing underscores the elusiveness of the subject more than the
lack of agreement among scholars regarding the dates of his birth and death. While
most concur that he lived to be approximately 80 years of age, there are different
calculations utilized to determine when those 80 years fall on the timeline. Depending
on the timing of the coronation of the emperor Ashoka, some argue that the Buddha's dates are 624–544 BCE, others say 570–490 BCE and a third group proposes
450–370 BCE.[16] Although most scholars now agree that the Buddha is a genuine
historical figure, the sources leave us with serious uncertainty about when he lived,
not merely in terms of the year or the decade but the century.

Gospel Portraits

In contrast to the vagueness concerning the Buddha's key dates, we are on firmer
ground in the case of Jesus, although there is still a lack of accuracy concerning the
precise year of his birth and his death. The gospel of Luke claims that Jesus was born
during the census of Quirinius, governor of Syria, which occurred in 6 or 7 CE
according to the historian Josephus. However, both Matthew and Luke indicate that
Jesus was born while Herod the Great was still alive. Given that Herod died in 4
BCE, most scholars ignore the census link and conclude that Jesus was probably born
between 6 and 4 BCE. This may sound odd given that the CE (Common Era) num-
bering is equivalent to the Christian system (Anno Domini) that supposedly begins
with the year of Jesus's birth. The explanation for the discrepancy is that Dionysius
Exiguus, the sixth-century monk who converted the Roman year numbers to the
new Christian version, made a minor miscalculation.

Pinpointing the year of Jesus's death is also somewhat frustrating. Jesus was
executed on the orders of Pontius Pilate who was prefect of Judea from 26–36 CE
and all agree it was a Friday, the day before the Sabbath. What is not clear is whether
that Friday was the preparation day for the Passover (14 Nissan), as stated in John's
gospel, or the first day of Passover (15 Nissan) as implied by the Synoptic gospels,
which describe the Last Supper on the previous evening as a Passover meal. Scholars
usually favor the former, given that activities would have been severely restricted on
the first day of a major annual festival. 14 Nissan fell on a Friday in the years 27, 30
and 33 CE. Moreover, Luke states that John the Baptist's ministry began in the "fifteenth year of the reign of the emperor Tiberius",[17] which would have been 28 or
29 CE. If that is true, then we are left with either 30 or 33 CE as the most likely year
of Jesus's death and the preference for one or the other depends on the length of
his public ministry.[18] In any event, it is clear that we have a much better idea of Jesus's
dates than those of the Buddha, but what are the main sources of information about
what happened between his birth and his death?

There are a few scant references to Jesus in secular Greco-Roman writing of the
period, but these are many decades later, typically brief and primarily concerned with

the fledgling Christian movement rather than Jesus himself. The Jewish historian Josephus mentions Jesus just twice, noting that he attracted large crowds and was crucified by Pilate.[19] The paucity of material in secular sources is echoed in Jewish writing. There are a number of references in the Talmud to a certain Yeshua, but they are all negative in tone, forming part of a later anti-Christian polemic and providing no real biographical information.[20]

Thus, the search for more detailed sources necessarily shifts to Christian writings, both canonical and noncanonical. In recent times, there has been heightened scholarly interest in early noncanonical Christian literature, particularly the apocryphal gospels, as a potential source for a more complete picture of Jesus. There are over fifty such gospels, which were not considered worthy of inclusion in the New Testament canon for a variety of reasons. Many of these are lost in the sense that we have no extant manuscripts but only indirect references to them in other writings. Others exist only in fragmentary condition. The main problem with these texts is that they date to the second century CE or later, and so are further removed from Jesus's time than the canonical gospels. Moreover, like the Buddhist Mahavastu and Lalitavistara, they abound in blatantly miraculous tales that are presumably the result of the religious imagination.[21] One apocryphal gospel, the Gospel of Thomas (not to be confused with the Infancy Gospel of Thomas), has caught the eye of scholars. It is ostensibly a product of second century Gnostic Christianity but it contains an earlier stratum of authentic sayings making it a "fifth gospel" of sorts.[22] Other Gnostic gospels have been discovered in recent times, including the Nag Hammadi library unearthed in Egypt in 1945, but all of these are late compositions.[23]

So the search for the most reliable sources necessarily narrows to the New Testament canon with its 27 books. Twenty-one of these are epistles written to specific groups of Christians, thirteen of which are associated with Paul. One might expect to find here a treasure trove of information about Jesus, but in fact the opposite is the case. Although Jesus occupies a central role in the message of the epistles, the overwhelming focus, especially in Paul, is on his death and resurrection. Even then, Paul is more interested in the theological meaning of those events rather than providing an in-depth description of what occurred. Somewhat surprisingly, Paul shows minimal interest in the period prior to Jesus's death. There is virtually no information in the Pauline corpus concerning the key events of Jesus's public ministry or his teachings, let alone his birth and childhood. If we relied solely on Paul as a source, we would know hardly anything about Jesus. For all of these reasons, most scholars admit that the most substantive biographical sources for Jesus are the canonical gospels of Matthew, Mark, Luke and John. John Meier concludes: "We are left alone – some would say forlorn – with the Four Gospels, plus scattered titbits".[24]

Although it is traditionally listed in second position among the four, Mark is generally considered to be the earliest of the canonical gospels. It is also the shortest, mainly due to its lack of an infancy narrative and the limited amount of Jesus's teachings. Mark begins his story when Jesus is already an adult and he includes only 13 parables in total, compared with more than 30 each in Matthew and Luke. Despite its brevity, Mark's style is dynamic and vivid, with one incident following the other at an almost breathless pace. The structure of the gospel is partially geographical in that Jesus commences his public ministry in Galilee, moves southward to Jerusalem, only entering Gentile territory on two occasions. The identity of the evangelists is perplexing since all four gospels are anonymous, their names only being added in the second century CE. In the case of the second gospel, tradition has identified him as the cousin of Barnabas known as John Mark, whose mother hosted Christians in her Jerusalem house and who accompanied Paul and Barnabas on their first missionary journey.[25] He is mentioned in several New Testament epistles[26] and was identified as Peter's secretary by the second century bishop Papias.[27] Many believe that the gospel was written in Rome for a Gentile Christian audience, not familiar with Jewish customs and facing persecution.[28] Most scholars have argued that it was probably composed just prior to the destruction of the Temple in 70 CE, although some prefer a date soon after that cataclysmic event. It was an unprecedented literary creation, in which Mark wove together preexisting units (pericopes) that had been transmitted orally within ecclesial settings during the 40 years since Jesus's death.

Readers of the New Testament have long noted the conspicuous similarity between the first three gospels. Matthew, Mark and Luke are so alike in content and order of events, that they are aptly described as the "Synoptic gospels". The general consensus of experts is that Matthew and Luke both borrowed extensively from Mark to create their own similar but distinctive versions of the Jesus story.[29] However, there is another interesting feature of Matthew and Luke that caught the scholarly eye. Not only have they borrowed heavily from Mark, but there is also a remarkable similarity in the material that is not from Mark. This extraordinary coincidence led to the hypothesis that a second common source was used, consisting mainly of Jesus's sayings. It was named "Q", from the German word Quelle (source), but no copy has ever been discovered.

Matthew and Luke are very different gospels, despite their common dependence on Mark and hypothetical Q. Each contains unique material from their own independent third sources. For example, both commence their gospels with a narrative about Jesus's conception and birth but, despite a common kernel, there are profound differences between the two versions. Only Matthew mentions Joseph's dream, Herod's jealousy, the magi and the escape into Egypt. Only Luke mentions the parallel with John the Baptist, Gabriel's appearance to Mary, her visit to Elizabeth, the angels' appearance to the shepherds and the presentation rite in the Temple. Yet it is not only the sources and contents of Matthew and Luke that ground their distinctiveness. The two evangelists also acted as final editors who selected, arranged and adapted Mark and Q for their own special purposes.

Matthew has always enjoyed first place in the order of gospels, reflecting not only the esteem with which it was held in the early Church but also the traditional belief that it was the first to be written and that the author was one of the Twelve. Modern scholarship has cast doubts on these presumptions, especially given that the gospel is written in Greek and not Aramaic. If Mark was composed just before or after the destruction of the Temple in 70 CE, then many scholars date Matthew to the following decade or two, around 75–90 CE. Indeed, its version of Jesus's prediction of the fall of the Temple contains details hinting that the event had already occurred when Matthew was writing.[30] There are a number of features of Matthew's gospel that indicate that his main audience were Jewish converts to Christianity. The gospel opens with a genealogy of Jesus that begins with Abraham and passes through the royal Davidic line; it cites the Hebrew Scriptures twice as frequently as Mark or Luke; it is divided into seven sections (a highly symbolic number in Judaism); and the middle five sections, each a combination of Jesus's deeds and teachings, mirror the five books of the Torah. Many scholars speculate that the gospel was composed in Antioch with its mixed community of Jewish and Gentile Christians.

If Matthew was primarily concerned with Christians of Jewish background, conversely, Luke wrote for a very different demographic. The third gospel is the largest book in the New Testament but, more importantly, it combines with the Acts of the Apostles to form an impressive two volume work by the same author. Both volumes are addressed to "most excellent Theophilus", which may refer to a Christian convert in public office. Indeed, a key theme of Luke–Acts is to demonstrate that Christianity is a legitimate religion in the Roman Empire. Luke is particularly interested in the expansion of Christianity beyond Israel and into all corners of the pagan world, including the capital, Rome. Luke's universalist thrust, combined with his lack of interest in Jewish themes and his limited knowledge of Palestinian geography and culture, has led scholars to conclude that the evangelist was writing for a predominantly non-Jewish (Gentile) audience. As to his identity, the author reveals at the very outset that he is not an eye-witness to the events of Jesus's life but rather that he received instruction from those who were.[31] Tradition has identified him as Luke, the doctor and companion of Paul mentioned in the letter to the Colossians.[32] Modern scholarship notes that the author possessed considerable literary talent given the superior quality of the Greek language used. The gospel is usually dated to about the same period as Matthew, namely 75–90 CE.

The fourth canonical gospel stands apart from the three Synoptics for a number of reasons. Although it relates the story of Jesus as they do, it is clear that John's perspective is a very different one. For one thing, the order of events in John does not correspond exactly with the Synoptic version.[33] Moreover, John describes only seven miracles ("signs"), using them as the basis for an extensive discourse by Jesus each time.[34] In these lengthy sermons, Jesus speaks more about himself than the Kingdom of God, which is the key theme in the Synoptic tradition. Consequently, Jesus's divine identity is more apparent in John; in fact, it is stated outright in the gospel's prologue, which functions like the overture to a grand symphony. Unlike Mark who starts his gospel with the adult Jesus, and unlike Matthew and Luke who commence the story with Jesus's conception and birth, John takes us back to the moment of creation itself. Jesus is identified as the unique incarnation of the divine Word (Logos) in time and space, neatly summed up in the classical verse: "And the Word became flesh and dwelt among us".[35]

Consequently, the fourth gospel is usually dated toward the end of the first century CE, although its original contents are based on the testimony of an eye-witness.[36] As with the Synoptic gospels, the author is not named, but the gospel indicates that the authority behind it is the "disciple that Jesus loved" – a member of the inner circle who leaned on Jesus's breast at the Last Supper. Second-century church fathers identified him as John, the son of Zebedee and brother of James, although this claim is debated among scholars today.[37]

John's gospel is something of an enigma for scholars in search of the earliest reliable sources for Jesus. On one hand, it is a later composition that has reworked the order of events as presented in the Synoptics, placed profound theological statements on the lips of Jesus and unequivocally portrayed him as an incarnate divine being, in some ways reminiscent of the superhuman Buddha found in the pages of the Mahavastu and Lalitavistara. On the other hand, John reveals firsthand knowledge of the geographical features of rural Palestine, the city of Jerusalem and the Temple precincts.[38] It is also intimately acquainted with cultural features, such as the Jewish religious calendar, Samaritan customs and the workings of the inner apostolic circle.[39] As a result, the fourth gospel deserves its inclusion as an important source alongside the Synoptics in the quest for Jesus.

The designation of the first four books of the New Testament as "gospels" only occurred in the second century CE. The literal meaning of gospel (Greek: evangelion) is "good news", and its original application was the oral preaching of the first Christian missionaries. A gospel is not a dispassionate, objective biography of Jesus as seen from outside Christianity. Rather, it is written with the intention of persuading the reader to embrace the Christian faith. A gospel is not just news but good news. It is meant not just to inform but to convince. As with Buddhism, the key sources for the story of Jesus are religious texts composed through the eyes of faith with the aim of winning minds and hearts. That is not to say that they are so distorted by faith that they contain no historical truth, but it does mean that the gospels cannot be read uncritically. Indeed, biblical scholarship has been looking critically at the four gospels for over 200 years in an attempt to uncover the "real" Jesus behind the layers of evangelical redaction, theological interpretation and devotional embellishment. This ambitious quest for the historical Jesus has thrown up some fascinating insights, but it has also suffered some dramatic vicissitudes.

The first author usually associated with this quest is Hermann Reimarus (1694–1768), who argued that Jesus was a failed revolutionary and that the first Christians stole his body to create the myths of resurrection and divine incarnation. The nineteenth century witnessed many similar works by authors such as Strauss, Wrede and Weiss, culminating in Albert Schweitzer's watershed 1906 publication, *The Quest for the Historical Jesus*. Schweitzer brilliantly exposed the inherent flaw in the entire project: the unconscious, anachronistic projection of modern presuppositions and values back onto Jesus. In the attempt to recover history behind myth, each author inevitably produced a new Jesus fashioned in the author's own likeness, much like the reconstructed historical Buddha of the same period. Schweitzer himself emphasized the chasm between the world of today and the world of the New Testament. In his view, Jesus was from a totally different age, dominated by messianic hopes and eschatological anticipation. There was little common ground and no bridge over the chasm. With that bleak assessment, the first phase of the quest came to an abrupt halt.

What followed in the first half of the twentieth century was a period of "no quest", and its dominant figure was Rudolf Bultmann, who resigned himself to the idea that the historical Jesus was irretrievable and ultimately unimportant. Just as the person of the Buddha was considered by some to be inconsequential to Buddhism, for Bultmann, the person of Jesus held little relevance for Christianity. For him, Christian belief was not based on certain dubious claims about a figure from the past, but a courageous leap of faith into the present. With his famous program of "demythologization", Bultmann purged the sources of their miraculous and eschatological contents, which only acted as barriers to the modern person, and recast Christianity in the framework of his favourite philosopher, Martin Heidegger.

The academic tide turned again soon after World War II when Ernst Käsemann kick-started the historical quest again. This New Quest (or Second Quest) argued against Bultmann that Jesus could not be ignored. Although it did not return to the heady optimism of the First Quest, it was hopeful that a reasonably accurate picture of Jesus could be salvaged from the sources. The Second Quest continued into the late twentieth century via the often controversial Jesus Seminar and its key spokesperson John Dominic Crossan. Methodologically, it paid closer attention to the Hellenistic background of the gospels. It moved beyond the canonical gospels and quarried the myriad of secular writings that open up the world of the Roman Empire, hoping to cast fresh, yet indirect, light on Jesus. According to Crossan, Jesus did not expect the world to end imminently as Schweitzer had claimed but, rather, the Kingdom was something to be found in the here and now of ordinary life. For Crossan, Jesus was not a Jewish apocalyptic prophet but a Greek-inspired wisdom sage. The key to understanding him is the figure of the itinerant Cynic philosopher-teacher who carried minimal possessions and offered insights via pithy aphorisms to whoever was interested.[40]

A further shift in direction came with the so-called Third Quest, which moved away from the broader context of the Mediterranean and focussed on the more particular context of Palestine and Second Temple Judaism. Thus authors such as Marcus Borg, Anthony Harvey, Geza Vermes, E.P. Sanders, Ben F. Meyer and John Meier have sifted through ancient sources in order to paint a more complete picture of Jesus in terms of his Jewish background rather than the Hellenistic world favored by the Second Quest. The Third Quest is also characterized by greater diversity in its various portraits of Jesus. For example, Meier returns to the eschatological emphasis of Schweitzer and sees Jesus as a Jewish apocalyptic prophet.[41] In contrast, Borg understands Jesus as a Spirit-filled mystic and social critic.[42]

After two centuries of biblical scholarship, there is still no meaningful consensus on which category of ancient religious figure best fits Jesus. Meanwhile, there are also many scholars who defend the plausibility and historicity of the miraculous claims in the canonical gospels and support the traditional position, made explicit in John's gospel, that Jesus is the incarnate Son of God. What is noteworthy is that the sources, both canonical and noncanonical, Christian and non-Christian, are rich and complex enough to provide supporting evidence for such a broad spectrum of academic opinion. What often differentiates each position on the spectrum is the set of philosophical presuppositions brought to the sources and the hermeneutical method used to interpret them.

Qur'an, Sira and Hadith

Muhammad lived 600 years after Jesus and a full millennium after the Buddha, making him clearly the most recent of the three founders. Such a gap naturally generates expectations that there should be significantly more material available concerning his life and teaching. Being a figure of the seventh century CE, it would seem that he is much more in the full light of history than his earlier counterparts. This is true to a degree although, as with Jesus and the Buddha, there are still limitations and challenges posed by the main sources.

One of the more reliable time references that we have is the date of Muhammad's death. The vast majority of commentators agree that this occurred on 12 Rabi al-awwal in the eleventh year of the Islamic calendar (11 AH), which converts to 8 June 632 CE.[43] The timing of his birth is more contentious given that neither Muhammad nor his family were public figures at the time. Bukhari states that Muhammad was 63 years old when he died and 40 years old when he experienced his first revelation.[44] Working backwards, we arrive at approximately the year 570 CE, which is commonly cited today.[45] As for the precise date, Sunni Muslims celebrate the birthday of the Prophet (Mawlid al-Nabi) on 12 Rabi al-awwal, the same date as his death, while Shi'ites prefer 17 Rabi al-awwal.[46]

In contrast to the Buddha, and to some extent Jesus, there are a reasonable number of non-Muslim references to Muhammad that are very close to the time that he actually lived. The oldest instance is a manuscript that mentions "the Arabs of Muhammad" at the Battle of Dathin in 634 CE.[47] The same phrase appears in a Christian codex concerning the Battle of Gabintha in Syria (636 CE), at which Arab forces defeated the Byzantines.[48] A more explicit and detailed reference to Muhammad is found in the chronicle of Sebeos, an Armenian bishop, which dates to approximately 661 CE, just 29 years after Muhammad's death.[49] The rapid expansion of the Arabian armies into the vacuum left by the Byzantine and Persian Empires catapulted Islam and its founder onto the world's stage much more quickly than in the case of Christianity and Buddhism. Consequently, it did not take long for Muhammad to attract the attention of chroniclers and historians outside Islam, but the references are still occasional and brief. So, as with the Buddha and Jesus, we must turn to Islamic sources in order to obtain more detailed biographical information, in particular the Qur'an, sira and hadith.

The Qur'an is the principal religious text for Muslims who believe that it contains revelations given by God to Muhammad via the angel Gabriel (Jibril) over a period of approximately 23 years, until his death. These revelations were memorized by the first followers and eventually recorded in written form. The book consists of over 6,000 verses (ayats) organized into 114 chapters (suras). Significantly, the chapters are not arranged in chronological or thematic order but roughly by decreasing length. This feature, along with the fact that the verses are not dated, makes the task of locating each passage in its original historical context a difficult one, although it is possible to distinguish verses from the Meccan and Medinan periods of Muhammad's life.[50]

Thus, the Qur'an is a unique text among the three religions in question. Muslims have always made a clear distinction between the revelations recorded in its sacred pages and the personal statements and sayings of Muhammad. It may be that the revelations were verbally recited by Muhammad but, for the Muslim, their true author is Allah and his prophet had no input in terms of content except to act as a human mouthpiece. There is no such two-tiered distinction between directly revealed messages and personal opinion in the case of the Buddha and Jesus. For Buddhists, the truths that the Buddha taught were insights that he himself gained in his long search for enlightenment. For Christians, all words spoken by Jesus intrinsically carry divine authority.

The process that eventually produced the written Qur'an has been the subject of scholarly interest for some time. The traditional view is that during Muhammad's lifetime, as the revelations were still occurring, a group of companions known as "qurra" were commissioned to recite the Qur'an daily and commit it to memory. Literate companions also began to act as official scribes, recording verses on stone tablets, bones and palm fronds.[51] Within a year of the Prophet's death, a significant number of those who had memorized the Qur'an were killed at the Battle of Yamama. This prompted the first caliph, Abu Bakr, to order Zayd ibn Thabit to gather the scattered private collections into one volume based on at least two witnesses for each verse.[52] A copy of Abu Bakr's volume was passed on to the second caliph, 'Umar, who gave them to his daughter, Hafsa, on his deathbed. By the time of the third caliph, Uthman (about 20 years after the death of Muhammad), there was a growing sense that a standardized version of the Qur'an was needed as the Islamic movement expanded into North Africa and Persia. Uthman established a committee headed by Zayd who utilized Hafsa's version to produce an official edition. The result is known as al-mushaf al-Uthmani (the Uthmanic codex). Uthman then ordered all remaining private versions to be sent to Medina where they were destroyed. Copies of the Uthmanic codex were then distributed throughout the Islamic world and this is essentially the Qur'an as we know it today.[53]

As with early Buddhist and Christian scriptures, secular scholarly opinion is divided on the early history of the Qur'an. Academics such as Richard Bell, William Montgomery Watt, Andrew Rippin, Fred Donner and F.E. Peters have supported the traditional picture. They assert that certain features of the Qur'an, such as its arbitrary order, its repetitions and its mixture of styles, suggest a collection process that was profoundly respectful of the original fragments. However, scholars such as John Wansbrough, Michael Cook and Patricia Crone are skeptical that the entire Qur'an can be attributed to Muhammad. In their view, there is no convincing evidence that it existed as a single book before 690 CE, and the most likely scenario is that the final text was composed gradually over several centuries as Islam encountered Jewish and Christian challenges.[54]

If the traditional picture is correct and the Qur'an is a genuine record of the revealed messages received by Muhammad, then it constitutes an invaluable source of information regarding his life. Apart from its central role in determining Islamic teaching, it also provides a direct link with the founder rather than a second-hand interpretation from a later generation. For this reason, many commentators describe it as the earliest and most reliable of sources.[55] One particular feature of the Qur'an reinforces this point. The revelations do not come in the form of timeless, absolute truths revealed in systematic fashion so as to form an Islamic catechism. Instead, the messages are highly contextualized, typically responding to a particular crisis or circumstance in the life of Muhammad and the early community. The Qur'anic voice may have been heard only inside Muhammad's mind, but the words reflected what was happening out there in his surrounding world. It is this dynamic, interactive character that makes the Qur'an a useful mirror on Muhammad's later life.[56]

Yet in another sense, the Qur'an remains an indirect and limited source for the life of Muhammad. Although its messages are responses to particular contexts, those historical contexts are rarely stated or explained by the Qur'an itself. Once the context is known, the message begins to make more sense, but the Qur'an seldom provides that vital information. Its allusive, enigmatic style makes it difficult to know precisely which persons and events are intended. Even Muhammad himself is only named on a handful of occasions. In this respect, the Qur'an is more reminiscent of Jewish prophetic books, such as Isaiah and Jeremiah, than the Christian gospels. As a collection of authoritative teachings without a narrative framework, it is also more akin to the Sutta Pitaka than the Buddhacarita. The Qur'an does provide a useful reflection of Muhammad's life story, but the reflection is dimmed and refracted.

About 100 years after Muhammad's death, a second type of source material appeared. The sira is a form of biography, tracing the key events of a person's journey from life to death. In the case of Muhammad, many siras were eventually produced, but the four most important are those of Ibn Ishaq, al-Waqidi, Ibn Sa'd and al-Tabari. [57] Ibn Ishaq (circa 704–767 CE) wrote several works but the most important is entitled Sira Rasul Allah – The Life of God's Messenger. No copy of his original work is extant, but it does survive in an edited version by Ibn Hisham (died 833 CE), and it is quoted verbatim and at length by al-Tabari. It is the earliest surviving biography of Muhammad even though it was penned more than a century after the Prophet's death. The Sira Rasul Allah is an extensive book, commencing with a genealogy that traces Muhammad's line back to Adam via Abraham and Ishmael. It continues with an account of his birth, his call to be Prophet of God, the beginning of his public mission in Mecca, the migration to Medina, his military campaigns and concludes with his death. Although Ibn Ishaq includes miracle stories, these are usually accompanied by guarded statements such as "only God knows whether a particular statement is true or not" or "it is alleged".[58]

The ninth century CE saw two more important siras appear, one of which is the Kitab al-Tarikh wa al-Maghazi (The Book of History and Campaigns) by al-Waqidi (died circa 822 CE). The work contains stories of Muhammad's military ventures (maghazi) during his time as leader in Medina. Not all Muslim scholars are convinced that al-Waqidi is a reliable source but his secretary, Ibn Sa'd (died circa 845 CE), enjoys a more positive reputation for his accuracy and trustworthiness. His major work is al-Kitab al-Tabaqat al-Kabir (The Great Book of Scholarly Classes), which is a compendium of biographical material regarding major Islamic figures from the first generations. It comprises eight books of which the first two concern Muhammad.[59]

The fourth important sira comes from the pen of al-Tabari (died 923 CE). His two principal works are al-Tarikh al-Rusul wa al-Muluk (History of the Prophets and Kings) – usually abbreviated as Tarikh al-Tabari – and the Tafsir al-Tabari (Commentary on the Qur'an). The former is a 40-volume universal history from the time of creation to the end of the caliphate of al-Muktadid in 915 CE, with four volumes dedicated to Muhammad. In the section of the History where he treats the Prophet, al-Tabari relies heavily on Ibn Ishaq and the material is virtually the same as in Ibn Hisham's edition. Nevertheless, there are important differences, such as the inclusion of the story of the Satanic Verses and their refutation, which are omitted by Ibn Hisham.

While they are not as late as the first written biographies of the Buddha, the siras are still separated from Muhammad by a century or more. Such a time gap rightly raises questions in the secular scholar's mind as to what degree the original material has been altered for religious reasons, especially if one of the main purposes of a sira was to provide a more detailed context for Qur'anic verses. The fact that later siras often contain far more details about a particular event than is provided in Ibn Ishaq's text tends to diminish confidence in their historical reliability, especially when the sources of that information are not clearly defined or filtered. In general, the siras were not particularly concerned with validating information for two reasons. First, the story of Muhammad's life was reasonably well known and recounted many times among the first generations of believers. Second, the siras were not used as the chief source for grounding and developing Islamic law. The literary genre that was employed for that purpose is known as hadith.

Hadiths are collections of individual reports concerning statements or actions of Muhammad as verified by a succession of witnesses. Consequently, there are two main components to a hadith: the narrative text itself (matn) and the chain of narrators (isnad) stretching back to the eyewitness at the time of the event or saying. Thus the chain determines the reliability of the source. In much the same way as the Sutta Pitaka sayings commence with the phrase "Thus on one occasion I heard the Buddha say . . .", a hadith often commences with the statement by a companion: "I heard the Prophet say . . .". The transmission of sayings and anecdotes from Muhammad began during his lifetime and continued for over two centuries in oral form.[60] It was not until the eighth century that authenticated collections of hadiths begin to appear. Scholars at the time had to trawl through an enormous body of traditions, some of which were partially incompatible or even outright contradictory. Their main task was to gauge the level of trustworthiness of each report. The process of textual criticism by which this was achieved is known as "the science of hadith" (ulum al-hadith), and it involves analysis of the text itself, the listed narrators and the pathway of the chain over time. [61]

The six classical Sunni hadith collections took final shape in the middle of the ninth century CE:

- Sahih Bukhari by Imam Bukhari (died 870 CE)
- Sahih Muslim by Muslim ibn al-Hajjaj (died 875 CE)
- Sunan al-Sughra by al-Nasa'i (died 915 CE)
- Sunan Abu Dawud by Abu Dawud (died 888 CE)
- Sunan al-Tirmidhi by al-Tirmidhi (died 892 CE)
- Sunan Ibn Majah (died 886 CE).

An earlier collection known as al-Muwatta by Imam Malik (died 796 CE) was largely incorporated into these six.[62] The first two on the list are considered the most reliable, as indicated by their title "sahih" (sound). In contrast, Shi'ite Muslims do not use these six collections but prefer their own traditions, which have passed through

Muhammad's descendants via his daughter Fatima, her husband Ali and other supporters.[63] Nevertheless, there are large overlaps in content.

Unlike siras, hadiths were used as a complementary source for Islamic jurispru-
dence since the Qur'an alone did not always provide clear instruction on the host of
religious, moral and legal issues that were arising as the Islamic Empire rapidly
expanded. The most obvious source to consult outside of the Qur'an was the Prophet
himself. His personal example (sunna) is regarded as a second source of guidance for
Muslims. It was this primarily legal application that generated the intense scrutiny
of sources that is so characteristic of the hadith but which is absent in the sira. In
that sense, hadith probably has a greater claim to reliability as an historical source.
Most Muslim scholars are confident that spurious reports were filtered out by Bukhari,
Muslim and their colleagues, and that the vignettes and glimpses that survived the
filtering process are authentic. However, it also means that the hadiths were not collected for biographical purposes. They may contain thousands of sayings and episodes
from Muhammad's life, which provide material for legal debate and spiritual nourishment but, like the sermons of the Sutta Pitaka and the pericopes of the pregospel
tradition, they are individual items without chronological order and outside a broader
narrative framework.

Secular scholarship's initial assessment was skeptical. At the beginning of the
twentieth century, many Western academics regarded hadiths as essentially fictitious
additions, invented to justify certain legal or theological opinions.[64] Skeptical views
continued into the late twentieth century with John Wansborough, Michael Cook and
Patricia Crone, who questioned any genuine historical link between Muhammad
and the hadith tradition. For such thinkers, the nature of the sources and the lack of
knowledge regarding pre-Islamic Arabia preclude an account of Muhammad's life
that would satisfy the demands of the modern historian.[65] However, there are scholars
who argue that many, if not all, hadiths do provide a genuine historical memory of
Muhammad. William Montgomery Watt admitted that some invention was possible
in the legal sphere but that material was more likely to have been reshaped rather
than completely fabricated. Others argue that wholesale rejection of hadith is unjusti-
fied and that, despite occasional contradictions and legendary forms, there is a
genuine core that can be recognized using the appropriate scientific methods.[66]

Observations

We began this chapter by noting that all three religious founders lived in the ancient
world and, like most figures from the distant past, each of them is shrouded to some
extent by the mists of time. In all three cases, there is a real problem concerning the
quantity and quality of material on which to build an accurate biographical picture.
The Buddha, Jesus and Muhammad did not actually write anything, and so there are
no primary written sources that come directly from their hand. They were not authors
in the literal sense. Instead, their message was communicated and transmitted orally
before eventually being recorded in writing at some point.

None of the three founders is mentioned in any sources external to their religious
tradition during their lifetime. This may seem surprising at first but such a mention

would only have been warranted if they had already made some sort of serious impact on their world. Of the three, the Buddha had the longest lifespan, living into his eighties, but it is unclear how widespread his new religious movement was at the time of his death. It is really only during the reign of Ashoka in the third century BCE, several hundred years after the founder's death, that Buddhism begins to appear on the radar screens of contemporary historians. Jesus died prematurely in his early thirties after a very brief public life and his circle of disciples was a small fledgling group within the complex world of Judaism at the time of his execution. The first secular references to Jesus only appear at the end of the first century, some 70 years later, when Christianity was beginning to attract attention in the broader Roman Empire. Given his astounding success in transforming the political landscape of Arabia, there is more reason to expect that Muhammad might have been mentioned in non-Islamic sources during his life or soon after. This seems to be the case with early references to the "Arabs of Muhammad" possibly dating to within a decade of his death in 632 CE as the Islamic army expanded into the Middle East and beyond.

Although some secular references to Muhammad and Jesus exist and thus lend support to the historicity of both figures, they are fleeting and provide no real detail. Thus, the main sources for the three founders are necessarily religious texts. There is nothing wrong with that per se, but historians have rightly pointed out that every text must be read critically with an eye to the author's fundamental presuppositions and inherent motives, whether it is religious or not. In other words, we must acknowledge that the texts that provide most information about the Buddha, Jesus and Muhammad were composed by believers who saw the world through the prism of their faith. These are not historical treatises in the sense that we might use such a term today. Their aim was not necessarily to produce a scientifically objective version of events or an unbiased portrait of the main subject. They were written within a community of belief, which saw the founder as unique and unrivalled. Hence, they often have an apologetic, kerygmatic or didactic purpose. For instance, the gospel of John candidly admits that it is written so that the reader may believe. This means that the authors involved not only had the duty to pass on what the founder had said and done, but they may have sincerely believed that they had a similar duty to select, expand, adapt, change, interpret and embellish in the process. The degree to which this has happened is the stuff of the contemporary scholarly debate in each case.

A second feature of these religious texts is the prescientific worldview that pervades them. Prior to the eighteenth-century Enlightenment, people viewed the cosmos and its processes in a different way. As one author colourfully stated, "the sky hung low in the ancient world".[67] Supernatural and natural forces intertwined with no clear boundaries and accounts of amazing events were not normally questioned. The miraculous element in a story did not meet with the sort of natural skepticism that characterizes the modern mindset. Thus, the presence of supernatural features in the sources presents a special challenge for today's reader and many have simply dismissed these as products of a more primitive religious imagination. The problem is more acute in the case of the biographies of the Buddha and the Christian gospels, whereas a miracle tradition was apparently not as central to the story of Muhammad (see Chapter 6).

A third factor is the time gap between the founder and the earliest written sources but there is a striking variation here. The gospel of Mark appears only about four decades after the death of Jesus, whereas the Pali Canon and the Mahavastu are several centuries after the Buddha. This is partially explained by the absolutely central role that Jesus occupies in the Christian message, which contrasts sharply with the total emphasis on the Buddha's teaching and an almost indifferent attitude to his life story in early Buddhism. Muhammad sits between these two positions with a time-lapse of approximately 120 years between his death and the Sira Rasul Allah of Ibn Ishaq. In one sense, that gap was bridged by the Qur'an, which represents a unique text in that it is claimed to be the carefully recorded *ipsissima verba* of the revelations that Muhammad received and communicated during his lifetime. In each case, the existence of a gap puts pressure on the oral phase of transmission and raises questions regarding the accuracy of the written sources. Critical scholarship has been quick to point out the potential for editorial alteration of the original material but the religious tradition in each case argues for a reliable link. Thus, Buddhism speaks of a double verbal tradition that goes back to Ananda and Upali; the gospel of John claims first-hand apostolic testimony and Luke refers to the eyewitnesses and ministers of the word in his preface; and the science of hadith involved meticulous filtering of the chain of witnesses behind each reported anecdote or saying.

Apart from the issue of the time gap, there is also the issue of an information gap within the sources themselves. The earliest material regarding the Buddha is in the form of individual sermons collected in the Sutta Pitaka. These are stand-alone teachings devoid of a narrative framework. When that framework finally appears as in the Mahavastu and the Lalitavistara, it covers only part of the story – from the Buddha's birth to the beginning of his teaching ministry. Admittedly, the Buddhacarita provides some information about the second stage of his career and his death, but the traditional focus has been squarely on his spiritual journey from protected prince to Enlightened One rather than the subsequent decades spent teaching on the road and establishing a new religious movement. In contrast, the canonical gospels turn their attention almost exclusively to the short public ministry of Jesus and say almost nothing about his youth and early adulthood, although Matthew and Luke both provide short infancy narratives. It is no wonder that Christianity describes that extensive period of Jesus's early life as "the hidden years". Similarly, the Qur'an, the siras and the hadiths provide quite detailed information about Muhammad's career as successful political leader in Medina in the post-Hijra period. There is much less information about his troubled time as persecuted preacher in Mecca and even thinner material concerning his childhood and early adulthood. Those gaps are reflected in the difficulty that scholars face in trying to determine exactly when each founder lived. The lack of precision is most acute in the case of the Buddha for whom the proposed dates vary up to a century. In contrast, Jesus and Muhammad are much more firmly grounded on the historical timeline, at least in terms of their death, but there is a good deal of haziness concerning the year of their birth.

While the sources have been accepted uncritically for centuries by each mainstream religious tradition, the assessment of modern Western scholarship has not been as positive. Where the believer sees a harmonious picture, the secular historian sees stress fractures: between the layers that make up the final edition; between the slight variations of a saying or an episode across the sources; between the natural and supernatural elements; between the religious version of the sources and information about the time and place gleaned from surrounding contemporary texts. In each case, this more critical, suspicious methodology has led to a search for the "real" founder behind the presumably obscuring and distorting layers of religious interpretation, exaggeration and amnesia. The quest for the historical Jesus began in the late eighteenth century, and it was quickly followed by the quest for the historical Buddha in the nineteenth century and a quest for the historical Muhammad in the twentieth century. Despite the earnestness of the quests, there is surprisingly little consensus among the scholars. Instead, a broad spectrum of opinion is evident, stretching from experts who support the traditional picture to those who are convinced that we know almost nothing about the founder, or in the case of the Buddha, even questioning whether he ever existed. So at the beginning of the twenty-first century, the debates continue, and while the paucity of sources is still a serious problem, each quest has been re-invigorated by progress in the field of archaeology. Although newly discovered manuscripts rarely pertain directly to the Buddha, Jesus or Muhammad, there is a growing confidence that we can learn more about them as we gain more knowledge of the ancient worlds in which they lived. The sources may be limited and frustrating at times, but there is a sense that more light can be shed on the subjects via a more complete picture of their original historical contexts, to which we turn in the next chapter.

Notes

1 Erich Frauwallner argued for a hypothetical text that was composed soon after the Buddha's death and upon which all subsequent biographies were derived, but most scholars have rejected this theory. See E. Frauwallner (1956) *The Earliest Vinaya and the Beginnings of Buddhist Literature*; Cohen 126.
2 Armstrong, Buddha xi; Nakamura I 20.
3 Foucher extensively used the artistic tradition unearthed at pilgrim sites for his classical biography.
4 Carrithers 8.
5 Armstrong, Buddha xvi.
6 Armstrong, Buddha xviii; Braden 17.
7 Reynolds & Hallisey 1063.
8 The Lalitavistara was the inspiration for the artwork of Borobudur temple and Edward Arnold's famous poem *The Light of Asia*.
9 Tradition holds that another "Buddhacarita" was composed within the Kanishka court by the poet Sangharaksa, although the original Sanskrit text is lost and only a Chinese translation exists today.
10 Pioneer scholars include Alexander Cxoma de Koros, Brian Houghton Hodgson, Franz Anton von Schiefner, Philippe Edouard Foucaux, Hermann Oldenberg and Thomas William Rhys Davids.
11 Thomas 233–234; Drummond 16; Reynolds & Hallisey 1061.
12 Guang Xing 7; Drummond 16.
13 Reynolds & Hallisey 1061; Foucher Introduction.
14 Strong 3.

15 Reynolds & Hallisey 1061–1062.

16 Nakamura I 68–72.

17 Luke 3:1–2.

18 On one hand, the Synoptic gospels imply a short interval of 1–2 years, suggesting 30 CE as the year of his death. That date is also supported by John 2:20, in which it is claimed that at the start of Jesus's ministry, work on the Temple extensions, which commenced in 19 BCE, had been underway for 46 years. On the other hand, John's gospel mentions at least three Passover festivals during the public ministry, which suggests the year 33 CE. Luke 3:23 states that Jesus was "about 30 years old" when he was baptized by John, but the phrase is ambiguous, and there is no certainty about the year of Jesus's birth. Third-century author Tertullian claimed that Jesus was crucified in the twelfth year of Tiberius' rule, which would be 25 or 26 CE. See Adversus Marcionem 15.

19 Antiquities 18.3.3; 20.9.1. For passing references to early Christians, see Pliny's Letters to Trajan 10.96–97 and Tacitus, Annals 15.44.

20 Yeshu ben Pandera is the teacher of Jacob, a second-century CE heretic; Yeshu Ha-Notzri is a sorcerer who is stoned and hanged on the eve of the Passover; Yeshu is also the name of a spirit summoned from the dead and who describes his punishment in the afterlife as boiling in excrement; another Yeshu is a son who burns his food in public; and Yeshu is the name of a prominent rabbi's student who, according to the Jerusalem Talmud, becomes a sorcerer and leads Israel astray. See Avodah Zarah 16b–17a; Sanhedrin 43a; Gittin 56b, 57a; Sanhedrin 103a, Berakhot 17b; Sanhedrin 107b; Chagigah 2:2.

21 Other Passion gospels include the Gospel of Nicodemus (also called the Acts of Pilate), the (lost) Gospel of Bartholomew, the Questions of Bartholomew and the Resurrection of Jesus Christ.

22 See Crossan's list of primary sources: Crossan 427.

23 The Nag Hammadi Library is a collection of thirteen ancient codices containing over fifty Gnostic texts.

24 Meier I 140.

25 Colossians 4:10; Acts 12:12, 25; 15:37, 39.

26 2 Timothy 4:11; Philemon 1:24; 1 Peter 5:13.

27 Eusebius, Ecclesiastical History 3.39.4, 15. See also Irenaeus, Adversus Haereses 3.1.1 and Tertullian, Adversus Marcionem 4.5.

28 Mark 13:9–13.

29 The evidence for Markan priority is very strong. Mark's material constitutes 90% of Matthew and over 50% of Luke. While the order of the pericopes is basically the same across the three Synoptic gospels, when one departs from the pattern, it is invariably Matthew or Luke alone.

30 Matthew 22:7.

31 Luke 1:2.

32 Colossians 4:14; see also 2 Timothy 4:11.

33 For instance, the disruption in the Temple, which the Synoptics identify as the immediate cause of Jesus's arrest and execution, comes at the very start of his ministry according to John 2:13-25.

34 John's seven miracles are: turning water into wine at Cana; the cure of an official's son at Cana; the cure of a paralytic; the multiplication of loaves; walking on the waters; the cure of the man born blind; and the raising of Lazarus.

35 John 1:14.

36 John 21:24.

37 Theophilos of Antioch (circa 180 CE) attributed the fourth gospel to John, the son of Zebedee. See Adversus Haereses 2.22.5; 3.3.4; Ecclesiastical History 3.23.3.

38 John 1:28; 2:1,12,14,20; 3:23; 4:20; 5:2; 8:2,20; 9:7; 10:23; 11:18,54; 12:21; 18:1,28; 19:17.

39 The Passover (John 2:13, 23; 6:4; 13:1; 18:28); the feast of Tabernacles (John 7:2, 37); the Dedication of the Temple (John 10:22); and purification rites (John 2:6; 3:25; 11:55; 18:28; 19:31).

40 Crossan's opus magnus is aptly entitled *The Historical Jesus: The Life of a Mediterranean Jewish Peasant*. One of the main criticisms of Crossan's thesis is the lack of evidence for a Cynic presence in Galilee at the time. See McClymond 321–322.

41 Meier's opus magnus is aptly entitled *Jesus: A Marginal Jew*, emphasizing Jesus's Jewish background rather than the Mediterranean Hellenism favored by Crossan.

42 See Marcus Borg, *Jesus. A New Vision* (1987) and *Jesus. Uncovering the Life, Teachings and Relevance of a Religious Revolutionary* (2006).

43 Al-Tabari favored 1 Rabi al-awwal, while Ibn Hajar al-Asqalani favored 2 Rabi al-awwal.

44 Bukhari 58.190, 242, 243.

45 Islamic tradition holds that he was born in the Year of the Elephant, which refers to the failed attack on Mecca by Abraha, ruler of Saba' in Yemen. Al-Tabari states that the attack took place in the forty-second year of the reign of the Sassanid ruler Khosrau I (531–579 CE), which would have been 573 CE. However, this may be too late for two reasons: the Sassanids overthrew Abraha's dynasty around 570 CE and historians estimate that Abraha himself did not reign long after 553 CE. Consequently, Armstrong claims that the Year of the Elephant was probably 547 CE; Armstrong, Muhammad 31. Thus, Ibn al-Kalbi's claim that Muhammad was born 23 years after the Year of the Elephant may be closer to the truth, but the effect is that Muhammad's birth year is still deemed to be approximately 570 CE.

46 Tradition states that Muhammad was born on a Monday; see Muslim 6.2603, 2606.

47 British Library (BL) Add. 14,643.

48 British Library (BL) Add. 14,461.

49 R.W. Thomson (1999) *The Armenian History Attributed To Sebeos Part I, Translated Texts For Historians*, Volume 31, Liverpool University Press, 95–96. Other translations can also be seen in Crone & Cook, 6–7.

50 Meccan suras are typically shorter prophetic utterances addressed either to Muhammad himself or people in general, and focusing on themes such as monotheism, the Day of Judgment and the negative response to Muhammad's message. The Medinan suras are longer, more ethical and legalistic, and usually addressed to the Islamic community via the phrase "O you who believe". See "The Meccan and Medinan Suras" in Oliver Leaman ed. (2006) *The Qur'an: An Encyclopedia*. Routledge, 398–401.

51 Twenty-two such persons are mentioned by name in the hadiths. Among them were Abu Bakr, 'Umar, Uthman, Ali, 'A'isha, Hafsa and Umm Salama.

52 Bukhari 60.201.

53 Bukhari 61.510. Sources indicate that there were versions owned by Abdallah Ibn Masud, Ubay Ibn Ka'b and Ali, although it is claimed that the variations are only minor.

54 Exponents of this position include Michael Cook, Patricia Crone, Christoph Luxenberg, Gerd R. Puin and Karl-Heinz Ohlig.

55 Welch 360.

56 Welch 361.

57 The earliest siras are thought to have been authored by 'Urwah ibn al-Zubayr (died 713 CE), Aban ibn Uthman (died 727 CE) and Wahb ibn Munabbih (died 737 CE), but none of these have survived.

58 Ibn Ishaq (Guillaume) xix. Because of his stress on human free will rather than God's omnipotence, Ibn Ishaq has often been criticized by traditional Muslim scholars. Moreover, Bukhari conspicuously avoided his narratives in his voluminous hadith collection.

59   Books 3 and 4 contain biographic notes concerning the companions of Muhammad;
      Books 5, 6 and 7 contain biographical notes on later Islamic scholars; and Book 8 contains
      biographical notes on important Islamic women.

60   Uthman was also concerned about opposition from a small minority of Muslims who
      rejected the hadith as a secondary written source of law and spiritual guidance. They find
      support in the Qur'anic verse: "Nothing have we omitted from the Book" (Qur'an 6:38),
      but they are considered heretical by many Muslims. The modern "Qur'an-alone" move-
      ment reached its peak in the middle of the twentieth century but is now in decline.

61   This led to the development of different levels of classification for a report. The standard
      version of Ibn al-Salah has the following categories: sahih (sound), hasan (good), da'if
      (weak), munkar (ignored) and mawdu' (fabricated). The first two categories are usually
      acceptable for usage in Islamic legal argument.

62   Some also argue for Sunan al-Darimi (died circa 877 CE).

63   Usul al-Kafi by Muhammad ibn Ya'qub al-Kulayni al-Razi; Man la Yahduruhu al-Faqih
      by Muhammad ibn Babuya; al-Tahdhib and al-Istibsar both by Shaykh Muhammad Tusi.

64   For example, Ignaz Goldziher, D.S. Margoliouth, Henri Lammens and Leone Caetani.
      In his *Origins of Muhammadan Jurisprudence* (1959), Joseph Schacht argued that isnads
      going back to Muhammad were in fact more likely to be spurious than isnads going back
      to the companions.

65   Nigosian 6.

66   For example, Herbert Berg (2000) *The Development of Exegesis in Early Islam*; Fred
      Donner (1998) *Narratives of Islamic Origins*; Wilferd Madelung (1997) *Succession to
      Muhammad*.

67   Quoted in Jaroslav Pelikan (1975) *The Emergence of the Catholic Tradition, Volume I
      (100–600 CE)* Chicago: University of Chicago Press, 132.

Chapter 2

CONTEXT

Individuality is a fundamental trait of being human. Every person is truly unique and unrepeatable, and this basic characteristic applies just as surely to the three founders. There will only ever be one Siddhattha Gotama, one Jesus of Nazareth and one Muhammad ibn 'Abdullah. Nevertheless, each person is also a product of their time and place, unavoidably shaped and influenced by their particular moment in history. We are powerfully forged and conditioned by the network of forces that surround us and constitute our particular context. This inescapable fact also applies to the three founders. Even though their followers see them rising above their narrow historical circumstances and representing a universal set of truths, none of the founders lived in a vacuum. Even though the Buddha, Jesus and Muhammad profoundly changed the path of history, they were also part of it. Thus, one key to gaining a more profound understanding of each man and his message is to look closely at their historical contexts. What were the dominant social, cultural, political, economic and religious factors of those times? What were the chief issues, the presuppositions and challenges, the dangers and expectations? What was it like to live in sixth-century BCE northern India, first-century CE Palestine or seventh-century CE Arabia?

The Ganges Plain

In terms of geographical context, the Buddha lived all of his 80 years in a region of northern India known as the Ganges Plain – an expansive, alluvial flatland created by the Ganges River and its main tributaries. In ancient times, its inhabitants called it Majjhima Desa (Middle Land) because it was believed to be the centre of the world. The area is bounded to the north by the soaring peaks of the Himalayas, whose snows feed the great river systems. Its southern edge is marked by the Vindhya Range and the Chota Nagpur Plateau. To the west lies the Great Indian Desert and to the east

Buddha, Jesus and Muhammad: A Comparative Study, First Edition. Paul Gwynne.
© 2014 John Wiley & Sons, Ltd. Published 2014 by John Wiley & Sons, Ltd.

is the lowland area of the Ganges Delta. The Plain runs for over 1,000 mi from the northwest to the southeast and it is several hundred miles wide in parts. The constant deposit of silt from flooding rivers has resulted in deep, rich soil, making it one of the most fertile areas in the Indian subcontinent. There are three seasons: a mild winter (November–February); a hot, dry summer (March–June); and the wet season (July–October). The monsoon rains account for most of the annual precipitation and are vital for the success of agriculture.

In terms of historical context, the Buddha lived during a transitional phase in Indian history, commonly referred to as the end of the Vedic Period, named after the principal Hindu scriptures of that time. Vedic society was characterized by social stratification in the form of the four traditional classes (varnas): the Brahmin or priestly class; the Kshatria or warrior class; the Vaishya or merchant class; and the Shudra or servant class. Over time there emerged a fifth class of "untouchables", who were considered to be beyond the pale of civilized society and whose very touch was deemed to be contaminating. Class was determined by one's birth and it was impossible to change during this lifetime. Class had serious practical consequences since it determined one's occupation, social status, suitable marriage partner, residential address, dining partners and so on. Although it supposedly gave society a degree of stability, class laws also made social change and mobility impossible and often generated imperious cruelty toward lower classes. The Rg Veda provides a mythical explanation for the four classes in terms of the various parts of a human body, with each part contributing to the efficient functioning of the whole.[1]

Between 900 and 500 BCE, Aryan groups had migrated onto the Gangetic Plain and began to establish Vedic civilization across northern India. Thus, the area became known as Aryavarta (Land of the Aryans).[2] With the assistance of innovative Iron Age technology, the newcomers cleared forests and began cultivation, gradually shifting from pastoral life to a sedentary agricultural system. Yet not all of the land was converted to farms, and the remaining jungle was a place where struggling farmers could still hunt game or gather fruits to supplement their diet. Technological advances also gave rise to a greater specialization of tradesmen, such as metal workers, carpenters and jewelers. Trade began to flourish as contact was established with the middle East and a new wealthy merchant class emerged. A money economy also replaced the older barter system in which cattle were a key measure of wealth. As the economy grew so too did the population, and cities and towns began to appear along the great rivers, just as they had in the ancient Indus Valley civilization. It was a time of rapid urbanization and swift economic change, which led to significant shifts in political structures as well.[3]

During the late Vedic Period, there was a distinct movement away from the tribal system toward a larger political unit known as the mahajanapada. Some mahajanapadas were hereditary monarchies, while others were oligarchies where the leader was elected or appointed for a term of office by a group of designated elders.[4] By 500 BCE, amalgamation and conquest had resulted in just four major kingdoms remaining: Avanti, Vamsa, Kosala and Magadha (see Map 1). Eventually, one of them, Magadha, would prevail over the entire region and become the kernel of the first imperial state in Indian history – the Mauryan Empire, which lasted from 321 to 185 BCE. It seemed that a robust, centralized monarchy was the best political system to capitalize on the changing economic environment. It was becoming clear that the future lay with kings and not with republics.[5]

In the story of the Buddha, Avanti was the least relevant, being situated at the extreme southwest edge of the Ganges Plain with its capital at Ujjain. Around 400 BCE it was defeated and absorbed by the expanding kingdom of Magadha. The second kingdom, Vamsa, was located east of Avanti, on the southern side of the Yamuna River, and included its confluence with the Ganges. Its royal capital, Kosambi, was a huge walled city situated on the banks of the Yamuna. It had become a bustling centre for trade and many wealthy merchants resided there.

The third kingdom, Kosala, was the second largest of the four, stretching from the Yamuna River north to the foothills of the Himalayas. Its capital, Savatthi, was situated on the banks of the Aciravati River and Buddhist texts describe it as a beautiful, populous city.[6] Savatthi features prominently in the story of the Buddha, since he spent 25 rainy seasons at its two main monasteries of Jetavana and Pubbarama. Consequently, many of his sermons were originally delivered in the city or its surrounds. Kosala's king Pasenadi is presented as a good friend of the Buddha who embraced his doctrine soon after he launched his preaching ministry.

On its northern edge, Kosala held sway over a number of smaller vassal states, one of which was the Sakyan kingdom where the Buddha was born and raised. The capital was Kapilavatthu, which was located near the present town of Lumbini in the lowland Terai region of Nepal. Nestled in the Himalayan foothills, the Sakyan territory was at the very edge of Vedic civilization, and some speculate that the Buddha's mother tongue was possibly not even an Indo-Aryan language. Its peripheral location also meant that Sakyan society may not have been organized according to the classical Brahmanic class system. As for its political structure, there are some who argue that it was more likely an oligarchy or tribal republic than a hereditary monarchy, although the tradition portrays the Buddha as a royal prince and heir to his father's throne. A more egalitarian form of government with a council of elders fits better with the model of monastic community life found in Buddhism and Jainism.[7] The Sakyans considered themselves Kshatria warriors but they were unable to remain independent of the more powerful states to the south and were effectively tied to Kosala both economically and politically.

The fourth kingdom, Magadha, was located at the eastern end of the Ganges Plain and its original domain roughly corresponded to present-day Bihar and parts of Bengal. The first capital, Rajagaha, frequently figures in the Buddha's life. The city was built among rugged hills and protected by massive stone walls whose shattered remains can still be seen today. During the reign of King Ajatasattu, the seat of power was moved to Pataliputta, which grew into one of the largest cities in the world and the political heart of the Mauryan Empire. The Buddha spent many years of his public life travelling within Magadha and several important events occurred there, including the most important of them all – his Enlightenment at Uruvela (Bodhgaya).

The Magadhan leaders during the time of the Buddha were Bimbisara (ruled 543–493 BCE) and his son Ajatasattu (ruled 493–461 BCE). Bimbisara is portrayed in Buddhist texts as a strong and effective leader who took a keen interest in religious matters, particularly the teaching of the Buddha, whom he met as a younger man still searching for enlightenment. According to Buddhists, Bimbisara became a devout adherent, although Jain texts simultaneously claim that he joined their movement. Whatever his religious allegiances, which were probably syncretic, Bimbisara undeniably pursued a policy of expansionism, with the aim of establishing Magadha as the most powerful of the four competing states. One of his strategies was the use of marriage alliances to secure his position and widen his dominion. His first wife was the daughter of the king of Kosala. As dowry for the wedding, Bimbisara received the region of Kasi, which was under Kosalan control at that time. More importantly, the marriage ended hostility between Magadha and Kosala and allowed Bimbisara to concentrate on other states.

Bimbisara ruled over Magadha for 50 years but his son, Ajatasattu, grew impatient for the throne. Fuelled by the Machiavellian plotting of the Buddha's cousin Devadatta, he imprisoned and starved his father to death. Immediately, the Kosalan king confiscated his sister's dowry, Kasi, which reignited military conflict between the two kingdoms. In the end, Magadha proved to be the stronger, recovering Kasi and annexing the entire Kosalan kingdom during the reign of Vidudabha. Ajatasattu was equally successful on the eastern front, conquering the adjacent state of Malla and the territory of the Vajji confederation with its capital Vesali. In his later life, Ajatasattu repented of his act of patricide and sought reconciliation and peace in the Buddha's teachings. Subsequently, he became a fervent supporter of the new movement, establishing monasteries and stupas throughout his realm, and hosting the first Buddhist Council outside of Rajagaha soon after the Buddha's death. Ironically, Ajatasattu was killed by his own son, Udayibhadda.

It was not only the political and economic spheres that were characterized by a critical questioning of traditional ways and an increasing willingness to adapt to the changing times. Things were also shifting in the religious and philosophical spheres. The main focus of the Vedic literature was liturgical ceremony. The correct performance of the sacred ritual was essential to its efficacy, whether it was for a successful harvest, victory in battle, rain, sons, healing, longevity or other blessings. The ritual was presided over by Brahmin priests who jealously guarded their secrets and were paid handsomely for their services. Only male members of the upper three classes were given access to the Vedic rituals, which usually involved a fire pit, symbolizing the presence of Agni, the god of fire and the divine messenger linking heaven and earth.

However, the new political and economic situation of the sixth century BCE created worrying cracks in the Vedic system and an array of new religious thinking began to surface. The Ganges Plain became a cultural cauldron in which a rich variety of spiritual ingredients were simmering. Different philosophical schools competed for the moral and financial support of kings and the merchant class. Buddhist texts speak of six contemporary "heretical" teachings: the antinomianism of Purana Kassapa; the determinism of Makkhali Gosala; the materialism of Ajita Kesakambala; the indifferentism of Pakudha Kaccayana; the skepticism of Sanyjaya Belatthiputta; and the Jain movement initiated by Nigantha Nataputta with its uncompromising stress on nonviolence toward all living things.[8] It truly was a time of intense intellectual competition.[9] Along with Buddhism, these schools are classified as nastika, meaning that they rejected the authority of the Vedas.

There were also astika schools that remained within Vedic orthodoxy even though they questioned aspects of traditional Brahmanism. The most noteworthy example is the Vedanta, which developed its own set of scriptural writings: the Upanishads.[10] These were attached to the Vedas and provided a supplementary lens through which the reader gained the "true" meaning of the Vedic text. Thus, they both complemented and questioned the Vedas. Although not an explicit protest, the Upanishads take a critical stance toward Vedic thought and practice at a number of levels. Whereas the Vedas provide the believer with liturgical chants and detailed instructions on how to conduct sacrifices, the Upanishads probe the relationship between the worshipper himself and the universe that surrounds him. Whereas the Vedas look outward to ritual purity, the Upanishads turn inward to the mystery of the self. Whereas the Vedic texts are primarily interested in ritual propriety, the Upanishads are concerned with philosophical truth. There was a growing sense that it was not ceremonial purity that mattered but a more profound understanding of human existence.

The Upanishads also called into question the polytheistic world of the Vedic hymns. Their interest in the relationship between the self (atman) and the world led them to see divinity in terms of one Absolute Reality rather than a pantheon of semidivine beings. Admittedly, there are already seeds of such monism in the Vedas,[11] but the concept of Brahman as supreme, all-embracing Reality becomes fully developed in the Upanishadic literature. Brahman is both transcendent and immanent – simultaneously beyond and within all things. The notion that the individual self is ultimately part of the One led to questions about physical death and the eventual reunification of atman with Brahman. Thus, the Upanishads developed the classical Hindu notion of reincarnation (samsara) driven by the law of karma. Individual beings are born, die and are reborn into the world in different forms. This occurs many times until they achieve their ultimate purpose, which is to be freed from the samsaric wheel forever. The crucial question was how to build up the good karma necessary to achieve liberation (moksha). The traditional Brahmanic system focused on blessings in the here and now, but gradually it absorbed the increasingly popular reincarnational worldview by teaching that good karma was generated by performing correct rituals and abiding by caste laws. However, the Upanishads declared that what really mattered was not liturgical conformity but ethical behavior. It was not proper ceremony but moral conduct that liberated.

The Upanishadic preference for ethics and philosophy over ritual, coupled with the new political and economic centres of power, created serious problems for a tradition that stressed sacrifices and caste. People were starting to ask how violence to animals could possibly help one advance on the wheel of reincarnation, especially when beings could be reincarnated as animals. The principle of nonviolence (Pali: avihimsa; Sanskrit: ahimsa) was in the air. In the urban centers questions were also raised about traditional caste theory, which did not easily accommodate the new, powerful merchant class. It was becoming obvious that a person's class did not necessarily determine their physical, psychological, intellectual or economic endowments. The caste theory was struggling to cope with the complexities of a world in which upper class persons could suffer and fail, while lower class persons could enjoy great worldly success. While the astika tradition faced such questions from within the ambit of orthodoxy, the nastika tradition was willing to go further. If the Upanishads typify the former, the shramana movement typifies the latter.[12]

The shramanas were radical ascetics who renounced normal life in search of a higher spiritual truth that could accelerate moksha. Theirs was a spartan existence, lived on the outskirts of the civilized world in an attempt to break the shackles that bind humans to the wheel of samsara. First and foremost, they were itinerants who had abandoned the household for the forest. Their new abodes were huts, caves or groves, and in these primitive conditions they discovered a freedom that could not be found in the cramped and dusty conditions of the domestic house. Leaving home involved leaving wife, children, family and friends. In some cases, the shramana embraced total solitude, living the life of a hermit and exchanged human company for the wild animals. In other cases, they replaced their familial network with a new spiritual community of fellow ascetics. Leaving home meant leaving behind the pleasures of marriage, including sexual activity. The life of the shramana was a celibate one in which powerful sexual energy was rechannelled up the spine and into the mind to enhance meditative states. Leaving home meant leaving the kitchen and the hearth and embracing a mendicant existence. Instead of regular, cooked meals, the shramana relied on the fruits of the forest or the generosity of others who would place morsels of food in their begging bowl. Leaving home meant leaving behind concerns about clothing and physical appearance. Many shramanas dressed in simple yellow colored rags or even went about naked ("sky clad") in an act of total detachment. Some shaved their hair while others allowed it to grow long and unkempt. Despite their dishevelled and emaciated appearance, they were highly respected as holy persons, on the verge of moksha. Yet shramanic life was not just renouncing ordinary physical pleasures. It also involved positive action, especially silent meditation. As a jobless, dependent wanderer, the shramana had plenty of time to devote himself to matters of the spirit. As the body was disciplined and tamed, the mind was to be expanded and enlightened. In the turbulent, rapidly changing world of sixth century BCE northern India, the shramanic lifestyle was extraordinarily popular. Shramana movements probably existed in the ancient Indus Valley civilization but the sheer numbers of young men joining at the time of the Buddha was unprecedented. It was a road of individual effort and self-discipline outside the distractions of ordinary social life, for anyone who had the desire and the strength.

Roman Palestine

The setting for the story of Jesus is a modest strip of land at the eastern end of the Mediterranean Sea variously known as Canaan, Palestine, Israel, the Holy Land and other titles, many of which carry religious and political connotations today (see Map 2). In terms of geography, the area can be divided into four natural regions. A thin coastal plain stretches over 100 mi from Lebanon to the edges of the Nile delta. The plain is bounded to the east by higher terrain that runs from Galilee in the north to the Judean hills in the south, broken only by the Plain of Esdraelon. To the east of the hill country lies the Great Rift Valley, an enormous fissure in the earth's crust that cuts through the entire region and continues through the Red Sea into East

Africa. Following the line of the Rift Valley is the most important watercourse in the area, the Jordan River. Fed by the mountains of Lebanon and Syria, the Jordan flows in a southerly direction and feeds the fresh waters of the Sea of Galilee, which abounds in marine life. It then continues south for another 60 mi before terminating in the lifeless, salt-saturated waters of the Dead Sea, which at 1,300 ft below sea level is the lowest point on the earth's surface. To the south of the Dead Sea lies a desert area known aptly as the Negev – a term that means both "dry" and "south" in the Hebrew bible. The latitude of the region places it in the subtropical zone, but the wetter climate of the north gradually gives way to a semi-arid climate in the south. The rains tend to fall in the cooler months between October and April, whereas the summers can be oppressively hot and dry. The area has seen cultivation since the dawn of civilization, including crops such as wheat, barley and other grains, as well as olives, figs, dates and grapes. Sheep and goat grazing, for the production of wool and flax, was the main pastoral activity since it was well suited to the terrain and climate.[13]

In the early first century CE, Palestine was a recent addition to the rapidly expanding Roman Empire, which at that point completely encircled the Mediterranean Sea (aptly nicknamed "the Roman Pond"). The dominion of Rome extended from Lusitania (Portugal and Spain) and Mauretania (Morocco) in the west to Cappadocia (eastern Turkey), Syria and Judea in the east. Across the Danube to the north lie the barbarian lands of Germania; to the south was the Sahara desert; and to the east was the Parthian Empire and the sands of Arabia. There is some debate as to the precise moment of transition from Republic to Empire, but one crucial point was the victory over Mark Antony by Julius Caesar's great nephew Octavian, at the naval Battle of Actium in 31 BCE. Octavian was subsequently given the imperial name Augustus by the Senate and he is often listed as the first of the Roman emperors, reigning from 27 BCE to 14 CE. Augustus was succeeded by his wife's son Tiberias (emperor from 14 to 37 CE). The Empire would continue to expand until the mid-second century when, under the emperor Trajan, it reached its geographical zenith, covering over 2,000,000 sq. mi.

In terms of culture and religion, Rome was the heir of Alexander's Hellenism. The gods of the Greek pantheon had been given new Roman names – Zeus became Jupiter; Aphrodite became Venus; Ares became Mars; Hermes became Mercury and so on. The Empire was also home to a myriad of religions from the diverse cultures that had been incorporated into it. The legions had brought back cults, such as those of Cybele, Isis and Mithras. These were the "mystery religions" – closed societies that practiced secret rituals of initiation, propitiatory sacrifices and symbolic communal meals. In contrast to the private, individual nature of the mystery religions, there was also the public, civil obligation on all citizens to acknowledge the divine status of the emperor.

Hellenism was also characterized by extraordinary advances in philosophical thinking. Apart from the great classical schools of Plato and Aristotle, new movements had also arisen and were widely disseminated by Roman times. Stoicism advocated calm indifference in the face of life's vicissitudes. Epicureanism proposed the pursuit of pleasure, albeit with modesty and balance. Skepticism criticized logic as an unreliable path to truth. Cynicism protested against the vanity of wealth. Its founder,

Diogenes of Sinope, had lived in a tub in the streets of Athens, and by the first century BCE, itinerant, celibate Cynic philosophers were preaching and begging in towns across the Empire, dressed in their standard uniform of cloak, wallet, staff but no sandals.[14]

The Hellenistic influence was ubiquitous throughout the Empire, even in Palestine despite its fiercely proud traditions. Aramaic (a variation of Hebrew) was the native tongue, but many educated and commercial folk spoke the lingua franca of the Empire, which was Greek rather than Latin.[15] The city of Sepphoris, the main administrative base for lower Galilee, was a typical cosmopolitan centre where Jewish and Gentile cultures mixed. Within a range of 50 mi were other Hellenistic cities such as Tyre, Sidon, Caesarea Philippi, Hippos, Gadara, Scythopolis and Gaba. Just a few miles down the road was the small single-well village of Nazareth, slightly off the beaten track but still near enough to be in contact with the complex Hellenistic world around it.[16]

In 64 BCE the Roman general Pompey marched into Syria and established it as a Roman province. At the time, the Jewish nation was in the grip of a civil war between two Hasmonean brothers: Hyrcanus II and Aristobulus II. Pompey supported Hyrcanus, the older brother, possibly because he was considered to be the weaker and thus more easily controlled. Aristobulus surrendered, but his forces ensconced themselves in Jerusalem, which was placed under siege for three months. In the autumn of 63 BCE, Pompey broke the siege and captured the city. Aristobulus was sent to Rome as a prisoner, Hyrcanus regained the office of High Priest and Judea had officially become part of the Roman Empire.[17]

After some time, Hyrcanus was also named ethnarch (something less than king), but the Romans dealt primarily with his chief advisor, Antipater, who became de facto decision-maker. As Antipater's power increased, he began to advance the interests of his own family and in 49 BCE he appointed his eldest son as governor of Jerusalem and his second son as governor of Galilee. Although the elder son, Phasael, faded from the scene, the second son, Herod, would have a profound impact on local history. After gaining support from Rome, where he was given the title "King of the Jews", Herod conspired to have the last surviving Hasmonean heir drowned in his Jericho palace. He was now sole effective ruler of Palestine and he reigned for nearly 40 years until his death in 4 BCE. Despite his efforts at legitimization and his epithet "the Great", Herod was not a popular king, being seen as a foreign usurper and a Roman puppet. His decadent lifestyle and the murderous treatment of his own family did not help his cause, and many devout Jews considered his ambitious extension of the Temple precincts as grandiose and self-interested, although such building projects brought considerable economic benefits.

After Herod's death, Roman authorities divided the kingdom between his three sons. The southern region, which comprised Judea, Samaria and Idumea, was entrusted to Archelaus; Herod Antipas became tetrarch of Galilee and the southern part of Transjordania known as Perea; and Philip received Batania and Traconitis, which were located beyond the Decapolis in the northern part of Transjordania. Archelaus proved to be such a brutal leader that his own populace appealed to the Emperor Augustus, who banished him to Gaul. His portion of the kingdom was placed under the direct authority of a Roman prefect.[18] Rome also controlled the office of High Priest, which was considered a political as well as a religious position. The High Priest presided over the chief council of Jews known as the Sanhedrin, which interpreted Jewish law, especially in those matters that pertained to ritual. Its 71 members were powerful and influential figures in Jewish society, including chief priests, elders, scribes and other leading citizens.[19]

The Empire was not primarily interested in the Romanization of the many cultures within its sway and, to a great extent, it allowed the local leader to rule with a considerable degree of autonomy, provided sufficient tribute was raised and the people were not driven to rebellion. Rome's real interest in Judea was its strategic location on the trade route between Syria and Egypt, and its potential as a buffer state to the Parthian Empire in the east. Despite a relatively hands-off approach, however, there were strong elements of disquiet and unrest around the Empire, particularly in Judea, where the potential for violent rebellion was never far away. Both the Roman and Jewish authorities knew this and endeavored at all times to avoid a spark flying into the tinderbox. One of the main sources of political trouble was the general discontent of the peasant class, especially as a result of heavy taxation.[20] Jewish tax collectors were employed by the government to implement the system and they were often despised by the common people as opportunistic traitors. Such taxes were common throughout the Empire, but in Israel, there was an additional layer: a religious tax. Jews were also required to offer support to the Temple priests, sometimes in the form of money, but also via the purchase of animals, which were offered in sacrifice.[21]

On the religious front, first-century Judaism was characterized by such a complex variety of factions that it seems more appropriate to speak of Judaisms in the plural rather than in the singular.[22] Most villages and towns had their local synagogue but the heart of Jewish religious life was the Jerusalem Temple. The original Temple had been constructed in the tenth century BCE by King Solomon but it was destroyed in 587 BCE by the Babylonians. A second Temple was constructed toward the end of the sixth century BCE, and it was substantially extended under Herod the Great. The Temple was not just an impressive physical edifice; it was also Israel's primary politico-religious symbol and its most prominent institution. It was a place where sacrifices were offered and sins forgiven, but it also stood for Jewish pride and national sovereignty. Offences against the Temple cut deeply into Jewish sensitivities and formal protests to the Roman prefect often concerned some sort of abuse against the Temple, such as the idolatrous instalment of the Emperor's image or the misuse of its funds.[23] The Temple precincts were constantly under the watchful gaze of the Roman authorities especially when large crowds gathered for festivals. Yet the Temple, or at least the priestly elite that controlled it and presided over its ritual system, was often the target of criticism from within Judaism.[24]

The historian Josephus speaks of three main groups within Judaism at the time: Sadducees, Pharisees and Essenes. The term Sadducee is probably derived from Zadok, the High Priest of the first Temple.[25] It is a fitting title for a group that consisted primarily of priests and their influential aristocratic allies, whose power base was Jerusalem. The Sadducees accepted only the written Torah as the definitive Word of God, disallowing any form of supplementary oral tradition. They also tended to interpret the Torah in a literalist manner. Some of the doctrinal consequences of this position included the rejection of the concepts of angels, bodily resurrection and the immortality of the soul. The Sadducees disappeared from history after the destruction of the Temple in 70 CE.

The main political and religious opponents of the Sadducees were the Pharisees, from the Hebrew word "perushim", meaning separated ones. The Pharisees insisted that sanctity could be found outside of the Temple and the priesthood, emphasizing the holiness of the nation itself and applying to all believers many laws that were originally intended for priests.[26] The Pharisees were mainly teachers and scribes who insisted that effective reform of Judaism required meticulous adherence to the divine commandments, especially rules concerning purity, fasting, tithing and the Sabbath.[27] In contrast to the Sadducees, the Pharisees admitted the validity of an unwritten tradition, which supplemented the written Torah and was passed down orally through the centuries. One important consequence of this position was that they accepted the concept of a postmortem judgment and bodily resurrection, which is not explicitly taught in the Torah but appears in Jewish thought around the time of the Maccabean revolt.[28]

Josephus' third group, the Essenes, is commonly linked to the collection of writings that was unearthed between 1947 and 1956 in caves near the ruins of the Qumran monastery on the northwest shore of the Dead Sea. The Dead Sea Scrolls reveal a group that were so utterly disenchanted with the Temple, including its priesthood, cult and calendar, that they retreated to the wilderness at some stage during the second century BCE.[29] In the isolation of the desert, the community followed a radical lifestyle, in protest against Hasmonean claims to the High Priesthood and the general corruption of the Temple elite. Members shared their material possessions, practiced elaborate cleansing rituals and many of them embraced celibacy. The community and its dwellings were destroyed by the Romans around 68 CE.

There was actually greater diversity within Judaism than Josephus' three groups suggests. One important category was that of the charismatic magician or wonder-worker, who performed amazing feats by channelling or controlling divine power over natural forces. The classical biblical cases are Moses, and the ninth century BCE prophets Elijah and Elisha, but they are the exception not the rule. The prophets of Israel did not normally work wonders and the figure of a miracle-worker does not feature again in the Hebrew bible after them. However, there are two cases mentioned in the Talmud. Both figures lived in the first century BCE and they are described somewhat enigmatically as "men of deed". The first is Honi the Circle-maker, who once successfully prayed for rain.[30] The second case is Hanina ben Dosa, who cured an official's son from a distance and survived a bite from a poisonous lizard.[31] These are rare cases but any miracle worker would have been considered inherently dangerous by the religious authorities because he represented a source of divine power and mercy outside of the central ritual system.[32]

Another type of religious figure at the time also took its inspiration from the Exodus story. The late Second Temple period witnessed a dramatic rise in the appearance of millennial prophets who saw themselves as harbingers of national liberation just as Moses and Joshua had led the Hebrew people out of Egyptian slavery and across the wilderness to a new promised land. Relying on their persuasive powers rather than on miraculous deeds or military force, they were able to rally hundreds and even thousands of people in the belief that God would act imminently to restore the kingdom of Israel. Examples include: an anonymous Samaritan who led a large group of followers to Mount Gerizim in 36 CE; Theudas who took his followers to the Jordan between 41 and 44 CE; and an "Egyptian Prophet" who gathered 30,000 people on the Mount of Olives sometime between 52 and 58 CE. On each occasion, the authorities intervened and the movement failed, in some cases resulting in the death of the leader.[33]

The millennial prophets not only saw themselves in the tradition of the great prophets of Israel, especially Moses, but they also sensed that they belonged to a special time in Israel's history. Like the Essenes, their worldview was apocalyptic in that they believed that a new age was about to dawn as a result of a definitive act of God, particularly through his "anointed one", the Messiah.[34] By the time of the Roman occupation, many Jews understood the term to refer to a descendant of King David who would rise up and establish a golden age of independence, justice and peace. Yet there was disagreement as to the process. Some stressed an apocalyptic version in which God would intervene to set up his earthly king via a cataclysmic overturning of existing powers, divine judgment and a completely new idyllic age. Others saw the hand of God working more subtly through an historical person who would literally drive out the Romans by very down-to-earth military means. Unlike the millennial prophets, these messianic movements involved the use of arms, and their leader modelled himself not so much on the figure of Moses but on the first kings of Israel: Saul and David.

There are three cases of messianic claimants in the chaotic period that immediately followed the death of Herod the Great in 4 BCE. The first instance is Judas, son of Ezekias, who gathered a large number of men and raided the royal palace at Sepphoris, the principal city in southern Galilee. With their booty and weapons, the group continued to attack powerful and wealthy targets.[35] The second occurred in the region of Perea when Simon, a former slave of Herod the Great, burned and plundered the royal palace at Jericho. He and his band roamed the countryside setting fire to other royal buildings. Simon was reputedly tall, strong and handsome – features reminiscent of Saul, the first king of Israel.[36] The third case is Athronges who attacked military targets throughout Judea and claimed to be the true king of Israel. Like Simon of Perea, Athronges possessed the physical prowess of Saul, but he also resembled the biblical figure of David in that he came from a lowly shepherd's background.[37]

Apart from these messianic claimants, there was also a broader armed resistance against Roman oppression, which Josephus called the "Fourth Philosophy" (alongside Sadducees, Pharisees and Essenes) – or more commonly the Zealots. One form of such resistance was the "Sicarii" (dagger men), who operated mainly in urban centers where they carried out secret assassinations against fellow Jews suspected of collaborating with the Romans. The members of the Sicarii were from the educated, urban middle class, but in the countryside the armed resistance took the form of banditry. In northern Galilee, the targets were the wealthy Jewish elite. One of the reasons that Rome imposed its most brutal forms of punishment against the bandits (crucifixion, being burnt alive or being fed to beasts) was the potential for the bandit chief to assume political power on the wave of widespread support. After all, King David had lived the life of a bandit under Saul before his ascension to the throne.[38]

As Roman forces concentrated on the north in their attempt to eradicate banditry, they effectively drove large numbers of peasants and bandits south toward Jerusalem where the groups began to coalesce into the Zealot movement proper. Its goal moved beyond the bandit's main concern with economic injustice to a political-religious one – the total eviction of foreign power and the establishment of an independent Jewish state. With them, the entire spectrum of economic, social, religious and political unrest came to a head in 66 CE with the outbreak of the Jewish–Roman War. It lasted four years but, unlike the successful Maccabean fight 200 years earlier, this time the foreigner proved too strong and the price was exceedingly high. In the catastrophic year of 70 CE, the Temple, the priesthood and a sizeable portion of ancient Judaism were swept away and lost forever.

Arabia Deserta

The Arabian Peninsula is a vast land mass, over 1,200 mi long, 600 mi wide and surrounded by water on three sides (see Map 3). To the east, it is separated from Asia by the Persian Gulf; to the west lies the shore of the Red Sea and beyond that the African continent; and to the south are the waters of the Arabian Sea, itself a part of the Indian Ocean. As one author describes it, Arabia is paradoxically "a desert in the midst of an ocean".[39] The southwest corner around Yemen experiences reasonable levels of rainfall making it greener than the rest of the peninsula. It boasts an amazing variety of tropical plant life, from which exotic spices, perfumes and other aromatic substances were produced, including the much sought after frankincense. But this fertile niche is the exception. Most of Arabia experiences an arid climate, making it one of the hottest, driest and most inhospitable habitats in the world.

The Romans used the term Arabia to designate three distinct regions. Arabia Petrae (centred on the ancient city of Petra) encompassed modern Syria, Jordan, the Sinai Peninsula and northwestern Saudi Arabia. Migrant Arab tribes, such as the Nabateans, had settled here over the centuries seeking arable land at the edge of the Fertile Crescent in Mesopotamia. This was the only part of greater Arabia that actually became a province of the Roman Empire. The second region was Arabia Felix ("fertile Arabia"), which referred to the cultivated terraces of the southwest. The peoples of this area were known variously as Sabaeans or Yemenites, and the wetter climate and fertile soils had allowed them to settle into the sedentary lifestyle of villages and towns surrounded by farmed areas. Yemen's commercial wealth and strategic location meant that it aroused the attention of the greater political powers.

The third Roman term was Arabia Deserta ("Desert Arabia"), which referred to the great unconquered (and unconquerable) interior of the peninsula. This was a very different world. In this harsh environment, settled agriculture was limited to a few oases where date palms were grown and harvested. By sheer necessity, the only realistic means of income was nomadic pastoralism. Whereas the Yemenites could live in concentrated towns and work their farms, the Bedouins of the desert had to form small tightly knit tribal groups and move their herds from place to place in search of water and suitable food. It was a grim, relentless struggle. Yet by the seventh century CE certain tribes had established towns at the vital natural springs that were sprinkled around the periphery of Arabia Deserta. Thus, a semi-urban, sedentary culture had started to grow up beside the more traditional nomadic one.

A major trade route ran from Syria, along the western coast of Arabia, to the Yemenite towns of the southwestern tip. There were typically two seasons each year. In winter, the caravans travelled southward and in summer they moved northward. Along this critical highway, three oasis towns had emerged as important centres under the management of Arabs who abandoned the nomadic life for the rewards of commercial prosperity. Those towns were Ta'if, Yathrib and Mecca. Ta'if was a walled citadel town about 40 mi southeast of Mecca on the slopes of the Sarawat Mountains. It enjoyed a milder climate than the lower regions near the Red Sea coast. Crops such as wheat, grapes and fruit could be grown, thus earning it the title "Garden of the Hijaz". Approximately 250 mi north of Mecca was the town of Yathrib. It had been built on an abundantly fertile oasis, which enabled the citizens to grow dates and cereals. One striking feature of Yathrib was its strong Jewish presence.

Unlike its northern neighbor, Mecca was located in a particularly barren area that was unsuitable for agriculture. However, it did have sufficient water from its natural spring, Zamzam, to sustain a reasonable population. The Quraysh tribe had become successful merchants, taking control of commercial interests by the early sixth century and promoting Mecca as an important stop on the trade route.[40] As the centre of a loose confederation of client tribes, Mecca was a potential binding force in a fundamentally disunited Arabia. The success of trade depended on the safe passage of the caravans and, to this end, the Meccan businessmen forged alliances with the local Bedouins who would offer protection at various stages of the journey. The Quraysh also worked toward some degree of intertribal peace by establishing a strict zone of nonviolence within a 20-mi radius of the centre of Mecca.[41]

On the broader political front, Arabia was located on the volatile border between two massive states: the Byzantine (Roman) Empire to the west with its capital of Constantinople and the Sassanid (Persian) Empire to the east with its centre at Ctesiphon (approximately twenty mi south-east of modern Baghdad). In the early seventh century, the two leviathans were locked in a series of military campaigns that left both financially, militarily and politically exhausted.[42] Although neither empire seriously contemplated incorporating the deserts of Arabia into its domain, the two superpowers were very interested in seeking allies and supporters from small satellite states in the region.

Yet the sphere of imperial influence could not penetrate into the heart of Arabia Deserta, where the tribe was the fundamental political and social unit. Although dialects were based on a common language, there was no real overarching sense of Arabian unity.[43] One's fundamental loyalty was to one's own tribe and all others were potential enemies unless a special alliance had been forged. The members of the tribe were usually blood kin and the name of each clan or tribe was usually prefaced with the term "Banu", which means the descendants of a common ancestor, historical or legendary.[44] Inter-tribal tension was a constant factor as rival groups competed with each other for the limited resources. Fighting frequently broke out over water or pastures since there were rarely clearly defined borders within the nomadic world. This was also the context for the acquisition raid (ghazu), although all military conflicts were supposed to cease during the four sacred months of the year.[45]

The classical Muslim term for the religious situation before Muhammad is "jahili-yya". Literally it means a time of ignorance, when the one true God was unknown and people wallowed in superstitious idolatry.[46] In fact, pre-Islamic Arabian religion was an interesting amalgam of various ingredients: native and foreign; polytheistic and monotheistic. The most basic form of religion was animistic polytheism, in which natural forces were deified. There were gods and spirits everywhere: in the sky and earth, hills and caves, wind and rain, oases and springs, trees and stones, especially meteorites that had fallen from heaven. The main deity of the Meccan pantheon was Hubal whose advice was sought by tossing arrows in front of his statue. The people of Mecca also acknowledged the existence of Allah, a high god who created the world and provided rain but, as a distant figure, one would only turn to him directly on rare occasions, such as a serious crisis.[47] Allah's very transcendence and remoteness meant that he had little practical relevance to the ordinary lives of Meccans. On the other hand, his three daughters – al-Lat (sun goddess), al-'Uzza (Venus) and Manat (Fate) – were seen to be more concerned with genuine, mundane struggles, and they were the object of frequent worship, sacrifice and petition throughout Arabia.[48] Although they had no dedicated shrine in Mecca itself, the citizens of that town had a special fondness for the three daughters, likening them to beautiful cranes that soared higher than any other bird.[49]

There were also the capricious spirits of the desert, known as jinn (singular: jinni) who played mischievous pranks on people. They were thought to be the mysterious inspiration behind the poet (sha'ir) and the soothsayer (kahin).[50] In a purely oral tradition, the recitation of poems was the key means of literary expression and the sha'ir often filled multiple roles: artist, historian, propagandist, social commentator and religious oracle. The poet played a vital part in the tribe's struggle for survival and supremacy over others. His poems would sing the praises of the tribe and recount the great deeds wrought by its heroes. Other poems would satirize enemy tribes, focusing on their weaknesses and mistakes. At the market town of 'Ukaz, near Mecca, a poetry competition was held at its annual trade fair.[51]

It is no coincidence that the 'Ukaz trade fair was held during the three-month period of truce at the turn of each year. It was a time when military activity was suspended and commercial activities were allowed to proceed unhindered. It was also the occasion for one of Arabia's most important religious practices – the annual pilgrimage, whose focus was a simple, cube-shaped edifice in the centre of Mecca known as the Ka'ba. The Ka'ba was essentially a repository for over three hundred idols, each one linked to a particular tribe. The most prominent was the statue of Hubal, the principal deity of the town.[52] In addition, a black stone was set into the outer wall at the eastern corner of the building. It was considered to be a holy item, similar in religious significance to the red stone in Ghaiman and the white stone near the town of Tabala.[53]

There were also Jews and Christians living in Arabia at the time. They spoke Arabic, organized themselves into tribes like the Bedouins, and had assimilated local customs and values. Yet they had retained their distinctive religious faith, and so Jewish and Christian ideas had slowly disseminated throughout the peninsula by the time of Muhammad. There was a large Jewish community in Yathrib but numbers were much lower in Mecca.[54] Small groups of Christians were also scattered about the peninsula, and an icon of Mary and the infant Jesus had even been painted on the inside wall of the Ka'ba. However, Arabs were wary of formal conversion since Christianity carried political ramifications, given that the Byzantines and Abyssinians were Orthodox Christian, while the Sassanid Empire was a mix of Zoroastrianism and Nestorian Christianity.[55] A consequence of this was the existence of a group of Arabs who were explicitly monotheistic in outlook but who professed neither Judaism nor Christianity. These were the "hunafa" (singular: hanif). The Qur'an uses the term to refer to those who profess the pure religion of Abraham, the first true hanif, in contrast to later Jewish and Christian variations. However, it also has come to mean believers in the one God prior to the coming of the Prophet, faint beacons of truth and hope in the dark days of jahiliyya.[56] The hunafa did not constitute a formal religion or an organized movement, but rather a minority group within Arabian society, which saw tribal polytheism as an aberration of true religion.

Jewish and Christian influence not only brought the idea of monotheism but also eschatological ideas, such as resurrection of the body, postmortem judgment, and the dual possibility of heaven or hell. The monotheistic faiths also presumed the idea of divine revelation via a series of chosen prophets and the expectation of the future coming of the Messiah (whether for the first time as in Judaism or for the second time as in Christianity). There was also a local tradition that God had sent three prophets to the Arabs in the distant past: Hud, Salih and Shu'ayb. According to tradition, Hud was one of the original Arabs who lived in the sands of the Hadramawt. Several shrines around Arabia are claimed to be his tomb. Salih was sent to the Thamub people of Arabia, but his plea for them to return to monotheism was met with scornful rejection for which the people were punished by a terrifying storm. Shu'ayb was thought to have preached against idolatry and social injustice in the area of Midian, although the Druze revere his tomb at Hittin in modern Israel. There was also a vague expectation among some Christians and Jews that a fourth prophet would soon be sent to the Arabs.[57]

Observations

The first noteworthy feature concerning the various contexts of the three founders is the sizeable temporal separation between them. It is not as if they are a few decades or even a few centuries apart on the historical timeline. There is half a millennium between the Buddha and Jesus, and another 600 years between Jesus and Muhammad, placing them in three very different stages of the human story. In itself, such immense gaps might suggest that their individual contexts will have very little in common, but there are some interesting intersections nevertheless. The chronological order of the three is important since it means that a later figure may be cognizant of an earlier figure and thus be open to some degree of influence. Neither Jesus nor Muhammad seems to have been aware of the Buddha or the religion that sprang from his life, even though it had been developing and expanding across Asia for five and eleven centuries, respectively. In contrast, Muhammad was very much aware of Jesus as well as the two religions associated with him. There were Jewish and Christian communities living in Arabia at the time, and Muhammad had direct, first-hand experience of both faiths in his earlier and later years. Consequently, and somewhat surprisingly for some, Jesus was accredited with an important role in Islam from the very beginning. Moreover, many elements of Jewish belief and practice are echoed in Islam, despite the serious politico-religious tensions currently plaguing their interrelationship.

A comparison of the geographical contexts also throws up some interesting patterns. From the traditional, and highly subjective, European cartographic perspective, all three founders hail from "the East" – namely that part of the world east of Europe. The Buddha's India is the most oriental of the three, placing him in at the edge of the Far East, although the members of his own society understandably called their territories "the Middle Land". In contrast, both Jesus and Muhammad lived in the Middle East, sharing a common cultural heritage that is encapsulated by the broader sense of the term "Semitic". From Jerusalem, it is nearly 3,000 mi to Bodhgaya but only 700 mi to Mecca. Although international trade links existed, India was a distant, unknown land that lay far beyond the everyday horizon of the Jews and the Arabs. While Alexander's Empire had started in Greece and extended east to the fringes of India, the Roman Empire encircled the Mediterranean Sea and Judea was on its eastern extreme. In Roman Palestine, the political and cultural centre of the world was to the occident rather than to the orient. Seventh-century Arabia was slightly different in that it lay beyond the boundaries of both the Western Byzantine Empire and the Eastern Sassanid Empire. But Syria, Egypt and Jerusalem were well within reach, and it is possible that a young Muhammad may even have travelled to some of those places. Certainly, Islamic tradition claims that he mystically flew to Jerusalem and then to heaven one night at the crossroads of his career. Moreover, the original direction of the daily prayers was towards that city until it was later changed to Mecca.

Although all three homelands share a similar northern latitude (Mecca 21°; Rajagaha 25°; and Jerusalem 32°), there is a striking contrast in climatic conditions as a result of the different positions of continents, oceans and mountain ranges. On one hand, the world of the Buddha was characterized by great rivers, rich cultivated floodplains and lush forests. On the other hand, Arabia is an arid, sun-scorched desert world where only the hardiest of plants survive, mainly in scattered oases. In Israel, the green pasturelands of Galilee give way to the semi-arid hills of Judea in the south, with the barren wilderness never far away. Although forest and desert seem to be opposite ends of the spectrum, both take on a similar religious meaning as a place of religious retreat. Both offer a space away from the din of human society, where the voice of the spirit can be more easily heard. It is no coincidence that the key events in the life of the Buddha occurred under a tree in a forest. Similarly, the quiet solitude of the desert features at the key turning points in the stories of both Jesus and Muhammad.

In terms of economic life, all three men lived in preindustrial societies where the majority of people eked out a living as agriculturalists or pastoralists, but there were also urban centres where tradesmen and merchants earned their keep. In the Palestine of Jesus, one of the main economic concerns was the crushing burden on the peasantry created by a double taxation system. For many, it was a fine line between surviving and being forced to break the law, either a civil or a religious one. In contrast, the Buddha and Muhammad both lived in a time when a merchant class was emerging due to the explosion of new forms of commercial activity. In Mecca, groups of Bedouins had given up nomadic pastoralism and become urban-based commercial brokers, establishing a thriving trade monopoly based on caravans. On the Ganges Plain, new technologies, specialized trades, a money economy and greater urbanization were all threatening the traditional social structures and providing lucrative sponsorship for new religious movements more attuned to the needs of the *nouveau riche*.

Economics is inextricably linked to politics, and the economic forces at work in each context had ramifications regarding the distribution of power and authority. In many ways, the three contexts are quite different when viewed through the political lens. The Buddha was born into a small vassal state under one of four expanding regional states. Small republics were giving way to larger kingdoms. It was a time of annexation, incorporation and monopolization of power as the four vied for ultimate supremacy. In the end, it was Magadha that triumphed, forming a viable political unit that would eventually become the seed of the first great Indian empire just over a century later. Jesus lived during a more advanced point in the empire-building process since Judea had been incorporated into the Roman state 60 years before his birth. Soon afterward, the Republic had evolved into the Empire with Augustus and Tiberius, both of whom feature in the gospel story, as the first two emperors. The Roman colossus would reach its greatest geographical extent a century later under Trajan. The occupation of Judea brought benefits for some Jews but generated widespread resentment among the masses, many of whom considered collaborators as traitors. Nationalist resistance was sky-high, and protests took both nonviolent and violent forms. The terrible climax would come several decades after Jesus's death with the destruction of the Temple in 70 CE, one of the darkest moments in Jewish history. In contrast, Muhammad's Arabia was at a much earlier point in the empire-building process than either of the above. While Israel was inside the borders of the dominant empire of the day, Arabia was just outside the periphery of two empires, protected from conquest by its inhospitable climate and terrain. Internally, there was little sense of Arabian unity. A fierce, proud loyalty to one's tribe was the major political determinant and the limited resources meant constant internecine competition and warfare. It was a fragmented world outside the pale of the great civilizations of the day. Yet history has shown that, given the right circumstances, the potential was there to unify the tribes and unleash a new political force into the vacuum created by the weakened Byzantine and Sassanid Empires.

Finally, and most importantly, it is imperative to compare the religious contexts in which each of the founders lived and taught. The first common feature is the tension between polytheistic and monotheistic/monistic views of transcendent reality. The notion that there is a pantheon of divine beings above us and around us is a feature of the Vedas, Roman religious mythology and Arabian tribal animism. Yet against these given systems, there is also a protesting voice that insists on the oneness and singularity of absolute being. The new Upanishadic movement of the Buddha's day proposed that the multitude of the Vedic gods were fundamentally manifestations of the one ultimate reality beyond all forms: Brahman. Since the time of Abraham, Judaism stood almost unique in its constant insistence on the one, true God and the utter emptiness and futility of worshipping any other gods. Biblical history reveals Israel's own struggle against the polytheistic temptations of Egypt, Mesopotamia, Assyria, Babylon, Greece and Rome. Finally, the Jews and Christians of Arabia represented a monotheistic presence in a world of tribal polytheism, but the hunafa also indicate the existence of local, nondenominational monotheists among the Arabs themselves.

The earlier geographical distinction between the Far East and the Middle East is also reflected in the fundamental religious anthropology of both worlds. Although Vedic religion focused mainly on blessings in this life, the new Upanishadic movement began to speculate on the fate of the person beyond death. Inspired by the cyclic patterns manifest in plants and crops, its thinkers developed a samsaric view of human life in which the essence (atman) of a person is reborn over and over again in different forms according to the law of karma. The cycle of birth, death and rebirth continues until the atman is eventually released from the wheel of reincarnation and achieves final liberation (moksha). In contrast, Jewish theology saw human existence essentially as a linear process in which the person is born and dies only once. Although some streams accept a limited notion of reincarnation,[58] the element of accountability, which is the primary function of karma, is captured via a postmortem judgment of each person by the divine judge. Whereas the Indian samsaric system sees liberation worked out over hundreds or thousands of lifetimes, the Semitic view gives each person a single opportunity to get it right. All of the pressure is on this one life, irrespective of how long or short it turns out to be. Moreover, while the Indian samsaric system accords no perpetual value to the physical body, since the atman will have many such bodies along the way, Judaism was beginning to see a role for the body in the afterlife via the concept of resurrection, which came to the fore in the Maccabean period, probably as a result of Zoroastrian influence. Yet the Sadducee–Pharisee debates about the fate of the body show that the issue was not fully resolved in Jesus's time. Meanwhile, Arabian polytheism was very much focused on the here and now, and had no developed philosophical notions of an afterlife, let alone the idea of bodily resurrection.

The models of revelation in each religious context also display interesting similarities and differences. The Vedic, Jewish and Arabian religious traditions all possessed the concept of special communication between the gods and humans. The Indian tradition held that the contents of the Vedas had been revealed in ancient times to sages who had entered into highly advanced states of consciousness. The art of meditation was considered to be the most reliable gateway to sublime truths. The Jewish religion also had its own sacred scriptures, which were thought to have been revealed via a long series of prophets, simultaneously commencing and climaxing with the unrivalled figure of Moses. The prophets were the human conduits through which divine commandment, admonition and consolation were conveyed. Many biblical books carry the name of the prophet concerned: Samuel, Isaiah, Jeremiah, Ezekiel and so on. Arabian society also had its prophetic figures although their messages were not stored in written form, but rather were memorized and orally recited generation after generation. The Arabian poets, who were thought to have been possessed or inspired by the desert jinn, delivered words of literary beauty, psychological motivation and incisive social comment.

In Jewish thinking, the age of the prophets was thought to have closed long before the time of Jesus, and within a century or two, the contents of the Hebrew scriptures would be definitively closed. Meanwhile, the general tenor of thinking and writing had shifted to the apocalyptic mode. The Maccabean rebellion and the Roman occupation had fuelled expectations of an imminent divine intervention. It was widely believed that a glorious new age would very soon be ushered in and presided over by God's anointed one, the Messiah. This pervasive sense that the end of days was nigh and that a long-awaited leader was on the horizon is an absolutely crucial ingredient in the Jesus story. There is a faint echo in the case of Muhammad with vague rumors circulating among some Christians and Jews of an Arabian prophet, but there was no such expectation among the polytheistic communities in general, nor was there a prevailing sense that the end-times were at hand. Similarly, Hinduism had not yet fully developed the myth of Vishnu's incarnations (avatars), the tenth of which is still to come. In fact, the Buddha was eventually added to that list as the ninth in the series, following Rama and Krishna. Thus, the question put to Jesus is unique among the three: "Are you the one who is to come?"[59]

Although the expectation of an imminent apocalypse is not found in the Buddha's religious world, there is an intersection in the shared tradition of renunciation. The discipline of meditation as a way of gaining wisdom had been given pride of place in the Upanishadic reforms and was typified by the shramanic movement. This was not an easy road to follow since it required a radical renunciation of the ordinary comforts of family and village life. The shramanas were celibate, homeless itinerants who relied on others for material needs, yet their detachment from mundane life provided them with the liberty to pursue the highest levels of wisdom and virtue. It was also a silent protest against the ritualism and sacerdotalism of the Brahmanic tradition. There is a strong echo of this in the Cynic philosophers who abandoned all desire for wealth and material pleasure, opting instead to wander the roads of the Roman Empire seeking and sharing wisdom with those who had ears. A similar attitude is found among the Qumran community whose celibate members, something very rare among Jews, forsook Jerusalem and established a monastery on the shores of the Dead Sea in protest against the illegitimacy and corruption of the Temple priesthood.

Mention of the Temple brings us to the final aspect of the religious context that deserves noting – the sacred building. While no particular edifice plays a key role in the Buddha's life, the situation was very different for Jesus and Muhammad. It is impossible to tell the story of these two men without reference to the Temple in Jerusalem and the Ka'ba in Mecca respectively. Both buildings were a central place of worship, a focus of official pilgrimage and a powerful carrier of political and religious symbolism. The Ka'ba was the repository of the tribal idols and protected by the defined zone of nonviolence. It was one place where the warring tribes could gather in peace and worship in harmony – and Muhammad's life very much revolved around it. The Temple had been the repository of the Ark of the Covenant and, although once destroyed and several times defiled, it represented the unbreakable faith of a nation that saw itself as God's Chosen People. Like the Ka'ba for Muhammad, the Jerusalem Temple would play a crucial role in the fate of Jesus.

Notes

1 Brahmins are the mouth; Kshatrias are the arms; Vaishyas are the legs; and Shudras are the feet. Rg Veda 10.90.
2 Von Pochhammer 82.
3 Carrithers 13–15.
4 Gokhale 57–58; Stein 57–58.
5 Carrithers 14.
6 Samantapasadika 3.614.
7 Thapar 137, 146; Gombrich, What 49–50.
8 The six are mentioned in context of the conversion of King Ajatasattu. Samannaphala Sutta in Digha Nikaya 2; Thomas 129–130.
9 Carrithers 28.
10 The principal Upanishads are: Aitareya, Brhadaranyaka, Isha, Shvetashvatara, Katha, Taittiriya, Chandogya, Kena, Mundaka, Mandukya and Prashna.
11 Rg Veda 1.164.46c: "To what is One, sages give many a title"; also 10.129.7.
12 Carrithers 18; Blomfield 39–46.
13 Safrai 61–63.
14 Crossan 80–84.
15 For example, many Jews in Israel used Greek for the epitaphs on their family tombs.
16 Crossan 15–19.
17 Sartre 40–41.
18 The first prefect was Coponius (6–9 CE), then Marcus Ambivulus (9–12 CE), Annius Rufus (12–15 CE), Valerius Gratus (15–26 CE), Pontius Pilate (26–36 CE), Marcellus (36–37 CE) and Marullus (37–41 CE) after which the office was renamed procurator.
19 Acts 4:5–6.
20 Local rulers, such as Herod Antipas in Galilee, were allowed to impose taxes on their citizens in order to pay the annual tribute to Rome and keep a handsome income for their own opulent lifestyle. The principal forms of taxation were land and poll taxes, but Herod added special levies for building projects and public works as well as customs and sales taxes. McClymond 361.
21 Crossan 220–221.
22 McClymond 365–366.
23 See Crossan's list of 7 protests between 4 BCE and 65 CE: Crossan 451.
24 Ezekiel 40–48.
25 2 Samuel 8:17; 15:24. See Meier III 394.
26 For instance, precepts concerning unclean meat that were originally intended for priests were extended to the entire people. See Ezekiel 44:31; Judges 13:4; Leviticus 11; Deuteronomy 14:1–21.
27 Meier III 330.
28 The two principal schools of thought within the Pharisaic tradition were those of Hillel (died circa 10 CE) and Shammai (died circa 30 CE). In general Shammai insisted on strict fidelity to the written word whereas Hillel was more liberal, usually taking into account extenuating circumstances and the welfare of the individual. Talmud Shabbat 31a.
29 Meier III 633–636.
30 Mishnah Ta'anit 3:8. See also Antiquities 14.2.1–2 where he is called Onias.
31 Babylonian Talmud, Berakot 33a.
32 Eve 272–295.
33 See Crossan's list of 10 "prophets" between 30 and 73 CE: Crossan 451.

34   Crossan 107–108.
35   Horsley, Galilee 268–271; Antiquities 17.10.5.
36   Jewish War 2.4.2; Antiquities 17.10.6; Tacitus, Histories 5.9.2.
37   Jewish War 2.4.3; Antiquities 17.10.7; 1 Samuel 16:11. Two other examples of military
     leaders who saw themselves in messianic terms occurred during the Jewish–Roman War:
     Menahem and Simon bar Giora. Jewish War 2.19.2; 2.20.2; Crossan 202–206.
38   See Crossan's 11 cases of "bandits" between 47 and 69 CE: Crossan 452.
39   Emerick 14.
40   Armstrong, Muhammad 22. Crone downplays Mecca's importance, arguing that if the
     town had been a well-known center of trade, it would have been mentioned by authors
     such as Procopius, Nonnosus and Syrian church chroniclers. Instead, it is absent from
     geographies or histories written in the three centuries prior to the rise of Islam. Crone,
     Makkan 137.
41   Armstrong, Muhammad 30.
42   Armstrong, Muhammad 34.
43   Peterson 10.
44   Armstrong, Muhammad 22; Peterson 9.
45   The months concerned were the consecutive eleventh, twelfth and first (Dhu al-Qi'da,
     Dhu al-Hijja and Muharram), thus forming a 90-day period, and the seventh (Rajab).
     The Qur'an criticises those who changed the order of the months in order to gain an
     unfair military advantage; see Qur'an 9:37.
46   Qur'an 5:50; 3:154, 33:33, 48:26.
47   Qur'an 13:16; 29:61–63; 31:25; 39:38.
48   Qur'an 53:19–22; 16:57; 37:149.
49   Rodinson 106; Peters, Hajj 26.
50   Zwettler 76–77; Peterson 16–17; Emerick 8.
51   Haykal 69, footnote 4. Among the most famous bards of the pre-Islamic era were Imru'
     al-Qays, al-Nabigha, Tarafa and Zuhayr.
52   Peters, Hajj 24–27. It is also possible that the Ka'ba housed the sacred utensils of a cult
     associated with the nearby Zamzam spring, which provided Mecca with precious water
     and set it apart as a sacred place. See Armstrong, Muhammad 29.
53   Von Grunebaum 24.
54   Emerick 9–10. One reason for the low numbers of Jews and Christians in Mecca was the
     mistrust that was generated when Abraha, the Christian ruler of Yemen, attacked Mecca
     in the Year of the Elephant (see Chapter 1).
55   Peterson 30.
56   Qur'an 2:135–136; 3:67–69, 95; 6:161; Peterson 29–30; Rodinson 36–37, 100.
57   Peterson 31.
58   The Jewish Kabbalistic tradition professes the notion of "gilgul neshamot" ("cycle of
     souls"), in which, as a result of divine compassion, a person is reincarnated a number of
     times so that they may fulfil the 613 biblical commandments.
59   Matthew 11:3; Luke 7:19.

Chapter 3

EARLY YEARS

Like the majority of famous historical figures, all three founders only came to public attention during the adult phase of their lives. None of them were child celebrities and so the circumstances and details of their boyhood were not widely known. The most reliable information that we have of them naturally stems from the later period, which was played out in the full glare of the public eye. Yet in time, their respective religious traditions understandably began to fill the information gap with various accounts of their conception, birth and other selected episodes from their youth. In general, these accounts tend to contain a higher proportion of theological embellishment and, thus, are usually considered less reliable from an historical perspective. That is not to say that they are totally devoid of credible information about what happened in those crucial formative years. Indeed, most scholars admit that there are genuine historical memories woven into the narratives, but those memories are heavily mixed with mythical elements that are inspired by faith and primarily aimed at expressing the religious significance of the child. For our purposes, both dimensions – the historical and the legendary – are worthy of consideration since together they have shaped the classical portraits of the Buddha, Jesus and Muhammad in their early years.

Heir to the Throne

In a famous passage from the Pali Canon, the Buddha explains his ethnic origins to King Bimbisara who has been struck by the graceful, regal nature of the young teacher:

> Straight ahead, your majesty, by the foothills of the Himalayas, is a country consummate in energy and wealth, inhabited by Kosalans: solar by clan, Sakyan by birth. From that lineage I have gone forth.[1]

Buddha, Jesus and Muhammad: A Comparative Study, First Edition. Paul Gwynne.
© 2014 John Wiley & Sons, Ltd. Published 2014 by John Wiley & Sons, Ltd.

Siddhattha's homeland was a modest territory at the very northern end of the Ganges Plain, near the present border between India and Nepal. There is little historical information available concerning the Sakyan people, but the name has been preserved in one of the most widely used titles for the Buddha – Sakyamuni ("the wise one of the Sakyans"). At the time, the Sakyan territory was under the political sway of Kosala.[2] It boasted no major cities and was situated at the very margins of Aryan civilization. Although the stories depict the Sakyans as a proud and noble race, in fact it was a peripheral vassal state.

The reference to the "solar lineage" of the Sakyans reveals the influence of classical Hindu mythology, which speaks of two great lines of rulers in northern India: the solar dynasty (surya vamsha) and the lunar dynasty (chandra vamsha). According to the Hindu epics, such as the Ramayana and the Mahabharata, the first solar king was called Okkaka (Sanskrit: Ikshvaku), and his descendents formed the majority of the Kshatria (warrior) caste of Aryan society. According to the legend, King Okkaka had five sons to his principal queen, Bhatta. However, Bhatta died and the king married a younger woman, promoting her to principal queen and promising to grant her any wish. Predictably, she insisted that her son become the next ruler, which created much anguish for the king and much jealousy on the part of the other wives. Eventually, he acquiesced and expelled the sons of Bhatta to the jungle. Their half-sisters were so disenchanted that they followed them into the Himalayan foothills where they settled. The princes named the place Kapilavatthu ("the farm of Kapila") after a local hermit who advised them to build a city there. Because the princes were too proud to marry the local women, they took their half-sisters as wives. When the king heard the news that his sons had not only survived in the wilderness but had bred a new generation, he exclaimed that they were indeed very clever ("sakya"). This is the main explanation for the derivation of the name although another theory suggests it was derived from the grove of "saka" trees that they chose as their new home.[3]

Buddhist writings have transformed Okkaka into the ancestor of the Sakyan people, even providing various versions of a royal genealogy down to the Buddha himself, who is consistently portrayed as the only son of the local ruler and heir to the throne. However, there is considerable doubt as to whether it is appropriate to speak of a Sakyan "kingdom", since the concept of hereditary monarchy was only slowly replacing the older and more common oligarchic systems of government in the region. Most scholars surmise that the Sakyans were actually ruled by a council of warriors and elders who chose a president or "raja" for a term of office.[4] The Buddha's father was one of these rajas, although it is possible that his term of leadership was an extensive one and other members of his family had occupied the position before him.

The sources agree that the Buddha's clan name was Gotama (Sanskrit: Gautama), which is unusual since it is a Brahmin (priest) class name rather than Kshatria (warrior) class as the Sakyans claimed to be.[5] There is also something anomalous about his father's personal name Suddhodana ("pure rice"), since it suggests that the family was originally involved in rural economic activities typical of the Vaishya (merchant) class.[6] The Sakyans practiced polygamy and endogamy, and so it is not surprising that Suddhodana married two sisters who were also his cousins, but their personal names vary slightly from source to source. In the Pali Canon and the Lalitavistara, the Buddha's mother is called Mahamaya (or Maya) and her sister is Mahapajapati. In the Tibetan tradition, they are known as Maya and Mahamaya, respectively, which naturally creates some confusion.[7]

The story of the Buddha's conception is given considerable space in the classical accounts and is characterized by lavish symbolism. Within the reincarnational scheme, the Buddha's previous existence was in Tusita Heaven where he waited for the propitious moment to be reborn for the last time. The oldest accounts imply that the Buddha was conceived in the usual manner by both parents whose qualities he inherited.[8] However, in later versions the father is no longer thought to have been physically involved, thus giving rise to the concept of a virginal conception. The mother was taken to Lake Anotatta in the Himalayas where she was bathed and escorted to a gold mansion on a hill. There she lay down on a couch with her head facing east. The future Buddha appeared as a white, six-tusked elephant, circling the couch three times and then entering her womb on the right side. The Lalitavistara and the Buddhacarita consider the entire event to be a dream, whereas other texts interpret it literally.[9] In either case, the albino elephant, which was one of the seven treasures of a universal monarch, represents regal wisdom and power, while the right side indicates a male child.[10] After the conception, it is claimed that Mahamaya took a vow of chastity and retired to a secluded room for a type of religious retreat. The underlying presumption is that the mother of a Buddha has no burning passion for men, including her husband. In some sources, even the father is said to have taken an oath of sexual abstinence.[11] As the texts describe the unusually long gestation period of 10 months, it becomes apparent that it is not only the father who has been removed from the process. The Buddha is said to have entered his mother's womb fully conscious, fully formed, albeit in miniature, and completely independent of any maternal sustenance, having drunk from an elixir of honey on the night of his conception. Almost every physical link with the mother has been removed, although the authors could not dispense with the fundamental fact that the Buddha was born of a woman.[12]

The Pali Canon claims that Buddha's birth occurred on the same day as his Enlightenment and death – the full moon of the lunar month of Vesakha (May/June), although the Lalitavistara identifies this as the night of his conception. In terms of location, all texts agree that it occurred in a grove at Lumbini, approximately 10 mi from the palace.[13] The reason for the unusual venue is that Mahamaya was on the way to her parents' home in Devadaha for the birth, although the Mahavastu claims that her motive was merely a recreational visit to a pleasure garden. In any case, labor pains came suddenly and she was forced to give birth, standing up and clinging to a tree, which graciously bent over to assist. It would not be the last time that a major event in the life of the Buddha occurred in the shade of a tree.[14]

There are traditionally four miraculous events linked to the moments immediately following the Buddha's birth, all of them underlining the special status of the child. The first was the child's reception by the gods Indra and Brahma so that the newborn does not touch the earth. Hindu deities often appear in the story of the Buddha, recognizing his greatness and delighting in the key milestones of his life, implying the supremacy of the new religion over the old.[15] The second event was the bathing of the child, which was a standard postnatal procedure, although it is not clear why it was necessary since the Buddha had been protected from any form of contamination since conception. Again, there are various forms of the story: two streams of warm and cool water naturally sprang from the earth and filled tubs; cleansing water fell like rain from heaven; two water spirits (nagas), in half-human, half-serpent form, poured water over the child in a manner similar to the anointing of kings.[16] The third event is perhaps the most startling, and possibly the oldest tradition. The texts describe how the infant took seven steps toward the north and prophetically declared: "I am chief of the world, I am the eldest in the world, I am the foremost in the world. This is the last birth. There is now no more coming to be".[17] The fourth event was the simultaneous birth of several other key characters, including his wife, his charioteer, his horse and others who would play a role in his future life. The auspicious concurrence of these births is another signal that a higher cosmic design was at work.

Two episodes feature the recognition of the child's special calling by astute observers. Asita (literally "black") was a wise and holy man (rishi) who lived as a hermit in a Himalayan retreat. When told of the Buddha's birth, he went to Kapilavatthu to see the child for himself. When the sage noticed the strange marks on his body, he began to weep from the realization that he was an old man and would not live long enough to witness this boy become a great religious leader. It was a bittersweet moment, but he returned home and told his young nephew, Nalaka, to watch the progress of the child carefully and to follow him when he eventually renounced his royal lifestyle.[18]

The Asita story is retold in the fifth century CE Nidanakatha with changes to the characters but with the same basic plot. Eight Brahmin priests examined the child's bodily marks. Seven of them held up two fingers, indicating that there were two possible paths for the boy: if he stayed at home then he would become a great political king; if he left home then he would become a great religious teacher.[19] However, the eighth Brahmin, a young man named Kondannya, raised only one finger, convinced that the child's destiny was religious not political, and he correctly predicted the catalyst that would alter his career path forever. Like Asita, Kondannya had no doubt as to the future role of the child. Unlike Asita, Kondannya would live long enough to hear the Buddha's liberating message and become one of his first five disciples. But there is a further twist – the other four (Assaji, Bhaddiya, Vappa and Mahanama) were the sons of the Brahmins present that day. Like Asita's nephew, they were counseled by their fathers to watch the child and follow him when the time came. [20]

The prophecies of Asita and Kondannya were the immediate context for the giving of the name Siddhattha (Sanskrit: Siddhartha), which literally means "one who achieves his aim". The Mahavastu uses a slight variant, Sarvarthasiddha, which translates as "one who has already accomplished all of his aims" and thus implies that it is the father who has fulfilled his aims in that he now has an heir.[21] However, the king's joy over the gift of a son was quickly undermined by the sudden death of Mahamaya just seven days after the birth. According to the tradition, she was reborn in Tavatimsa Heaven in male form. The medical cause of the death is not clear, but there are various theories concerning the theological reason. One hypothesis is that the mother of a Buddha must abstain from any sexual activity and thus it was better that she pass from this world. Another suggests that she died of a broken heart in the knowledge that her son would one day leave home. The most common explanation is a sort of cosmic rule that the mothers of all Buddhas must be surrendered in order to balance the great gift that has been received. In a sense, the lack of physical connection between mother and son that characterized the gestation and birth now becomes a complete severance with her death. In her absence on earth, the child was suckled and raised by her sister, Mahapajapati, Suddhodana's second wife.[22] Thus his aunt also became his stepmother and nurturer.[23]

Siddhattha's upbringing remained the responsibility of women until he was seven years old. There are three episodes frequently selected from his childhood that highlight his exceptional talents, presenting a foretaste of things to come. The first occurred when Siddhattha was still an infant and was taken to the countryside.[24] The nurses placed the toddler on a couch in the shade of a rose-apple tree, where he began a breathing exercise and attained his first state of advanced meditation. The second episode took place when Siddhattha attended school for the first time, which was the appropriate setting to highlight his superhuman intellect. The youthful student asked his teacher about the form of writing that he would be taught and then produced a list of 64 potential alphabets. The teacher was suitably overwhelmed and fell to the ground in humble reverence.[25] The third episode concerns his physical education, which would have been a standard component of Kshatria class training. The Lalitavistara lists running, jumping, wrestling and archery while other sources add horse-riding, chariot racing, as well as the use of the sword and lance. In all categories, Siddhattha proved to be a natural champion but his mastery of martial arts is combined with a profound sensitivity to life rather than an instinctive preference for violence.[26]

Meanwhile, Suddhodana was unsettled by the confident predictions of Asita and Kondannya that the young Siddhattha would follow a religious calling as an adult, and the ambivalence of the other priests who could not rule out that possibility. Naturally enough, Suddhodana expected his son to follow in his footsteps as raja. Thus, he set out to ensure that the boy was utterly content in the palace and would never entertain thoughts of an alternative career. Consequently, the texts describe his youth as a life of extravagant luxury and abundant pleasure. According to the Pali Canon, Siddhattha had access to a different residence for each of the three seasons – hot, cold and wet. He enjoyed the finest clothes of silk and wool, the most delectable food and drink, and the most beautiful surroundings.[27]

The Buddhist texts openly admit that the founder married and had a child. While there is an understandable tendency to portray Siddhattha as compelled to do so rather than acting on his own volition, the inclusion of these stories is strong evidence that his status as husband and father is historical. Marriage and children (especially sons) has always been a serious religious duty for a young Hindu adult, and his father would have been particularly keen to see a grandson born to secure the lineage. Thus, when Siddhattha was approximately 16 years of age, a suitable wife was found for him. However, it is difficult to establish the precise details since even her name is somewhat elusive. Whilst she is most commonly referred to as Yasodhara, following the Mahavastu and the Buddhacarita, the Pali Canon does not use this name, preferring the generic Rahulamata (Rahula's mother). In other texts she is variously called Bhaddakacca, Gopa or Bimba.[28] Even the name of the son, Rahula ("fetter"), looks suspiciously like a later invention by monastic authors who would have seen any child as a serious impediment to Siddhattha's true vocation.[29] Moreover, it was no coincidence that Rahula was born just prior to the turning point in Siddhattha's life, which would see him radically renounce both family and throne.

Son of the Carpenter

The classical account of Jesus's birth is derived from just two of the four canonical gospels. Matthew and Luke both dedicate two chapters to this earliest stage of the founder's life and these are the main source of material for the Christmas story. Commentators generally agree that there is less historically reliable information in the infancy narratives than in the accounts of Jesus's public ministry. One reason is the inclusion of miraculous events that create problems for modern minds, such as angelic apparitions, a virginal conception and a marvellous wandering star. There are also public events that have no confirming evidence in nonbiblical sources, such as the massacre of male babies in Bethlehem and a worldwide census during the reign of Herod the Great. Nevertheless, the canonical accounts are rich in theological symbolism and meaning, revealing a fascinating portrait of the founder's childhood as seen through the eyes of early believers.

Both evangelists include a genealogy of Jesus, but there are noteworthy differences. Matthew traces Jesus's lineage back as far as Abraham, the father of Judaism, whereas Luke takes the bloodline back to Adam, the father of humankind. Both versions agree that Jesus is a descendant of King David, and the names on both lists generally correspond for the generations between Abraham and David. However, the lines part ways immediately after David. Matthew traces the royal pedigree through Solomon, but Luke opts for Solomon's elder brother Nathan. The number of generations also differs in each case, and the names of the generations just prior to Joseph do not correspond. Matthew's genealogy displays a mathematical pattern consisting of three sets of 14 generations, understood as a sign of the divine plan behind Israel's history. Moreover, Matthew includes the names of five women, including Jesus's mother, all of whom are involved in some sort of irregular relationship.[30] The primary purpose behind both genealogies is to demonstrate that Jesus is a descendent of King David via Joseph. The very first verse of Matthew's gospel is an explicit claim that Jesus is "son of Abraham, son of David", and Luke describes how Mary was "engaged to a man whose name was Joseph, of the house of David".[31] There was a general expectation at the time that the Jewish Messiah would come from the Davidic line, which was also reflected in early Christian writing.[32] The problem is the related claim that Jesus was not the biological son of Joseph, and thus was not literally in the royal bloodline, even if Joseph was.[33] One traditional response is to claim that Mary was also a descendant of David but this has no support in the New Testament. A more common solution is to appeal to Joseph's legal paternity of Jesus, which would render the child a "son of David" in the eyes of the law at least. This was accomplished when Joseph officially named the child and took him as his own. The Aramaic "Yeshua" (from which the name Jesus is derived) is an abbreviated form of the Hebrew "Yehoshua" (Joshua) meaning "God saves".

The miraculous nature of Jesus's conception is attested to in both gospels. His mother Mary fell pregnant during the two-year period of betrothal, but Joseph was not the father. Although the couple did not live together during this period, sexual intercourse with a third party constituted adultery rather than fornication. Matthew tells the story from Joseph's perspective, explaining how he is shocked and perplexed by the situation, but being an upright man, decided to end the relationship informally. This possibly meant avoiding an official investigation that would lead to Mary being convicted of adultery and facing death by stoning.[34] However, an angel appeared to Joseph in a dream, explaining that the child was "from the Holy Spirit" and should be named Jesus. The implication is that the child did not have a human father at all.[35] Thus, Joseph abandoned his plans for divorce, agreeing instead to become the legal foster-father of the child.

In contrast, Luke presents the entire episode from Mary's perspective. In the famous Annunciation scene, the angel Gabriel informs Mary that she will become pregnant and that she must name the child Jesus. Thus, in both gospels, the name is provided by the heavenly messenger and not the parents. Like Matthew, Luke refers to the Holy Spirit as the immediate cause of Mary's pregnancy:

> The Holy Spirit will come upon you, and the power of the Most High will overshadow you; therefore the child to be born will be holy; he will be called son of God.[36]

Some interpret this as metaphorical language designed to cover up the embarrassing fact that Mary had fallen pregnant to another man, either through adultery or rape. Opponents of Christianity generally accepted that Joseph was not Jesus's biological father and focused on his illegitimacy, possibly hinted at in John 8:39, where the Jews declare to Jesus that they are not illegitimate (like him?). The second century CE writer Celsus claimed that Jesus was the son of a Roman soldier named Panthera and that he learned magic in Egypt – themes that became part of later Jewish writing. More recently, it has been speculated that Mary may have been a victim of rape, but there is no explicit evidence for this in the New Testament.[37]

The traditional interpretation has instead been a miraculous, virginal conception. This is supported by Luke's deliberate comparison of Jesus with John the Baptist, aimed at demonstrating the preeminence of Jesus over John. In both instances, there is a serious obstacle that is overcome by divine power. In John's case, it is the fact that his parents, Zechariah and Elizabeth, are too old to have children.[38] In Jesus's case, the problem is that Mary is a virgin. Thus, it is understandable that in the next scene Mary went "with haste" to see if Elizabeth was really pregnant and, hence, confirm the angel's message.[39] While the pregnancy of an elderly and barren Elizabeth is amazing, a virginal conception is more amazing and without precedent in the story of Israel. Luke confirms his intention by noting in his genealogy that Jesus is the son of Joseph "as it was thought".[40] Commentators have speculated that the notion of a virginal conception, which is foreign to Judaism, may have been borrowed by the early Christians from the Greco-Roman or other gentile traditions. Figures such as Perseus, Romulus, Alexander, Augustus, Plato and some Egyptian Pharaohs were all said to have been conceived by a union of a god and a young maiden. Moreover, Luke's description of the Holy Spirit "coming upon" and "overshadowing" Mary has been understood by some in a sexual sense with the divine spirit adopting the male role. However, opponents point out that the Hebrew noun for God's spirit (ruah) is feminine, while the Greek equivalent (pneuma) is neuter. They argue that the overshadowing is more likely linked to the biblical image of the divine cloud that covers Israel in the wilderness and is a prominent feature in Jesus's transfiguration later in Luke's gospel.[41]

Matthew and Luke both agree that Jesus was born in the town of Bethlehem, about 6 mi south of Jerusalem. However, they do not agree on the reason for this location. Matthew presumes that Joseph and Mary live in Bethlehem since he describes how Joseph took Mary "home" after the birth and the wise men visit a Bethlehem "house" where they find the child. In the Matthean account, the parents naturally return to Bethlehem after their exile in Egypt, and only move to distant Nazareth when they discover that Herod's eldest son, Archelaus, now rules in Judea.[42] In contrast, Luke presumes that their permanent residence was always Nazareth, in Galilee, and that the birth took place in Bethlehem because of a census that required all persons to travel to their familial town for registration. However, there is no evidence of a universal census under Augustus. Quirinius did oversee a local census while he was governor of Syria, but it took place in 6 CE, 10 years after Herod's death. Some surmise that Luke has either mistakenly confused or deliberately combined the turmoil that followed Herod's death in 4 BCE with the turmoil that followed the deposition of Archelaus in 6 CE and Quirinius' attempts to restructure Judea as a Roman province in the aftermath.

Neither evangelist takes much interest in the actual birth. Matthew passes over it in one sentence, while Luke focuses on the unusual venue, explaining that Jesus's parents were unable to find accommodation in the local "inn".[43] We are not told precisely where the birth took place but only that Mary wrapped her baby in swaddling clothes and laid him in a manger – a feeding trough for animals. So the traditional image of a stable at the back of the lodgings has merit. Christian devotion has emphasized the paradoxical poverty in which the world's King and Savior was born, although the biblical image of swaddling clothes evokes luxurious comfort, since a young Solomon was swaddled and nursed, not unlike the infant Buddha.[44]

Matthew and Luke both recount visits to the infant Jesus soon after his birth. In Luke, they are shepherds from the surrounding fields who have been told by an unnamed angel that the Messiah has been born in Bethlehem and the sign to seek is a child wrapped in swaddling clothes and lying in a manger.[45] Like Mary, they hasten to see the evidence for themselves.[46] In Matthew's case, the visitors are pagan sages from distant lands. Matthew describes them as "magi" – a general term that could be applied to astrologers, dream interpreters, visionaries, enchanters or anyone who practiced secret lore and magic.[47] They come "from the east", but the precise country of origin is not specified.[48] Matthew does not say how many there were but tradition suggests three, probably based on the number of gifts presented to the child.[49] The reason for their journey to Jerusalem, and then Bethlehem, is a new star, which they have interpreted as a heavenly sign announcing a royal birth. The idea of a celestial portent linked to a great event is common enough in ancient literature and there have even been attempts to identify it as a real astronomical event.[50] According to Matthew, the magi were warned in a dream to avoid the jealous Herod and return to their homeland by another route. Enraged, Herod ordered the death of all male children less than two years old in Bethlehem and its surrounds, but Joseph, also warned in a dream, took his family to Egypt until the death of the king. Once again, there are historical problems. Herod the Great did perpetrate terrible acts of cruelty, even on members of his own family, but there are no records of a mass killing of young children in Bethlehem. There are, however, strong literary parallels with the murder of the Hebrew children by Pharaoh in the book of Exodus.[51]

The gospel of Luke also has two visits to the Jerusalem Temple during Jesus's early years. The first is the purification of the mother, although Luke seems to confuse this with another obligation – the redemption of the firstborn son.[52] While the parents are in the Temple, an elderly and devout man named Simeon acclaimed the child as the Messiah. Simeon thanked God for allowing him to live long enough to witness this moment and predicts that Jesus will cause the "fall and rise of many in Israel" – ostensibly a reference to a deep-seated division within the community. He adds that the mother's heart will be pierced with a sword, traditionally interpreted as the agony of witnessing her son's death, but more likely a reference to future divisions within the family over Jesus.[53]

Luke narrates a second visit to the Temple for the Passover when Jesus was 12. Like the purification scene, it reveals the extraordinary qualities of the boy and hints at his future religious role. When the festival was over, the parents headed home but after a day's journey, they discovered that Jesus was not with their group. After three days of frantic searching, they found him in the Temple, sitting and conversing with the teachers who were astounded at his depth of understanding. When quizzed about his strange, almost precocious behavior, the young Jesus enigmatically explained that he must be "in my father's house" (alternatively translated as "about my father's affairs"). As with Simeon's prophecy, division is hinted at again, this time between Jesus's natural parents, who do not fully understand him, and his true parent, the One whom he will call "abba" (father).

Apart from this incident, the canonical gospels have no further information about Jesus's youth or early adulthood. Luke simply states that Jesus returned to Nazareth and "increased in wisdom and in years, and in divine and human favour" while Matthew closes his infancy narrative by explaining that Joseph "made his home in a town called Nazareth".[54] The next chapters of both Matthew and Luke take us immediately to the commencement of the public ministry when Jesus is about 30 years of age. It is a frustrating gap that has led to this unknown period of Jesus's life being aptly described as "the hidden years". The biographical hole has been partially filled by later apocryphal gospels that are highly imaginative in content. The most well known is the Infancy Gospel of Thomas (not to be confused with the Gospel of Thomas), which was probably written during the second century CE. It portrays the child Jesus as something of a supernatural trickster and an all-knowing pupil who is impossible to teach.[55]

The issue of Jesus's siblings is a much disputed point among Christians. The key theological issue at stake is the perpetual virginity of Mary, which is a deeply cherished belief in Catholic and Orthodox traditions. The doctrine holds that Mary and Joseph never consummated their marriage but lived in a celibate relationship instead. Thus, Jesus was not just her firstborn but also her only child. The perpetual virginity of

Mary is explicitly developed in the post-New Testament period, especially via the second century CE work known as the Protoevangelium of James, which asserts that Mary, like Siddhattha's mother, physically remained a virgin even during the birth process itself. Prominent patristic writers of the following centuries, such as Athanasius, Hilary, Ambrose and Jerome, all lent their support to this tradition, but it faces several challenges.[56] At the sociocultural level, celibacy has always been rare in Judaism.[57] It would have been utterly strange for a young, betrothed Jewish maiden to vow lifelong celibacy, although proponents point to the extraordinary nature of her child as the primary motive. More significantly, there are several New Testament passages that may suggest otherwise. First, Matthew writes that Joseph "had no marital relations with her until she had borne a son", although commentators note that the Greek term "eos" does not imply a change in status whereas the English term "until" does.[58] Second, there are several references to Jesus's "adelphoi" ("brothers and sisters"), including the scene in Mark 6:3 where some are actually named: "Is not this the carpenter, the son of Mary, and brother (adelphos) of James and Joses and Judas and Simon, and are not his sisters (adelphai) here with us?" Moreover, Paul refers to James, one of the apostles and a leader of the Christian community in Jerusalem, as "brother of the Lord" twice in his letter to the Galatians.[59] There are two main responses from the traditional point of view. The first is found in the Protoevangelium, which claims that these brothers and sisters were children of Joseph from a previous marriage.[60] The Protoevangelium portrays Joseph as an older man who marries Mary in order to protect her but who never consummates the union.[61] The second response translates the Greek "adelphos" as "cousin" or "kinsman", which is a possible rendering, rather than "brother" in the strict sense. A similar interpretation is also possible in Hebrew and Aramaic.[62]

Although the tradition locates Jesus's birth in Bethlehem, all sources agree that he grew up in the village of Nazareth in the territory of Galilee, in northern Israel. His mother tongue was Aramaic or, more accurately, the Galilean dialect of Aramaic, which was distinguishable from the Judean form. Galilee was generally considered by those living in southern Israel as culturally inferior and compromised by foreign influence. Yet such exposure to Hellenistic culture meant that Jesus and many of his compatriots may have also spoken Greek.[63] It is not known whether he attended a rabbinical school. On one hand his knowledge of the Jewish scriptures was impressive but, on the other hand, his listeners presumed that he did not have any formal training.[64]

The gospel of Mark describes Jesus's occupation as carpentry, although Matthew changes the phrase to "son of a carpenter". The shift may be due to an element of embarrassment, but it was common that sons followed their father's trade.[65] According to the second-century CE author Justin Martyr, Jesus made ploughs and yokes for local farmers but the Greek term "tekton" was broad and could mean a skilled worker who specialized in wood, stone, metal or construction in general.[66] Some have even speculated that the original Aramaic term, "naggar", was also an oblique reference to a man of letters, in which case Jesus may have been the son of a scholar rather than the son of a carpenter.[67] Whatever the precise trade, it did not turn out to be his lifelong career, nor was it the reason that history so vividly remembers him.

Orphan and Merchant

Muhammad was born into the Hashim clan of the Quraysh tribe in Mecca. Like Jesus, there were Abrahamic links. It is believed that the northern Arab tribes had descended from Ishmael, Abraham's first son, who had been banished to the desert with his mother Hagar as recounted in the book of Genesis.[68] The Quraysh were the majority tribe in Mecca at the time and essentially ruled the town via a council of elders. In the late sixth century CE, it had been subdivided into numerous clans, including the Banu Hashim, which was characterized by a peculiar mix of nobility and poverty. Although the clan was one of the more distinguished Meccan aristocratic families, its members had lost out in internecine conflicts and consequently found themselves up against challenging economic circumstances.[69] The Hashim clan had traditionally been responsible for supplying water for the Ka'ba in Mecca and Muhammad's grandfather, 'Abd al-Muttalib, is credited with rediscovering the ancient spring, Zamzam, near the shrine itself.

'Abd al-Muttalib had 10 sons, but his favorite was 'Abdullah, who had married Amina, the daughter of a local tribal chief. Soon after their wedding, 'Abdullah was struck down with a viral infection and died suddenly. Upon hearing the news, a pregnant Amina collapsed and fell ill, but her African servant girl, Baraka, tended to her. The prospects were not rosy for the young expectant widow and fears for a precarious life of prolonged penury were well based. However, 'Abd al-Muttalib took it upon himself to provide for her as best he could.[70]

During her pregnancy, Amina dreamed that radiance came from her womb and lit up the mountains and valleys around Mecca. In one version, she was even able to see the distant fortresses of Syria. Then she heard a voice speaking:

> You carry in your womb the lord of his people and when he is born say "I place him beneath the protection of the One from the evil of every envier". Then you must name him Muhammad.[71]

The name Muhammad literally means "he who is worthy of praise". According to Ibn Ishaq, it was rare at the time, although today it has now become one of the most common personal names throughout the world. Tradition holds that the birth was exceptionally easy for Amina. Her servant Baraka was the first to hold the child, but then his grandfather, 'Abd al-Muttalib, took the boy to the Ka'ba, circumambulating it seven times, thanking God for a new life that replaced the tragic loss of his son.

It was a long-established custom among Meccan nobility to entrust their newborn babies to a Bedouin wet nurse. The air was considered cleaner in the desert than in Mecca, which was surrounded by high valley walls and was prone to epidemics. Even after weaning, children sometimes spent most of their infancy among the desert-dwellers before returning home. The Bedouins' spartan existence, traditional values and purer form of the Arabic tongue also made an excellent educational mix that produced strong, well-mannered and eloquent children.[72] The practice also constituted a lucrative source of income for the nomads who would visit towns seeking the employment of aristocratic families with young babies. However, Amina's widow status meant that it was difficult to find a Bedouin who was willing to take on her newborn son. After many rejections, she finally contracted a woman named Halima to be Muhammad's wet-nurse. Thus, the child Muhammad was raised in the harshness and beauty of the desert environment. He learned the Bedouin dialect and began to absorb the songs and poems of the nomadic culture.

Islamic tradition claims that Muhammad's presence brought tangible benefits to Halima's family. While the boy was in her care, she reported that her goats gave better milk, her chickens grew fatter and her donkey walked faster, but the miraculous incident that features most prominently in the infancy stories occurred when Muhammad was about three or four years old.[73] One day, Halima's son came rushing to the tent exclaiming that two men dressed in white had laid Muhammad on the ground, opened up his chest and placed their hands inside. The foster-mother raced to the scene and found the boy unharmed with no sign of the angelic strangers. Later in life, Muhammad explained how they had split open his chest and removed an ugly black clot from his heart, which they threw away, washing his chest with melted snow from a golden basin. The removal of the clot is traditionally understood as the purification of Muhammad's heart from temptation and sin.[74]

Muhammad spent about four years with Halima before he was eventually returned to his natural mother. He had already lost his father, and tragedy struck again when Amina suddenly fell ill on her way home from a family visit to Yathrib. She died and was buried in a humble grave, dug by her servant girl Baraka. The six-year-old boy was now fully exposed to the perils of being both fatherless and motherless.[75] Baraka brought the boy to 'Abd al-Muttalib who took them into his own home. Fortunately for Muhammad, his grandfather was very fond of him, showering him with great affection. The young boy's daily playmates were Hamza and Safiyya, children of 'Abd al-Muttalib from his last wife.[76] But 'Abd al-Muttalib was already in his 80s, and he passed away when Muhammad was only about eight years old. It was the third time that the primary caretaker of the boy had died but on his deathbed 'Abd al-Muttalib entrusted the care of the bereaved boy to his son Abu Talib, the full brother of Muhammad's father 'Abdullah. Abu Talib had become the leader of the Hashim clan but this did not mean that he was prosperous or powerful. His business was struggling and the prestige of the clan was on the wane. Yet Abu Talib still commanded respect among the Meccans and he honored his father's deathbed wish by taking his nephew into his care.

Much of Muhammad's childhood involved tending Abu Talib's flocks of sheep and goats on the hills around Mecca. Some say that the natural solitude of the shepherd's life imbued in him a spirit of meditation and reflection.[77] Yet there would also have been opportunities for Muhammad to experience the richness of human culture when he accompanied Abu Talib on commercial journeys within and beyond Arabia. According to one story, the caravan rested near a Christian hermitage in the region of Bostra in southern Syria. The monk living in the hermitage was named Bahira, and he noticed that a cloud was following the group and sheltering them from the scorching sun. Curious to discover more, he invited the travelers to dine with him. After questioning Muhammad at some length, he inspected the boy's back and found a slightly raised egg-shaped birthmark between his shoulder blades. In Bahira's mind, the boy's answers and the mysterious mark confirmed that he was the long-awaited prophet to the Arabs and he instructed Abu Talib to protect him from the machinations of his enemies.[78]

The portrait painted of the young Muhammad is that of a sensitive, caring person with a strong sense of social justice. He also enjoyed a good dose of providential protection from the vices into which young men of his town often fell, such as drinking, gambling and prostitutes. His work as a shepherd limited his exposure to the seedier side of urban life and even when he came into town, we are told that he would be distracted by a haunting song or a sudden bout of somnolence and, thus, be prevented from placing himself in moral danger. He had gained the reputation of being honest and dependable, earning the sobriquets al-Sadiq ("truthful one") and al-Amin ("trustworthy one").[79] Most commentators agree that Muhammad received no formal education, yet there is debate as to whether he was illiterate or not. On one hand, some argue that he must have been able to read and write since he was entrusted with managerial roles in the trade caravans. On the other hand, many Muslims argue that literacy in Mecca was rare, quoting the Qur'an, which describes Muhammad as "ummi", a term commonly translated as "unlettered" or "illiterate".[80] Such an interpretation has a clear apologetic advantage, since it serves to highlight the supernatural nature of the Qur'an itself. Simply put, an illiterate Muhammad could never have produced such a masterpiece. However, others have argued that "ummi" is more correctly translated as "without scripture". In other words, unlike Jews and Christians, the Arabian tribes did not possess revealed sacred writings. Thus, the miracle is not so much that Muhammad could neither read nor write, but that he was a prophet uneducated by a scriptural tradition and sent to an unscriptured nation.[81] During his youth, Muhammad may have had limited contact with local Jews and, in his later years, he would have been exposed to Nestorian Christianity on the caravan routes to the north. It is possible that he gained his knowledge of the biblical stories and their characters by hearing them recited rather than by reading or studying the written text, as there were no scriptures available in Arabic at the time and there is no evidence that he spoke Hebrew or Greek.

As a young man Muhammad had hoped to marry his cousin Fakhita, the daughter of Abu Talib, but her father pointed out the painful truth that he could not afford to support a wife.[82] However, a dramatic and unexpected turn occurred when he was about 25 years of age. Khadija bint al-Khuwaylid was a distant relative from the influential Asad clan. She was about 40 years of age and twice widowed, but she had inherited a considerable fortune. She was not only wealthy but also shrewd, and her acumen had enabled her to build up a very successful trading business. She was seeking a manager for her Syrian caravan, and Abu Talib took the opportunity to recommend his nephew. Khadija had heard that Muhammad was honest and efficient and so she agreed to the terms on the proviso that the venture was profitable. Ever canny, Khadija sent along her manservant to observe the new employee carefully.

Muhammad's first commercial journey to Syria for Khadija is the setting for an incident that strongly parallels the earlier story of Bahira the monk. In this version, the monk is named Nestor and it is two angels that afford protection from the scorching sun although the location is still Bostra and the outcome is the same: a Christian holy man recognizes the prophetic status of Muhammad.[83] The commercial enterprise was very successful, and the manservant provided a glowing report on Muhammad's mercantile skills. However, Khadija was not only impressed with Muhammad as a capable business manager. She was also deeply attracted to him personally. So she asked a friend to investigate subtly whether Muhammad was interested in marriage. His initial response was to explain his difficult financial position, but when the friend clarified that it was Khadija who was seeking his hand, he was both surprised and deeply honored. Consequently, the 25-year old, single, male employee agreed to take the hand of his 40-year-old, twice-married female employer. It was a most unusual match for its time and place. History testifies that the monogamous union lasted for two and half decades until Khadija's death in 619 CE. Muhammad's later wives were occasionally infuriated by the fact that he constantly sang her praises, and all too often reminded them how no other woman could ever be compared to her. In many ways, she was the first to recognize his true genius.[84]

Although Khadija already had a daughter and two sons from her previous two marriages, she bore six more children to Muhammad.[85] The firstborn was a boy named Qasim, but he died at two years of age. Then came four girls, all of whom safely reached adulthood: Zaynab, Ruqayya, Umm Kulthum and Fatima. Finally, another son, 'Abdallah, was born, but like Qasim, he also died in infancy. In a culture that valued male offspring, it is very significant that the Prophet had only daughters to succeed him. Yet there was a "son" of sorts. On his wedding day, Muhammad freed a slave whom he had inherited from his father. In exchange, Khadija gave him a slave boy named Zayd, who had been captured in a tribal raid. Some years later, Zayd formally chose to stay with Muhammad rather than return with his natural parents, who had come to Mecca and offered to purchase his freedom. Immediately, Muhammad declared him to be his son and heir, giving him the name Zayd bin Muhammad.

The other boy who was a vital part of Muhammad's family life was his cousin Ali, son of Abu Talib. Muhammad took him into his home when the boy was about five years of age as a gesture of support for Abu Talib, who was experiencing financial difficulties. Years later Ali would marry Muhammad's youngest daughter, Fatima, forming one of the most influential matches in early Islamic history. Muhammad's other daughters also wedded kinsmen: Zaynab married her cousin Abu al-'As, and Ruqayya and Umm Kulthum married two sons of Muhammad's uncle, Abu Lahab.

Without doubt, his relationship with Khadija was a transforming moment, lifting him out of a marginalized existence as shepherd and providing him with greater social status and a comfortable lifestyle. In time, he consolidated his reputation as a trustworthy, ethical person, joining the Hilf al-Fudul ("League of the Virtuous"), which was established to ensure fair and just commercial transactions in Mecca. He also enjoyed a reputation as a competent mediator. The most quoted example of his ability to resolve conflicts is the episode of the Black Stone. When Muhammad was about 35 years old, the Quraysh leaders decided to rebuild the Ka'ba, which was in dire need of repair. A minor crisis arose at the end of the project when the time came for the Black Stone to be placed in its position on the outside wall. Each tribe felt that it deserved to be the one to perform the task and a dangerous stalemate quickly developed. After four days, someone suggested that the next person to enter the sacred area would carry the solution. Sure enough, Muhammad walked in just at that moment and so was given the challenge of overcoming the deadlock. Seizing the opportunity, he laid a large cloth on the ground, placed the Black Stone on it, and then invited a representative from each tribe to take hold of the fringe and lift together. Then Muhammad himself placed the Stone in its setting to the satisfaction of all parties.[86] Although he was not tribal chief, Muhammad's uncanny ability to analyze a situation quickly and to produce a workable solution was already displaying itself – a sign of the outstanding leadership potential that would come to the fore in time.

Observations

Although their stunning impact on history only occurred in their adulthood, the religious tradition behind each of the three founders provides a considerable amount of material – some historical and some mythological – that fills the information gap concerning those earlier years. A closer comparative look at this material reveals interesting areas of similarity and contrast.

The first point for consideration is the common concern to establish the ancestry of each founder via a genealogy. Siddhattha is presented as the descendant of the royal Hindu solar dynasty. His forefathers were banished princes who set up a new home in Kapilavatthu, the capital of the Sakyan kingdom in northern India. Siddhattha himself is portrayed as the oldest son of the local raja who raised the child in luxurious comfort to ensure that the heir was not distracted from his political vocation as future king. Royalty was his pedigree and aristocratic affluence was his actual circumstance. In contrast, the socioeconomic stratum of Jesus's family was Galilean working class. Yet the gospel tradition traces his bloodline back to Abraham via King David. Descent from Abraham via his son Isaac is the basis of Jesus's Jewish identity, but the Davidic factor is an important element in the Christian claim that the carpenter's son is the long awaited Messiah. Jesus was from peasant stock, but with allegedly royal blood. Muhammad, like Jesus, is also seen as a descendant of Abraham who is revered in both Christianity and Islam as the father of monotheism. As an Arab, Muhammad's genealogy runs through Abraham's older son Ishmael, bypassing the line of Israel's kings. Thus, there is no claim to royal pedigree in his case although, as member of the Quraysh tribe and the Hashimite clan, Muhammad enjoyed a certain patrician status in Meccan society. Yet the Hashimites were struggling on the financial front at the time of his birth and, like Jesus, his background is a disjointed mix of inherited nobility and economic hardship.

A comparison of the immediate families reveals something unusual in each case. One of the main factors that contributed to the difficult economic circumstances of Muhammad's childhood was the death of both parents. Muhammad never knew his natural father since 'Abdullah passed away before he was even born. One must also wonder how well he knew his mother, Amina. She died when Muhammad was around 6 years of age, but most of his infancy had been spent in the desert under the maternal care of Halima, his Bedouin wet-nurse. In the following years he was cared for briefly by his paternal grandfather and then by his paternal uncle, Abu Talib whose death many years later would trigger a serious crisis. In similar fashion, tradition says that Siddhattha lost his natural mother just one week after his birth. Her role was taken over by her sister Mahapajapati, who married his father. Consequently, Siddhattha's aunt-stepmother exercised a crucial influence in his formative years and would eventually play a vital role in the establishment of the order of nuns.

The surrogate parent theme is also a feature of the gospel story in that Jesus is not understood to be the biological son of Joseph. There has been much speculation, ancient and modern, as to the identity of the true father, but the infancy narratives in Matthew and Luke explain the embarrassing dilemma via the claim that Jesus was virginally conceived. He was born of Mary but he had no human father and thus is "son of God" in a truly unique sense. Joseph is foster-father to the miraculous child who has a growing perception that his real "abba" (father) is supernatural rather than natural. Almost no information is available concerning the fate of Joseph, but the common presumption is that he died before Jesus's public ministry began. In contrast, Mary survived her son and was eventually accorded a highly elevated status in some branches of Christianity. In time, Christian writers extended Mary's virginity beyond the moment of conception to the birth process itself and then to the entirety of her life. In some traditions, she is deemed the ever-virgin Mother of God, who never consummated her marriage to Joseph. The theme of the virgin mother is also a feature of later versions of the Buddhist story, in which Mahamaya not only conceived her child without the involvement of her husband, but also gave birth without any compromise to her physical virginity. In contrast to Mary, Mahamaya died prematurely, with the traditional explanation that the mother of a Buddha must remain pure and, thus, should not linger in a tainted world.

The question of Mary's and Mahamaya's virginal purity touches on another feature of the founders' early experience. All three men were the firstborn sons, but did they grow up in the company of siblings? The gospel references to Jesus's "brothers and sisters" are interpreted in various ways. For those who believe that the marriage between Joseph and Mary was a genuine one, these are literally Jesus's younger blood brothers and sisters. For those who consider Mary as ever-virgin, they are either cousins or Joseph's children from an earlier marriage (stepbrothers and stepsisters). However, in popular piety, the siblings are often ignored, and the Holy Family is commonly imagined as an intimate three-person circle. Effectively, Jesus is portrayed as an only child. In Muhammad's case, the death of his father and the fact that his mother did not remarry meant that he was theoretically an only child. Yet Muhammad spent his infancy in the company of de facto siblings: initially the children of Halima in the Bedouin desert community and, then, Hamza and Safiyya. Similarly, the early death of Siddhattha's mother meant that he did not have any full brothers and sisters. However, tradition states that there was a half-brother, Nanda, and a half-sister, Sundari, who were born of the marriage between his father and aunt-stepmother.

The claim of a virginal conception in the case of Siddhattha and Jesus raises another significant feature of the three stories: namely, the miraculous element. This is most apparent in the Buddhist tradition, where extraordinary events occur with unremitting frequency from conception to young adulthood. The nativity of Siddhattha is a striking example. Not only does the birth itself bypass normal biological processes, but four miracles are added that accentuate the uniqueness of the newborn: the reception by the gods, the water bath, the seven steps and the concurrent births. The supernatural happenings continue as Siddhattha grows: his strange bodily marks, the rose-apple tree incident, his astonishing intellect in the classroom and his outstanding prowess on the athletic field. In the Christian tradition, the apocryphal gospels display a similar tendency, describing a precocious Jesus who makes clay birds fly, stretches beams of wood, multiplies food, strikes people blind but also heals injuries. The canonical gospels of Matthew and Luke are much more restrained, but they are not devoid of unusual events, such as angelic appearances, a virginal conception, a moving star and mysterious visitors from the East. The tendency is less obvious in the narrative concerning Muhammad, but even there one can find supernatural features: the light that shines from his mother's womb, the angelic voice that provides the child's name (as in the case of Jesus), the opening of Muhammad's chest and the moving cloud over the caravan at Bostra.

Mention of Bostra touches on another theme common to all three traditions: recognition of the child's significance by wise and holy persons. Commentators have frequently been struck by the parallels between the stories of Asita and Simeon, but we should also include here the story of Bahira (or Nestor). Both Asita and Bahira are hermits whose attention is caught by a supernatural sign: the rejoicing of the gods and the cloud that hovers over the caravan troop. In the Christian story, Simeon is a righteous man who is urged to visit the Temple by the Holy Spirit. In the Buddhist and Islamic stories, the curious gentlemen notice bodily marks on the child, which constitute the key to his identity and future. For Asita, they were an unambiguous sign that Siddhattha was destined to become a great religious leader. For Bahira, the birthmark between Muhammad's shoulders was an indication that he was the foretold prophet to the Arabs. We are not told what convinces Simeon that Jesus is different from other children, but his recognition that the child is the long-awaited Messiah leads him to utter his heartfelt song of thanksgiving. Simeon can now die in peace since he has been privileged to live long enough to witness this moment. In contrast, Asita's reaction is bittersweet: he has lived long enough to see the Buddha as a child but he will not be alive when the child becomes Buddha. However, Asita is consoled by the thought that his nephew will and, thus, advises him to watch and be prepared for the moment when it comes. There is no such rejoicing or weeping for Bahira who, instead, warns Abu Talib that the future prophet will need protection from his enemies. Indeed, it is Abu Talib's death many years later that places Muhammad and his young community in serious jeopardy. The same ominous note of danger is found in the gospels. In Luke's account, Simeon perceives that Jesus will bring division within his own family and his nation. In Matthew's narrative, the magi function in much the same way as Simeon. They too are wise men, albeit pagans, who recognize the sign (the star) and acknowledge the special nature of the Christ child with their gifts. But they also sense the jealous opposition that is brewing in Jerusalem and prudently avoid the treacherous Herod on their way home.

Although all three founders are portrayed as exceptionally intelligent children, their contrasting socioeconomic circumstances are reflected in different educational experiences. As a young prince, we are told that Siddhattha received the very best of a royal education with a curriculum that involved rigorous mental and physical discipline. The highly embellished stories of his childhood give the impression that the young prodigy has already mastered all fields of knowledge and that there was very little that a schoolmaster or sports coach could teach him. In contrast, the gospels are silent on Jesus's education and commentators have speculated whether or not he was literate, whether or not he attended rabbinical school, and whether or not he spoke Greek as well as his native Aramaic. Luke's story of the 12-year old Jesus sitting with the teachers in the Temple does not depict him as an all-knowing divine child but, rather, notes the acuity of his mind and his eagerness to listen and learn. Apart from that, commentators can only presume that Jesus received practical training in his father's trade as would have been the customary practice. The Islamic tradition provides slightly more information about Muhammad's formal education, although there are still frustrating gaps in the picture. As with other children of noble families, he spent his earliest years with the Bedouin desert nomads, where it is presumed he learned a purer form of Arabic and became acquainted with the grand tradition of oral poetry. The loss of his parents and the hardships suffered by Abu Talib probably meant that he did not receive further official schooling and spent much of his child-hood working as a shepherd. This corresponds to the general notion that he was brilliant but illiterate, although he must have been numerate if he was a successful commercial manager as a result of his providential marriage to Khadija.

Muhammad's marriage raises the final significant point of comparison concerning the early years prior to each founder's emergence in the public eye: their marital status. The young nephew of Abu Talib, talented but faced with limited scope due to difficult circumstances, had suddenly been given an unlikely opportunity with the marriage proposal of an older and wealthier Khadija. Their monogamous relationship, unusual in a polygamous society, yielded four daughters and enabled Muhammad's reputation in Mecca to grow and consolidate. The orphaned shepherd boy had become faithful husband, loving father and successful merchant. Similarly, the young prince Siddhattha found a suitable wife and fathered a son, fulfilling the expectations of both his Hindu culture and his father, who was preoccupied with a smooth politi-cal succession. His was a courtly life of affluence and comfort, protected from the ills of the world that lay beyond the palace walls. Similarly, Jewish culture would have expected the young adult Jesus to find a wife and start a family, but the gospels make no mention of spouse or children. On the verge of his 30s, it would seem that the carpenter's son was still unmarried – a highly unusual state for a young Jew, especially one who may have considered becoming a rabbi.

Notes

1 Sutta Nipata 405–424.
2 Digha Nikaya 27.8.
3 Digha Nikaya 1.92,98; Mahavastu (Jones) I 338,348: Mahavamsa 2.1–24.
4 Nakamura I 36, 46; Blomfield 20–21.
5 Carrithers 13; Thomas 22.
6 Nakamura I 48–51. The names of Suddhodana's four brothers also follow the agricultural theme: Amitadana (unmeasured rice), Dhotodana (washed rice), Sukkodana (white rice) and Sukkhodana (fine rice).

7 Digha Nikaya 14.3.30; Thomas 24–25; Ashvaghosha (Beal) 1.1–2. The Pali Canon claims that their father was Anjana, whereas the Lalitavistara and the Tibetan writings identify them as daughters of Suprabuddha.
8 Digha Nikaya 4.5; Thomas 36.
9 Lalitavistara (Foucaux) 61; Buddhacarita I.34; Nakamura I 54.
10 Buddhacarita I.20; Lalitavistara (Foucaux) 63; Foucher 22–25.
11 Majjhima Nikaya 3.118; Lalitavistara (Foucaux) Chapter 5; Mahavastu (Jones) I 147; Thundy 83–85.
12 Foucher 27–28.
13 There is a major pilgrimage site near Rummindei in the Nepalese Terai district. However, the precise locations of Kapilavatthu and Lumbini are still a matter of debate today, based on various interpretations of the accounts of two Chinese pilgrims: Fa Hsien (circa 400 CE) and Hiuen Tsiang (circa 640 CE).
14 Foucher 30. Some versions describe the birth as painless and from the mother's right side, possibly suggesting a Caesarean section. See Buddhacarita I.9; Mahavastu (Jones) II 20; Nakamura I 66.
15 An alternative version speaks of the "four celestial kings" who were the guardians of the cardinal points of the compass. See Nakamura I 65; Foucher 33.
16 Foucher 34.
17 Nakamura I 77–83; Foucher 35.
18 For variations of the Asita story, see Sutta Nipata 689–697; Buddhacarita I.54; Nakamura I 72–75.
19 Nakamura I 84–85; Thomas 43–44; Braden 18.
20 The bodily marks included dark, curly hair with a protuberance on the top of the head; a broad even forehead with a circle of silver hair between the eyebrows symbolizing the third eye of wisdom; dark blue or black eyes; a long, flexible tongue; a perfect set of pure white teeth and a lion-like bottom jaw; fine golden skin; long slender arms stretching down below the knees; webbed fingers and toes; and the impression of a wheel on the soles of the feet. Digha Nikaya 32; Brahmayu Sutta in the Majjhima Nikaya 91.
21 Nakamura I 84; Mizuno 15; Foucher 36.
22 Buddhacarita II.19.
23 Foucher 46–47; Mizuno 16–17.
24 Majjhima Nikaya 36. The Nidanakatha fills in the gaps by explaining that it was the annual festival at the opening of the ploughing season: Nakamura I 91–92.
25 For example, Gandhara artwork shows the Buddha holding a reed in his right hand and with a slate tablet on his knees.
26 Foucher 62.
27 Anguttara Nikaya 3.38–39.
28 Buddhacarita II.46; Buddhavamsa 26.15; Anguttara Nikaya 1.25.
29 Anguttara Nikaya 1.24. Rahula may have been named such because he was born during or around the time of a lunar eclipse (rahu).
30 Tamar slept with her father-in-law (Genesis 38:15–19); Rahab was a prostitute (Joshua 2:1); Ruth seduced her future husband (Ruth 3:6–14); Bathsheba committed adultery (2 Samuel 11:2–5); and Mary fell pregnant during her betrothal.
31 Matthew 1:1; Luke 1:27.
32 Romans 1:3; 2 Timothy 2:8. There were also exceptions such as the priestly (Aaronic) Messiah anticipated by the Qumran community and the second century CE messianic claimant Bar Kokhba who was not Davidic. Brown, Birth 507.
33 Brown, Birth 511.
34 Deuteronomy 22:23–24.

35 The virginal conception of Jesus is sometimes mistakenly described as an "immaculate conception", but this is a Catholic term that refers to Mary's conception in her mother's womb without original sin. Similarly, "virgin birth" is misleading, since technically, this implies that Mary miraculously gave birth to her son without loss of her virginity, namely without rupture of the hymen.

36 Luke 1:35.

37 Brown argues that Paul's statement that Jesus was "born under the Law" (Galatians 4:4) suggests that Paul was not aware of anything untoward. Brown notes Jane Schaberg's thesis that Mary may have been raped, based on Deuteronomy 22:23–27, but argues that Matthew is not implying this since he does not refer to that passage. See Brown, Birth 601, 637–638.

38 Overcoming a woman's barrenness is a classical Old Testament theme and features in the conception stories of Isaac, Samson and Samuel. See Genesis 21:1–8; Judges 13:2–25; 1 Samuel 1:1–20.

39 Luke 1:42–43. See Deborah's greeting in Judges 5:24 and Uzziah's greeting in Judith 13:18.

40 Luke 3:23. There are some biblical precedents where the mother's name is used but it is very rare: see 1 Chronicles 2:16 ("the sons of Zeruiah").

41 Bovon argues that pagan parallels are crucial, but Mussner claims that Luke's "semantic universe" is Jewish. See Brown, Birth 124, 314, 602; Johnson, Elisabeth 244–247.

42 Matthew 2:19–23.

43 Luke uses another word (pandocheion) for the public inn that features in the story of the Good Samaritan; see Luke 10:34.

44 Wisdom 7:4–5.

45 Brown thinks the key text here is the Septuagint version of Isaiah 1:3: "The ox knows its owner and the donkey knows the manger (phatne) of its Lord but Israel has not known me". Brown, Birth 419.

46 The shepherds are seen as representatives of the "common man" in popular imagination even though, at the time, shepherds were probably feared by many as a dishonest and dangerous lot. Luke's point may be to demonstrate how Jesus is associated with sinners and outsiders from the very start. There is also a connection with King David, whose provenance was Bethlehem and who started his career as a shepherd. Brown, Birth 673.

47 Daniel 1:20, 2:2, 5:7; Acts 8:9–24, 13:6–11; Didache 2.2.

48 The term "magi" suggests Parthia or Persia; their interest in astrology suggests Babylon; the gifts of gold and frankincense suggest Sheba, Midian and Arabia. See Isaiah 60:6; Psalm 72:15.

49 Tradition has transformed them into three "kings" and even supplied the names: Balthasar, Melchior and Gaspar. Brown, Birth 193–198.

50 There are three main hypotheses: a 5 BCE supernova mentioned in Chinese chronicles; the planetary conjunction of Jupiter, Saturn and Mars in 7 BCE; and Halley's Comet which appeared in 12 BCE. Brown, Birth 610–613. See also Numbers 24:17.

51 Brown, Birth 615.

52 Leviticus 12:1–8; Numbers 18:15–16.

53 Brown, Birth 462.

54 Luke 2:51; Matthew 2:23.

55 The difficult child makes clay birds fly, causes a boy to wither, curses another boy who dies, and strikes his critics blind. There are some benevolent acts as well, such as reviving a person who fell from a roof, healing a man who had severed his foot, multiplying a wheat grain into a banquet, and stretching a beam of wood to help his father construct a bed.

56　Athanasius, Orations against the Arians 2.70; Hilary of Poitiers, Commentary on Matthew 1:4; Ambrose of Milan, Letters 63:111; Jerome, Against Helvetius, 21.

57　The case of the Qumran community is more akin to the temporary priestly abstinence prior to offering sacrifice. Brown, Birth 305.

58　Matthew 1:25. See also Acts 8:40.

59　Galatians 1:19; 2:9. See also Matthew 12:46, 13:55; Mark 3:31–32; Luke 8:19–20; John 2:12, 7:3–5; Acts 1:14; 1 Corinthians 9:5.

60　Exodus 13:12–16.

61　Protoevangelium 9.13.

62　Genesis 13:8, 14:14–16; Leviticus 10:4; 1 Chronicles 15:5–10, 23:21–22.

63　Matthew 26:73.

64　John 7:15; Mark 6:2–3.

65　Mark 6:3; Matthew 13:55.

66　Justin, Dialogue with Trypho 88.

67　Vermes, Jew 26.

68　Genesis 16:1–15; 21:9–21.

69　Ramadan 10; Armstrong Muhammad 35; Peterson 34. See Qur'an 93:6–11.

70　Ramadan 10.

71　Ramadan 10, footnote 6.

72　Ramadan 10; Peterson 36–37; Armstrong Muhammad 36.

73　Ibn Hisham 1.301–302.

74　Qur'an 94:1–4.

75　The Qur'an refers to the Prophet's own painful experience and reminds him of the constant need for compassion toward the orphan. See Qur'an 93:6–11.

76　Armstrong Muhammad 36; Emerick 32.

77　Ibn Hisham 1.303. Peterson quotes Widengren, who noted similarities with Krishna, Cyrus, Faridun and David; see Peterson 37, footnote 10.

78　Ibn Hisham 1.319–321; Ramadan 19; Emerick 34; Peterson 42.

79　Peterson 44; Emerick 38.

80　Qur'an 7:157–158.

81　Peterson 40; Rodinson 240; Qur'an 7:157.

82　Armstrong, Muhammad 37.

83　Peterson 44.

84　Ibn Ishaq (Guillaume) 150; Emerick 44.

85　Shi'ites believe that Khadija only bore Muhammad one daughter, Fatima; the others are considered to be children of her earlier marriage.

86　Emerick 46; Peterson 47; Ramadan 25.

Chapter 4

TURNING POINT

The course of a human life is best depicted not as a perfectly straight line but as a meandering path, with a mix of gentle bends, sharper twists and occasionally complete divergences. The shifts reflect those moments in life when external events and internal decisions bring about profound changes and long-term consequences for the person concerned. Life literally heads off in a new direction – sometimes foreseen and sometimes unforeseen. In one sense, there are many turning points in a human life, and this is true of Siddhattha, Jesus and Muhammad. However, this chapter focuses on one very important change of direction in each of their stories – the one that marks the decision to abandon their existing lifestyle in favor of a religious vocation. What were the factors and circumstances that led the prince, the carpenter and the merchant to leave behind their careers and embark on a new path that would eventually transform each into the founder of a major religious system? How and why did Suddhodana's heir end up in a Sarnath deer park sharing his newly discovered insights with five transfixed colleagues? How and why did an anonymous carpenter from Nazareth suddenly appear in the synagogues of Galilee with a fresh interpretation of an old faith? How and why did a respected Meccan merchant dare to challenge openly the sacrosanct traditions of his fellow citizens?

The Four Sights

The life of Prince Siddhattha had been one of opulent splendor from the very beginning. He enjoyed the very best of food and clothing. He had unlimited servants at his beck and call. He had constant access to all forms of entertainment, including dancing, singing, music and women. He even had a residence constructed for each season of the year.[1] Such sumptuousness was hardly unusual for royalty, but his father's ulterior motive was a long-term strategy aimed at ensuring a seamless succession. In other words, he wanted to ensure that the prince eventually became king.

Buddha, Jesus and Muhammad: A Comparative Study, First Edition. Paul Gwynne.
© 2014 John Wiley & Sons, Ltd. Published 2014 by John Wiley & Sons, Ltd.

The hope was that Siddhattha would be so utterly content in his palatial existence that he would never want to leave it. There would be no greener grass anywhere else than at home.

Suddhodana had good reason to fear that his boy might possibly be distracted from his princely life. The sages at his birth mentioned two possible future paths: one political and the other spiritual. The first corresponded precisely to the father's aspirations but the second constituted a genuine threat to those plans. Another cause for concern had occurred when the child experienced his first meditative trance under the rose-apple tree. For the king, it was a disturbing sign that confirmed the veracity of the sages' double prediction.

Despite his father's anxieties, Siddhattha appeared reasonably settled in his late twenties. He had been married to his wife for 10 years and she was now pregnant with their first child. However, something else would soon shake his equilibrium and revive the vivid memories of the rose-apple tree incident. The critical catalyst that irreversibly changed the direction of his career is commonly described as "the four sights".[2] As the term implies, it was something that Siddhattha saw that profoundly affected his worldview and eventually led him to the most important decision of all. After years of being protected inside the pleasure dome of palace life, one fateful day, the young man stepped out into the real world and was never the same again. It is difficult to know precisely what happened. Some sources describe four separate excursions in his royal chariot. Others speak of a single springtime journey into the surrounding forest. Some even describe how Suddhodana himself organized trips, lining the streets with healthy, smiling folk to give a positive impression. Yet the gods conspired to ensure that Siddhattha encountered a hitherto unknown and darker aspect of human existence. Others see the entire story of one or more physical journeys as a metaphor for a young man's inner, spiritual quest over a considerable time – a literary symbol of his gradual conversion due to years of genuine searching and meditation.[3]

The tradition speaks of *four* sights: an old man, an invalid, a corpse being carried on a funeral stretcher and a holy ascetic.[4] The first three sights – ageing, illness and death – represent the fragility of existence and the inevitability of suffering, even for the powerful and wealthy. These are the very things that Suddhodana did not want his son to encounter before taking the throne. Now a new grim reality was thrust upon Siddhattha, and the fact that he had been sheltered only served to intensify the impact of the experience. The realization dawned on him that his comfortable life had been an illusion. Material pleasure and political sway were utterly transient and eventually gave way to suffering and death. The fourth sight is different, even though the ascetic himself was probably aged, sick and not far from death. If the first three sights represent the problem, then the saintly beggar represents the solution. While the first three reveal the futility of investing one's time and energy in passing realities, the fourth sight reveals a way that transcends such temporariness and points toward lasting happiness and fulfillment. But it is a path that was diametrically opposed to Siddhattha's current situation. The stark choice predicted by the sages at his birth had now become a reality. Siddhattha had arrived at the crossroads and an alternative future suddenly opened up before him, much to his father's chagrin.

The tradition indicates that Siddhattha was profoundly affected by the experience. He had been startled out of his complacency and shocked into a new perspective, although it would take some time before he finally made the crucial decision. As the weeks passed, Siddhattha became increasingly restless. He was now convinced that the palace was really a prison and that domestic life was essentially trivial and meaningless. The dominant image used in the early texts is that of dust. In Siddhattha's mind, the royal residence was covered in a pall of suffocating dust whereas, in contrast, the outside world was clean and pure like a polished shell.[5] He had glimpsed a different reality outside the walls and now he was inextricably drawn to that space where perennial truth could be found. The memory of the fourth sight began to crystallize into a profound desire to take the path of wandering ascetics in those wide, open spaces. He was not the first Indian to believe that liberation is found away from home under an open sky.[6]

Meanwhile, Yasodhara had given birth to a boy. Tradition calls him Rahula, meaning "shackle" or "fetter", but the name is probably a later creation, reflecting the bias of monastic editors who would have viewed marriage and children as hindrances to advanced spiritual states.[7] Despite having a newborn son, Siddhattha's anguished soul-searching continued and eventually came to a head one night when he saw a room full of dancing girls, sprawled asleep on the floor. He was overcome with nausea as he gazed at the "sea of human flesh still moist with sweat".[8] Normally sensual, ravishing women were lying in unflattering positions, grinding their teeth, dribbling, snoring and muttering incoherently. It was the final straw and it convinced Siddhattha that he had to leave home immediately. The night in question is appositely described by Buddhists as the Renunciation.

The earliest sources suggest that Siddhattha's family were a witness to his departure, weeping and begging for him to reconsider as he resolutely shaved his head and donned the yellow robe of the shramana.[9] However, the more common account has Siddhattha stealing away in the dead of night while the entire household is in a deep slumber, possibly the result of supernatural assistance. Even in this version there is a farewell of sorts. Before leaving, Siddhattha went to the room where his wife and his newborn son were sleeping and, without waking them, silently promised to return one day.[10]

At this point, the tradition introduces the figure of Mara, the lord of illusion and temptation.[11] Representing those distractions that hinder true progress toward enlightenment, Mara appeared to Siddhattha at that very moment, sowing seeds of doubt and uncertainty. Mara reminded Siddhattha that he was only a few weeks away from becoming a powerful king and that, in this role, he could achieve great good. It would be foolish to miss such an opportunity in order to become a monk instead. Siddhattha resisted the misleading advice but Mara vowed to follow him and wait for another opening.

Accompanied by his personal groom Channa, Siddhattha mounted his white steed, Kanthaka, and rode off into the night. There are different versions as to the length of the ride but at some point the prince dismounted and sent Channa back to his father's house with the horse. In some accounts, this occurred just outside the city, while in other accounts Siddhattha rode all night, or even for several days, until he reached the border of the Sakyan territory.[12] The intention was clearly to be distant enough from his father's house to ensure that he was not intercepted and forced to return. Just as in the tradition where he leaves during the day in the company of his family, this stealthier version of the Great Departure (Abhinikkhamana) has

Siddhattha cut his long hair and shave his beard as a sign of total severance with the past. Similarly, he discarded his princely robes, exchanging them for the tattered garments of a local huntsman. He then gave his jewelry to Channa and ordered him to return home. Buddhist legend claims that the horse died of grief while Channa broke the distressing news to a shocked palace.[13]

The shaving of the hair and the donning of the yellow robes represent not only a drastic change in physical appearance but a fundamental shift in status. With these simple gestures Siddhattha had abandoned the noble Kshatria (warrior) class and declared himself to be a shramana. Without income, he would now rely on the goodwill of others for survival. Without home or family, he was free to go to any corner of the earth in search of higher truth. It was a radical decision but not unique since the tradition of wandering ascetics had been a long established one in Indian society and functioned almost like a fifth class.[14] He had lost his blood family but he was now a member of the broader family of forest dwellers, some of whom lived solitary lives while others banded together in small communities.

Siddhattha headed south, toward the kingdoms of Kosala and Magadha. Their capitals, Savatthi and Rajagaha, were popular centers of learning where religious ideas were openly debated and intellectual leaders had established well-known schools. Either would be a good place to start his epic quest for higher truth. Savatthi was probably too close to the Sakyan kingdom and so Siddhattha crossed the Ganges and headed for Rajagaha, which was ruled by a young regent, named Bimbisara.

The traditional story sets up a double encounter between Bimbisara and Siddhattha soon after he arrived in Rajagaha. Despite the shaved head and tattered clothes, Siddhattha still possessed an unmistakable aristocratic appearance and this caught the attention of the king.[15] Impressed by the majesty that was only thinly covered by a mendicant's garments, Bimbisara offered Siddhattha control of one of his regiments, possibly motivated by the desire to establish an affiliation between Sakya and Magadha.[16] Siddhattha graciously declined and retreated to a residence outside the city. Dissatisfied with the first response, the king visited him and made a second, more substantial proposal. Some sources suggest that it was half of the kingdom while others state that Bimbisara offered to make him heir to the throne.[17] Both are historically unlikely, but they serve to continue the theme of resistance to temptation, echoing the earlier encounter with Mara. The tradition is keen to emphasize that Siddhattha's choices were real and that his path to enlightenment required a steely determination to overcome all distractions and obstacles.

Although Siddhattha declined the two royal propositions, he did promise Bimbisara that he would return one day when he had reached his goal. Yet the journey to that point would not be a quick one. According to tradition, it would take seven long years of commitment and struggle. Scholars usually divide that period into two distinct phases based on the methodology adopted: a phase of meditative practices and a phase of rigorous self-denial.

The first phase commenced in Rajagaha when Siddhattha joined a group of shramanas at a rocky outcrop outside the city known as Vulture Peak. There he took up the esteemed Hindu tradition of yoga. According to the sources, Siddhattha possessed exceptional skill in this area. Even in those first weeks, he was able to attain an advanced state of consciousness known as "pure form", but he also realized that he would need specialist guidance if he was to progress to the even more advanced state called "no form".[18] There was no shortage of schools with renowned teachers scattered across the Ganges Plain, but Siddhattha was looking for an expert and he heard that a guru named Alara Kalama had achieved the second highest level within the realm of "no form": the plane of nothingness. Kalama lived with a community of three hundred disciples near Vesali and so Siddhattha left Rajagaha and travelled north, back across the Ganges. Kalama warmly welcomed the eager, young student, who quickly mastered the relevant techniques and attained the plane of nothingness to the absolute amazement of the old master. As a result, Kalama offered Siddhattha co-leadership of the community.[19]

Once again Siddhattha declined a tempting offer, although in this case it was much closer to his heart than Bimbisara's political–military position. Siddhattha heard that another teacher, named Uddaka Ramaputta, had surpassed Alara Kalama and achieved the next level: the plane of neither perception nor nonperception. So he headed back to Rajagaha and joined Ramaputta's community of over 500 disciples.[20] The outcome was much the same as with Alara Kalama. Siddhattha was welcomed into the community and displayed exceptional ability at mastering the guru's techniques. Within no time, he attained the desired level, but he was frustrated to discover that not even this lofty plane brought ultimate satisfaction. One was still reborn into a world of suffering. All of these superior levels of consciousness were still temporary. Overwhelmed by the unique ability of his pupil, Uddaka Ramaputta invited Siddhattha to accept sole leadership of the community but, once again, he graciously declined and moved on.

Faced with the limited capacity of yogic meditation to provide definitive liberation from suffering and rebirth, Siddhattha turned to another esteemed Hindu tradition: asceticism. Thus, the second phase of his quest was characterized by intensive self-mortification. The aim was to weaken and ultimately break the power of the body over the soul, which was trapped in its corporeal prison. Siddhattha practiced rigorous self-denial for five or six years along with the five companions that he met soon after leaving the monastery of Uddaka Ramaputta. It was during this phase that Siddhattha became widely known as Gotama the Ascetic. But as the years went by, it became more and more apparent that such extreme measures were not leading him to enlightenment. He was becoming emaciated rather than emancipated. The physical beauty, which caught the eye of Bimbisara years earlier, was waning. His body weight dropped dramatically, his bones protruded like a "row of spindles" and his spine was visible through his abdomen.[21] A crisis point was looming and finally, one day, he collapsed in a river while bathing, nearly drowning as a result. In this dire moment Siddhattha realized that the way of asceticism, like the way of yogic meditation, was ultimately inadequate. He would never reach enlightenment while his body was so broken. There must be another way.

It was another moment of utter clarity and decisiveness. Asceticism had to be abandoned and the catalyst came in the form of a young girl named Sujata. When she saw Siddhattha lying semi-paralyzed under a tree, she was not sure if he was even human and mistakenly took him for the tree spirit. Sujata offered him rice and milk pudding and Siddhattha gladly accepted. It was his first solid meal in a long time and it immediately renewed his bodily strength. Seeking a sign from the gods, Siddhattha then placed Sujata's tray on the river and when it began to float upstream he knew that he was capable of achieving enlightenment.[22] His five companions were under-standably upset and scandalized. In their eyes, he had capitulated to basic physical desire and compromised his status as an ascetic. Disgusted, they left behind their colleague and headed toward the city of Baranasi (Benares).[23] Yet Siddhattha now realized that such radical denial of physical needs did not help in the search for enlightenment; in fact it seriously undermined one's well-being. Truth lay via a "middle way" between two extremes: indulgent hedonism on one side and sterile austerity on the other.

Following the "via media", Siddhattha quickly regained his health and pondered his next move. According to the accounts, he recalled the incident under the rose-apple tree as a young boy, when he had effortlessly entered a state of blissful peace. If an untrained child could almost reach enlightenment, then it was surely now within his grasp as long as he allowed nature to take its course. What was needed was a quiet, secluded place, preferably in the cool shade of a tree. So he walked westward and soon reached the village of Uruvela on the banks of the Neranyjara River, at the place now known as Bodhgaya. A local cutter offered him some bundles of soft grass, from which he made himself a comfortable seat under a pipal (fig) tree.[24] Sitting down in lotus position, he faced toward the east and vowed that he would not budge until he had achieved his goal.[25] It was dusk on the full moon of the month of Vesakha, his birthday according to tradition. It was to be a night of destiny – the night of his Enlightenment.[26]

Although the earliest Pali texts describe the Enlightenment without any reference to the tree or the tempter, later accounts include Mara who is intent on thwarting Siddhattha's plans.[27] The duel with Mara would recur many times throughout his life, but the eve of the Enlightenment was the most demanding test. For this reason, the episode is often described as "the Victory over Mara". There is considerable vari-ation as to the contents and timing of the temptations on that fateful night. In the Sutta Nipata, Mara focused on Siddhattha's weakened physical condition, urging him to choose an easier path and simply offer libations to the gods on a holy fire.[28] However, the two forms of temptation that dominate the later biographies and artis-tic renditions are fear and lust, symbolized by the violent attack of Mara's forces and the lascivious dance of Mara's daughters.

In the first test, Mara appeared as a grotesque beast riding a war elephant and accompanied by ten squadrons of hideous monsters. He then unleashed the forces of nature in order to terrify Siddhattha into fleeing. Torrential rain (water), whirlwind (air), flaming spears (fire), rock showers, sandstorms and mudslides (earth), and boundless darkness (ether) were flung at the former prince who remained unmoved. Mara then challenged Siddhattha's right to be seated under the bodhi tree but Sid-dhattha calmly stretched forth his right hand and touched the ground, requesting that earth itself testify to his worthiness. With a shattering roar, it answered back "I bear witness to you" – a moment that is frequently represented in Buddha statues with the master's right arm in the "earth touching" pose. At this, the elephant fell to the ground in submission, the soldiers fled and a vanquished Mara disappeared.

Fear had failed to dissuade Siddhattha from his destiny, but the ordeal was not over since a second temptation arose based on lust.[29] Mara's daughters appeared in forms ranging from nubile virgins to mature women and drew on their arsenal of song, dance and speech to arouse sexual desire in him.[30] Yet it was all in vain. Just as the terrifying display by Mara's army failed to move Siddhattha, so too the voluptuous wiles of his daughters were unable to distract him from his purpose.

Having overcome these final temptations, Siddhattha moved quickly toward his destiny, which is said to have occurred during the three watches of that night. Some consider this a literary device that has compressed a longer, involved process into one fateful evening.[31] During the first watch, Siddhattha focused on his own personal past, gradually recalling all of his former reincarnations. In the second watch, he expanded his inner gaze to take in all other beings, perceiving how each one dies and is reborn in different forms and different planes according to the law of karma. Finally, in the third watch, Siddhattha grasped with unprecedented clarity the fourfold principle that was the key to liberation from the wheel of reincarnation. With this insight, he ascended to the very summit of spiritual knowledge. It was as if he had awoken from a great sleep. The former prince Siddhattha, who had developed into Gotama the Ascetic, was now a totally enlightened being – a Buddha. In that instant, he extinguished the fires of desire that bound him to the cycle of reincarnation and now, as a Buddha, he would never be reborn again. Although still physically alive, he had entered nibbana.

At the end of that momentous night, the new Buddha appropriately exclaimed: "What had to be done has been accomplished; there is nothing else to do".[32] In one sense, this was true. Siddhattha had come to the end of his epic personal journey after seven years of arduous discipline as yogin and ascetic. It was natural for him to want to savor the sublime peace that only nibbana could bring. The traditional narratives describe how he spent seven weeks in blissful meditation in the immediate vicinity of the bodhi tree.[33]

The story could have ended there if not for another turning point. Petrified that the Buddha would pass on his knowledge to other beings and thus open up the path of liberation for all, Mara returned to convince him to leave the world and enter fully into nibbana. Indeed, the Buddha himself had doubts about the wisdom of trying to communicate to others what he had just discovered. His audience would probably not have the capacity to appreciate what was being offered. However, we are told that the god Brahma descended from the higher realms and implored him to become a teacher. The earnest appeal struck a chord in the heart of the Enlightened One and, inspired by his unbounded compassion for all beings, the Buddha made the critical decision.[34] He would not remain locked away in his private nibbana just as he did not remain locked away in his pleasure palace as a youth.[35] Although he had a sense that his teaching would eventually fade away, as it had with previous Buddhas, he resolved to share his wisdom. Once the decision had been taken, the next question was who should be his first pupils.

Waters of the Jordan

All four canonical gospels agree that the commencement of Jesus's public life is linked to the ministry of the prophetic figure known as Yohanan ha-Matbil (John the Baptist). According to Luke, these events occurred in the fifteenth year of the reign of the Emperor Tiberius, making it either 28 or 29 CE.[36] John had deliberately chosen the wilderness of Judea as the setting for his particular religious mission. Although the Jewish tradition viewed the desert as the abode of wild beasts and demons, there was also a well-known theme in the Hebrew Scriptures that saw this barren world as a place of revelation and purification, especially in the stories of Elijah and Hosea.[37] In fact, John's dress of camel's hair and leather belt was unmistakably reminiscent of the former.[38]

The second geographical feature associated with John's ministry was the river. His famous epithet aptly captures the conspicuous symbolic action that underpinned his message. John not only invited people to travel to the fringe of the Judean desert, but he simultaneously invited them to be baptized in the waters of Israel's most important waterway – the Jordan.[39] The imagery of the river evoked the crossing of the Jordan and the conquest of the land under Joshua. John's choice of location fitted well with his claim that God would soon act in a powerful way just as he had at the beginning of Israel's history.

The concept of full immersion in a water bath (mikveh) was hardly foreign to Judaism. The Hebrew Scriptures prescribe immersion in "living water" to wash away spiritual impurity generated by causes such as menstruation or contact with a corpse.[40] The High Priest would also take a full bath each year before the Day of Atonement (Yom Kippur). However, John's one-off invitation to repentance was more akin to the mikveh that was required of a convert to Judaism, symbolizing the washing away of past idolatry and initiation into the people of Israel.[41]

John's actual message was more disturbing than consoling: God would soon come down in blazing wrath to judge all people. Borrowing from the imagery of Isaiah and Jeremiah, John declared that the ax was already at the root of the tree. Those that did not bear fruit would be cut down and burnt in the fire of God's justice. Appealing to membership of the Jewish nation would have no consequence in the eyes of the divine judge, since God could conjure up children of Abraham from the very stones along the river bank.[42] Moreover, John spoke of a mysterious figure that was to come after him and carry out the act of judgment in God's name. Continuing with the agricultural imagery, the anonymous Coming One would wield a winnowing fork to separate the wheat (the virtuous) from the chaff (the wicked). John was unsure of the identity of the Coming One, although there was no doubt about their relative status: John would not even be fit to undo his sandal strap. Furthermore, while John baptized in water, the Coming One would baptize with God's dynamic Spirit and unquenchable fire.[43]

Despite the grim nature of his message, the Baptist attracted considerable crowds. The gospels and Josephus both speak of people flocking from all over Judea to hear his message and submit to his baptism of purification and renewal.[44] Among those who thronged to hear this outspoken prophet was Jesus of Nazareth, who was about 30 years old at the time.[45] The gospels do not reveal what triggered Jesus's decision to travel from his native Galilee to the Judean wilderness. Some have speculated that 30 was the minimum age to become a rabbi, but there is no evidence of such a custom in biblical times, and it has not applied to rabbinical ordination in subsequent history.[46] More likely, Jesus was impressed by the reports of John and felt a need to see and experience the preacher for himself. It is unlikely that the later Christian community would have invented the story of Jesus's baptism given its awkward implication that he had sins that needed washing away. In fact, Matthew contains a dialogue between John and Jesus explaining its propriety.[47] However, unlike the many others who were immersed in the river, Jesus experienced something more than a symbolic water-bath of purification and repentance; it was nothing less than a life-changing theophany.

The theophany consisted of two elements: a heavenly voice that declared Jesus to be God's "beloved Son" and the descent of God's Spirit on Jesus in the form of a dove. There is some ambiguity as to who was actually privy to the supernatural words and vision. Mark and Luke imply that it was primarily Jesus since the celestial voice uses the second person.[48] In contrast, the voice uses the third person in Matthew, implying that it was addressing either John alone or others who were present.[49] The fourth gospel does not explicitly mention the baptism but instead refers to a revelation given personally to John that the person on whom he saw the Spirit descend would be the one that he was expecting.[50]

While it is possible that the theophany and baptism may have been separate events, the traditional picture combines the two into a single scene that constitutes a dramatic turning point in the life of Jesus.[51] The silence of the gospels with regard to his adult life prior to his baptism is frustrating, opening up a vast array of speculation as to the development of his self-understanding and vocation. Did the theophany merely confirm what he had already known since childhood, giving him the green light to proceed? Or was it a powerful, unexpected summons to a new career path in the style of the biblical prophets? The canonical texts do not provide the answers. Whatever Jesus himself was thinking, there is no doubt that, from that moment, the unknown woodworker from Nazareth would never again work with wood, and would soon become very well known.

According to the Synoptic gospels, Jesus did not immediately take up a public role. Instead, he was led by God's Spirit into the Judean wilderness where he fasted for a symbolic period of 40 days and nights, in the pattern of Moses and Elijah.[52] In this inhospitable place of demons and wild animals, and in a state of physical weakness, Jesus encountered Satan. In later Jewish and Christian thinking, Satan is understood as the leader of the rebel angels who were cast out of heaven.[53] However, the name is derived from the Hebrew verb "to oppose" or "to obstruct", and the Hebrew Scriptures apply it to the spirit whose role was to test people's virtue by accusing them before the court of God, much like an official prosecutor in human legal systems.[54] While Mark briefly notes the encounter, Matthew and Luke provide details of three tests, although in a slightly different order. Luke opts for a geographical sequence from desert to mountain to temple, whereas Matthew's arrangement reflects increasing moral gravity in each case.

The first test sounds authentic given that Jesus would have been feeling real pangs of hunger and thirst. In a reference to the declaration of the heavenly voice at the Jordan, Satan challenged: "If you are the Son of God, command these stones to become loaves of bread." But Jesus resisted the suggestion to satisfy his physical cravings and pointed out that the soul needs nourishment as much as the body: "It is written, 'One does not live by bread alone, but by every word that comes from the mouth of God'".[55] The quotation is from Deuteronomy, and Jesus cites the same Torah book in each of the three tests. In Matthew's version, Satan then took Jesus to the parapet of the Temple and invited him to test God by literally jumping off. Emulating Jesus's own strategy, Satan cited Psalm 91, which promises that God will send angels to protect his own from injury, but Jesus countered with another Deuteronomy quote that forbids Israel from putting God to the test.[56] Finally, the tempter took Jesus to a mountain summit and offered him all of the world's kingdoms if Jesus fell at Satan's feet and worshiped him. But a steadfast Jesus drove him away, once again using a verse from Deuteronomy: "You must worship the Lord our God and serve him alone".[57]

Christian writers have often interpreted the temptations as symbols of three addictive vices: pleasure, fame and power. Indeed, it is quite possible that such thoughts may have crossed Jesus's mind from time to time as he became increasingly aware of his commanding sway over natural forces and human beings. Shifting the focus from Jesus's morality to his mission, some argue that the temptations represent a compromised view of his true role as Messiah: focusing on alleviating physical hardships; performing magical tricks to win converts; and liberating Israel from Roman occupation by political force. Behind all of these interpretations is the more fundamental point that, at the very outset of his public life, Jesus was victorious over Satan. He emerged as the "stronger one" who had authority over demons and the kingdom of darkness – an idea that would be central to his message.[58] As with the Buddha and Mara, this would not be the last encounter between the two, and Luke notes that the devil departed from Jesus "until an opportune time".[59] A victory had been established at the start, but the full struggle would still be played out in the months and years ahead.

What happened next is not exactly clear. According to the Synoptic version, the critical development was the arrest of John the Baptist by Herod Antipas. At this point, Jesus returned to Galilee and began a preaching tour of synagogues with his own distinctive message. Matthew adds that he moved out of Nazareth and set up residence in Capernaum on the shores of the Sea of Galilee. There are various explanations given for the arrest and eventual execution of John by Herod. The gospel accounts claim that it was John's candid criticism of Herod's marriage to Herodias, the wife of his brother Herod Philip 1.[60] Herodias instructed her daughter Salome to request the head of the Baptist after Herod was delighted by her dancing and promised to grant her any wish.[61] Josephus' version confirms that Herodias did have a daughter Salome, but suggests that the real motivation for the incarceration and execution of the Baptist was that he had a large following and, thus, constituted a real political threat.[62]

The key question is: what was Jesus doing between his baptism and John's arrest? The fourth gospel provides some interesting clues since it describes how Jesus and some associates engaged in a period of baptizing either within John's own community of disciples or alongside them. The gospel speaks of both groups working at Aenon because of its abundant water, although it is unclear if Jesus himself baptized. That gospel also hints at a certain competition between the two groups as outsiders noted the increasing popularity of Jesus over John.[63] Moreover, there is evidence that some of Jesus's key disciples were formerly followers of the Baptist but eventually chose to align themselves with Jesus.[64] In time, that early tension was diluted and Christian tradition cast the Baptist as the Elijah-like forerunner of the Messiah.[65]

So the figure of John the Baptist played a crucial role at the start of Jesus's public ministry. Although the precise timing is unknown, his personality and message must have struck a resonating chord in Jesus's mind, prompting him to travel from Nazareth to the Judean wilderness in order to see firsthand and to be baptized. At some stage, Jesus also experienced a powerful prophetic call that identified him as God's beloved "Son" and special recipient of God's Spirit. The Synoptic gospels link the theophany to his baptism in the Jordan, but some speculate that it may have been the initial catalyst in Nazareth or even a subsequent event that further delineated Jesus's career path. Initially, that path meant participating in John's baptizing mission, but at some point, probably as a result of John's arrest, Jesus decided to launch out and offer his own distinctive reinterpretation of John's call to repentance. One of the first differences was the choice of location. Unlike John's preference for the highly symbolic combination of Jordan River and Judean desert, Jesus opted for the village synagogues of his native Galilee.

Night of Power

By the time Muhammad was 40 years old, it seemed that his life was stable, with little hint of the unsettling events that would soon occur. He had been in a happy monogamous marriage with Khadija for 15 years. Tragically, the couple had lost two sons in infancy, but they also had four young daughters aged between 6 and 11. His mercantile career had been successful and it provided him with adequate income to support his family. In terms of his broader social standing, Muhammad was a well-respected citizen of Mecca, as indicated by his popular nicknames Al-Sadiq ("truthful one") and Al-Amin ("trustworthy one"). He was also reputed to be an excellent mediator in disputes but he felt dissatisfaction with the growing injustices in Mecca's stratified society.[66] On the verge of middle age, Muhammad was keenly aware of the malaise that was pervading his community. Many customs and practices troubled him: incessant tribal warfare, the torture and murder of enemies, slavery, female infanticide, lack of women's rights, drunkenness, gambling and the cult of idols.[67]

The last point raises the issue of Muhammad's religious faith. There are vague hints that a younger Muhammad may have shared the surrounding polytheism of his world. The Qur'an states that "God found you astray and guided you",[68] and many of his family remained pagan despite Muhammad's attempts to convert them during his public career. Yet the Islamic tradition strongly insists that Muhammad was a monotheist from his earliest days, placing him within the hanif movement. It is possible that these loosely organized Arabian monotheists saw the high god of the Arabian pantheon, Allah, as the same deity as the Jewish and Christian God.[69]

It is difficult to determine the extent to which Muhammad was influenced by the monotheistic ideas and movements in early seventh-century Arabia. What is clear is that something happened that transformed his whole consciousness.[70] While some have argued that the turning point was actually a gradual process based on prolonged periods of meditation,[71] the traditional account speaks of a sudden, compelling experience. The growing restlessness in his soul and the availability of leisure time led Muhammad to withdraw from Mecca and seek spiritual inspiration in the solitude of the surrounding desert hills. His favorite place of retreat was a small cave on Mount Hira, just a few miles northeast of the town. Here he would meditate for days and nights at a time.[72] During his sleep, he would experience vivid dreams that were like the breaking of dawn, convincing him that this time spent alone was not in vain. It was on one such evening near the end of the month of Ramadan, probably in the year 610 CE, that something more powerful than a dream seized upon him and changed his life forever.

Muhammad had been dozing off when suddenly he was overwhelmed by the sense of another presence in the cave. He opened his eyes and saw a luminescent being in human form standing before him. Then Muhammad heard a booming voice uttering the word "iqra" – a term that can mean either to recite from memory or to read aloud from a written text.[73] Quivering with fear, Muhammad responded by explaining that he was not one of those who read or recited. The angel then seized Muhammad and placed him in an overpowering embrace, forcing the very air from his lungs. Once again, the angel ordered him to recite, once again Muhammad honestly explained that he could not read and once again the angel squeezed him until he nearly fainted. This happened three times until Muhammad relented and asked the spirit what it was that he was meant to recite. Suddenly, he was released from the suffocating grip and found himself effortlessly uttering strange words in melodious Arabic verse:

> Read in the name of your Lord Who created.
> He created man from a clot.
> Read and your Lord is Most Honorable,
> Who taught (to write) with the pen
> Taught man what he knew not.[74]

Then, the spirit vanished as abruptly as it had appeared, leaving Muhammad terrorized in the eerie silence of the cave. His immediate thought was that he had been the victim of an attack by one of the jinn – the fiery desert spirits who played capricious tricks but also inspired the poets and soothsayers, sometimes throwing them to the ground and forcing verses from their lips.[75]

In a state of fear and panic, he rushed out of the cave and raced down the hillside. He had only managed to stumble halfway down the rocky slopes of Hira when the ghostly figure returned in a gigantic form that stretched from horizon to horizon, filling the entire night sky. No matter which way Muhammad turned, he was confronted with his frightening, supernatural pursuer. According to some authors, it is at this point that the angelic presence identified itself as Jibril (Gabriel) and declared Muhammad to be a messenger of God.[76] Even more terrified and confused, Muhammad staggered home to Khadija. Shaking convulsively, he cried "cover me" and threw himself into his wife's comforting arms. She wrapped her distressed husband in a blanket, holding him gently until he calmed down and eventually fell asleep.

Khadija's first instinct was to consult with her elderly Christian cousin, Waraqa ibn Nawfal.[77] When Khadija described Muhammad's perplexing experience, Waraqa surprisingly reacted with excitement and joy. In his mind, the strange celestial being that had appeared to Muhammad was a genuine envoy from the one, true God.[78] He was convinced that the same angel who had communicated with Moses in ancient times had now contacted Muhammad. Waraqa confirmed what Khadija was already thinking, namely that the enigmatic experience that Muhammad had undergone was not the work of a desert jinni but an authentic encounter with the divine. Her conclusion was not based on whim or even intuition but on a logical premise: God would not play a cruel trick on a good man who was considerate to others, especially the poor. The very trustworthiness of Muhammad's character suggested to her that not only was his story credible but also that its cause was genuine. At that moment, Muhammad had his first convert.

The tradition continues that when Khadija arrived home, she found Muhammad still shivering and sweating. He had just awoken from his sleep and found himself once again uttering words that seemed to be placed on his lips by another speaker:

> "O you who are clothed (wrapped in a blanket)!
> Arise and warn."[79]

This verse is often coupled with another, which also addresses Muhammad as "wrapped up" (mutazammil) and speaks of a "weighty word" that he would soon receive.[80] Some scholars think that these "mantle" passages may have been the first revelations to Muhammad and that the wrapping in clothing may refer to Muhammad's preparation for prayers.[81]

The explosive, life-changing impact of Muhammad's encounter with the angel is reflected in the traditional names for both the place and the time. Mount Hira is commonly referred to as Jabal al-Nur ("Mountain of Light"), and the cave itself is a popular place of visitation for the annual religious pilgrims in Mecca. The momentous event has its place in the Islamic calendar as Laylat al-Qadr ("Night of Power") and is commemorated toward the end of Ramadan.[82] Another passage in the Qur'an describes it in this way:

> Surely We revealed it on the grand night.
> And what will make you comprehend the grand night.
> The grand night is better than a thousand months.
> The angels and Jibril (the Spirit) descend in it by the permission of their Lord for every affair.
> Peace! It is till the break of the morning.[83]

Here the Qur'an is referring to its own descent from heaven, but there is no reference to Muhammad and the turbulent, frightening aspects have been replaced by a gentler, feminine tone, more like the conception of Jesus in Mary's womb. A new era of divine communication had driven away the darkness of ignorance and ushered in peace like the daybreak.[84]

As abruptly and unexpectedly as the first revelations had came upon Muhammad, they suddenly and inexplicably ceased. Although Muhammad had been expecting further revelations from the angel, there was only silence instead. The days turned into weeks, which subsequently turned into months. Estimations of the length of the "fatra" (pause) range from six months to three years. Whatever the exact interval, it was a prolonged period that began to take a serious toll on Muhammad. Feelings of anxiety and desolation were coupled with an increasing sense of doubt about the veracity of the entire experience. Perhaps God was displeased with him in some way and had abandoned his plan to make Muhammad his prophet. Perhaps it was the result of a capricious jinni after all. Worse still, perhaps he was suffering from delusional madness.[85] The most drastic and serious consequence of this troubled time was that Muhammad started to entertain thoughts of suicide. Several hadiths describe how a distressed Muhammad felt like throwing himself off a mountain top but it is unclear as to the timing and the frequency.[86]

Then, just as abruptly as the fatra had begun, it ended. After a seemingly endless period of divine silence, the spirit returned and the terrible ordeal of self-doubt passed. Tradition holds that the episode is captured in the 93rd sura of the Qur'an, appositely entitled al-Duha (Morning):

> I swear by the early hours of the day,
> And the night when it covers with darkness.
> Your Lord has not forsaken you, nor has He become displeased,
> And surely what comes after is better for you than that which has gone before.
> And soon will your Lord give you so that you shall be well pleased.[87]

It was as if the dark shadow of despair and anxiety had been swept away by the blinding glory of a new dawn. From this point on, there would be no more extended pause in the revelations and no more wavering doubts on Muhammad's part. While the precise timing of each revelation was never predictable, an overall realiability was established that would continue for the next 20 years until his death. Muslims see the perplexing silence as an initial test that pushed Muhammad's faith, patience and sanity to the very limits but, nevertheless, one that he passed in the end.[88]

The original revelatory experiences are described as both visual and auditory – Muhammad saw the angel and heard it speak. But as time passed, auditions replaced visions as the norm. There are occasional references to further visionary experiences in the Qur'an, but the vast majority of the divine messages that Muhammad received came to him in the form of words heard internally either in his dreams or during the unusual trances that would overcome him.[89] For some, the graphic descriptions of these trances reinforce their authenticity since their embarrassing manner is unlikely to have been invented by later tradition.[90] The sources speak of trembling, profuse sweating, fever and chills, and an intense pain as if he had been struck by a heavy blow. Muhammad felt as if his soul had been torn away from his body.[91] In such a state, he would hear strange, incoherent sounds, such as bells tolling, which would slowly crystallize into a meaningful message.[92]

The striking, physical nature of Muhammad's revelatory experiences has given rise to the theory that he suffered from a type of epilepsy.[93] Indeed, certain characteristics of Muhammad's trances resemble symptoms of temporal lobe epilepsy: the sudden onset, falling to the ground, loss of muscle control and hallucinatory imagery. Yet arguments against this theory include: the advanced age of Muhammad when the trances commenced; they were always associated with revelations; Muhammad's consciousness was not impaired; he was able to utter highly organized, poetic statements immediately after the event; and there is no evidence of mental or physical degeneration over time.[94]

In Muhammad's day, such experiences would have been interpreted as an attack by the jinn. Indeed, this was Muhammad's own instinctive response to the first revelation, confiding in Khadija that he was afraid that he might be "majinun" (possessed). His later enemies would dismiss him in the same way. It was not an unreasonable conclusion given that the soothsayer (kahin) and magician (sahir) were familiar cultural figures, whose inspired trances, produced by the desert spirits, bore some resemblance to Muhammad's episodes.[95] Tradition tells us that Khadija had her own idiosyncratic way of testing whether the spirit was benevolent or malevolent. The next time the mysterious messenger was present, Khadija asked Muhammad to sit on her lap. "Do you see the spirit?" she asked. When he replied in the affirmative, she audaciously removed some of her clothing and exposed herself. "Do you still see the spirit?" she inquired. When Muhammad responded in the negative, she confidently explained that this could not be a devil, but must be a genuine angel from God.[96] The Qur'an also explicitly affirms that Muhammad was neither mad nor a poet nor a soothsayer.[97]

The Qur'an describes the agent of revelation in a number of ways: the Spirit, our Spirit, the Honest Spirit and the Holy Spirit.[98] In two places the Qur'an explicitly identifies the heavenly messenger as Gabriel.[99] This name is highly significant since it places Muhammad's prophetic calling squarely in the monotheistic stream of Judaism and Christianity, rather than Arabian polytheism. In the book of Daniel, Gabriel appears in human form, providing the young visionary with the key to interpreting his strange dreams.[100] In the gospel of Luke, Gabriel is the angel who appears to Zechariah and Mary, announcing the imminent births of John the Baptist and Jesus, respectively.[101] In many places, the Qur'an confirms the fundamental connection between Muhammad's experience and the divine revelation of the Jewish and Christian scriptures, recognizing the same Spirit at work in all three.

> And most certainly We gave Musa the Book and We sent apostles after him one after another; and We gave Isa, the son of Marium, clear arguments and strengthened him with the holy spirit.[102]

The resumption of the revelatory experiences after a long and frustrating period of silence had a powerful and lasting effect on Muhammad. From that moment, there was no further mention of confusion or despair. The feelings of self-doubt evaporated, replaced by an unswerving, rock-solid conviction that he had been chosen by God for a purpose. It had been a painful, unsettling process that had taken him to the brink but now it was time for action and the message was clear. Muhammad had been called to "recite". Like the angel, he, too, was being sent as a messenger and he would have to start speaking on behalf of the elusive, powerful God who had selected him. However, Muhammad was neither naïve nor reckless. He did not rush headlong into the public eye. He courageously decided that he would accept the role of prophet, but he would do so initially with prudence and patience.

Observations

This chapter has focused on the pivotal transition from private life to public religious career in the case of each founder. It has attempted to identify the main catalysts that prompted Siddhattha, Jesus and Muhammad to leave behind their existing lifestyle and step into the public domain with a particular message to communicate. It has endeavored to trace the persons and events that constitute such a major turning point in their respective lives.

One striking feature is that the traditional sources devote more attention to Siddhattha's career shift from prince to teacher than in the case of Jesus or Muhammad. Several of the Buddha's earliest biographers thought that there was no need to go beyond that crucial phase of his life. For example, the Mahavastu terminates with the conversion of the earliest disciples and Buddha's return to his home. Similarly, the author of the Lalitavistara thought it fit to wind up the narrative with the first sermon, just weeks after the Buddha's Enlightenment. Neither work is interested in recounting the decades to follow: the itinerant preaching, the establishment of the monastic community and the Buddha's death. The Buddhacarita provides a more complete account, which includes the last days of the Buddha and his passing into nibbana, but the earlier texts provide only limited information on the 45 years between the Enlightenment and the death. This narrowed focus is understandable, since it is the seven-year journey to Enlightenment that is the heart of the matter for Buddhism. In one sense, once Siddhattha becomes the Buddha and achieves nibbana, the story is over. Hence, the early writers provide us with ample material regarding the details of that fascinating journey: the initial curiosity, the shock of the four sights, the pain of leaving home, the initial confidence, the disappointment in the spiritual schools, the dangerous extremes of asceticism, the option of the middle way and finally the bliss of nibbana that came under the tree at Bodhgaya.

In contrast, there is frustratingly little information about this formative phase of Jesus's life. The canonical gospels leave us with no information about the "hidden years" at Nazareth. We can only speculate on his growing sense of a religious calling and his search as a young adult to understand his self-identity. There appears to be no indication that there was anything special or exceptional about Jesus although the potential was obviously there. The focus of the gospels, and subsequent Christian theology, is elsewhere: his short but powerful ministry and his premature death. It is a similar situation with Muhammad. Admittedly, there is slightly more information available regarding the period just prior to his public career and much interest in his first revelation. Yet the material is still scant and pales into insignificance against the main focus of the biographies: the painful trials in Mecca and the astounding success in Medina.

The timing of the turning point makes for an interesting comparison. None of the three founders appear in the public eye as child prodigies or teenage celebrities, nor were they old men steeped in the wisdom of the years. They are all more or less in that period often described today as "thirty-something". Siddhattha is traditionally reckoned to have been 29 years old when he experienced the four sights and decided to abandon his family for the forest. After an epic seven-year quest, he became the

Buddha and began to attract followers in his mid-30s. We are told that Jesus was about 30 years old when he was baptized by John and soon thereafter began a preaching career in Galilee. If he was born prior to the death of Herod the Great, as the gospels suggest, then he may actually have been in his mid-30s when the turning point came. Muhammad was slightly more senior in that the tradition puts him around 40 years old when he experienced the first revelation in the cave, although some have argued that his later dynamic career hints at a slightly younger age. Like Siddhattha, he had a wife and family at the time, although his calling did not require him to emulate Siddhattha's drastic step and literally leave them behind.

The turning points are also a fascinating mix of internal and external factors. In regard to the inner, mental predispositions of the three founders, the most explicit account by far is that of Siddhattha. The Buddhist texts explore in considerable depth the inner yearnings of the restless prince who had already experienced a higher state of consciousness as a young boy under the rose-apple tree. That moment of extraordinary insight had been smothered by the opulent lifestyle of the palace but the seed of intellectual and spiritual curiosity never disappeared entirely. The kindling was already in place and it only needed a spark to be reignited – a spark that came in the form of the four sights. Siddhattha's desire to venture outside the safety of the palace walls was symbolic of his innate drive to know more and for the first time he saw human existence as it really was and not as his father had deceptively presented it. The impact of the four sights profoundly unsettled him and although he did not act immediately, the deep-seated unease eventually led to his life-changing decision to leave the palace. During the next seven years of searching, the story traces his unrelenting determination to discover supreme liberation despite the disappointing inadequacies of two spiritual schools and the dangerous extremes of asceticism. In the end, it was an extraordinary achievement grounded in his patience, perseverance and prudence.

At first glance, it would seem that the opposite is the case with Muhammad who did not become prophet as a result of his own desire or disciplined effort. Instead, his turning point was a frightening encounter with a powerful other being who issued him with a solemn and mysterious command. The initiative seems to come entirely from without rather than within. However, one must ask what was Muhammad doing in the cave on his own in the first place? The answer is that he was praying, fasting and meditating. In other words, he was already seeking something or someone that transcended the aggressive materialism and small-minded tribalism of Meccan society. As a result of his stable economic situation, Muhammad could afford to take the time to seek out the one true God of the hunafa. But not every successful merchant with plenty of leisure time retreated to Mount Hira. When the angel suddenly appeared, it was not to a man who was intrinsically incapable of responding in the appropriate way. God chooses his prophets for a reason.

In the case of Jesus, it is even more difficult to make statements about his personal faith just prior to his public ministry. Undoubtedly his mindset was partially shaped by the chief concerns of the Galilean peasantry among whom he grew up: Roman occupation, crippling taxes and empty religious legalism. More importantly, there must have been something about the message of John the Baptist that resonated in Jesus's heart and made it a natural decision to leave Nazareth and travel south to the banks of the Jordan. Most likely, Jesus shared with John the firm expectation of an imminent apocalyptic event of some sort, although it quickly became apparent that Jesus had his own very different interpretation of what God had in mind.

Alongside the internal mental world of the three founders, the turning points also involve external stimuli, which are naturally more accessible to biographers. Siddhattha's inherent curiosity led him to leave the palace, but it was the four sights that made the difference. The discovery of sickness, old age and death starkly revealed the transient nature of all physical pleasure, while the fourth sight unveiled a new possible career path that promised ultimate truth and lasting happiness. With the four sights, a chronic disillusionment with palace life set in and the final straw was yet another sight: the dancing girls sprawled in unbecoming manner across the room. There are other external factors that keep prompting Siddhattha inexorably toward Bodhgaya: the sleeping of the palace guards, the unquestioning obedience of his chauffeur, the inadequate yet valuable training under two masters, the companionship of his fellow ascetics, the milk pudding of Sujata and the kindness of the grass cutter. Buddhist mythology sees behind these occurrences, the clandestine assistance of the gods who are committed to clearing the way for the one destined to be the Buddha.

These "gods" are merely agents of the dhamma rather than a supreme deity that has planned a special role for his Buddha. In contrast, the chief external factor in the stories of Jesus and Muhammad is the God of biblical monotheism. Muhammad was not the only hanif who earnestly sought the one true God with prayer and meditation but it was not to them that Gabriel was sent. The Night of Power is partially about a spiritual man climbing a mountain in search of answers but it is also about the inscrutability of divine choice and the primacy of divine initiative. As with the experience of other prophets in the biblical tradition, it is God who acts and man who reacts. According to Muslim faith, Gabriel is not conjured up by Muhammad but is truly an "angel" in the root sense of the word – one who has been sent from beyond. Muhammad is the privileged recipient of a divine call, via a messenger, to become a messenger himself. Yet God is not the only agent. There are also other mundane factors, including Khadija's crucial support and Waraqa's consoling assessment.

For those who see Jesus in the same biblical tradition, the turning point of his life can be interpreted as a type of prophetic call. The important clue here is the theophany in which Jesus is identified as God's beloved son and recipient of God's Spirit. In the gospel accounts, it is linked to the baptismal scene itself, but irrespective of whether it occurred before, during or after the actual baptism, the voice of the Father and the descent of the Spirit hint at a life-changing vocational experience that, as with Muhammad, originated from beyond. It may well have been the trigger that convinced Jesus to abandon his life as a tradesman and take up a religious vocation. But there is no account in the gospels of Jesus's reaction to the theophany, and so we do not know if it only confirmed what he already knew or if it was a moment of genuine revelation about his identity and his role in God's plan. While the theophany represents the heavenly dimension of Jesus's turning point, the earthly dimension is undoubtedly the figure of John the Baptist. All four gospels link the commencement of Jesus's public career with the Elijah-like prophet who was eventually assimilated into Christian tradition as the subordinate but vital precursor of Jesus. His commanding personality and fiery warnings of impending judgment made an impression on many Jews, including Jesus, who left Nazareth and travelled to the Jordan in order to be baptized by John and probably join his movement for a short time. The subsequent arrest of John by Herod Antipas should have sent alarm bells ringing for anyone indulging in similar activity, but it seems only to have convinced Jesus to return to Galilee and launch his own religious project with a distinctive variation of the Baptist's theme.

The three stories also contain an element of struggle or obstruction, although it takes a different form in each case. In the Buddhist accounts, a spirit known as Mara ("death") appeared at critical moments and attempted to distract Siddhattha's focus from his noble goal. Just as the prince was about to leave the palace, Mara endeavored to cajole him into staying, reminding Siddhattha that he would soon become king and, thus, be in a position to do wonderful deeds. Siddhattha ignored him and forfeited his royal inheritance. Mara is reintroduced into the narrative at the very climax of the story when Siddhattha was on the verge of attaining enlightenment. This time the assault was more aggressive as Mara utilized the weapons of fear and lust. He unleashed an army of grotesque monsters, symbolizing the vices, followed by the full fury of natural forces but Siddhattha remained calm and unmoved. Mara then called in his voluptuous daughters who tried with all of their wiles to arouse sexual desire in Siddhattha, but again it was to no avail. Siddhattha kept his poise and touched the earth in a gesture that has become one of the common mudras of Buddha statues. He called on the earth to witness that, against Mara's claim, he was worthy of enlightenment and the earth thundered back its approval. Defeated but persistent, Mara would continue to surface on subsequent occasions, with the same agenda of opposition and obstruction. Despite the fact that Siddhattha is portrayed as one who is supremely above all temptation and doubt, the inclusion of Mara in the story suggests that there was a real struggle within his soul. For many, Mara symbolizes natural psychological desires and fears that Siddhattha had to conquer in order to attain his destiny. Along with Mara, there are human obstacles as well. Siddhattha's own father was committed to keeping his heir safely ensconced in palace life in the hope that he would succeed him as political ruler. Another king, Bimbisara, would present him with a tempting offer to act as his deputy. Even Siddhattha's own wife and child are seen as a constraint that holds him back from his true destiny, as reflected in the very name of his son, Rahula, which means chain or fetter.

The story of Jesus also includes a spiritual foe that appears at the very outset of his public ministry. The Synoptic gospels describe how Jesus was "tempted" by Satan in the wilderness immediately after his baptism. These temptations were not attempts to coax Jesus into committing a sin. They are more concerned with whether Jesus would misuse his genius and authority: to satisfy physical desires, to impress others with amazing feats and to acquire political might. In the end, Jesus rejected the lure of pleasure, popularity and power in favor of another form of kingship. As with the Buddha, there is no reference to the real possibility that Jesus might have failed and his adversary might have triumphed but, once again, the inclusion of Satan in the story suggests that there was a genuine internal struggle at the key turning point of his life.

The element of struggle in Muhammad's case is quite different from the Buddha and Jesus. Although Satan is part of Islamic belief, he does not appear at the start with the aim of tempting Muhammad away from his calling. In fact, the real hindrance comes from the confusing and frightening nature of the revelatory experience itself. Muhammad's initial reaction to Gabriel was not unlike that of Zechariah or Mary who, according to Luke, were also terrified and perplexed.[103] Muhammad rushed out of the cave in a state of great anxiety and fear, collapsing into the arms of Khadija. His first instinct was to presume that he was a victim of the mischievous pranks of the jinn, although his wife offered valuable consolation, assuring him that it was God and not the fickle desert spirits who had contacted him. It would take considerable time before a troubled Muhammad was convinced that he was neither mad nor a victim of supernatural trickery. His agitated state was not helped by the inexplicable pause in revelations that possibly lasted up to several years. So serious was the frustration and desolation that Muhammad even began to consider suicide. In hindsight, the entire period is seen as a test of faith and patience – one that Muhammad passed. When the revelations finally resumed, it not only brought an enormous sense of relief but it also cemented in his soul a lasting and unbreakable confidence that he was truly a prophet of the one God. There would be more trials to come, but an unwavering conviction in his vocation would be one of Muhammad's most outstanding traits.

In the prime of adulthood, the prince, the carpenter and the merchant had each passed through a series of intensive experiences that totally altered the orientation of their life journey. They would never be the same again and nor would the world since their new sense of self-identity was not just a private matter. Each one of them also experienced the obligation to communicate something to others. For the Buddha, it was compassion that compelled him to leave the sublime bliss that he had found in Bodhgaya and seek out those with whom he could share his newly discovered secret. For Jesus, the arrest of John the Baptist was a signal that the time had come for him to share with fellow Jews his interpretation of the imminent coming of God pronounced by John. For Muhammad, the mandate to speak is most explicit. The very first utterance of Gabriel in the cave was the command to "recite" the words that God would place in his mouth. Who, then, would be their audience and what would be their message?

Notes

1 Anguttara Nikaya 3.38.
2 Nakamura I 95; Thomas 51, footnote 1; Mizuno 18.
3 Blomfield 31.
4 These are often linked to the four gates of the city through which Siddhattha passed on each journey. Buddhacarita III.26–55; Armstrong, Buddha 29–30. A similar story is told of the earlier Buddha Vipassi in Digha Nikaya 14.
5 Majjhima Nikaya 36; Anguttara Nikaya 3.38.
6 Foucher 67; Nakamura I 105–108.
7 An alternative interpretation is that it refers to the astrological sign Rahu under which the child was born. Armstrong, Buddha 1.
8 Foucher 75; Lalitavistara (Foucaux) 197–198; Buddhacarita V.44–65.

9 In response to his father's final plea not to leave, Siddhattha promised that he would remain if the king could guarantee that he would not suffer old age, disease and death. Majjhima Nikaya 26, 36, 85, 100.

10 Foucher 76; Lalitavistara (Foucaux) 187; Buddhacarita V.65–87.

11 Foucher 110; Armstrong, Buddha 32.

12 Armstrong, Buddha 31; Mizuno 19.

13 Mahavastu (Jones) II 156; Buddhacarita VI; Nakamura I 115–116.

14 Armstrong, Buddha 25; Ling 76–82; Oldenberg 66–71.

15 Sutta Nipata 405–422; Mahavagga 1.22; Buddhacarita X–XI.

16 Sutta Nipata 419–421.

17 Nakamura I 123; Mizuno 20–22; Thomas 69.

18 The realm of "no form" consisted of four levels: boundless space; boundless consciousness; nothingness; and neither perception nor non-perception. Carrithers 32–34; Armstrong, Buddha 55.

19 Majjhima Nikaya 26; Lalitavistara (Foucaux) 228; Mahavastu (Jones) II 115; Buddhacarita XII.15–80.

20 Majjhima Nikaya 26; Mahavastu (Jones) II 117.

21 Cullavagga 6:4, 7:1; Majjhima Nikaya 36; Buddhacarita XII; Armstrong, Buddha 58.

22 Lalitavistara (Foucaux) 257–260; Buddhacarita XII.

23 Majjhima Nikaya 27, 38, 39, 112.

24 Buddhacarita XII; Nakamura I 142–144.

25 Lalitavistara (Foucaux) 261–279.

26 Mahavamsa 1.12; Nakamura I 187.

27 Majjhima Nikaya 19, 36.

28 Sutta Nipata 425.

29 Most versions agree that the appearance of the daughters occurs after the defeat of Mara's army but the timing varies from the same night to seven years later. See Sutta Nipata 424–448; Lalitavistara (Foucaux) 286–328, 359–370; Mahavastu (Jones) II 354; Buddhacarita XIII, XIV.

30 Nanamoli 64.

31 Carrithers 53.

32 Majjhima Nikaya 36.

33 The themes of each week are the chain of dependent origination, the bodhi tree, walking meditation, the jewelled staircase, rest, the serpent king protects him from a storm and the joy of nibbana. Nakamura I 220–223; Lalitavistara (Foucaux) 350–357; Mahavastu (Jones) III 261–266. The timespan is 4 weeks in the Mahavagga. Nakamura suggests that this was a method of abandoning his attachment to the bodhi tree. See Nakamura I 219.

34 Mahavagga 1.5; Buddhacarita XV; Lalitavistara (Foucaux) 376–378.

35 Armstrong, Buddha 87–88.

36 Luke 3:1–2.

37 Exodus 19; 1 Kings 19:1–18; Hosea 2:14–23.

38 2 Kings 1:8. Some translations prefer "a hairy man" to camel's hair or a hair shirt. The diet of locusts and wild honey is possibly a protest against material indulgence.

39 There is still debate over the exact location. The fourth gospel identifies it as "Bethany beyond the Jordan", which accords well with modern day Al-Maghtas on the eastern bank. However, most pilgrims and tourists today visit a nearby spot on the western bank known as Qasir al-Yahud (Jew's Castle). Both locations are east of Jericho, at the southern end of the Jordan River just a few miles from its entrance into the Dead Sea.

40 Numbers 19:19; Leviticus 15.

41 McClymond 377; Meier II 52–53.

42 Matthew 3:7–10.

43 Matthew 3:11–12; 11:2–3; McClymond 377–378.

44 Antiquities 18.5.2.

45 Luke 3:23.

46 Conybeare 177. See also Genesis 41:46; 2 Samuel 5:4; Numbers 4:3.

47 Matthew 3:14–15.

48 Mark 1:11; Luke 3:22.

49 Matthew 3:17.

50 John 1:29–34.

51 Meier II 108–109.

52 Exodus 34:28; 1 Kings 19:4–8.

53 The first-century CE work 2 Enoch contains an early reference to Satanael and other "Watchers" being expelled from heaven. 2 Enoch 18:3; 29:4. See also Martyrdom of Isaiah, 2:2; Book of Jubilees 17.18.

54 Job 1–2; Zechariah 3:1; 1 Chronicles 21:1.

55 Deuteronomy 8:3.

56 Deuteronomy 6:16.

57 Deuteronomy 6:13.

58 Mark 3:27.

59 Luke 4:13.

60 Also called Herod II (c. 27 BCE–33 CE), he should not be confused with Philip the Tetrarch (also known as Herod Philip II). See Leviticus 20:21; 18:16.

61 Mark 6:17–29.

62 Antiquities 18.5.2–3.

63 John 3:22–24; 4:1–2.

64 Acts 1:21–22; John 1:35–42.

65 See Luke 1, 2; John 3:30. The Christian calendar symbolizes the superior–inferior relationship by linking the birthdays of Jesus and John to the two solstices in December and June. The effect in the northern hemisphere is that days grow longer after Jesus's birthday and shorter after John's birthday.

66 Peterson 49.

67 Emerick 55.

68 Qur'an 93:7; see Peterson 50, including footnote 5.

69 Emerick 55.

70 Welch 363.

71 Welch 363.

72 Bukhari 87.111; Peterson 50; Rodinson 70; Emerick 57; Armstrong, Muhammad 45.

73 Peterson 51, Ramadan 29.

74 Qur'an 96:1–5.

75 Peterson 52; Armstrong, Muhammad 21.

76 Emerick 59; Armstrong, Muhammad 47.

77 Peterson 62; Emerick 60; Armstrong, Muhammad 47; Ramadan 30.

78 Bukhari 87.111. Riaz Hassan argues for greater recognition of the role of Khadija as the key influence on Muhammad's self-understanding as God's Prophet. See Hassan chapters 5–6.

79 Qur'an 74:1–2; Emerick 60; Ramadan 32.

80 Qur'an 73:1–8.

81 Welch 363.

82 The precise date is not known, although it is presumed to be an odd number late in the month, thus giving rise to the custom of "seeking" the Night of Power by praying and meditating in a mosque for the last week of the fasting season.

83 Qur'an 97:1–5.

84 Armstrong, Muhammad 48–49.

85 Peterson 52.

86 In some versions, the temptation to commit suicide occurred as Muhammad was hurriedly descending from Mount Hira immediately after the initial revelation. What stopped him was the second appearance of the angel, who filled the sky and confirmed that he was truly God's prophet. In other versions, the temptation arose on several occasions during the "fatra", possibly because Muhammad continued to withdraw to the isolation of his cave. See Ibn Hisham 1.237, 238; Bukhari 87.111; Ibn Ishaq (Guillaume) 106; Watt, Mecca 40–41.

87 Qur'an 93:1–5.

88 Welch 363.

89 Peterson 53; Qur'an 8:43; 48:27; 53:12; 81:22–23.

90 Welch 363.

91 Bukhari 1.2; 60.478; 87.111; Armstrong, Encyclopedia 6221; Peterson 54.

92 Armstrong, Encyclopedia 6221.

93 The earliest known record of such a diagnosis is the eighth-century historian, Theophanes the Confessor, but the claim was common throughout the medieval period and into the modern age. Peterson 54. See also Frank R. Freemon, "A Differential Diagnosis of the Inspirational Spells of Muhammad the Prophet of Islam", *Journal of Epilepsia* (1976) 17:423–427; Margoliouth 46.

94 Andrae 51; Rodinson 56; Rahman 13; Watt, Statesman 19.

95 Welch 363; Ibn Ishaq (Guillaume) 106.

96 Emerick 61.

97 Qur'an 68:1–4; 69:40–43.

98 Qur'an 26:192; 16:102; 42:52.

99 Qur'an 2:97; 20.96.

100 Daniel 8:15–26; 9:20–27; 10:5–12:13. Later rabbinical writings speak of Gabriel as one of the four supreme angels that attend the throne of God. Gabriel is also linked to the three angels who appear to Abraham, the fiery destruction of Sodom, the protection of the infant Moses and the angel that wrestled with Jacob.

101 Luke 1:10–20, 26–37.

102 Qur'an 2:87. See also 19:17; 2:253; 5:110.

103 Luke 1:12, 29.

Chapter 5

MESSAGE

Each founder stands at the head of a major religious tradition that claims to provide definitive responses to the most fundamental questions of human existence, especially in terms of our origin, purpose and destiny. The Buddhist, Christian and Islamic answers to life's great issues have been developing for centuries and have branched out over time into a complex range of denominational variations. Despite this current diversity, most schools share an essential core of teaching that is rooted in the original message of the founder. Indeed, all three founders were messengers in a sense. In their own distinctive ways, each of them felt the need to communicate something profound and urgent in their time. This chapter will explore those messages. What did the Buddha, Jesus and Muhammad have to say during their public careers? What was the essential wisdom that they wanted to convey to their contemporaries? What was the vision that inspired them to become preachers of a transcendental truth?

Four Noble Truths

There is an immense number of sermons and sayings attributed to the Buddha, making the task of producing a succinct summary of his teaching considerably challenging. However, most commentators point to his First Sermon as a good place to start. Even if it is not the verbatim record of a single homily delivered by the Buddha himself, many agree that it contains the essence of his life-changing insight.[1] The most commonly cited version of the First Sermon is located in the 56th chapter of the Samyutta Nikaya.[2] The context is the first encounter between the Buddha and his five former companions, just weeks after his Enlightenment. The full title of the sermon is the "Dhammacakkappavattana", which can be translated as "the truth of the turning of the wheel". It was a momentous occasion of cosmic significance since this speech set in motion the process of ultimate liberation. After he had spoken, a new religious movement was born and the world would not be the same.

Buddha, Jesus and Muhammad: A Comparative Study, First Edition. Paul Gwynne.
© 2014 John Wiley & Sons, Ltd. Published 2014 by John Wiley & Sons, Ltd.

The Sermon opens with the Buddha expounding the importance of choosing a balanced middle way between extreme forms of human lifestyle. Both materialistic hedonism and masochistic asceticism are to be avoided since neither brings ultimate benefits. The memories of his own experience are just beneath the surface here: the opulent lifestyle of his father's palace and the unhealthy self-mortification of his time in the forest. The Buddha then announces that he has discovered four noble truths that address the fundamental problem of human existence and point the way to ultimate freedom and happiness. The four noble truths are often formulated in the following way:

1. *The Nature of Suffering:* This is the noble truth of suffering: birth is suffering, ageing is suffering, illness is suffering, death is suffering; sorrow, lamentation, pain, grief and despair are suffering; union with what is displeasing is suffering; separation from what is pleasing is suffering; not to get what one wants is suffering; in brief, the five aggregates subject to clinging are suffering.
2. *The Origin of Suffering:* This is the noble truth of the origin of suffering: it is this craving that leads to renewed existence, accompanied by delight and lust, seeking delight here and there, that is, craving for sensual pleasures, craving for existence, craving for extermination.
3. *The Cessation of Suffering:* This is the noble truth of the cessation of suffering: it is the remainder-less fading away and cessation of that same craving, the giving up and relinquishing of it, freedom from it, nonreliance on it.
4. *The Path Leading to the Cessation of Suffering:* This is the noble truth of the way leading to the cessation of suffering: it is the Noble Eightfold Path – that is, right view, right intention, right speech, right action, right livelihood, right effort, right mindfulness and right concentration.

It is often observed that the structure takes its inspiration from the world of medical practice. The Buddha diagnoses the fundamental illness afflicting humankind; he identifies the cause of that illness; he confirms that the illness can be cured; and, finally, he provides a detailed prescription for the cure. It is little wonder that the Buddha has been described as a "great physician of the spirit".[3]

The first noble truth represents the starting point of the Buddha's central message, namely that suffering is an unavoidable, all-pervasive feature of the human condition. Wherever we turn, we encounter pain and unhappiness, which seem to be woven into the very fabric of our existence. But what exactly does the Buddha mean when he speaks of suffering? The original Pali term is "dukkha", which literally means "unsatisfactoriness". In other words, the Buddha is thinking of suffering on several levels. At the most basic level is physical pain. Given that our bodies are prone to injury, illness and gradual deterioration over time, physical suffering is never far away. The Buddha explicitly mentions old age, sickness and death in the standard formulation of the first noble truth, and it is no coincidence that these constitute three of the four sights that he experienced on that fateful expedition outside the palace walls.

The second level of meaning captured by the term dukkha refers to mental suffering. Here the Buddha is thinking of the psychological states of discomfort and distress that also go with being human. Because of our psychosomatic nature, mental suffering is often directly linked to physical suffering. Falling ill or being injured is frequently a cause of anxiety, depression, anger and fear. But such states of mind can also arise even when the person enjoys good physical health. Thus "sorrow, lamentation, pain, grief and despair" are explicitly listed as forms of dukkha in the classical formula of the first noble truth. Yet there is a further level of dukkha in the first noble truth, hinted at by the clause "not to get what one wants". Beyond the physical and mental pain, there exists a more fundamental form of "unsatisfactoriness". This is more akin to an existential angst: a nagging, long-term sense of the evanescence of happiness and the futility of life. It speaks of a lingering dread that our deepest yearnings will never be fulfilled and our efforts will ultimately come to nothing.[4] This profound sense of unease is only magnified in the reincarnational worldview that the Buddha inherited from his Hindu background. Rebirth means a return to the world of physical, emotional and existential suffering. The prospect of apparently endless and aimless reincarnation only adds another stratum of futility. As one author puts it, dukkha operates "against the background noise of samsaric existence".[5] The Buddha has occasionally been criticized for an overly pessimistic assessment of human existence in his first noble truth. Indeed, choosing suffering as the most salient feature of life seems gloomy and imbalanced, especially for one who advocated a "middle path". Yet, drawing once again on the medical analogy, it is argued that the doctor cannot hope to cure the patient unless there is a frank admission of the existence and seriousness of the illness.[6]

The first noble truth is traditionally expanded via a discussion of the three marks of existence. According to the Buddha, all aspects and dimensions of our world are characterized by three features: dukkha (suffering), anicca (impermanence) and anatta (non-self). The first mark is central to the first noble truth and has been spelled out in the comments earlier. Simply being in the world brings with it suffering at the physical, mental and existential level. Yet if we dig a little deeper, we uncover the real reason for all of this suffering. The second mark (anicca) refers to the fact that everything in our spatiotemporal world is in a constant state of flux. Things come into being and then cease to be. Change, like suffering, is ubiquitous and nothing remains the same even if it appears to be permanent and immutable. The Buddha had an acute awareness of the innate transience of all conditioned things.

The third mark of existence takes the concept of anicca to another level – that of the self. The Buddha called into question the basic Hindu ideas of Brahman and atman. In his view, there was insufficient evidence to justify either concept. In fact, they constituted an impediment to enlightenment. One can follow his logic. The second mark of existence – impermanence (anicca) – also pertains to the atman. When one examines our "self" in detail, what one discovers is not a solid integrated core or a permanent indivisible essence from which we derive the term "individual". According to the Buddha, the "self" is composite and ever-changing – a loosely bound mix of elusive, ever-shifting phenomena. In other words, the "self" is a mirage; the atman (self) is really an-atman (non-self). This is anatta – the third mark of existence – and it is the most original and radical of the three.[7]

Consequently, the most common metaphors used to capture the Buddha's analysis of the self are dynamic processes. The person is like a raging bushfire moving from tree to tree, a stream of flowing water, or a monkey swinging through the forest and grasping fruit from branches as it goes.[8] Similar metaphors are used to explain how samsara can occur even if there is really no permanent "self" to be reincarnated each time. The image of a flame passing from one candle wick to the next is frequently utilized. Although the Buddha dispensed with the notion of the self as a solid vessel, he still envisaged the last impulses of the dying person leaping across to the next reincarnational form.[9] Anatta does not mean the rejection of samsara. In fact, it holds the key to liberation from it. The illusion of the self binds us to that wheel, and only its overturning can bring release.[10]

If the first noble truth targets the unsatisfactory, impermanent and insubstantial nature of the world, the second shifts the focus to the human subject who is bound on a seemingly endless cycle of reincarnation back into this world of suffering. Returning to the medical paradigm, the next step after recognizing the disease is to identify its cause. The second noble truth asserts that suffering is the direct result of "tanha". The Pali term originally meant "thirst", but here it is more aptly translated as "craving". This is not a mild, occasional desire; it is more an insatiable, chronic, pathological addiction that afflicts all of us.

So the Buddha locates the cause of suffering in the human will. Our desires create our prison; our cravings create our chains. But it is not just a volitional problem. There is also an intellectual element since not all desires are harmful. For example, the desire to seek enlightenment and the desire to help others are both extremely worthwhile. The problem arises when craving is mixed with ignorance. The second noble truth is not speaking simply of desire but of misplaced desire. Suffering arises when we crave transient things that cannot bring ultimate happiness or satisfaction. There is an endemic blindness within us that blocks us from perceiving the impermanent nature of reality, and this combination of volitional desire and intellectual myopia can only mean frustration. When the third element of negative sentiment is added, a vicious circle is set up, trapping us on the wheel of reincarnation. This is graphically portrayed in traditional Buddhist art via the image of three animals chasing each other's tails in a closed loop. The rooster represents greed, the pig represents ignorance, and the snake represents hatred. The three animals are usually placed at the hub of a six-sectioned wheel that symbolizes the samsaric process, powerfully reinforcing the notion that it is the disastrous combination of these three attitudes that binds us to the cycle of rebirth. This is the essential message of the second noble truth.

The other image often used to encapsulate the second noble truth is fire. In contrast to Hinduism, where fire stands for divine presence and is a common element in sacred rituals, the Buddha used the symbol of burning to illustrate the destructive effects of ignorant craving. The point is highlighted in what is known as the Fire Sermon, which is traditionally placed early in his career.[11] Every facet of our experience is aflame but the fire is not the spark of the gods; rather it is an all-consuming conflagration that gradually devours us. Continuing with the imagery of combustion, what is clearly required is that the triple fire of greed, ignorance and hatred be doused. This is precisely the theme of the third noble truth, which is essentially a statement of hope. It is possible to overcome suffering by tackling its root cause. Returning to the medical paradigm, the physician has named the disease, identified its cause and is now in a position to declare confidently that a cure is possible.

Technically, the third noble truth speaks of the "nirodha" ("cessation") of craving and suffering, but the more commonly used term is "nibbana" (Sanskrit: nirvana). The word literally means "no blowing", as in a blacksmith's shop when the bellows no longer provide oxygen for the furnace and, thus, the fire goes out. Similarly, it can refer to the dying of a lamp when the wick and oil are exhausted. It is not so much an external agent that blows out the flame as the fuel feeding the flame runs out. In the Buddha's scheme, cyclical reincarnation back into a world of suffering ends when ignorant craving ceases.

Given that Siddhattha achieved enlightenment and liberation in his mid-30s but lived until he was in his 80s, the tradition speaks of two levels of nibbana: one attainable during life and the other at physical death. The former is sometimes known as nibbana "in-this-world" or "with residue".[12] The Buddha was still subject to the aches and pains that came with bodily existence, but his mind was free from misplaced cravings and, thus, he enjoyed a state of sublime bliss. He was beyond the turbulent passions that disturb our equanimity and calm. In a true sense, he was "in the world but not of the world".[13] In the end, he passed away and entered into nibbana beyond death – his Mahaparinibbana. Reincarnation had ended since there was no more residual karma, no more misplaced craving and no more factors of the illusory self. There was literally now nothing to follow. However, at this point, the Buddha's message becomes notoriously difficult to pin down, especially in terms of the fate of the one who has escaped the wheel of rebirth. What actually happens to the person who achieves final nibbana?

There is a natural temptation to imagine final nibbana as an eternal postmortem existence characterized by unsurpassable happiness, possibly in the company of the Buddha and all other liberated beings. Some argue that the Buddha hinted at such a transformed state of personality via such phrases as "blessed coolness", "entering nibbana" and "the city of nibbana".[14] But there are two serious dangers in adopting such an interpretation. First, such paradises are typically extrapolations and extensions of worldly experiences, which are necessarily temporary, finite and conditioned and, thus, should not be applied to nibbana. Second, such images imply that a form of the self survives final death and subsequently exists in a state of nibbana beyond time and space. However, this seems to ignore the Buddha's tough teaching regarding anatta. Given that the self is really an ever-changing mixture of fleeting factors, it is ultimately an illusion – a product of ignorant craving. Therefore, some argue that hoping for ongoing existence in nibbana is essentially pathological. Only by letting go of the ego is nibbana possible. There is no need to mourn the vanishing of the self since it was only ever a mirage that pinned us to the wheel of reincarnational suffering in the first place.

Applying anatta to nibbana in this radical way has led many to criticize the Buddha's message as annihilation of the self and denial of the eternal soul. However, others argue that the negative language surrounding nibbana is not about the extinction of the person but the limits of our understanding and language. With nibbana, we have reached the boundary of our capacity to comprehend and describe. It simply does not correspond to anything that we have ever experienced, forcing us to apply the "via negativa".[15] The issue was a pressing one among his own followers but the Buddha remained elusive. His classical response to such questions was the story of a man who was shot in the eye with an arrow. Instead of attending to his wound and saving his life, he began to ask himself where the arrow came from and who had fired it.[16] In other words, queries about the details of nibbana were irrelevant and contributed nothing to one's quest for enlightenment and liberation. The urgent priority was to attend to the arrow and not worry about the archer. The Buddha's most succinct statement on the issue is his enigmatic claim that the person in nibbana "neither exists nor does not exist". Nibbana lies beyond even the most basic distinction between what is and what is not, stretching the fundamental norms of classical Western logic to their extreme.[17]

Having described the disease, identified its cause and declared that it can be overcome, the final step in the medical paradigm is the prescription for the cure. The fourth noble truth provides the means whereby one can move toward and eventually achieve the cessation of all suffering. The medicine is presented as an eightfold strategy:

1. Right view
2. Right intention
3. Right speech
4. Right action
5. Right livelihood
6. Right effort
7. Right mindfulness
8. Right concentration.

In contrast to the third noble truth, the fourth is an eminently practical one. It spells out what can be done, here and now, to facilitate the defeat of ignorant suffering. Here is the Buddha's pragmatic prescription for overcoming the curse of all-embracing dukkha.

It would be a mistake to treat the eight aspects as sequential steps indicating a certain degree of advancement along the way. The disciple does not progress from one aspect to the next in chronological order as each item is mastered. Rather, all eight should be applied concurrently as one might take eight different tablets to deal with a particular illness.[18] The point is also well made by the popular image of the eight-spoke wheel that often serves as an identity badge for the Buddhist religion. The spokes symbolize the fourth noble truth and all eight work simultaneously and equally to keep the wheel turning.

The traditional order of the eight aspects is not arbitrary. The oldest sources recognize a distinct threefold division under the following headings: wisdom (1 and 2); virtue (3, 4 and 5); and meditation (6, 7 and 8). The list begins with two aspects connected to the concept of wisdom (panynya). Right view refers to the correct understanding of ourselves and the world in which we live. It means knowing the Buddha's teaching and acknowledging its validity. The second aspect, right intention, adds a volitional element. It is not enough simply to know and understand the Buddha's teaching. An act of commitment is also required because, without such resolve, one will not persevere in this path. Wisdom needs both intellect and willpower.

The second grouping sits under the umbrella of virtue (sila). In the Buddha's thinking, wisdom alone cannot bring nibbana. It is not enough to know the path and to want it in the inner working of our minds. One must also act it out in the external world of behavior. The road to nibbana can only be walked by a person who is both wise and virtuous. The first of the three "virtuous" aspects is right speech. What is relevant here is honesty and sensitivity in our communications with others. The second aspect, right action, is more generic and covers all moral actions but, in particular, it often means avoidance of three specific vices: killing, stealing and sexual misconduct. The third virtuous aspect, right livelihood, implies that certain careers are morally unacceptable and, thus, should be avoided.

The final three aspects are usually gathered together under the subheading of meditation (samadhi). Right effort refers to the need to control one's thoughts, steering them away from what is distracting, and directing them toward what is wholesome, beneficial and liberating. Right mindfulness involves constant, enhanced awareness of oneself and the surrounding circumstances. There should be no blind spots in our self-knowledge. Finally, right concentration marshals the mind's ability to focus on an object and, when properly cultivated, takes us beyond mere awareness to complete absorption in the moment and the merging of subject and object. The fact that three of the eight aspects involve the art of meditation is a testimony to its central importance in the Buddha's teaching and in Buddhist practice. Even though Siddhattha felt frustrated by the limitations of the schools of Alara Kalama and Uddaka Ramaputta, it was the result of a night of intense meditation that he was able to transcend those masters and achieve complete enlightenment as the Buddha. Wisdom and virtue alone will not result in nibbana. What is also needed is time spent in skilled reflection.

There is much more that could be said about the teaching of Siddhattha Gotama, who lived and instructed his followers for another 45 years after that initial sermon in the deer park at Isipatana (also known as Sarnath). Yet the Four Noble Truths are considered by most Buddhists as the heart of his message, focusing as they do on the universal plight of human suffering, identifying its fundamental causes and offering a way out of its enslaving grip. In that sense, it is an eminently practical message, with little apparent interest in many of the traditional aspects of religion. There is no reference to a divine creator or redeemer or judge; no instructions on prayer; no sacred, authoritative text; no list of rituals or worship practices. Instead, the Buddha invites his listeners to embark on a journey of profound self-discovery. It is a quest for wisdom, virtue and insight, but always with the overarching purpose of ultimate liberation from suffering. This was the Buddha's primary goal, and he had little interest in other areas of theological or philosophical speculation. He was essentially a spiritual physician who diagnosed the most serious of all illnesses and provided an effective cure.

Kingdom of God

According to Mark's gospel, Jesus commenced his public ministry in Galilee with the announcement: "The time is fulfilled, and the Kingdom of God has come near;

repent, and believe in the good news".[19] Most commentators agree that Mark's identification of the "Kingdom of God" as the kernel of Jesus's message is historically correct. In a rare case of genuine consensus, scholars point to the Kingdom as the linking thread that integrates Jesus's teachings and other activities, such as the healings, the gathering of followers, the socializing with outcasts and even his untimely death.[20] It is the central notion that sums up Jesus's pedagogical vocation and prophetic mission.

The original phrase, "basileia tou theou" ("Kingdom of God"), is found more than 100 times in the Synoptic gospels while, in contrast, it is virtually ignored by John and Paul.[21] The common English translation "Kingdom" is somewhat problematic since the word tends to suggest a geographical territory with demarcated borders. Better translations are "kingly rule", "sovereignty", "reign" or "kingship" since the intention is not a location somewhere on the surface of the earth but a dynamic relationship between God and human persons.

The precise term "Kingdom of God" is not used in the Jewish scriptures, suggesting that it originated with Jesus himself. Nevertheless, his Jewish listeners would have been familiar with the general concept. In Jewish thinking, God rules over the entire cosmos as its creator but he is also the true king of his own people.[22] The failure of most of Israel's earthly kings led to the notion of a future "Messiah" ("anointed one") who would establish a universal reign of peace and justice on earth, ensuring security and prosperity for the poor.[23] This idea is articulated in the biblical prophets but further elaborated in the apocalyptic writings of the second and first centuries BCE. A final cataclysmic intervention by God would shake the heavens and the earth, the wicked would be punished and the just rewarded in a newly created order under God's Messiah. The timing of that fateful day had been determined by God but its advent could be anticipated by carefully recognizing signs in the natural and political world.[24] All of these rich ideas and anguished hopes would have filled the minds of those who heard Jesus announce the impending arrival of God's reign.

Despite the many references to it in his recorded teachings, one searches the gospels in vain for a precise, scientific definition of the Kingdom. Jesus never offered his own univocal interpretation of this familiar yet slippery religious term. Rather than state what the Kingdom is, Jesus often stated what the Kingdom is like, drawing on the most common, mundane images that were an intrinsic part of his world.[25] Using the traditional Jewish "mashal" (parable), Jesus compared God's Kingdom to everyday experiences, such as finding a lost object, attending a wedding feast, herding sheep or planting a seed. These simple pictorial lessons have a genuine ring of originality about them, suggesting that his listeners were the rustic peasants of Galilee and its surrounds.

One of the most debated aspects of Jesus's understanding of the Kingdom of God has been the timing of its coming. In the summary passage from Mark quoted above, Jesus declares that the "time is fulfilled" and the Kingdom of God "has come near". The burning question is whether Jesus was expecting an imminent apocalyptic event or something less dramatic that was already taking place. Both sides of the argument are able to point to pertinent gospel passages to support their position. Supporters of the former emphasize those sayings where Jesus seems to refer to the coming of the Kingdom as a pending event such as the verse from the Lord's Prayer: "your

Kingdom come". There are also passages that imply that the Kingdom would arrive before the passing of the present generation or the death of some of his listeners or the time it would take for his followers to travel around the towns of Israel.[26] This strong sense of an imminent eschatological event is carried over into Paul's early letters where the apostle clearly anticipates that he will still be alive when Jesus returns in glory.[27] If this interpretation is correct, then the obvious dilemma for Christianity is that its founder and the first generation of believers seem to have been terribly mistaken since history did not end and the cosmic order was not overturned in the first century CE.

In contrast, it is possible to identify passages from Jesus's teachings that indicate a very different understanding of the manner and timing of the Kingdom's arrival. These sayings suggest that the Kingdom had already begun to break into the world via Jesus's own activity and that its development is more organic than apocalyptic. It is more like the mysterious, steady growth of a plant than a violent, abrupt cosmic revolution. There are some who argue for a "realized eschatology", namely that Jesus had no intention of proclaiming an imminent end of the world but that he did correctly predict the inevitable destruction of the Temple.[28] Others admit that the eschatological element is present but hardly primary in his teachings. For them, the coming of the Kingdom is proleptic – already commenced but yet to be fulfilled.[29] Both positions argue that Jesus's principal focus was not a looming judgment day but the establishment of a fresh interpretation of the Jewish faith. The evidence for this downplaying of the eschatological element can be found in a number of passages from Luke's gospel.[30] Thus, Jesus speaks of the Kingdom already "among you" and interprets his healings as evidence that Satan had been effectively defeated and the Kingdom was already breaking into the world.[31]

The ongoing question concerning the coming of the Kingdom is linked to the nature of the Kingdom itself. Although Jesus left no succinct definition, what do his sayings tell us about his understanding of God's reign? At the heart of the matter is the gentle paternity of the deity. According to Jesus, God is not a distant, aloof Creator nor a narrow-minded, vengeful Punisher but a loving, caring Father. This theme is not lacking in the Jewish scriptures where Israel is described as God's first-born son and his dear child.[32] Similarly, God is portrayed as the Father of Israel and is occasionally addressed in prayer as "our Father".[33] So Jesus has taken a minor theme in the Hebrew Scriptures and converted it into the centrepiece of his religious vision. The Greek term "pater" ("father") is used over 100 times in the gospels when Jesus is speaking of God, usually in the form "my Father" or "your Father". There is also one occasion in Mark where the original Aramaic "Abba" is added.[34] While there is still some debate over its precise connotation, the term is quite intimate and many argue that, as a form of address, it would be better translated into English as "dad" rather than the more formal term "father".

Such a warm, close relationship with God is the key to being "in the Kingdom" and it is echoed in Jesus's prayer life in general. Although he is often present in synagogues and the Temple, the gospels suggest that he preferred individual prayer in solitude or at least at a physical distance from his companions.[35] His advice to others was to do the same: "But whenever you pray, go into your room and shut the door and pray to your Father who is in secret; and your Father who sees in secret will reward you".[36] Moreover, there is no point in being loquacious since the Father already knows our needs before we even ask for them. The classical model of such simple, heartfelt communication and a useful summary of key Kingdom themes is the prayer formula that the gospels claim was composed by Jesus himself, although it is structured for a group rather than an individual. Matthew's version is as follows:

> Our Father in heaven,
> hallowed be your name.
> Your Kingdom come.
> Your will be done on earth as it is in heaven.
> Give us this day our daily bread.
> And forgive us our debts,
> as we also have forgiven our debtors.
> And do not bring us to the time of trial,
> but rescue us from the evil one.[37]

Although the Father is "in heaven", he is also directly accessible in the privacy of our own prayer room where we can place before him our most fundamental needs: daily bread, forgiveness and deliverance. A consequence of Jesus's understanding of God as a loving Father is his striking optimism about divine providence. There is no need to be unduly anxious about food, clothing and other material needs since the God who cares for the birds of the air and the lilies of the field will not abandon his human children who are worth more than hundreds of sparrows.[38] Moreover, when sickness and accidents occur, such as someone born blind or a tower collapsing on people, these are not to be interpreted as divine punishment for sin or inherited karmic guilt.[39]

The fatherhood of God not only means that daily bread will be provided but that heavenly forgiveness is readily available on earth. Being in God's Kingdom means not only food for the body but also healing for the soul. Unexpected and unmerited divine clemency is one of the most pervasive themes in Jesus's teachings. God is like a shepherd who would leave a flock of 99 in order to seek out one single lost sheep. God is like a woman who would frantically sweep the house until she recovers one lost coin. God is like a father who would patiently wait years for his self-centred, wayward son and then throw an excessively lavish banquet upon his sheepish return. The doors of the Kingdom are open until late and even workers who only put in one hour of labour will receive a full day's pay.[40] Jesus was fully aware that such apparently unfair treatment of the sinful might naturally cause resentment among the righteous of society. The older brother of the prodigal son stubbornly refused to join the celebrations and the vineyard workers who put in a full-day's work grumbled that their wages were not increased proportionately. In Jesus's eyes, they should rejoice in the Father's abundant mercy instead of indulging in bitter resentment and jealousy. Those who appreciate the incredible compassion of the Father, such as harlots, tax collectors and pagans, will flock into the Kingdom while self-righteous do-gooders may find themselves outside claiming that they knew God when they really did not.[41]

The "good news" of the Kingdom is grounded in the nature of the God whose reign it is: a caring, forgiving Father who invites all His earthly sons and daughters into a profoundly intimate relationship with him. But God's invitation is only half of the story; the invitees must also respond if they are to gain entry. The coming of the

Kingdom is not entirely a divine project; it requires human cooperation as well. Similar to John the Baptist and the prophets of Israel's past, Jesus's announcement of the nearness of the Kingdom is accompanied by a sincere plea to repent and believe. The repentance that Jesus seeks is not a superficial gesture but a genuine turning around of one's entire life. The New Testament term "metanoia" means a total change of mind and heart, which results in a complete U-turn in one's life direction. It is the death of the old self and the start of a completely new relationship with the Father.[42] Without such a radical reorientation, Jesus's message will not take hold. It will be like sewing a patch of new cloth onto an old garment, putting fresh wine into used skins or seed falling into thorns or onto rock and never germinating.[43]

Given Jesus's stress on the fatherhood of God, it is not surprising that he frequently speaks of childlike trust as the fundamental attitude required for entry into the Kingdom: "Unless you change and become like children, you will never enter the Kingdom of heaven."[44] This is not infantile naivety but an innocent, unadulterated trust in one's heavenly Father. It is the pure in heart who will see God.[45] The metaphor of the child also implies a healthy dose of self-effacement and, on this point, Jesus has some stinging criticism for the arrogant and the conceited. Members of the Kingdom do not parade themselves in public for gratification, seek the most prominent places at dinners or stand at the front of synagogues singing their own praises. God does not see us through the lens of our human socio-religious hierarchies. In the Kingdom, the exalted are humbled and the humble are exalted. For Jesus, it is the meek who will inherit the earth.[46]

If members of the Kingdom are those who accept God as their loving Father with childlike trust and humility on the vertical axis, then there are far-reaching consequences on the horizontal axis of interpersonal relationships. As sons and daughters of the Father, humans are brothers and sisters to each other. Love of God must be supplemented by love of neighbor. Thus, when asked to provide his "kelal" (summary statement of the Torah), Jesus quoted two well-known passages from Deuteronomy and Leviticus, combining wholehearted love of God with wholehearted love of neighbor.[47] The intrinsic connection between these two aspects of life was already a widely accepted principle in Judaism. Its classical symbol is the two stone tablets on which the Ten Commandments are inscribed: five on the first tablet for the relationship with God and five on the second for the relationship with others. Prophets such as Amos had also emphasized the need to match devotion in the Temple with justice in the marketplace.[48] What is distinctive and challenging in Jesus's approach is his definition of "neighbor". Traditionally, this applied to members of one's own people, and, more specifically, only those who were deemed to be living righteous lives within the Law. It was imprudent to mix with pagans, outcasts and sinners since they were beyond the pale. In contrast, Jesus pushes social and religious boundaries to the very limit. He deliberately associated with lepers, tax collectors and prostitutes claiming that it was the sick, and not the healthy, who need the physician. Moreover, one of Jesus's most scandalous stories was precisely his response to the question: who is my neighbor? It was provocative enough to tell the story of a Temple priest and a Levite who callously ignored a fellow Jew left beaten on the roadside by highway robbers. But to choose a Samaritan as the hero who takes time to care for the victim would have deeply shocked Jewish ears, given the deep-seated mistrust and tension between the two contiguous communities.[49] Today, the term "good Samaritan" has come to mean a compassionate person who would stop to help a total stranger but its original meaning is more poignant. It is really the person who would stop and help a despised enemy:

> You have heard that it was said, "You shall love your neighbour and hate your enemy." But I say to you, Love your enemies and pray for those who persecute you, so that you may be children of your Father in heaven.[50]

Jesus knew that such an astonishingly inclusive ideal cuts against the deeply engrained human propensity to create enemies as a result of prejudice, fear and resentment. It can only be remotely possible via utter commitment to the processes of reconciliation. Once again, it is ultimately a question of imitating the divine Father. God's mercy to us must be mirrored in our mercy to each other. We cannot expect to be forgiven our debts in heaven if we are unwilling to forgive each others' debts on earth. Moreover, there is no real comparison. God's mercy to us is like cancelling a debt of 10,000 talents (20,000 years' wages), whereas we often refuse to write off petty debts among ourselves worth a hundred denarii (100 days' wages). There is no cap on forgiveness in God's Kingdom; not seven times nor even seventy times seven.[51]

Such was Jesus's vision for a revitalized and reformed Israel. The coming of the Kingdom meant rediscovering God as an infinitely merciful Father and rediscovering others, even sinners, strangers and foes, as one's brothers and sisters. This was essentially his message, his "good news". It was like finding treasure hidden in a field or a priceless pearl. The appropriate thing to do was to buy the field or the pearl, but that could mean selling everything that one possessed.[52] For Jesus, there could be no half-hearted commitment to the Kingdom. It was all or nothing. As every farmer knew, once the ploughing has begun, one cannot afford to look back, otherwise the result is crooked furrows.[53] This presented a problem for those who had more to sell and for whom the Kingdom did not sound like good news at all. Jesus made no bones about the fact that material wealth was a very serious obstacle. Hoarding monetary assets was ultimately a futile exercise since the hour of death was unknown and none of it could be taken to the other side. Jesus's advice was to store up treasure in heaven where savings were not threatened by moth or rust. However, it was unwelcome counsel for those who had already invested in affluence as their highest priority. Jesus warned that one cannot serve both God and mammon. Indeed, it was easier for a camel to pass through the eye of a needle than for a rich man to enter the Kingdom.[54]

If the message of the Kingdom was awkward, if not downright threatening, to the rich, it also sat uneasily with the pious and devout. Particularly grating was Jesus's claim that God was more interested in the repentant sinner than those who scrupulously followed their religious duty to the letter. Jesus's teachings contain a significant amount of criticism aimed squarely at those who considered themselves righteous according to the divine Law. Moreover, Jesus occasionally displayed an unsettlingly liberal attitude, especially in regard to Sabbath activity and kosher rules regarding washing. Yet in each case he defended his position not by undermining the Law but by pointing to its true meaning or citing precedents from history.[55] Indeed, it would be grossly incorrect to think that Jesus was fundamentally opposed to his own Jewish tradition and intended a complete replacement of the Torah. In many instances, he adhered to the prescriptions and traditions of his people.[56] For Jesus, unless moral and religious principles are authentically internalized, there is a real danger of superficial literalism and hypocritical ritualism. In the true spirit of the Israelite prophets, Jesus did not come to abolish the Law but to plant it deeply in the heart.

Despite the stress on God's magnanimous compassion, there is a sterner side to Jesus's teaching. The Father is a God of justice as well as mercy. The graciousness of God does not mean that there is no human accountability in Jesus's religious vision. The master of the household may be temporarily absent but the servants are expected to be going about their business, least of all because they do not know precisely when he will return. Because the arrival of the groom could be at any hour of the night, wise bridesmaids would carry enough oil to keep their lamps burning whereas foolish ones would not and be badly caught out.[57] There will be a final sorting of sheep and goats; there will be wailing and gnashing of teeth; there will be burning of chaff in an unquenchable fire.[58] Furthermore, it is so serious that if a part of our body represents a stumbling block then it is better to cut off a hand or foot or cast out an eye than to lose oneself.[59] In the end, the Kingdom is open to all, but even Jesus acknowledged that not all will accept the invitation. Human freedom meant that choice was real and, while he never indulged in quantification, Jesus soberly acknowledged that the Kingdom was only accessible via a narrow road and a small gate.[60]

The Straight Path

The message that Muhammad was commissioned to proclaim on behalf of Allah can be found in the pages of Islam's holiest book. In the eyes of Islam, the Qur'an is a precious collection of divine utterances, delivered to Muhammad via the angel Gabriel over a period of more than two decades. Although Muhammad's own statements, actions and general example complement the sacred text, there is no substitute for the revealed word when it comes to ascertaining what the Prophet was commanded to communicate to his listeners. The hadith is an important element, but the Qur'an holds the key.

One obvious place to start is at the beginning and indeed the opening chapter of the holy book, aptly named al-Fatiha (The Opening), functions much like the overture of a classical opera, previewing the major themes that are to follow.[61] After the standard invocation of the divine name, the text reads:

> All praise is due to Allah, the Lord of the Worlds.
> The Beneficent, the Merciful.
> Master of the Day of Judgment.
> Thee do we serve and Thee do we beseech for help.
> Keep us on the right path.
> The path of those upon whom Thou hast bestowed favors.
> Not of those upon whom Thy wrath is brought down, nor of those who go astray.[62]

The very first verse of al-Fatiha immediately directs our attention to the One who is considered the true author and source of its message: Allah, the one and only God. It mentions His two roles at the beginning and end of time (Creator and Judge), as well as his merciful nature. It then introduces the human subjects who acknowledge Him, praise Him, serve Him and seek help from Him. Finally, it mentions two possible paths that humans can follow: a straight path that is taken by those who receive divine favors; and an ominous, alternative path that brings divine anger and leads nowhere. As with the Buddha's teaching, the straight path, which is mentioned 34 times in the Qur'an, is understood as a balanced, middle way between extremes. Here, in essence, is the Qur'an's vision of human existence. Each person stands at existential crossroads, facing a critical choice between two possible routes, one of which leads to a blessed destination and the other literally to perdition.

The first key point in the Qur'anic message is that our world is the cosmic project of a single creator deity. The idea that supernatural beings exist would not have been particularly surprising or new to Muhammad's contemporaries since the pre-Islamic Arabian pantheon was replete with gods, angels, spirits and jinn. What was novel and unsettling in Muhammad's revelations was the relentless insistence that there was only one true God above all creatures, visible and invisible. In direct opposition to entrenched Meccan polytheism, the Qur'an declares an uncompromising and strict monotheism. This belief is succinctly expressed in the first part of the "shahada", Islam's fundamental creedal statement: There is no god but (the one) God. This is the expression of the principle of "tawhid" – the absolute unity and uniqueness of God – and it is not surprising that Sunni Muslims consider the shahada to be the first of the five pillars of Islam.[63]

Conversely, the most serious sin in Islam is "shirk", which literally means to assign partners to God. According to the Qur'an, idolatry in any form is unacceptable and inexcusable: "God will not forgive shirk, but may forgive any sin lighter than that".[64] Thus, Meccan polytheism is the prime target of Muhammad's mission, and it is understandably compared with the Israelites' worship of the golden calf at the base of Sinai.[65] Other gods, whether they are from biblical Canaan or from Muhammad's own Meccan culture, are ultimately false gods. As empty idols, they offer as little security as the house of a spider, which is so easily destroyed.[66] Those who vacillate between polytheism and monotheism, depending on the circumstances, are not spared criticism either.[67] This is the context for the famous incident of the Satanic Verses as attested by al-Tabari and Ibn Sa'd. Frustrated by slow progress in his preaching, Muhammad thought that he had received a revelation allowing the Meccans to intercede via Allah's three daughters:

> Have ye thought upon al-Lat and al-'Uzza
> And Manat, the third, the other?
> *These are the exalted cranes (intermediaries)*
> *Whose intercession is to be hoped for.*[68]

The response of the Meccans was favorable since it allowed them to retain a much loved element of their existing religion. However, Muhammad received a corrective revelation indicating that the italicized verses were not from God but from Satan.

Consequently, they were expunged from the Qur'an and replaced by words that sarcastically note the hypocrisy of the Meccans in ascribing daughters to God when they themselves consider female children to be inferior to male children.[69] It was one thing for Muhammad to employ successful missionary strategies to win over his audience, but it must not be at the expense of tawhid. There is no god but God and he has no daughters.

Nor does God have a son, and on this point the Qur'anic critical focus shifts away from the Meccan pantheon to the Christian Trinity:

> O followers of the Book! do not exceed the limits in your religion, and do not speak (lies) against Allah, but (speak) the truth; the Messiah, Isa son of Marium is only an apostle of Allah and His Word which He communicated to Marium and a spirit from Him; believe therefore in Allah and His apostles, and say not Three. Desist, it is better for you; Allah is only one God; far be it from His glory that He should have a son.[70]

God is One, not Three. On this point, readers of the Qur'an would notice that the divine author uses a variety of pronouns and nouns as self-designation: "I", "We", "He" and "Allah". In the eyes of Islam, the first person plural form should be understood, as with similar verses in the Hebrew bible, as the "royal We" rather than an implication of actual plurality within the Godhead.[71]

Tawhid means that there is only one God, without partner or equal. Allah alone is infinite and independent while all other beings are finite and utterly dependent. There is no more fundamental ontological distinction than the one between Creator and creatures. The entire universe owes its existence to Him. Echoing the first creation story in Genesis, including reference to the six-day period, the Qur'an affirms that the cosmos and all of its contents came into being as a result of God's simple command.[72] Moreover, the divine power that ushered the world into being, continues to sustain it in being. The natural world, with all of its intricate patterns, processes and laws, is completely under the control of the Almighty. Nature itself is "Muslim" since it humbly and unquestioningly submits to Allah's will, thus glorifying its Creator.

The Qur'an speaks not only of Allah's omnipotence but also of His omniscience. Although the pre-Islamic Arabs acknowledged a creator deity, Allah, among their many gods, the general presumption was that Allah was basically uninterested in the affairs of his creation and too remote to be approached in supplication. One would be better served turning to other more proximate gods and spirits, but the Qur'an rejects the connection between divine power and divine indifference. As Lord (Rab) of the worlds, Allah knows and takes a keen interest in all things within His creation. Not a leaf falls without him knowing and not one atom is beyond his notice. He is like a sentinel on a watch tower; he knows the whisperings of our very souls; he is nearer to us than our jugular vein.[73]

As the Qur'anic messages come to Muhammad, a portrait of its divine Author builds up over time, revealing a range of attributes that are neatly summed up in the Islamic tradition of the 99 names of God. Without compromising the fundamental principle of tawhid, the litany of qualities reflects the richness of the divine personality. The names can be divided into various categories, but arguably three main qualities are evident: power, justice and mercy. Traditionally, the first two names listed are those that feature in the standard preface to each chapter of the Qur'an: "In the name of God, the merciful, the compassionate". Despite the common perception in Western literature that the Islamic God is a strict, unforgiving deity, the Qur'an is literally replete with verses that speak of the graciousness of Allah.

According to the Qur'an, this all-powerful, all-knowing God of mercy and justice has created the world and its inhabitants for a purpose, directly challenging the Meccan presumption that blind fate lies behind all events. Allah does not act on a whim or for sport or play.[74] There is an overarching divine plan and it involves the cooperation of God's creatures, especially human beings who have been given the ability to choose for or against their Maker. It is this priceless gift of freedom that opens up the two possible pathways that are mentioned in al-Fatiha. Moreover, there is no guarantee that those who are on one path will always remain there. Freedom also means that humans can move from one to the other as a result of their thoughts and actions. It is possible to slip off the straight path as a result of sin, and it is possible to return to it as a result of repentance.[75]

Although Islam does not profess a doctrine of original sin, the Qur'an implies that there is an innate proclivity to wrongdoing in all persons. Sadly, sin comes relatively easy to the human person.[76] The reason for this is complex. At one level, the Qur'an agrees with the Jewish–Christian tradition and acknowledges the existence of a spirit known as Iblis (Devil) or Satan who disobeyed Allah and has become the enemy of humankind. It is Satan who tempted Adam and Eve in the garden, and their descendants must engage in an ongoing struggle to overcome his wiles and temptations.[77] At another level, the Qur'an sometimes so stresses God's omnipotence that God himself is ultimately responsible since he determines who is on the right path and who is not. It is almost as if God deliberately leads some astray, setting a seal on their ears, eyes and hearts so that they cannot and will not listen to wise counsel.[78] Yet the Qur'an also contains many verses insisting that the cause of sin is not God but the stubborn imperviousness of individuals.[79]

It may be relatively easy to stumble off the straight path into the wilderness, but the Qur'an constantly holds up the hope that errant travellers can also find their way back. The voice of revelation warns of dire punishment to wrongdoers, qualifying this with phrases such as: "except those who repent" and "surely Allah is forgiving".[80] Thus, it is never too late to turn one's life orientation around. Yet prevention is better than cure, and al-Fatiha itself is a fervent plea for God to keep the believer on the right path at all times. Moreover, God has provided the map and compass for life's precarious journey: the teachings of the line of authentic prophets culminating in Muhammad's ministry and the sacred words revealed through him.[81] Ultimately, the preaching of all true prophets and the contents of all valid scriptures stem from the one divine source, which is described as a heavenly Book predating creation itself. This is the archetype from which all earthly scriptures are derived, including the most reliable of them all – the Qur'an itself:

> I swear by the Book that makes things clear:
> Surely We have made it an Arabic Qur'an that you may understand.
> And surely it is in the original of the Book with Us,
> truly elevated, full of wisdom.[82]

Yet the Qur'an has its predecessors. The Jewish Torah and the Christian Gospel are genuine expressions of this eternal truth and, thus, the Qur'an acknowledges Jews and Christians as "followers of the Book". Their fundamental monotheism sets them apart from the polytheistic majority of Mecca and, thus, they enjoy a special standing in the eyes of Islam. Muhammad is commanded to explain to them that "our God and your God is One, and to Him do we submit".[83] However, while their scriptures contain much that is valid, they are imperfect and incomplete, having overlooked or obscured aspects of that heavenly Book:

> O followers of the Book, indeed Our Apostle has come to you making clear to you much of what you concealed of the Book and passing over much; indeed, there has come to you light and a clear Book from Allah.[84]

Christians are often surprised to discover the status accorded to Jesus (Isa) in the Qur'an. It seems to accept his virginal conception and explicitly acknowledges his miracles.[85] Jesus is a "rasul" (messenger) of the true God and brings the "Injil" (gospel), which is true revelation. He ascended to heaven and will return at the end of time, although it is thought that he did not actually die on the cross.[86] He is given the title "Messiah" and can be called a "son of God" in the same sense as Adam, since neither had a human father. However, to profess that he or his mother is divine is a grave error.[87] In the end, the Qur'an understands Jesus as an eminent prophet but he does not share the same level of authority and prestige as the last in that distinguished line of divine spokesmen. In the court of God, some messengers are "more excellent than others", but Muhammad holds a preeminent place as the "Seal" of the prophets.[88]

Muhammad's vocation as Final Prophet brings with it an onerous burden of responsibility: "Surely We will make to light upon you a weighty Word."[89] The word that he must faithfully and courageously deliver to his contemporaries is the Qur'an itself – the definitive message from God that completes the long process of revelation. In one sense, it is not a novel doctrine but the final exposition and summation of God's core message. Likewise, Muhammad is told not to view himself as an innovator or the founder of a new sect but as a "plain warner".[90] His plea is not that his fellow Meccans turn to monotheism for the first time in their history but that they return to an already revealed monotheism. Rather than the establishment a new faith per se, the Qur'an endeavors to "remind" its hearers of a long forgotten truth. It reaches back behind Judaism and Christianity to the figure of Abraham who, according to the Qur'an, was neither Jew nor Christian but "Muslim" in the true sense of the word – one who professed and submitted to the one true God in a world of polytheism and idolatry.[91] True religion is the pristine faith of Abraham, the champion of tawhid and a paragon of virtue. This is where the Qur'an points as guide; this is the right path.[92]

Thus, the key to finding the right path is the wholehearted acceptance of monotheism, exemplified by Abraham and exhorted by the prophetic line that culminates in Muhammad. However, this is only part of the story. Pure faith in the one God must be complemented by appropriate behavior toward many neighbors. Proper relationships on the horizontal axis are just as important as a proper relationship on the vertical axis, including care for the orphan, the wayfarer, the beggar and the captive.[93] Professing monotheism and saying one's prayers is not enough to be a true Muslim if a fundamental commitment to the poor is absent.[94] The problem is not wealth per se. After all, despite prolonged disadvantage as an orphan in his early years, Muhammad had married a rich woman and enjoyed considerable commercial success as her business manager. Moreover, the Qur'an recognizes the recent Meccan prosperity generated by the trade routes as a blessing from God.[95] The problem is the addictive fascination with and pursuit of wealth. The Qur'an would be in total agreement with the famous New Testament passage that identifies the *love* of money as the root of all evil.[96] Ruthless competitive greed can easily enslave the soul and blind it to the foolishness of relying on financial assets as an ultimate security.[97] Muhammad's audience is urged to invest with God who pays a much better rate of interest in the long term.[98] In fact, the very practice of charging interest is frowned upon and eventually prohibited by the Qur'an. While Allah causes acts of charity to prosper, he does not bless usury, which is linked to the works of Satan.[99] True believers not only avoid taking interest on a loan but they also give generously to those in need. Almsgiving is often mentioned in the Qur'an as a worthy cause but even charitable acts must be performed with the correct intention.[100] Alongside alms, the Qur'an also speaks of zakat, an annual contribution to the common purse for the benefit of the needy.[101] The Qur'an often links zakat with salat (the five daily prayers), reinforcing the notion that vertical devotion goes hand in hand with horizontal compassion. In time, both salat and zakat were listed by Sunnis among the five pillars of Islam.

The Qur'an has much to say about other important social reforms, including women's rights and the role of politics, but these will be dealt with later chapters. However, there is one final all-pervasive theme that must be included in this brief summary: the eschatological dimension. Like many of the biblical prophets, Muhammad is commanded to remind his listeners that their time on earth was limited and that all would be held accountable for their actions by the divine Judge. The Qur'an frequently describes Muhammad's role as that of a "warner", drawing people's attention to their mortal nature and reminding them of the eternal consequences of their attitudes and actions. Muhammad cannot be responsible for the dead, but his pressing task is to galvanize the living into choosing the right path before it is too late.[102]

While most humans lived their lives in ignorance and heedlessness, the day of postmortem judgment will be a "moment of truth" when each person will become painfully aware of the consequences of their actions.[103] Apart from individual death, the Qur'an also speaks of a day when the cosmos will come to a tumultuous end, although there is no hint of imminence as in Jesus's proclamation of the Kingdom. Thus, the Qur'an frequently speaks of the Last Day (Yaum al-Din) and the World to Come (Akhira), drawing on classical apocalyptic language to describe what is to occur. There will be a cataclysmic upheaval in which the natural order will be thrown into disarray.[104] The world will be utterly shaken but it will not be obliterated. Instead, the Qur'an speaks of a "new creation" that will be fashioned out of the old.[105] This concept of transformation rather than destruction is also relevant to the human person. Not only will God transfigure the physical cosmos, but he will also bring the bodies of the dead back to life. Once again echoing the Jewish and Christian tradition, the Last Day will also be a Day of Resurrection (Yaum al-Qiyama).[106]

Thus we come to the question of what lies at the end point of the two paths that are described in al-Fatiha: the path of God's anger and the path of God's blessing. As in the Christian worldview, the Qur'an proposes that each route leads to a very different outcome. The terminus of the path of God's anger is described as "Jahannam" (Hell). Like the Jewish Gehinnom, it is an "evil place" where fire is the main form of punishment and the Qur'an provides graphic descriptions of the excruciating tortures suffered by its inhabitants.[107] The Qur'an also identifies various types of persons who are doomed to its flames, including the proud, the ignorant and the deceitful. But the most frequently mentioned is "the unbeliever".[108] This is normally understood to mean the idolatrous polytheist, especially those who heard Muhammad's preaching but refused to accept it.[109] As to the duration of the fiery punishment, there are Qur'anic passages implying that Jahannam is permanent, but there are others that speak of "a long time" and, thus, raise the possibility of divine reprieve.[110]

In stark contrast to the horrific pains of Jahannam, the destiny of those on the straight path is a wonderful existence forever in Janna – the heavenly gardens "beneath which rivers flow".[111] Like an earthly oasis in the middle of a scorching desert, Janna is a place of cool shade where crystal-clear water flows from fountains in abundance.[112] The lifestyle is replete with the full array of sensuous pleasures, yet without the sinful dimension. The fortunate inhabitants will live like royalty in magnificent mansions. Clothed in fine silk garments, they will sit on golden thrones or recline on finely crafted cushions. They will feast on delicious fruits of all kinds and drink from goblets filled with exquisite wine that does not cause intoxication.[113] They will enjoy the company of demure, chaste companions (houris) of equal age with large, lustrous eyes like pearls.[114] They will never again suffer toil or illness or fatigue or death, but the greatest reward is seeing God and finding blissful tranquility in his presence.[115] This is God's preferred destiny for all human beings but, in the end, the decision rests with each individual as to which path they will choose: the wayward path that leads to the fire or the right path that leads to the garden. The Qur'an declines to provide statistics but it constantly warns that Jahannam is a very real danger for many and that it will be filled with large numbers since God is just. However, it also frequently speaks of the mercy of God and describes Janna as being wider than the sky and the earth, hosting "a numerous company".[116]

Observations

At the most basic level, all three teachings claim to address the most fundamental questions about the meaning and purpose of existence. They all claim to have discovered the keys that unlock the riddle of human life and the signposts that point us to where we are meant to be heading. In this sense, they are universal messages, like the religions that they spawned, reaching beyond the particular time and place in which they were initially proclaimed. They are also transcendent in the sense that they envisage the meaning of existence as grounded partially in this present world and partially in another world. Each in their own way speaks of a dimension of reality beyond the here and now, beyond the empirical and beyond physical death. In the broadest sense of the term, they are "religious" messages.

All three messages also require a response of some sort from the listener, and all three readily acknowledge that not everyone will respond favorably. The first and second elements of the Noble Eightfold Path outline the need to know what the Buddha has taught and to commit oneself to it as a genuine road to liberation, but it may take many turns of the samsaric wheel before nibbana is attained. Jesus invites his listeners to repent and believe his good news. They must set their hands to the plough and not look back, but he admits that the seeds of his teaching will fall on rocky ground as well as fertile soil. The Qur'an speaks of the two possible paths between which each person must choose, and it endeavors to convince its audience that only one is worth following in the long run.

Given that all three teachings locate our ultimate destiny beyond this life but also insist that it is contingent on attitudes and actions within this life, it is not surprising to note the common themes of detachment and moral rectitude. The third, fourth and fifth aspects of the Eightfold Path specifically highlight the importance of ethical behavior, and the entire thrust of the Four Noble Truths is to make people realize that craving for transient things is ignorant and cannot lead to happiness. Similarly, Jesus links love of God with love of neighbor and warns that those who store up treasure on earth will find it very difficult to enter the narrow door of the Kingdom. In the same way, the Qur'an urges believers to invest in God rather than earthly wealth, and sees a fundamental connection between authentic worship of Allah on the vertical axis and sincere concern for the poor on the horizontal axis. Both salat and zakat are pillars of Islam.

However, there are also significant dissimilarities between the messages and the roles of the messengers themselves. One important difference exists between their respective understandings of human life, in particular between the cyclic, reincarnational model of the Far East and the linear, resurrection model of the Middle East. A son of Indian culture, the Buddha accepted the emerging Upanishadic notion of samsara whereby a human person is born, dies and is reborn into this world. This cycle can occur hundreds or thousands of times and a being can be reincarnated in the form of a human, an animal, a hungry ghost or a godlike spirit depending on the amount of good or bad karma generated in each time. Because there are so many reincarnations, any one particular bodily form carries no abiding significance since it is discarded each time. Moreover, the Buddha agreed with the Upanishads that the ultimate goal is to escape from this reincarnational merry-go-round once and for all. What Hindus call moksha, the Buddha called nibbana, but in both cases, it means the end of reincarnation and escape from the samsaric prison.

In complete contrast, the Semitic worldview is a linear one in which each human person is born, lives and dies just once, with their ultimate fate resting upon their behavior during that one single life. Whereas accountability is captured by the law of karma in the samsaric scheme, the Semitic worldview has the Day of Judgment. In one system, karmic consequences mean that a being can be reincarnated in better or worse circumstances each time. In the other, divine justice awaits the dead, whose divinely willed destiny is to abide in perfect happiness in the company of the Creator, but whose free will opens up an ominous alternative fate. Jesus and his Jewish audience would have presupposed such a linear model although there was debate among first-century Jews as to whether the physical body played any role in the afterlife via physical resurrection or not. Pre-Islamic Arabian culture and the Qur'an also presume a similar linear view of human life, but the Qur'an's insistence on bodily resurrection was foreign and difficult for Meccan ears. Moreover, the Qur'an essentially agrees with Jesus and the Jewish tradition that the ultimate goal of human life is blissful communion with the Creator beyond death, but it also concurs that another darker fate is possible for those who choose it.

Closely linked to the contrast between linear and cyclic worldviews is the role, or lack of role, of the deity. Once again, this element sets the Buddha's message apart from that of Jesus and Muhammad but it also highlights points where all three figures challenged the existing tradition. In the case of the Buddha, his Hindu background included a pantheon of gods and demigods, but they play no significant role in his message. Like the Upanishads, the Buddha also saw the dangers of empty ritualism in the prevalent Brahmanic religion of his day. Yet the Buddha went even further than their penetrating critique, calling into question the existence and ultimate pertinence of two fundamental Upanishadic concepts: Brahman and atman. Here the Buddha's message takes a radical turn. While he agreed that release from the vicious cycle of reincarnation was our ultimate aim, his concept of nibbana was not the same as moksha, which is usually understood as absorption of the atman back into Brahman or at least perfect communion between the two. Instead, the Buddha refuses to supply details of nibbana, preferring negative language and suggesting that any attempts to provide positive descriptions are distracting and irrelevant. Moreover, his doctrine of anatta shakes the very notion of the self, reducing it to a loosely connected series of fleeting elements. When pressed on the issue, the Buddha left us with the enigmatic statement that, in nibbana, the self "neither exists nor does not exist". As a result, the Buddha's message is often described as nontheistic. While such branding can be dangerous, it is true that a striking feature of his teaching regarding the solution to human unhappiness and suffering is the absence of any role for a deity or deities. There is no divine creator, such as Brahma; there is no divine savior, such as Vishnu or Shiva; there is no divine destiny such as union with Brahman. Human suffering is analyzed in terms of a profound pathological craving that needs to be overcome and the Buddha offers a raft of practical prescriptions that deal with the problem. It is no wonder that it is often described as psychology rather than theology.

In contrast, Jesus and Muhammad stand firmly in the tradition of monotheistic religion. The assertion that there is a single deity who is intimately involved in the human story is central to both. The universe exists because it was created by God with a specific purpose in mind and humans play an important role in that purpose. Our divinely willed destiny is joyful communion with God in the next life but evil and sin have marred the project and opened up the possibility of alienation from God. For both Jesus and Muhammad, God is Creator, Redeemer, Judge and Destiny, but their messages have different focuses, in no small way due to the different historical contexts of the messengers.

Jesus's Jewish audience would have needed no persuading that there was one, true God, although the reversion to idolatry was a constant struggle in Israel's history and a common theme of the prophets. Hence, Jesus's primary concern is not polytheism. Rather, his focus is on the divine nature or, rather, misconceptions of it among his Jewish contemporaries. At its most fundamental level, Jesus's enthusiastic announcement of the Kingdom is a declaration of the surprising, almost scandalous, mercy of God who is best understood as a loving father. Jesus's intellectual energy is not directed at deniers of the one, true God but rather at Jewish compatriots who indulge in narrow legalism, self-righteous arrogance and hypocritical smugness. These are the caricatured "scribes and Pharisees" of the gospel accounts. While the Buddha offers a pathway to happiness for those who unwisely crave for transient things, Jesus offers abundant and unexpected divine compassion for those who are plagued with guilt and unworthiness.

In contrast, Muhammad's religious context was Arabian polytheism. Although monotheism was not a totally foreign concept, it was peripheral at best. Thus, the Qur'an's main thrust is to convince its listeners that there is no god but Allah and that other gods are empty idols. In many ways, Muhammad's mission echoes the struggle of Abraham, Moses and the earlier prophets of Israel whose task was to establish and consolidate a robust monotheism amid a sea of polytheistic beliefs and practices. His commission was to convince his listeners that the remote god that they knew as Allah was the only true deity, supreme in power and knowledge, yet keenly interested in the welfare and fate of each individual. His task was to persuade the Arabs to move Allah from the margins of their spiritual world and place Him firmly and unrivalled in the centre.

The involvement or noninvolvement of a deity impacts on the source of the message and the mandate of the messenger. From where does each founder obtain the truth that they proclaim and on whose authority do they speak? Although Hindu gods feature in the narrative of Siddhattha's search for enlightenment, it is not they who choose him or call him to become the Buddha. These gods manipulate events from time to time in order to ensure that Siddhattha's quest for enlightenment progresses, but they are really secondary characters in the drama. The main protagonist is Siddhattha himself, whose insight and willpower inspire him to leave home and spend seven years in the search for a higher truth. The main focus of the story is this relentless quest. This is the most "bottom up" of the three stories– a man who dedicated years of his life, experimenting with existing philosophical schools and extreme ascetical practices, until he found the spiritual secret that leads to supreme happiness. It is an extraordinary accomplishment for which the Buddha is admired and respected. However, his accomplishment was not to invent the Four Noble Truths – only to discover them or, rather, rediscover them. Subsequent Buddhist tradition teaches that Siddhattha was not the first Buddha; nor will he be the last. He is one in a long series of enlightened beings who recover these truths that are lost over time. Siddhattha happens to be the Buddha for our era, but the Truth that he recovered has always been there and always will be there, in much the same way as a scientist does not create or invent the laws of nature but merely uncovers them. Moreover, his authority as teacher is also akin to that of the scientist. There is no power bestowed upon him by a superior Being for whom he acts as spokesperson. Rather, any authority that he enjoys rests on the veracity of his message and its success in overcoming suffering. The Buddha never commanded anyone to follow him on blind trust but, rather, he invited listeners to see for themselves if the Four Noble Truths worked in practice.

The notion of recovering a long lost truth is also an element in the case of Muhammad. Although monotheism may have seemed novel to the Meccans, Islam does not see the Prophet as the founder of a brand-new religion, but rather as the restorer of an ancient one. Muhammad is the last of the prophets, not the first. The Qur'an directs its audience back to the primordial faith of Abraham, the father of Ishmael as well as Isaac. The Qur'an is seen as the perfect articulation of the heavenly book that was already partially revealed via the Jewish and Christian scriptures. Yet the role of Muhammad is very different from that of the Buddha. While the latter sought after the long lost truth as a result of his own vocational decision and personal drive, Muhammad was chosen to be a recipient of the forgotten truth by another. While the Buddha found the message from within, the message finds Muhammad from above. The tradition is most careful to distinguish between the words of the Qur'an and the words of Muhammad. In the eyes of Islam, the former does not derive from Muhammad's own spiritual insights but, rather, they are literally dictated to him via revelatory trances. Even then, the voice that he hears is only that of another intermediary, the angel Gabriel. In contrast to Siddhattha, this is very much a "top-down" dynamic. Consequently, the ultimate authority of Muhammad as messenger resides not in the man himself, but in the God who mysteriously chose him as spokesperson. Such a claim seemed incredible and unsubstantiated to many of his fellow citizens but, in time, Islam would recognize supporting evidence in the extraordinary religious and political success of the Prophet and the miraculous nature of the Qur'an itself.

On this point, Jesus sits somewhere between the Buddha and Muhammad. Like Muhammad, Jesus speaks for God and, in this sense, fulfils a prophetic role – a role recognized by many in his audience. His call for repentance and his offer of divine consolation are classical themes in the Jewish prophetic tradition. Yet unlike Muhammad, Jesus does not clearly distinguish between his own words and the words of the Father. Even though Jesus spends considerable time in solitary prayer, there is no intermediary angel or revelatory trances or translation of a heavenly book into human language. Nor does he use the classical phrase of the Hebrew prophets: "The word of the Lord came to me". In a style more reminiscent of the Buddha, the gospels give the impression that Jesus's teaching comes from his own personal store of wisdom and knowledge, raising questions in the mind of his listeners as to the nature of his relationship with the one he often called "my Father". Moreover, according to the gospels, his authority as teacher was not only grounded in his pedagogical methods or his striking message but, to a considerable extent, in his extraordinary powers over natural forces – a theme that is explored in the next chapter.

Notes

1 Cohen 153–154; Armstrong, Buddha 93.
2 Samyutta Nikaya 56.11. A similar account is also found in the Mahavagga. Parallel texts can be found in other Buddhist sources as well, such as the Lalitavistara and the Mahavastu.
3 Mizuno 45.
4 Keown 46.

5 Cohen 155.

6 Cohen 155.

7 The classical elaboration of the concept of anatta is provided in the Second Sermon where the Buddha describes the five factors (khandas) that constitute the person: body; sensations; perceptions; volitions; and consciousness. See Samyutta Nikaya 22.59.

8 Armstrong, Buddha 100–102; Foucher 147; Carrithers 58–59.

9 Carrithers 69–70; Armstrong, Buddha 99.

10 Cohen 158.

11 Samyutta Nikaya 35.28.

12 Cohen 164.

13 Cohen 165. Carrithers notes that the first controversy in Buddhism was whether one who had attained nibbana could slide back. Later debates focus on whether awakening was gradual or instantaneous. See Carrithers 74–75.

14 Armstrong, Buddha 78; Cohen 165.

15 For Cohen, the best analogy is "empty space". See Cohen 166.

16 Majjhima Nikaya 63.

17 Panikkar interprets the Buddha's silence regarding ultimate reality as legitimately "apophatic". See Panikkar 14, 102, 130.

18 Mizuno 53.

19 Mark 1:15.

20 McClymond 380.

21 Matthew's preference for "Kingdom of Heaven" (basileia ton ouranon) avoids the divine name out of deference to his Jewish audience, although the effect of using "Heaven" is to relocate the Kingdom in an otherworldly location beyond death.

22 See the Enthonement Psalms 11, 24, 29, 47, 75, 82, 93, 96–99; Exodus 19:5–6.

23 Isaiah 11:1–9; 9:6–7; 10:20–23.

24 Daniel 7:9–14; Psalms of Solomon 17.23–28. See also 2 Baruch, 4 Ezra, Assumption of Moses. The War Scroll from Qumran speaks of the 12 tribes that will be represented in the Temple service 1 QM 2.2.

25 Matthew 13:34. Norman Perrin describes the Kingdom as a "tensive symbol", which cannot be fully expressed by any one referent, unlike the simpler "steno symbol". Perrin 30–31.

26 Mark 9:1; 13:24–30; Matthew 10:23.

27 1 Thessalonians 4:13–17; 2 Thessalonians 2:1–12; 1 Corinthians 7:25–31.

28 Mark 13:1–2. Authors who support this view include Funk, Dodd and Crossan.

29 Proponents of the proleptic interpretation of the Kingdom include Jeremias, Cullmann, Kummel and Ladd.

30 Luke wrote his gospel for those already coming to terms with the delayed parousia.

31 Luke 17:20–21; 10:18; 11:20.

32 Exodus 4:22; Jeremiah 31:20.

33 Deuteronomy 32:6, 18; Jeremiah 3:4; Numbers 11:12; Malachi 2:10; Isaiah 63:16; 64:8.

34 Mark 14:36. Paul also uses the term in Romans 8:15 and Galatians 4:6.

35 Mark 1:35; 6:46; 14:32–35; Luke 5:15–16; 6:12; Matthew 14:23.

36 Matthew 6:6.

37 Matthew 6:9–13; Luke 11:2–4.

38 Matthew 6:25–34; 10:29–31; Luke12:6–7.

39 Luke13:1–4.

40 Luke 15:3–32; Matthew 20:1–16.

41 Matthew 21:31–32; Luke 13:28.

42   McClymond 415; Drummond 110.
43   Luke 5:36–39; Mark 4:3–20.
44   Matthew 18:3.
45   Matthew 5:8.
46   Luke 18:9–14; 14:7–11; Mark 12:38–40; Matthew 5:5.
47   Mark 12:29–32; Deuteronomy 6:4–5; Leviticus 19:18.
48   Amos 5:21–24.
49   Luke 10:29–37; Matthew 9:9–13; John 4:5–42.
50   Matthew 5:43–44.
51   Matthew 18:21–35.
52   Matthew 13:44–45.
53   Luke 9:62.
54   Matthew 6:24; 19:23–24; Luke 12:13–21.
55   See the incidents regarding healing and eating corn on the Sabbath and the dispute over washing before meals in Matthew 12:1–13; Mark 7:1–23.
56   Matthew 5:21–30.
57   Matthew 24:45–51; 25:1–30; 13:40.
58   Matthew 8:12; 13:42, 50; 22:13; 24:51; 25:30.
59   Mark 9:42–48.
60   Matthew 7:13–14.
61   Cook, Koran 8–20.
62   Qur'an 1:1–6.
63   Qur'an 40:65–66. See also 3:18; 16:51; 17:42.
64   Qur'an 4:48.
65   Qur'an 7:138–140.
66   Qur'an 29:41. Sura 29 is aptly named "The Spider".
67   Qur'an 29:65.
68   Qur'an 53:19–20.
69   Qur'an 53:21–22.
70   Qur'an 4:171.
71   Genesis 1:26, 3:22, 11:7; Isaiah 6:8; Armstrong, Muhammad 60.
72   Qur'an 3:47, 59; 50:38; 6:73; 16:40; 19:35; 36:82; 40:68; 41:11.
73   Qur'an 6:59; 50:16; 89:14; 10:61; 34:3.
74   Qur'an 3:190–191; 38:27; 21:16–17; 23:115; 59:22–24; 27:60–64.
75   Qur'an 67:2.
76   Qur'an 12:53.
77   Qur'an 7:11, 27; 4:119; 2:30; 20:116; 18:50; 38:74–75.
78   Qur'an 2:6–7; 16:93; 2:142, 213, 272; 14:4; 16:93; 24:35; 28:56; 30:29; 35:8. Such verses push the principle of divine omnipotence to extremes, attributing all events (good and bad) to God's will and potentially undermining the reality of human freedom.
79   Qur'an 2:264; 5:51; 6:144; 9:19, 24, 37, 80, 109; 12:52; 16:37, 107; 28:50; 39:3; 40:28; 46:10; 61:5, 7; 62.5; 63:6.
80   Qur'an 2:160; 3:89; 4:146; 5:34; 24:5.
81   The Qur'an recognizes nearly 30 religious figures of the past as authentic spokesmen of the one true God. The key figures primarily belong to the Jewish or Christian tradition including Adam, Noah, Abraham, Ishmael, Isaac, Jacob, Moses, Job, Jonah, David, Solomon and Jesus. Yet the group also includes several Arabian prophets: Hud from Ad, Salih from Thamud and Shu'ayb from Midian. There are also others that are not named as such. See Suras 7 and 11; also Qur'an 4:163.
82   Qur'an 43:2–4. See also 42:15–16; 26:195; 39:28.

83 Qur'an 29:46.
84 Qur'an 5:15; 3:65.
85 Qur'an 3:47; 2:253; 5:110. The reference to the clay birds is reminiscent of the Infancy Gospel of Thomas.
86 Qur'an 2:87; 4:157, 171; 3:45, 55; 5:46.
87 Qur'an 3:59; 4:171; 5:116.
88 Qur'an 2:253, 285; 17:55; 33:40.
89 Qur'an 73:5.
90 Qur'an 46:9; Peterson 60.
91 Qur'an 3:67; 16:123.
92 Qur'an 6:161; 16:120; 60:4.
93 Qur'an 2:177. See also Sura 90 (The City).
94 Qur'an 107:1–7.
95 Qur'an 106:1–4; also 62:10; 73:20; 5:2; 24:2; 2:105, 215, 272–273; 11:84; 22:11.
96 1 Timothy 6:10.
97 Qur'an 3:14, 185; 4:77; 9:38; 10:23, 70; 13:26; 28:60; 40:39; 90:5–6; 102:1–4; 104:1–6.
98 Qur'an 30:39; 57:11.
99 Qur'an 2:275–276; 30:39.
100 Qur'an 2:261–274.
101 Qur'an 9:60.
102 Qur'an 6:19; 11:12; 26:214; 35:22–23; 38:70; 88:21–22.
103 Qur'an 79:34–35; 50:20–22; 6:94; 19:95; 4:41–42; 28:75.
104 Qur'an 81:1–14.
105 Qur'an 29:20; 53:47; 13:5; 32:10; 34:7; 14:19; 35:16; 50:15.
106 Resurrection was a difficult concept for Meccans to accept but the Qur'an argued that if God can create an entire world then He could bring the dead back to life in a bodily fashion. Qur'an 23:83; 27:67–68; 36:26–27, 77–83; 31:29; 35:13; 57:6; 30:19–24, 50.
107 Qur'an 3:162; 4:56, 97; 22:19–20; 14:49–50; 23:103–104; 21:39–40; 33:66 ; 54:47–48; 40:69–72.
108 Qur'an 39:72; 2:206; 16:27–29; 3:12; 9:49; 7:179; 8:36–37; 9:68; 17:8, 18, 39; 21:98; 39:60, 71.
109 Qur'an 66:9; 48:6; 4:140; 18:106.
110 Qur'an 72:23.
111 Qur'an 2:25; 4:57; 9:72.
112 Qur'an 15:45; 76:13–15.
113 Qur'an 37:42; 38:51; 43:71–73; 55:48, 66, 68; 69:23–24; 56:20.
114 Qur'an 55:56–58, 70–76; 56:22–24, 35–37; 78:33; 38:52; 44:53–54.
115 Qur'an 35:35; 75:22–23; 9:72; 89:27–30.
116 Qur'an 3:133; 56:39.

Chapter 6

MIRACLES

Reports of amazing feats that defy natural processes are a common feature in the stories of religious figures of the past and the Buddha, Jesus and Muhammad are no exception. The marvelous events that are associated with their infancy are carried over into the traditional accounts of their adult careers. All three are said to have worked powerful deeds that lie beyond the scope of the normal human person often generating astonishment and wonder in the onlookers. This chapter focuses on the miraculous element in their stories. What sorts of miracles are involved? How should these events be understood and interpreted? Are they central or peripheral to the message? What theological weight should be accorded to them?

Iddhi

Accounts of the Buddha's 45-year career after his Enlightenment typically include reference to a host of spectacular actions. While there is a definite tendency in later texts to expand and multiply the miracles of the Buddha, even the earlier versions portray him as a man with an impressive array of extraordinary powers to say the least. On the physical level, there were occasions when the Buddha displayed the ability to levitate and to fly. He could suddenly vanish and just as suddenly reappear. He was able to pass through solid objects, travel to distant worlds and even multiply his body many times. On the mental level, he was able to recall past lives on the cycle of reincarnation, to see objects and to hear sounds at enormous distances, to move material objects with only the mind and to access the secret thoughts of others.

The first important point to note is that the Buddha was not unique in this respect since many of his closest disciples also displayed a similar mastery of bodily movement and mental capacity. Perhaps the best known examples are Anuruddha, who enjoyed extraordinary perception, and Moggallana, who was able to transport himself with

Buddha, Jesus and Muhammad: A Comparative Study, First Edition. Paul Gwynne.
© 2014 John Wiley & Sons, Ltd. Published 2014 by John Wiley & Sons, Ltd.

absolute ease over any distance. Moreover, these amazing powers were not restricted to the Buddha and his disciples since they were actually an aspect of the preexisting tradition of yoga.[1] According to that tradition, these amazing physical and mental powers could be gained by anyone who had mastered the art of samyama meditation and gained complete control over the object of contemplation. It is said that the ability to levitate or to vanish, to practice telekinesis or clairvoyance arises when subject and object are perfectly united. Thus, these powers are not, strictly speaking, supernatural miracles, but rather they are the supernormal products of the inner power of meditation.[2] They demonstrate the dominance of the trained mind over matter.

So the "miracles" of the Buddha are actually signs of his absolute mastery of the noble Indian tradition of meditation. These powers were not given to him by the gods nor are they proof that he is a divine being of some sort. Rather, they naturally arise out of the dedicated application of meditation methods in his search for truth. The technical term for the amazing abilities that are acquired by the expert yogins is iddhi (Sanskrit: siddhi). The word literally means "power", and the Buddhist tradition speaks of six iddhis in total.[3] The first is perfect freedom of movement. It refers to the physical skills listed earlier, including levitation, flying, passing through solid objects, disappearing and reappearing at will, and multiplying one's bodily form.[4] The second iddhi is known as the "divine ear". This is the vastly superior perception that comes with advanced meditation so that the subject is able to hear the faintest sounds at enormous distances and to discern distinct strains within a complex array.[5] The third iddhi is insight into others' minds, especially the ability to discern the three main vices of greed, hatred and ignorance.[6]

The final three iddhis are usually linked to the three watches of the night of the Buddha's Enlightenment. The fourth iddhi is the recollection of one's former lives on the wheel of reincarnation and this was achieved in the first watch of that fateful evening. Normally, such memories are suppressed in the process of death and rebirth but, according to the Hindu tradition, a person in an advanced state of meditation can delve into the depths of the subconscious and retrieve them. The fifth-century CE commentator, Buddhaghosa, claimed that arhants could only recall up to forty cycles, but the Buddha himself recovered in great detail all of his former lives, which numbered in the thousands.[7] The fifth iddhi, the "divine eye", was gained in the middle watch of the night of Enlightenment. As implied by the term, this power enables the exponent to view anything in the realm of forms, both present and past. In other words, the Buddha extended the perception of his own samsaric journey to those of all beings in the cosmos. With panoramic vision, he was able to see how the law of karma applied to each individual just as if he was standing on a tall building in the centre of a town square observing people coming and going below him.[8] Some also interpret the divine eye to include the ability to see into the future.[9]

Finally, during the last watch, Siddhattha achieved full enlightenment and became the Buddha. In that moment he attained the sixth iddhi, which is translated as the "termination of effluent or outflow", referring to the definitive breaking of the chains of sensual desire brought about by clearly discerning the origin of suffering. It is the moment when the Four Noble Truths are grasped and the subject realizes that they will never again undergo rebirth.[10] While the first five iddhis are impressive, Buddhist teaching insists that the sixth is the most important since only it leads to nibbana, thus setting the Buddha apart from other virtuosi of the yoga tradition.

This point touches on the first theological meaning of these amazing powers in the story of the Buddha. These miraculous occurrences are often aimed at demonstrating the Buddha's superiority over rival figures and, thus, the superiority of his teaching over rival schools. Quite often the display of power by the Buddha is aimed at casting the guardians of the Vedic religion or other contemporary groups in an inferior light, especially given Siddhattha's background as Kshatria (warrior) and not Brahmin (priestly) class.[11] Thus, there are traditions that speak of explicit contests of power between the Buddha and his opponents.[12] The most prominent example is the Great Miracle that the Buddha is said to have performed at Savatthi in the sixteenth year of his Enlightenment.[13] For some scholars, the Great Miracle is a literary condensation of many competition stories into one great colloquium where the Buddha vanquishes, at once, all of his competition, usually represented by the six heterodox teachers.[14]

The setting is a magical tournament between the Buddha and his enemies, the Ajivakas. The Buddha had announced that he would work a miracle under a mango tree outside the city but, upon arriving, discovered that all of the trees had been uprooted by the opposition. Nevertheless, a local gardener named Ganda offered him a piece of mango fruit. The Buddha told Ganda to plant the seeds in the ground and immediately a mature tree grew from the soil, heavily laden with fruit.[15] Impressive as this was, it was only a preamble to the main event. In fact the tradition speaks of two feats. The first is called Yamaka Patihariya, usually translated as "the Twin Miracle". The Buddha rose into the air and began to gyrate rapidly. Then hundreds of jets of fire flared from his upper body while a similar number of jets of water streamed from his lower body. The positions were then reversed. Next fire and water alternately ushered from his right and left sides. The point of the story is that the Buddha not only had mastered yoga technique, but that he was also able to control the fundamental elements of the material world: earth, air, fire and water.[16]

The second feat is called Mahapatihariya ("Great Miracle") in which the Buddha multiplied himself many times over. The witnesses saw hundreds of Buddhas standing and walking, sitting and lying down. The narrative claims that every person present conversed with their own Buddha.[17] Thus, the sheer power that lies behind the Great Miracle is seen as proof of the Buddha's unrivalled mastery over the material world and his unique status among all exponents of the iddhis. According to the Buddhist stories, the people consequently showered the Buddha and his followers with gifts and ignored the Ajivakas.

The Great Miracle at Savatthi is usually coupled with another amazing event that occurred at Sankassa, namely the Descent from Heaven. It is significant that these two events occurred, respectively, at the beginning and end of the annual monsoon retreat.[18] Immediately after the Great Miracle, the Buddha disappeared from sight, travelling secretly to a spiritual world known as Tavatimsa Heaven, where his mother, Mahamaya, had been reincarnated. According to the tradition, the Buddha spent the entire wet season there, teaching the dhamma to his mother and other inhabitants.[19] As time went by, his earthly companions became concerned and Anuruddha used his divine eye to discover the Buddha's precise whereabouts. He then dispatched Moggallana to fly to Tavatimsa Heaven and urge the master to return. The Buddha agreed and indicated that after seven days he would descend to earth at Sankassa.[20] If the ascension of the Buddha was a barely noticed affair, his return to earth was the opposite. Replete with all the pomp and ceremony of a royal visit, the Descent from Heaven is once again meant to demonstrate the supremacy of the Buddha over rival claimants, including Hindu gods.[21] The rulers and citizens of eight neighboring kingdoms gathered at the designated spot and beheld a magnificent triple staircase reaching to the sky. The Buddha appeared on the golden staircase accompanied by Brahma on a crystal staircase to the right, Indra on a silver staircase to the left and an immense host of Hindu gods in train.

The miracles of the Buddha are also linked with his teaching mission, and they are often used as a means to gain skeptical people's attention, such as during the visit to his hometown where the Twin Miracle is said to have been repeated.[22] However, the effect was only temporary. Although the Sakyans bowed down and acknowledged their former compatriot as truly enlightened, the miracle failed to lead them to a deeper understanding. The story confirms another important theme concerning miracles in the Buddhist tradition: their limited usefulness for conversion and instruction. The classical case is Uruvela-Kassapa and his brothers, who witnessed hundreds of miracles performed by the Buddha but obstinately refused to believe. In the end, it was a blunt verbal statement by the Buddha that shocked Uruvela-Kassapa out of his self-delusion and onto the path of conversion.[23] The point is that iddhis can mesmerize but they do not necessarily enlighten.

This is one of the reasons for the Buddha's persistent reluctance to use such powers. Many of his amazing deeds were in response to a basic need or dangerous situation, such as controlling a rampaging elephant in order to save his own life and that of a young child. Yet on other occasions, he withheld this power. One example is the story of the young monk, Tissa, who suffered from a malignant skin disease. Instead of curing the ailment, the Buddha taught him about the transience of the physical body, allowing Tissa to accept his ailment and to die in peace. The moral of the tale is that healing of the mind is more important than healing of the body. A similar story is that of Kisagotami, who asked the Buddha to bring her dead son back to life. The Buddha agreed provided she brought him a mustard seed from a family in which no one had ever died. After searching vainly, Kisagotami finally grasped the point: death was inevitable, even as it is unpredictable and sometimes premature.[24]

The tradition also reveals other reasons for the Buddha's disinclination to use miraculous powers. Not only can they engender a misleading, shallow faith, but astonishing displays of power can easily create adulation among the crowds and an inflated ego in the performer. The Buddha was concerned that such shallow exhibitionism was a real temptation for monks and it had the potential to undermine all that he had taught about the need to overcome the ignorant craving that leads to rebirth.[25] The classical example is the story of Pindola-Bharadvaja, who used his iddhi powers to fly up and take a valuable bowl that had been placed on top of a tall pole in the centre of the village as a prize for anyone who could retrieve it. A disappointed Buddha chastised him and subsequently banned all of his monks from displaying iddhi power in public.[26] In the end, iddhi powers are of limited polemical and pedagogical use. They are not essential to the message; in fact, they constitute something of a hindrance. The Buddha himself insisted that the greatest of all miracles was not about making material objects or processes do amazing things, but rather the miracle of someone listening and surrendering to his teaching. Perhaps the most overt statement of this position is in his dialogue with Kevatta, where he declared: "I despise, loathe, abhor and reject miracles of magic power and divination. My disciples and I gain adherents only by the miracle of instruction".[27]

The Finger of God

It is difficult to read the canonical gospels and not be struck by the prominence of miraculous works wrought by Jesus during his short but dynamic public career.[28] If one sets aside epiphanies, such as Jesus's baptism, transfiguration, resurrection appearances and ascension to heaven, there are over 30 miracles specifically recounted in the pages of the gospels, as well as summary statements suggesting that this is just a sample of many more awe-inspiring deeds that he performed. Moreover, some of these astonishing powers are also passed on to his closest disciples who, in their turn, carry out extraordinary feats in the same style as their master. This sharing of power is said to have commenced prior to his death but continued afterwards for an unspecified period in the early church.[29]

Scholars have usually divided the miracles of Jesus into various subcategories in order to facilitate analysis and interpretation. The first category consists of healings from a wide variety of physical ailments. The gospels record over a dozen extraordinary cures from the following conditions: fever, leprosy, paralysis, hemorrhaging, deafness and dumbness, blindness, dropsy, a withered hand, and a severed ear.[30] In addition, one could include three resuscitations of persons who were diagnosed as deceased: the daughter of Jairus, the son of the widow of Nain and Jesus's close friend Lazarus.[31]

The second category is exorcism. The Synoptic gospels record a number of instances where Jesus drove out an evil spirit or spirits from a possessed person: a man in the Capernaum synagogue, the Gerasene demoniac possessed by Legion, the daughter of the Canaanite woman, a boy whose demon could not be expelled by Jesus's disciples, a mute man, a blind and mute man, and Mary Magdalene from whom Jesus cast out seven demons.[32] Some cases overlap with a physical disability, such as blindness, dumbness and possibly epilepsy. In other cases, the problem involves a severe mental disorder with the potential to cause physical injury.[33]

The third category has traditionally been labelled as "nature miracles" based on the idea that these wonders involve control over physical processes and objects rather than healing of minds or bodies. They are more about the laws of physics than the laws of medicine. Thus, this type includes: the calming of the storm on the Sea of Galilee; Jesus walking on the waters of the Sea of Galilee; the two versions of the multiplication of the loaves and fishes; the transformation of water into wine at the wedding feast of Cana; the amazing catch of fish; the finding of a coin in the mouth of a fish; and the cursing of the fig tree.[34]

One category that is often overlooked is Jesus's superhuman knowledge. In a similar vein to the extraordinary consciousness ascribed to the Buddha, the gospels also refer to occasions when Jesus displays a mental awareness far beyond normal capacity. We are told that he could read minds and hearts with ease; he knew the name of the stranger Zacchaeus and he saw Nathanael under a fig tree long before they actually met; he accurately foretold where his followers would find a colt for his entry into Jerusalem and, a few days later, where they would find a man with a pitcher who would lead them to an upper room for their Passover celebration. There are also Jesus's somber predictions about his own premature death and the eventual destruction of the Temple.[35]

The miraculous element in the gospels often constitutes one of the major obstacles to belief for the modern mind. There are many today who adopt a skeptical approach to these stories, convinced that they cannot possibly have happened as described. Many modern biblical scholars proceed on such a basis, presupposing that anything miraculous in the gospels must be redefined and tempered so that the story of Jesus becomes credible for the educated person of today.[36] Yet there are other scholars who reject such "a priori" positions as inherently prejudiced, insisting that a truly scientific approach is to keep an open mind. They point out that not all educated people today reject the possibility of the miraculous outright.[37]

One of the most serious problems for those who would expunge the miraculous element from the story of Jesus in the name of scientific credibility is that the baby is easily thrown out with the bathwater. Far from being of marginal consequence, the miracles of Jesus seem to occupy a central role in the original story, especially as evidenced by the earliest gospel. If the miracles are extracted from Mark's narrative, then there is little left except the account of Jesus's death. This does not prove that the miracles occurred precisely as claimed, but it does indicate that, at the time, his wondrous deeds were hardly considered to be a dispensable addendum to his mission.[38] In fact, the miracles serve as the most satisfactory explanation for the large crowds that were attracted to Jesus at the commencement of his career. Although it is possible that Jesus initially made his mark as a preacher with an alluring message, the gospel testimony suggests that the real reason behind his meteoric rise to local fame was his reputed ability to perform supernatural deeds.[39]

The importance of miracles at the start of Jesus's public mission is reflected in all four gospels. According to Mark, Jesus commenced his ministry by exorcising a demon in the Capernaum synagogue and then healing Simon's mother-in-law of fever. Immediately, word of these incidents spread like wildfire throughout Galilee and, in the evening of the very same day, the entire town gathered around the door seeking help from ailments and evil spirits. The resultant clamor for his attention forced Jesus to rise early the next morning and clandestinely retire to a private place but his disciples found his whereabouts and reported that everyone was looking for him. He then announced that he would leave Capernaum and travel through other towns in the district. The same pattern continued with great multitudes flocking to him in the hope of gaining or seeing a miraculous cure. At one point, Jesus was forced to sit in a boat moored just off the shore in order to avoid being crushed by the throngs seeking cures. Mark summarizes the situation:

> Wherever he went, into villages or cities or farms, they laid the sick in the market-places, and begged him that they might touch even the fringe of his cloak; and all who touched it were healed.[40]

So the Synoptic tradition identifies Jesus's power as exorcist and healer as the critical factor that propelled him into the limelight.[41]

The question arises as to how Jesus's miraculous deeds would have been perceived in his day? Were these utterly unique acts that set him apart from and above any other historical person? Or were there other instances of exorcism, healing and nature miracles in the ancient world with which Jesus should be compared? There are scattered reports of wonder-workers (thaumatourgoi) in the Greco-Roman world, although the term "thauma" could mean either genuine "wonder" or deceptive "trickery". The fact that Greco-Roman polytheism was not a proselytizing religion meant that miracles were not required to convert the masses and thus explains the relative paucity of such accounts. However, there are claims of healings, the most famous of which is the cult of the god Asclepius, who is said to have cured hundreds of visitors at his shrines.[42] There were also individual wonder-workers who seemed to be a mix of holy men, gurus, shamans, exorcists and magicians.[43] The Jewish biblical tradition also contains instances of amazing healings brought about by God either directly or indirectly, via the intercession of holy men. The main instances can be found in the two concentrations of miraculous happenings associated with Moses and the prophets, Elijah and Elisha.[44] There are also the postbiblical figures of Honi and Hanina that are described in the Talmud.[45] Thus, Jesus is not the only one who healed in God's name. Yet his extraordinary powers and the sheer number of healings attributed to him by the gospels place him firmly in the company, if not at the head, of the most prominent religious figures of Judaism.

Nature miracles also have strong roots in the Jewish biblical tradition, once again with most examples found in the Exodus and Elijah–Elisha stories. One prominent theme is the provision of food or drink in dire circumstances. Examples include the desert manna, the sweetening of bitter water, a jug of oil that was not exhausted and the feeding of a crowd with a small amount of barley.[46] Another prominent theme is control over natural forces, including the waters of heaven and earth. Examples include the partings of the Red Sea and the Jordan, drought-breaking rain, fire from heaven and a floating axe.[47] Similar to the healings, Jesus's nature miracles link him with the greatest religious figures in Jewish history, through whom divine power over cosmic forces was patently at work – a key theme in the gospel Transfiguration scene where the two biblical giants appear alongside a glorified Jesus.[48] In contrast to the healing and nature miracles, there is a striking absence of exorcisms in the pages of the Hebrew Scriptures. There are no references to driving out demons in the stories of Moses, Elijah, Elisha or any major biblical character. However, interest in demons and exorcisms increased during the Second Temple period as recorded in the books of Tobit and the Wisdom of Solomon.[49] The gospels also speak of other Jewish exorcists apart from Jesus, some of whom were using Jesus's name.[50]

What sets Jesus's miracles apart from those of Moses, Elijah, Elisha, Honi and Hanina, is his own distinctive interpretation of their meaning and purpose. The most revealing text is found in Luke's gospel where Jesus is accused of working on behalf of Satan. He replies:

'Every kingdom divided against itself becomes a desert, and house falls on house. If Satan also is divided against himself, how will his kingdom stand? – for you say that I cast out the demons by Beelzebul. Now if I cast out the demons by Beelzebul, by whom do your exorcists cast them out? Therefore they will be your judges. But if it is by the finger of God that I cast out the demons, then the kingdom of God has come to you.[51]

The original phrase "finger of God" (Hebrew: etsba elohim) is only used three times in the Old Testament: once when God works through Moses to show the inferiority of the Egyptian magicians; and twice to refer to the divine author tracing the Ten Commandments on the stone tablets.[52] This rare phrase, connected to the foundational events of Israel's history, was applied by Jesus to his own miraculous actions. In his understanding, the amazing power that he possessed over demons, sickness and cosmic forces was a sign that, with his ministry, Satan's grip on this world was being replaced by a new order: the Kingdom of God. He was not working for Satan but against him, with the power of the God of the Exodus and Sinai. The same point is made often in summary statements that follow particular miracles.[53]

There is a double effect here. First, all of Jesus's miraculous activity now comes together under one overarching theme. The exorcisms, healings and nature miracles are not unrelated, ad hoc reactions to particular situations. Rather, they are all aspects of one single project. At times, this connection is made explicit. For example, the casting out of a demon is often accompanied by the return to physical health. Similarly, Jesus's power over the waters, seen in Jewish tradition as the symbol of chaos, is reminiscent of an exorcism.[54] Second, the miracles themselves are not just a magical show on the side, but they are integrally linked to his message. His verbal proclamation that God's reign was imminent is supported by evidence that divine power was flooding into the world to restore order and well-being. Words are backed up by actions. The curing of sickness, the driving out of demons and the channelling of natural forces were all seen as signs that his message was not hollow. God's Kingdom truly was at hand, and this is why the crowds were quick to acknowledge that the rabbi from Nazareth brought a new teaching with true "authority" behind it.[55]

In Jesus's teaching, the coming of the Kingdom was primarily the initiative of God, but it could only take root if the human subject was open and receptive, in the same way as a seed requires fertile soil in which to germinate. Similarly, a certain degree of openness and receptivity were required in the case of Jesus's miraculous actions. Thus, it is quite common to find Jesus attributing a successful healing or exorcism to the faith of the recipient or their family and friends.[56] In contrast, lack of faith could be a serious impediment. For example, when the disciples queried Jesus as to why they were unable to perform a difficult exorcism, he explained that it was their lack of belief. Even with the faith of a tiny mustard seed they could move a mountain.[57] The most striking demonstration of Jesus's apparent reliance on others' faith was his visit to Nazareth. Like the Buddha, Jesus met with skepticism in his hometown, and was amazed at their lack of belief although he also acknowledged that familiarity was the problem. Unlike the Buddha, Jesus "could do no deed of power" there except to cure a few sick persons by laying hands on them.[58]

Likewise, Jesus refused to perform a sign to the skeptical who demanded it as proof of his authority. Even King Herod had heard of Jesus's reputation as a wonder-worker and was hoping to witness a miracle first hand during Jesus's arrest and interrogation but Jesus did not respond.[59] Thus, the Synoptic gospels present Jesus's miracles as the effect rather than the cause of faith. These mighty deeds (dynameis) arouse curiosity and wonder in those who do not yet believe but they do not necessarily win over converts. In contrast, John's gospel is more optimistic regarding the capacity of miracles to generate faith. His seven miracles are explicitly called "signs" (semeia) and are deliberately chosen in order to convince the reader that Jesus is truly the source of life and truth. On some occasions, the sign does not presuppose but, rather, leads to faith even if it is in rudimentary form. Thus, Nicodemus recognized that Jesus was "from God" because of the signs; the crowds who witnessed the multiplication of the loaves professed that Jesus was "the prophet who is to come into the world"; and the blind man cured by Jesus confessed his belief and "worshipped" him.[60]

The intrinsic connection between Jesus's miracles and his proclamation of the Kingdom echoes Jewish apocalyptic writings that portray the coming of the Messiah as being accompanied by eschatological wonders such as the restoration of health, the lengthening of the human lifespan, abundance of food, harmony between animals and the establishment of peace.[61] Thus, the miracles of Jesus not only give tangible support to his message but also touch on the issue of his true identity. The demons recognized him immediately as the "Holy One" and "Son of the Most High God".[62] In contrast, humans needed more time to fully understand but the miracles triggered the relevant question in their minds. After the calming of the storm, the terrified disciples asked themselves "Who then is this, that even the wind and the sea obey him?"[63] Their pondering was shared by others and led to speculation as to whether Jesus was perhaps Elijah returned, or one of the prophets or even the Messiah himself.[64]

One or Many?

Whereas the respective sources generally agree that the Buddha possessed advanced iddhi powers and Jesus performed many healings, exorcisms and nature miracles, the situation is somewhat different in the case of Muhammad where mixed signals are given. On one hand, the hadith collections and later biographies abound in accounts of amazing happenings associated with the Prophet. On the other hand, the most important text of all, the Qur'an, scarcely mentions miracles and even seems to imply that such events play only a minor role, if any, in Muhammad's story.

The hadith tradition provides scores of miracles attributed to Muhammad and, in many cases, these echo similar occurrences in the Jewish and Christian biblical traditions: for example, the provision of water in the tradition of Moses or the ability to bring rain in the tradition of Elijah and Honi.[65] The recognizable biblical theme of supplying food also appears, such as multiplication of dates and the feeding of 80 men with a few loaves of barley.[66] Although there are no exorcisms attributed to Muhammad, hadiths report a number of healings, such as the cure of sore eyes, a wounded leg and a snake bite.[67] Animals also feature in other miracle stories, such as a slow camel that could sprint, a wolf that spoke, and the spider's web and pigeon's nest that concealed the hiding place of Muhammad and Abu Bakr during the Hijra.[68] As with the Buddha and Jesus, Muhammad is also attributed with superhuman knowledge, quite apart from the occasional revelations that give rise to the Qur'an itself. For example, he was able to detect poison in a roast sheep that had been prepared by the Khaybar Jews, and he was aware of the terrible defeat at distant Mu'ta via dreams and visions, recounting the battle as if he had been present.[69]

Although many devout believers accept these stories as factual accounts that should be interpreted literally, many scholars suspect that, as with similar miracle stories concerning the Buddha and Jesus, there is a healthy dose of later folk legend at work here. Such stories may have evolved as an expanding Islam began to engage in serious apologetic debate with Christianity and Judaism.[70] There have been prominent Islamic philosophers, such as al-Kindi, who took a more skeptical approach to all miracle stories, including those connected with Muhammad. Moreover, as one of the earliest champions of scientific rational thought, Islamic scholarship was not a natural ally for the propagation of a miracle tradition. Similarly today, many modern biographies of Muhammad pay minimal attention to the miracles, portraying him as a reformer whose real miracle was the social, religious and political transformation of Arabia. This reluctance to include the hadith-based miracles of Muhammad is not only grounded on the presupposition that the modern educated person finds such ancient stories difficult to believe. Such a predisposition may be a factor but there is also a solid basis for downplaying the relevance of miracles, even casting doubt on whether Muhammad performed any miracles, in the most important Islamic text of all: the Qur'an.

It should be noted that the Qur'an is not totally bereft of references to miraculous events in the life of Muhammad. The tradition mentioned in Chapter 3 concerning the opening of the Prophet's chest by two mysterious strangers during his childhood is usually justified by a verse in sura 94: "Have We not expanded for you your breast, and taken off from you your burden, which pressed heavily upon your back?"[71] The Qur'anic text is characteristically elusive but the hadiths have supplied the details. Less ambiguous are the Qur'anic verses that refer to Allah's direct intervention to thwart the governor of Yemen's military assault on Mecca in the Year of the Elephant, reckoned to be about 570 CE.[72] Of course, this is not a miracle brought about by Muhammad himself since it is said to have occurred around the time of his birth. However, the theme of divine assistance in battle is repeated on a number of occasions in the Qur'an. For instance, the astonishing Muslim victory against the odds at the Battle of Badr in 624 CE is interpreted by the Qur'an as another example of much needed divine aid in a threatening military situation.[73] Outnumbered, three to one, the Muslim fighters later claimed that they had seen angelic figures fighting for them in the heat of the conflict, the turning point of which is identified as the moment that Muhammad threw a handful of dust at the attackers in a gesture of defiance.[74] The unexpected victory at Badr certainly buoyed the faith and hope of the fledgling Muslim community at Medina, but the same, divine assistance would not be experienced two years later at Uhud where the Muslims were soundly beaten and Muhammad was almost killed. Like most religious cultures that turn to the deity in time of conflict, Muhammad and his followers had to learn what it meant that Allah would deliver them triumph on one occasion but humiliating defeat on another.

Yet this is a very different type of miracle to those described in the hadith tradition such as the multiplication of food, the control of the weather and the ability to cure illness. Are any such occurrences found in the Qur'an? One common answer is to point to the most prominent supernatural event in Muhammad's adult life that is explicitly mentioned in the Qur'an: the Night Journey. Known in Arabic as the Isra' and Mir'aj, this mystical, nocturnal flight has been elaborated in literature, celebrated on the annual calendar and featured in rare artistic depictions of the Prophet's life. The key verse is found in the 17th chapter of the Qur'an, aptly entitled al-Isra':

> Glory be to Him Who made His servant to go on a night from the Sacred Mosque to the remote mosque of which We have blessed the precincts, so that We may show to him some of Our signs; surely He is the Hearing, the Seeing.[75]

Once again, the hadith fleshes out the enigmatic Qur'anic material. No dates are given, but the general consensus is that the Night Journey occurred in either 620 or 621, just prior to the Hijra. One evening, Muhammad was visiting the Ka'ba when the angel of revelation, Gabriel, appeared to him and announced that they were about to embark on a journey. Suddenly, there appeared a white, winged animal that resembled a mule.[76] Named Buraq by the tradition, its stride reached to the horizon and so Muhammad mounted it and was rapidly carried away into the night.[77]

The two terms – Isra' and Mir'aj – indicate the two stages of the journey. Isra' denotes the first stage, which ended at "the furthest mosque" (al-Masjid al-Aqsa). Although no specific earthly location is named, tradition has identified it as the Temple Mount in Jerusalem, now known in Islam as the Holy Sanctuary (Haram al-Sharif).[78] Mir'aj (literally "ascent") refers to the second stage, from Jerusalem to the various levels of heaven. According to Bukhari, Muhammad met key biblical figures in each of the seven celestial echelons: Adam in the first; John the Baptist and Jesus in the second; Joseph in the third; Enoch (Idris) in the fourth; Aaron in the fifth; Moses in the sixth; and Abraham in the seventh.[79] At this point, Muhammad reached the absolute limit for any creature seeking to approach the Creator – a boundary symbolized by the heavenly Lote Tree.[80]

In the classical period of Islamic theology, scholars debated whether the Night Journey was physical or spiritual. On one hand, authors such as al-Tabari and Ibn Kathir presume that Muhammad's body actually travelled to Jerusalem and then to the heavens. On the other hand, Ibn Ishaq and others interpret the experience as occurring in Muhammad's spiritual consciousness. They are supported by 'A'isha, Muhammad's third wife, who stated that "the apostle's body remained where it was but God removed his spirit by night".[81] Irrespective of the actual manner of the journey, the key point here is that it was not a public miracle such as the Buddha's magnificent descent from Tavatimsa Heaven or the Transfiguration of Jesus, which occurred in the presence of Peter, James and John.[82] In contrast, there were no witnesses to the Night Journey. It was essentially a private mystical experience, albeit one that had tremendous impact on Muhammad and constitutes a second turning point in his career. Disheartened by years of rejection in Mecca and saddened by the recent deaths of Khadija and Abu Talib, the Night Journey could not have come at a better time for Muhammad. However, the private nature of the Night Journey meant that it could not function as an unambiguous confirmation of Muhammad's claim to prophetic authority. Most people simply did not believe Muhammad when he recounted his adventure, although Abu Bakr did and is consequently admired as the epitome of trusting faith. Al-Tabari adds that Muhammad was able to describe in considerable detail a caravan that was headed to Mecca at the time. When it arrived several days later, its appearance corresponded to Muhammad's account, demonstrating his veracity.[83]

The problem of Meccan skepticism regarding Muhammad's prophetic claim, highlighted by reactions to his claims about the Night Journey, touches on a crucial aspect of the role of miracles in Muhammad's ministry. After nearly a decade of preaching in his hometown, his message was not only falling on deaf ears but his young community was suffering serious and prolonged persecution. In some ways, the situation was reminiscent of Jesus's problem in his hometown, Nazareth, where familiarity was an obstacle to faith and the possibility of working miracles. Significantly, the Qur'an suggests that this was also happening in Mecca. The townsfolk wanted proof that Muhammad was an authentic prophet but apparently no heavenly sign came to vindicate his claim or support his message. The implication is that Muhammad did not work the requested miracle and that this was a cause of some concern.

It is not as if the Qur'an rejects the notion that Allah can work, and has worked, wondrous deeds through his prophets in the past since there are references to miracles worked by Abraham, Moses, Solomon and Jesus.[84] Understandably, the leaders of Mecca expected Muhammad to possess a similar ability, especially if he was claiming to be the final spokesperson for the one true God in the line of the same biblical prophets. Hints of the taunting demands of the Quraysh leaders are discernible in a number of Qur'anic passages. The list of suggestions that would allegedly constitute proof for them included: a written parchment descending from heaven; the appearance of an angel; turning Muhammad into an angel; Muhammad becoming suddenly rich; the provision of a miraculous garden so that Muhammad need not go to market for food; a fountain that gushed forth from the earth; fragments of the heavens falling from the skies; the construction of a house of gold; and Muhammad ascending to heaven and bringing back a divinely authored book.[85]

The implication is that none of these signs were provided, thus leaving the Quraysh with some justification for dismissing Muhammad as lacking credibility. There are moments when the Qur'an offers Muhammad consolation for the ongoing rejection by his own townsfolk and the frustration in his heart that Allah did not seem willing to silence their criticism with a miraculous display of power. This is ultimately the background for the famous Western adage: "If the mountain will not come to Muhammad, then Muhammad must go to the mountain". The saying is not from the Qur'an, hadith or any known Islamic source. It first appeared in a 1625 publication of essays by Francis Bacon and eventually made its way into later anthologies of English proverbs.[86] The context is an invented story that describes how Muhammad, after assembling the Meccans, called on Mount Safa to come to him but it failed to move. After several attempts, the Prophet explained the reason for the lack of divine cooperation: "God is merciful. Had it obeyed me it would have fallen on us and destroyed us. I will therefore go to the mountain and thank God that He has had mercy on us". The contemporary meaning of the proverb is that sometimes one must bow to the inevitable and adapt one's strategy accordingly. However, the inclusion of Muhammad reflects a longstanding Christian critique of Islam's founder and essentially draws on the original Meccan skepticism hinted at in the Qur'an.

There is one passage in the Qur'an that does imply that a miraculous sign was granted to the Meccan skeptics. The two opening verses of the 54th sura, aptly entitled "The Moon", state: "The hour drew nigh and the moon did rend asunder. And if they see a miracle they turn aside and say: transient magic".[87] Once again, the hadith fills in the missing details, claiming that, on one occasion, the moon appeared to split into two before a group of onlookers.[88] In one sense, the mountain did come to Muhammad, or at least the lunar disc divided for him. However, the same Qur'anic passage adds that, despite this spectacular celestial display, the witnesses refused to believe and dismissed the entire event as a magic show. This is an important observation. Even in the face of overwhelming evidence, the intransigence of the Meccans did not allow them to convert. Moreover, this hardness of heart is the common explanation in other Qur'anic passages for the failure of Allah to yield to their demands and supply a miraculous sign. Allah advises his troubled messenger that, as with his predecessors, an obdurate predisposition renders futile any attempted miraculous verification of a prophet's authenticity.[89] Furthermore, Muhammad himself displayed considerable caution when it came to interpreting astronomical events as supernatural omens. The tradition narrates that a solar eclipse coincided with the death of his son Ibrahim but Muhammad refused to see any connection between the two.[90] The regular movements of the sun, moon and all objects in the heavens are part of the intricate order of creation and one of the most fundamental signs of the existence and ongoing sustaining power of the Creator. Nature itself is the primary miracle.

There is one more crucial, oft-quoted response in the Qur'an to the ridicule heaped upon Muhammad due to the apparent lack of miraculous proofs. The Prophet was instructed to acknowledge his humanity humbly and to declare that an adequate sign had already been given:

> The signs are only with Allah, and I am only a plain warner. Is it not sufficient for them that We have sent down to you the Book which is recited to them? [91]

While other prophetic spokespersons were granted miracles to vindicate their claims, Muhammad had been given something even more convincing – a "divine inspiration" crystallized into human language and captured in the pages of a book.[92] Thus, a specific form of Islamic apologetics arose in response to the criticism concerning Muhammad's lack of miracles. The greatest proof of all was not some wondrous deed that defied the normal course of nature but the holy text. The supreme miracle is the Qur'an itself, and it is not surprising that the term used for a verse of the sacred book (ayat) literally means "sign".

A consequence of the appeal to the Qur'an as the ultimate testimony to Muhammad's divine call is the need to demonstrate its miraculous status. Hence, the doctrine of the exceptionality of the Qur'an was developed to stress its unique qualities. This theological enterprise was grounded in the Qur'an's own self-assessment as sui generis. The voice of revelation urged Muhammad to challenge his critics to produce a similar work if they thought it was spurious or commonplace, but they were warned that even if humans and jinn worked together on such a project they would never succeed.[93] There are usually three dimensions to the argument. The first is the confident claim by Muslims that the Qur'an is a superior literary work. Not only are its contents seen to contain the most profound truths, but its exquisite language and haunting style are extolled as the product of sheer genius. The second dimension draws on the dichotomy between the book and its presumed human author. The Islamic tradition holds that such a superb piece of writing could not possibly have been composed by an illiterate, middle-aged merchant.[94] The third dimension is the potent, hypnotic impact that the Qur'an had on many who listened to it. The most celebrated case is 'Umar, the former enemy of Islam, who became spellbound upon hearing the holy text for the first time. The catalyst for his spontaneous conversion was Islam's paramount miracle. The point of the story is that there is really no need for other wondrous signs; the Qur'an is more than enough.

Observations

Accounts of miracles that occurred during their public adult careers are a feature of all three traditions, just as they were in their infancy narratives. Although there is a tendency to expand and embellish these stories in later literature, reports of amazing deeds also exist in earlier accounts. The inclusion of the miraculous element is well established in the case of the Buddha and Jesus, but a mixed signal emanates from Islamic sources. On one hand, the hadith collections contain many tales of supernatural happenings linked to Muhammad. On the other hand, the Qur'an is more circumspect, even implying at certain points that no divine signs were provided in support of his prophetic claim. This ambiguity is reinforced by the fact that the closest followers of the Buddha and Jesus performed similar deeds in imitation of their master. In contrast, and apart from the Shi'ite tendency to ascribe supernatural powers to Ali, there is no strong tradition in Sunni Islam asserting that Muhammad's closest companions worked miracles.

A comparison of the types of miracles reported for each founder shows both similarity and difference. All three are attributed with amazing powers in both the physical and mental worlds. The Buddha is able to levitate, to fly and to disappear at will, but these extraordinary feats of the body are subordinated to powers such as reading minds, recalling past reincarnations and, ultimately, discovering the detachment needed to reach nibbana. The opposite tendency is discernible in Jesus's case. His ability to know the thoughts of others and predict future events is acknowledged in the gospels, but these are overshadowed by the numerous accounts of his ability to heal bodies, to exorcise demons and to control natural forces. The hadith-based miracles of Muhammad are similar to those of Jesus and the biblical tradition, although there are no exorcisms. Along with physical healings and nature miracles, events involving animals also feature frequently.

The miracles alleged to have been worked by each founder do not automatically establish him as utterly unique. There is no claim that the Buddha, Jesus and Muhammad had an absolute monopoly on such powers. On the contrary, there is a well-established, preexisting miracle tradition in each case, providing the appropriate context in which to understand the full significance of these events. In the story of the Buddha, the background for his miraculous deeds is the yoga tradition of Hinduism, which teaches that certain powers (iddhis) can be summoned from deep within the human spirit. Such abilities are only available to those who have mastered the art of yoga – a term linked to the English word "yoke", highlighting its fundamental emphasis on strict discipline of mind and body. There were many yogins before and after the Buddha who were allegedly able to levitate, to fly, to appear and to disappear, to read minds and so forth. While the Buddha may have been the greatest master of these arts, he was not alone. Moreover, his miracles should be seen as the unleashing of a hidden, yet natural, capacity by anyone advanced in the ways of meditation.

The context of Jesus's and Muhammad's miracles is quite different given their monotheistic framework. In the case of Jesus, there is a twofold background to consider: pagan and Jewish. There are claims of miraculous occurrences in the broader Greco-Roman culture, including religious figures that healed the sick and exercised control over the elements. However, there are stronger links with the miraculous events recounted in the Hebrew bible, especially in the two main concentrations found in the Exodus and the Elijah–Elisha cycles. A number of Jesus's miracles seem to echo these earlier examples, such as the provision of food and the manipulation of natural forces. The one element in Jesus's miraculous activity that is absent from the biblical tradition is exorcism, which developed in the Second Temple period but was a relatively widespread practice by the time of Jesus. The situation is similar for Muhammad. As the final prophet in the monotheistic tradition, the hadith-based miracles also display many similar features to those wrought by Moses, Elijah, Elisha and other biblical figures. The Qur'an explicitly acknowledges that it is the same God who worked these miracles in the past and the present.

While it is openly admitted that the Buddha, Jesus and Muhammad are not the only exponents of such powers within their own contexts, the intent of the miracle stories, in each case, is to establish the founder's excellence within that same tradition. There may have been earlier yogins or miracle working prophets, but the underlying objective is to demonstrate the superiority of the Buddha, Jesus and Muhammad vis-à-vis their predecessors. They may not be the only possessors of such powers but they are portrayed as the best. Thus, in many of the stories where the Buddha displays iddhi powers, rival schools or Hindu gods appear as inferior or subordinate. The Great Miracle itself is a formal contest in which the Buddha emerges as the victor over his opponents. Likewise, in the Descent from Tavatimsa Heaven, the Buddha takes centre stage while his entourage includes the major Hindu deities Brahma and Indra. The theme of competition can be found in the Hebrew biblical tradition as well. Moses defeated the Egyptian magicians at their own game and Elijah called down fire from heaven to light the sacrifice on Mount Carmel, which was beyond the capacity of the prophets of Ba'al. While Jesus does not engage in a direct competition with rivals, the gospels explicitly depict him in the Transfiguration scene as superior to the celebrated miracle workers Moses and Elijah, in a manner similar to the Buddha's Descent from Heaven. The same notion of favorable comparison is evident in Muhammad's Night Journey where he not only joins but also leads other prophets in prayer. Moreover, it is Muhammad who travels to a higher level of heaven than any of the others, even higher than Gabriel is capable of venturing. The theme is extended to the Qur'an itself, which is considered to be the greatest of all books, proving not only that the illiterate Muhammad is a genuine prophet, but that he is the most elevated of all prophets, standing above even those who worked miracles before him.

At times, miracles are used as a means to instruct the listener, especially in the Buddhist tradition, where their pedagogical value is more openly commended. Thus, the Twin Miracle is sometimes interpreted as a lesson in the transience of material reality. In the gospels, miracles help to explain Jesus's popularity among the crowds and, once he has their attention, he does not waste the opportunity to teach them – a technique that is extensively utilized in John's gospel. However, all three traditions acknowledge the limitations of using such amazing events as an educational tool. Muhammad is told that Allah had not provided signs precisely because such displays rarely change the intransigent skeptic. Similarly, Jesus refused to produce miracles for his unconvinced opponents for the same reason and the texts admit that the Buddha's spectacular display at Kapilavatthu only generated an inquisitive, shallow response at best.

The reference to Kapilavatthu raises another theme that is common to all three traditions: doubt and rejection in one's hometown. For the Buddha, his dazzling performance at Kapilavatthu should have won over everyone but, sadly, deep-seated attitudes remained an insuperable obstacle. The Buddha worked a miracle but it had no impact on entrenched disbelief. In Jesus's case, the order is reversed: he could not work miracles at Nazareth because of entrenched disbelief. Muhammad experienced the most protracted native opposition of all three figures: 10 years of rejection, ridicule and persecution in Mecca. As much as he would have appreciated a sign, none was given, and this only added fuel to the local skepticism. If one accepts that the Meccans were granted a sign – the splitting of the moon – the point is still the same as the Buddha's experience at Kapilavatthu: even the most amazing miracles cannot overcome the obdurate mind.

Allied to the limited pedagogical value of miracles is the sense that they can also be dangerous, especially in the Buddhist context. Not only are iddhis ultimately ineffective at generating true faith, but such powerful displays can be downright misleading. Thus, the Buddha explicitly forbade his monks from performing iddhis in the public forum, since they could easily beguile people and distract them from what really matters. Moreover, they also have the potential to generate vanity in the exponent himself, as illustrated by the story of Pindola. The theme is not as overt in the gospels, since Jesus actually encouraged his followers to heal and to exorcise as he did. However, there were times when he was reluctant to use his powers, slipping away from the pressing crowds rather than basking in their adulation. This is consistent with the frequent condemnation of ostentation in his teachings and his rejection of Satan's attractive offer of fame and glory at the start of his public life.

The source of miraculous power varies considerably across the three founders as a result of different theological frameworks. Because Buddhism does not posit a supreme divine being, the miracles of the Buddha are not amazing powers invested in him from above. Rather, the iddhis are skills that reside deep inside all human beings. They can be tapped only via the art of advanced meditation, but ultimately they are of the natural, rather than the supernatural, order. Potentially, iddhis are within reach of everyone. Moreover, the iddhis are best understood as part of the dhamma. They cannot stand alone, but must be integrated into the Buddha's overall doctrine. Amazing as they are, the iddhis are ultimately subordinate to the Four Noble Truths that lie at the core of the teaching. This is reflected in the minimal space dedicated to them in modern works on the Buddha's life, arguably removing one serious obstacle for some modern readers. In the end, the Buddha's miracles are peripheral to the message.

An entirely different set of theological presuppositions is at work in the stories of Jesus and Muhammad. In their cases, the miracle tradition rests firmly on the presumption that the source of these powers is the one, omniscient and omnipotent God. When food is multiplied, storms cease at one's command and sicknesses are suddenly healed, this is the result of divine not human action. The emphasis on God's role is felt more strongly in Islam. It is Allah who works all miracles, although at times he may make use of human agents, such as Moses, Jesus and other prophets. Even the hadith-based miracles attributed to Muhammad are God's doing and not the Prophet's own. Thus, the Qur'an has Muhammad expressly remind himself and his listeners: "I am but a man". The principle applies not only to the many miracles recounted in the hadith, but also to the Qur'an itself. In Islamic thinking, such an unparalleled literary work cannot be the creation of an illiterate Meccan but must be the product of the divine mind. The claim that the Qur'an itself is Allah's supreme miracle has a similar effect as in Buddhism. It highlights the marginal relevance of miracles to the key message of Muhammad. Indeed, this is also reflected in contemporary biographies of the Prophet where little or no attention is given to the hadith miracle tradition. As with the Buddha, telling the story of Muhammad without the need to include frequent supernatural interventions potentially renders it more credible to the modern ear. If the hand of God is sought, then it is to be found in the holy book itself and the Prophet's unexpected success on the politico-religious stage.

The same monotheistic framework in Christianity means that, like Muhammad and the Old Testament prophets, Jesus's miraculous powers are seen as unambiguously supernatural. Such abilities are not an untapped potential residing deep within every human person as in the iddhi tradition. Rather, they are the unmistakeable intervention of a higher power. Miracles point upward rather than inward. However, in contrast to Muhammad, the gospel tradition tends to locate the source of this divine power within Jesus himself. The miracles come "naturally" to Jesus, who works them through his own volition and ability, often without any prayerful petition to heaven. Such close association between divine power and Jesus's own person understandably raises questions about his true identity and the nature of his relationship to the God of Israel's miraculous past. Indeed, the gospels describe how witnesses to his miracles subsequently wondered who this person could be. As a result, it is much more difficult to set aside Jesus's miracles and treat them as peripheral than it is with the Buddha or Muhammad. The earliest traditions suggest that these wonders were considered to be an indispensable element in the story, explaining the heightened attention that Jesus received initially. Moreover, Jesus himself interprets them as integral to his mission. For him, they are the deeds that lend authority to his words; tangible evidence that that the Kingdom was breaking into the world as he proclaimed. However, this tight intersection between Jesus's prophetic words and his miraculous deeds comes with a price in terms of credibility today. The problem is reflected in the ambivalent, even evasive, ways in which Jesus's miracles are treated in contemporary works. While Jesus's message is often appealing, many modern readers cannot easily overcome an instinctive doubt that such extraordinary events really happened.

Notes

1   A systematic treatment of these powers from the Hindu perspective can be found in Patanjali's Yoga Sutras. Armstrong, Buddha 114; Foucher 202.
2   Weddle 114; Thomas 185.
3   Mizuno 163–165.
4   A common example is the Buddha's crossing of the flooded Ganges "in the time it takes a strong man to flex his arm". Digha Nikaya 2; Samyutta Nikaya 51.22; Mizuno 164–165.
5   Digha Nikaya 2; Samyutta Nikaya 51.26.
6   Digha Nikaya 2.
7   Samyutta Nikaya 51.26.
8   Samyutta Nikaya 51.26; Thomas 213.
9   Mizuno 164–165. Another example is when the Buddha sees powerful earth spirits at the village of Patali and correctly predicts that a city will be built there one day. Mizuno 167.
10 Samyutta Nikaya 51.26.
11 Armstrong, Buddha 114.
12 For example, the annual Day of Miracles (Chotrul Düchen) in Tibetan Buddhism commemorates the Buddha's victory over six teachers during a 15-day competition of miraculous power. It also symbolizes the overcoming of the original Bon religion, and even serves as an inspiration for Tibetan resistance to Chinese rule. Weddle 107.
13 Buddhaghosa claims it was the seventh year after the Enlightenment (Sumangala Vilasini 1.57), but Cohen and Foucher state it was the sixteenth year. Cohen 185; Foucher 205.
14 Foucher 207.
15 Gandhara art depicts the Buddha seated on an enormous lotus.
16 In some versions, the spectacular display occurs while the Buddha walks on a jewelled bridge that stretches from horizon to horizon. Weddle 106.
17 Cohen argues that this constitutes the greater of the two feats since each cloned Buddha acted independently. Cohen 194.
18 Foucher 208; Cohen 205–206. These two events, along with the subjugation of a mad elephant at Rajagaha and the gift of a bowl of honey by a monkey at Vesali, constitute the four secondary pilgrimage sites.
19 Mizuno 142.
20 This is the most western of the pilgrimage sites and may have been inspired by the huge earthen ramps constructed besides wells. See Foucher 205.
21 Upon reaching the bottom of the stairs, the Buddha noticed one of his nuns, Uppala-vanna, had disguised herself as a great emperor and had taken pride of place in the welcome party. The Buddha castigated her for presumptuousness, which possibly reflects early concerns about the status of nuns. See Cohen 198–199.
22 Armstrong, Buddha 120.
23 Mahavagga 1.15.1–20.

24 Weddle 115. A similar story is that of Patacara, who experienced terrible afflictions like the biblical character Job. Consequently, she lost her mind and went about naked until the Buddha restored her sanity.

25 Armstrong, Buddha 108, 114.

26 Weddle 116.

27 Digha Nikaya 11; Cullavagga 5.

28 John's gospel agrees, although it contains only seven of Jesus's miracles, each of which is a springboard for an extensive sermon by Jesus.

29 John 14:12; Luke 10:1–12; Mark 3:15, 6:7; Acts 3:1–11; 5:1–16; 9:33–41; 12:7–17; 14:8–10; 16:16–18.

30 Blackburn 114.

31 Mark 5:21–24; Luke 7:11–17; John 11:1–44.

32 Mark 1:23–26; 5:1–20; 7:24–30; 9:25–29; Matthew 9:32–34; 12:22–32.

33 Mark 5:3–5; 9:22–27.

34 Mark 4:39; 6:51; 8:1–9; 11:12–14, 20–24; John 2:1–11; Luke 5:1–10; Matthew 17:24–27.

35 Mark 2:8; 11:2; 13:1–37; 14:13–16; Matthew 9:4; 12:25; John 1:48; Luke 19:5.

36 McClymond 397. Reimarus understood the gospel miracles as naturally explainable events but Strauss argued that they had no historical basis whatsoever.

37 McClymond 397.

38 Blackburn 117, 124.

39 McClymond 403.

40 Mark 6:56. Luke changes the order of events by placing Jesus's visit to Nazareth before the healing at Capernaum; Matthew simply makes a general statement about Jesus's early fame. Luke 4:16–30; Matthew 4:23–25.

41 John also states that many believe in Jesus because of his "signs". See John 2:23.

42 Garland 81.

43 Examples include Aristeas of Proconnesus, who died and reappeared 7 years later; Empedocles, who controlled the winds, healed the sick and resuscitated the dead; Pythagoras, who predicted earthquakes, calmed storms and averted plagues; Vespasian who cured a withered hand; and Apollonius of Tyana who repelled plagues, cast out demons, cured the sick, revived the dead and miraculously escaped from prison. Garland 83–87.

44 Numbers 16:41–50; 21:5–9; John 3:14–15; 1 Kings 13:4–6; 17:17–24; 2 Kings 4:8–37; 5:1–27.

45 See Talmud passages: Abot 3.10–11; Sotah 9.15; Berakot 5.5; Ta'anit 23a.

46 Exodus 15:23–25; 16:4–36; 17:1–7; Numbers 20:7–11; 1 Kings 17:4–16; 2 Kings 2:19–22; 4:1–7, 38–44; Mark 6:30–42.

47 Exodus 14:21–22; 2 Kings 2:8, 14–15; 1 Kings 17:14; 18:41–46; 2 Kings 6:1–7; 1 Kings 18:30–40.

48 Mark 9:2–8; Matthew 17:1–8; Luke 9:28–36.

49 Tobit 6–8.

50 Matthew 12:27; Mark 9:38; Acts 19:13–17; McClymond 400.

51 Luke 11:17–20.

52 Exodus 8:19; 31:18; Deuteronomy 9:10; Mechilta Beshallah 6.

53 Mark 1:39; 3:14–15; 6:12–13.

54 For example, Jesus "rebukes" the wind in a manner reminiscent of an exorcism. Note also that the Gerasene demons enter a herd of swine and throw themselves into the lake. See Mark 4:39; 5:8–13.

55 Mark 1:27.

56 Mark 2:5; 5:34; 10:52; Matthew 8:13; 15:28.

57 Matthew 17:20; 21:21; Mark11:22–23.
58 Mark 6:1–6.
59 Mark 8:11–12; Matthew 12:38–40; Luke 23:7–9.
60 John 3:2; 6:14; 9:35–41.
61 Jubilees 23:26–30; Messianic Apocalypse 4Q21.5–8; 4 Ezra 7:27; 2 Baruch 73:1–7. See Novakovic 106–108. See also Isaiah 61:1; Luke 4:18; Matthew 11:2–6.
62 Mark 1:24, 34; 3:11; 5:7.
63 Mark 4:41.
64 Mark 8:27–30; 10:47.
65 Bukhari 4.170, 194; 7.340; 17.126; 56.777, 779.
66 Bukhari 56.778, 780; Peterson 122.
67 Gabriel 115–116; Bukhari 52.253; 59.517.
68 Ramadan 82–83; Bukhari 34.310; 47.795; 39.517.
69 Bukhari 53.394; Ramadan 171.
70 Thomas, Miracles 207.
71 Qur'an 94:1–3. There is reference to a second opening of the chest during the Night Journey in Bukhari 8.345.
72 Qur'an 105:1–5.
73 Qur'an 8:9–11.
74 Qur'an 8:43–44.
75 Qur'an 17:1.
76 Bukhari 58.227.
77 Buraq is a popular symbol of protection for road vehicles in Muslim cultures and it was also the name of a domestic Indonesian airline company in the late twentieth century. Similarly, the Indonesian national carrier, Garuda, is named after the mythical bird that carries Vishnu according to Hindu tradition.
78 Some argue that the "farthest mosque" denotes a mosque in Medina or possibly heaven itself.
79 Bukhari 58.228.
80 Qur'an 53:13–18.
81 Ibn Ishaq (Guillaume) 183.
82 Matthew 17:1–6; Mark 9:1–8; Luke 9:28–36; 2 Peter 1:16–18.
83 Ramadan 69; Ibn Ishaq (Guillaume) 183.
84 Qur'an 21:68–69; 28:30–31; 38:34–38; 5:110–114; 3:49.
85 Qur'an 6.50; 25:7–8; 17:90–96.
86 See Essays of Francis Bacon (1625) Chapter 12.
87 Qur'an 54:1–2.
88 Bukhari 60.388; Muslim 39.6728.
89 Qur'an 6:7–10; 17.59; 6:34, 37, 109–111; 20:133–134.
90 Bukhari 18.151.
91 Qur'an 29:50–51. See also 18:106–110; Ramadan 46; Emerick 69.
92 Bukhari 61.504; 92.379.
93 Qur'an 2:23; 10:38; 11:12–13; 17:88.
94 Schimmel 376; Qur'an 7:157–158.

Chapter 7

FOLLOWERS

The focus of the last few chapters has been squarely on the individual founders themselves: the turning points that led them into the public domain; the essential message that they felt compelled to communicate; and the miraculous elements that supplemented their project. In this chapter, the focus shifts to those persons who were part of that public domain, who listened to the teachings and committed themselves to the founders in various ways. These earliest companions constitute a vital link in the causal chain since, without their support, the Buddha, Jesus and Muhammad would never have become household names. Their lasting influence would have been impossible without a community of believers who embraced their vision and carried it beyond their death into the broader historical stream. Who were the first followers and what were their backgrounds? What modes of attachment do we find among them? What were the costs and benefits involved? To what extent did they form organized communities with defined structures and practices?

The Third Jewel

The common image of the Buddha is that of a solitary man with legs folded and eyes shut, seated in perfect peace, untouched by the turbulent world around him. However, the lone contemplative was also the active leader of a vibrant religious movement that started with a handful of members and eventually grew into a sizeable community by the time of his death. A hint of the forthcoming emergence of a new community occurred while he was still savoring the moment of enlightenment at Bodhgaya. Tradition claims that he spent seven weeks there, contemplating various aspects of nibbana. During that time, two merchants, Tapussa and Bhalluka, appeared on the scene. They kindly offered the Buddha some rice cakes and honey, which he accepted in bowls that were miraculously created for him by the gods. The Buddha then delivered a brief discourse after which the men professed their faith via a twofold

Buddha, Jesus and Muhammad: A Comparative Study, First Edition. Paul Gwynne.
© 2014 John Wiley & Sons, Ltd. Published 2014 by John Wiley & Sons, Ltd.

formula, taking "refuge" in the Buddha and his teaching (dhamma). They had effectively become his first lay disciples.[1] The encounter raised the critical question whether the Buddha should share his newfound insight with others or not, and the narrative reflects the intense mental debate that he experienced. On one hand, he was concerned that no one would be intellectually capable of understanding the complex message and, thus, it would ultimately be a futile exercise. On the other hand, the high Hindu god Brahma pleaded with him to preach so that the prevailing darkness and ignorance could be overturned.[2] In the end, motivated by compassion, the Buddha decided to offer his wisdom to those who would listen. The next issue was where to start. The most obvious candidates were his former teachers, Alara Kalama and Uddaka Ramaputta, but they had died. He then thought of his five former ascetical companions and promptly set off toward Baranasi (Benares) to find them.

The tradition inserts another brief encounter prior to that historical meeting. On the way, we are told that he came across a young man named Upaka who, like the Buddha, was seeking a higher truth via the path of self-sacrifice and abstinence. As with the two merchants, this was an unexpected opportunity to share his truth with another and, given Upaka's spiritual background, one would have expected him to convert quite readily. Upaka acknowledged that the Buddha might be "the absolute victor" as claimed but surprisingly took his leave and continued on his journey.[3] So, at the very beginning of the mission there is a sobering reminder that not everyone would accept the message or the man.

The Buddha finally found his former colleagues in a deer park at Isipatana (Sarnath), which was a well-known gathering place for hermits.[4] The painful memories of the Buddha's earlier decision to break with their strict regime were still raw and understandably they gave their visitor a frosty reception. Yet they also recognized a radiant dignity about him and so they agreed to listen to his story. Thus, the First Sermon was delivered and the "wheel of the law" was turned. One of the five, Kondannya, grasped the truth immediately and achieved the first stage of advancement known as "stream-enterer".[5] The Buddha responded by saying: "Come, O bhikkhu, well taught is the doctrine. Lead a holy life for the sake of the complete extinction of suffering."[6] The summons was to a more radical level of commitment than the two merchants at Bodhgaya. In this case, it meant formal ordination as a monk (bhikkhu) in a new religious order. After further instruction, the other four ascetics – Vappa, Bhaddiya, Mahanama and Assaji – also joined Kondannya as stream-enterers and the nascent Buddhist monastic community (sangha) was formed. So precious is the sangha in Buddhist thinking that it is considered to be the "third jewel" alongside the Buddha and the dhamma.

Whereas the first monks were all experienced ascetics and former acquaintances of the Buddha, the next convert, Yasa, was a total stranger and the son of a wealthy Baranasi banker.[7] Yasa's background is suspiciously identical to the Buddha's own personal journey. He was married with a beautiful wife and was surrounded by opulence and luxury, yet he experienced an acute sense of the futility of material riches and earthly pleasures. The Buddha beckoned him to join his newly created group and Yasa professed, for the first time in history, the triple refuge: "I go for haven to the Buddha; I go for haven to the dhamma (teaching); I go for haven to the sangha (community)".

From this point on, the pace of conversion accelerated and the sangha experienced rapid expansion. Yasa's drastic decision to cut off his hair and enter a "houseless state" made an immediate impact on four of his closest friends who, like him, all hailed from affluent backgrounds. They joined their comrade and soon afterwards another 50 youths from noble families followed.[8] The trend of rich young men abandoning their comfortable lifestyle and adopting the Buddha's path of renunciation continued when, soon afterwards, the Buddha recruited 30 more youths who had been sporting with their wives in a grove.

The focus of recruitment then shifted back to ascetical forest dwellers. With a solid group of ninety monks, the Buddha now took on his main competition – the Brahmanic brotherhoods, symbolized by the communities of the three Kassapa brothers in Uruvela. The conversion took some time since the brothers were unimpressed with the Buddha's miraculous powers, including the slaying of the serpent demon. However, the Buddha's frank declaration that they would all fall short of nibbana had the appropriate effect. They cast their ceremonial implements into the river and accepted the Buddha's teaching. These were large communities, and it was nothing short of a mass conversion, swelling the sangha to over 1,000 members.[9]

The community had now become so large that it was not sustainable to stay in Uruvela and its surrounding hamlets.[10] The move to a larger urban centre was necessary for basic economic reasons and the Buddha chose Rajagaha. The move was strategically beneficial for two reasons. First, it was there that the Buddha would recruit his two most outstanding pupils: Sariputta and Moggallana. Both from Brahmin backgrounds, they were introduced by Assaji to the Buddha who exclaimed, "These two will become my greatest disciples".[11] Sariputta became renowned for his intelligence and Moggallana for his iddhi powers.[12] Three other names are often listed alongside Sariputta and Moggallana as the five most prominent of the Buddha's disciples. Maha-Kassapa was famous for his deep commitment to reclusive asceticism; Ananda was the Buddha's cousin and became his personal assistant for the last 25 years of his life; and Anuruddha purportedly had the ability to see at great distances.[13]

Second, the visit to Rajagaha was the fulfilment of Siddhattha's promise to King Bimbisara that he would return after he had found the secret to permanent happiness. The citizens immediately inquired about the identity of the newcomer who had converted the most prominent spiritual virtuosi in the region, the Kassapa brothers. The news reached Bimbisara and the regent visited the Buddha for a meal during which he accepted the dhamma and became a lay disciple. Bimbisara's conversion provided influential royal sponsorship and consolidated a long-term friendship. It also resulted in a practical gift from Bimbisara to the new, fast-growing community: land for a monastic residence.

The community of followers had a twofold structure: an inner group of ordained monks who adopted an ascetical, itinerant lifestyle; and a larger, outer group of lay disciples who remained in their homes and careers but provided support to the founder and his monks in practical ways. Given that a period of four and a half decades would pass until the Buddha's death, there was ample time for the significant growth of the community and for the ongoing development of a set of principles and rules for its two basic subdivisions.

The new order was called the "shramana children of the Sakyan" to distinguish them from other renouncer groups. An alternative title was the "bhikkhu sangha" ("Union of Monks").[14] The term "sangha" originally meant a guild of craftsmen or merchants but, by the Buddha's time, it was commonly applied to shramana groups. It effectively captures the notion that the followers of the Buddha were not isolated hermits existing in seclusion but, rather, a genuine religious family that ate, slept and travelled together. The point is well made via the story of the Buddha's return to his hometown Kapilavatthu. The reunion between the Buddha and his father was cordial, but there was an underlying sense that things had fundamentally changed. Suddhodana noticed that the visitors sought alms as a means of support and remarked to the Buddha that this was not fitting for someone who had been born into the Kshatria (warrior) caste. The Buddha replied that this may not be the custom of Suddhodana's "royal lineage", but it was the custom of his "Buddha lineage". It was a confirmation of his decision years earlier to abandon the palace for the woods. He did not need a royal parasol since he now had the trees of the forest.[15] In short, he was no longer the son of a king. He had a new name, a new identity and a new family. The household of Sakya had been replaced by the household of the Sangha.

The same point is made in the scene where the Buddha meets his own son, Rahula. The name itself, which is usually translated as "shackle" or "fetter", is a graphic statement of the subordination of blood to belief. This biological child was an obstacle to the Buddha's true parental calling, which was to be father to his spiritual sons and daughters. When the Buddha's former wife, Yasodhara, urged the boy to ask his father for his inheritance, the Buddha explained that the greatest gift that he could offer was the dhamma itself.[16] The harshness of this apparent rejection of his own blood family is softened by the claim that most of them accepted his teaching and became followers. Rahula was ordained a monk even though he was still only a child of seven or eight years of age. The Buddha's cousins, Ananda and Anuruddha, joined as well and would be numbered among his chief disciples in the years to come. Another cousin, Devadatta, also joined but would later become a dangerous enemy within the fold. Even his father, Suddhodana, became a stream enterer, although he was reluctant at first and only did so after his brothers had converted. According to one tradition, the king decreed that all families with two or more sons should turn one over to the order.

The membership criteria for this new religious family were surprisingly liberal given the strong emphasis on hierarchy in the contemporary Brahmanic society. Admittedly, not just anyone could join. The Buddha rejected criminals, those in debt, those who were physically disabled or ill, and those whose departure from their homes would cause harm to others.[17] Yet the classical Hindu concerns about caste, age and gender did not constitute insurmountable obstacles. In terms of caste laws, the Buddha had already abandoned his Kshatria warrior duties when he had left the palace many years earlier. It was clear that caste regulations did not feature highly on his list of priorities, and this is consistent with his policy not to restrict entry into his order to those of a particular class or caste. The relevant story here is that of Upali the barber, who was treated in exactly the same manner as more aristocratic colleagues who had joined.[18]

The issue of age is dealt with in the story of the Buddha's son who asked for his inheritance and was granted ordination at the tender age of seven or eight. However, Suddhodana came to the Buddha and reminded him of the distress that his family had suffered when he had left the palace. Consequently, he requested that, in future, no minors should be ordained without the express permission of their parents – a request that the Buddha granted.[19] In addition, the standard minimum age for ordination was set at 20 years, at which point it was deemed that the individual would be capable of making an informed decision and of coping with the arduous lifestyle. Yet this was still a relatively early age for the ascetical life, especially in a society where young adults were expected to marry and have children during the householder stage.[20]

The issue of gender is also a theme in the narrative of the visit to Kapilavatthu. According to the Mahavagga, "the first females in the world who became lay-disciples by the formula of the holy triad" were the mother and wife of Yasa.[21] Indeed, many lay women would offer their support for the monks in various ways, but the crucial question was whether women should be allowed into the inner circle of the monks. While the Buddha was staying at Kapilavatthu, his aunt-stepmother, Mahapajapati, approached him and requested to join the sangha with several other women. The Buddha initially refused on the basis that the monastic life would be too perilous for them. However, his cousin, Ananda, intervened on behalf of the importunate Mahapajapati and changed the Buddha's mind.[22]

The lifestyle that the Buddha's monks (bhikkhus) and nuns (bhikkhunis) were invited to undertake was not an easy one and required a high level of dedication and self-sacrifice. Initiation into the order of monks was marked in two very graphic ways: the shaving of the hair and the donning of the yellow monastic robes.[23] The monk was to be utterly detached from concerns about physical appearance. Such radical simplicity was also symbolized by the five basic items that constituted a monk's entire possessions: one set of robes; a needle; a razor; a strainer and a bowl. The needle indicated the monk's responsibility to care for his garments and the razor was to shave the head on a regular basis. The strainer reflected the principle of nonviolence and was used to strain out small insects that may have fall into the monk's drink. Finally, the bowl was used during the daily alms-round, reflecting the fundamental dependence of the monks and nuns on the generous support of laity in terms of food, clothing, money and the essentials of life. In return, the bhikkhu would offer wise instruction and the blessings of good karma. It is significant that the term "bhikkhu" literally means "one who begs", and the mudra (hands position) of Buddha images sometimes depict him holding his bowl as a sign of the mendicant life that he and his followers embraced.

The typical day was spent in meditation, study, instruction, confession, community chores and hospitality toward visitors and guests. As the order grew, circumstances and incidents occurred from time to time, which required the Buddha to clarify an existing guideline or develop a new one. Consequently, there emerged a collection of formal disciplinary rules. According to tradition, the monastic rules developed and endorsed by the Buddha during his lifetime were recited by the monk Upali at the First Council, held soon after the Buddha's death. Centuries later, these memorized rules were eventually put into written form in the Vinaya Pitaka (Basket of Discipline), which is part of the Tipitaka or Pali Canon. It is difficult to know precisely which of the many Vinaya precepts actually date back to the Buddha's own day but the general picture that emerges is one of an evolving monastic community, concerned with safeguarding and handing on its fundamental values to posterity.[24]

Among the myriad of Vinaya regulations commentators often refer to a list of ten precepts that form a convenient summary of early Buddhist monastic life. They are expressed in the first person and identify a range of activities or attitudes that must be avoided at all costs:

1. I refrain from destroying living creatures.
2. I refrain from taking that which is not given.
3. I refrain from inappropriate sexual activity.
4. I refrain from incorrect speech.
5. I refrain from intoxicating drinks and drugs that lead to carelessness.
6. I refrain from eating at the forbidden time (after noon).
7. I refrain from dancing, singing and music.
8. I refrain from wearing garlands, using perfumes and cosmetics.
9. I refrain from lying on a high or luxurious bed.
10. I refrain from accepting gold and silver. [25]

The first five items are known collectively as the Pancasila (five precepts) and are commonly understood as the basic moral norms that apply to all followers of the Buddha. The second five are specifically for bhikkhus and bhikkhunis, although the laity was invited to undertake these extra degrees of discipline at certain times, such as during the annual rains retreat. In addition to avoidance of the five cardinal vices of the Pancasila (violence, theft, fornication, lying and intoxication), the celibate monks and nuns also fasted daily from noon, forsook the usual forms of entertainment, downplayed physical beauty, disregarded material comfort and transcended concerns about money or property.

The monastic followers of the Buddha were not only meditative mendicants. They were also itinerant, at least for the majority of the year. Like its founder, who travelled incessantly until his death, the sangha was a peripatetic organization. After the Buddha had called a new recruit with the command "Come, monk", the next imperative was a missionary mandate. "Go now and travel". The Buddha did not specify precisely where his envoys should go, and there is no evidence that he restricted them to any particular kingdom or region. Eventually, they would journey beyond India and take the dhamma to the four corners of Asia. Unlike its mother religion, the Buddha's new spiritual movement was outward-looking and willing to share the dhamma with anyone and everyone. The drive behind this external thrust was compassion – the same motivation that had convinced the newly enlightened Buddha to leave the bliss of Bodhgaya and share his wisdom with his five former friends.

The itinerant nature of the early sangha meant that the first generations of monks often slept in caves, graveyards, under rocks or in makeshift shelters in the forest. However, the Indian climate meant that this was not always possible. The heavy rains of the monsoon season, which stretches approximately from June to September, caused rivers to flood and roads to become muddy. In such circumstances, it was difficult and dangerous for monks to move about on foot. Moreover, there was a general fear of stepping on submerged animal life and unwittingly causing death. Ever practical, the Buddha instructed his bhikkhus to remain in one place for the duration of the wet season and to utilize this time for their spiritual renewal. Thus, two important institutional practices were linked: the annual rains retreat (vassa) and the adoption of a semi-permanent residence (vihara).[26]

There were two basic forms of abode: the "avasa" and the "arama". The avasa was a large, circumscribed area in the forest. Here the monks would erect simple huts, abandoning them at the end of the monsoon period. Some monks would return to the same avasa year after year. In contrast, the arama was a tract of land usually located near a town or city. Often it was in the form of a flower garden, fruit tree grove or hunting ground. The arama was typically donated by a wealthy benefactor who frequently maintained the site while the monks were away wandering. The ideal location was far enough from town so that the monks would not be distracted, but close enough so that the monks could perform their alms rounds and the laity could visit.[27] The first arama was King Bimbisara's gift of the Veluvana bamboo grove on the outskirts of his capital Rajagaha. In time, 60 huts were erected there, along with a hall for ceremonies. A second arama at Jetavana, just outside Savatthi, was donated by Anathapindika, a wealthy merchant from that city.[28] Soon afterwards, a third arama was established at Pubbarama, also near Savatthi. In his later years, the Buddha is said to have spent most of his rains retreats at either Jetavana or Pubbarama.[29] As the years progressed, the sangha continued to benefit from the generosity of wealthy sponsors in this most practical way, and the number of arama-monasteries steadily grew.

The occasional donation of monastic residences and the more regular provision of food and clothing highlight the symbiotic relationship between the two principal subdivisions among the Buddha's followers. The inner circle of monks and nuns (bhikkhus and bhikkhunis) relied heavily on material assistance provided by the lay supporters (upasakas and upasikas). In return, the monks and nuns offered spiritual nourishment, guidance and consolation to the laity, especially at key moments of the annual calendar or the human journey from birth to death. As the third jewel of Buddhism, the sangha was a precious "field of merit", where ordinary folk could find refuge and good karma.[30] Yet this third jewel could not survive in practice without the aid of the upasakas who, whilst not abandoning home or family, nevertheless committed themselves to the Buddha's teaching and played a key role in the growth of the new movement. Although the five former companions of the Buddha are usually presented as his first disciples, it is important to recall the earlier reference to Tapussa and Bhalluka while the Buddha was still at Bodhgaya. Although the five were the recipients of the First Sermon and the first to receive ordination as fully fledged monks, nevertheless, the inclusion of the two lay followers who provided the Buddha with food prior to his departure for Baranasi is an important acknowledgment of the vital part that the laity plays. Despite the emphasis on the bhikkhus, the Buddha's movement was never a purely monastic one. From the beginning, it was always a two-dimensional phenomenon that saw the importance of a social solidarity between monk and layperson.

The Twelve Disciples

Jesus's entry onto the public stage as a healer and preacher quickly captured the attention of many people. The gospels frequently refer to the throng ("ochlon") that gathered around him, especially during his early ministry in Galilee.[31] The historian Josephus noted that Jesus "gained following both among many Jews and among many of Greek origin" in a similar way to John the Baptist.[32] Indeed, it was precisely such politically dangerous levels of popularity that eventually caught Herod's eye and led to John's execution. Although there is a traditional notion that the crowds abandoned Jesus halfway through his ministry (the "Galilean spring" theory), it is more likely that large numbers continued to follow him to the very end and ultimately this "fatal attraction" cost him his life.[33] However, the crowds were hardly followers in a religious sense. They flocked to Jesus primarily because of his reputation as a miracle worker, but often their curiosity did not progress to an enduring commitment. They may have been loosely sympathetic to his main ideas but the majority of them did not take the next step of genuine discipleship.

Apart from the anonymous crowds, the gospels also speak of "disciples" (mathetai).[34] The closest equivalent to this term is the master–disciple relationships that were sprouting up around Palestine as a result of Hellenistic influence.[35] In both the Greco-Roman and the contemporary Jewish cultures, there were schools in which disciple-students gathered around religious leaders and imbibed their wisdom.[36] Although the boundaries of Jesus's group are not precise, it is possible to identify at least three key criteria of membership. The first of these criteria touches on one of the most unusual and distinctive features of Jesus's disciples: namely, that the initiative lies not with the follower but with the master. In most cases, it is not the disciple who makes the first move but Jesus. According to Mark, the first four disciples, who were all fishermen, were recruited when Jesus spotted them by the Sea of Galilee and issued the startling command "Follow me". Amazingly, they downed tools, abandoned their careers and joined company with this apparent stranger.[37] Jesus issued the same authoritative instruction to a local tax collector named Levi with the same obedient reply.

Yet a positive response was not always guaranteed, as is demonstrated by the story of the rich, young man who was unable to accept Jesus's invitation to forsake all of his possessions.[38] Not all who were called ended up following. The converse was also true: not all who offered to follow were called. One example is the Gerasene demoniac who, after being freed, begged that he be allowed to accompany Jesus. However, Jesus refused his request and ordered him to remain in the Decapolis region and recount his story there.[39] In contrast, the fourth gospel shifts the initiative away from Jesus and onto those who guide others to Jesus. For example, the Baptist sent his pupils, Andrew and Philip, to Jesus. Andrew then brought along his brother, Simon, and Philip recruited his friend, Nathanael.[40]

The confident and imposing manner in which Jesus called strangers to join his company was rare, if not unique, in the Judaism of his day. It was not customary for a rabbi to confront a total stranger and order them in a peremptory manner to join his school or to become his pupil. Students would normally choose their rabbi. The nearest equivalent to Jesus's action is Elijah's unconditional call of Elisha who reasonably asked to bid his parents farewell first.[41] In contrast, Jesus refused similar requests from potential disciples, suggesting that even basic filial duties, such as saying goodbye to one's family or burying one's father, were subordinate to the exigency of the mission.[42]

The second criterion of discipleship was that the person called be willing to leave home and accompany Jesus on his preaching tours. Once again, this is a much more radical lifestyle than a pupil going away for a set number of years and attending a rabbinical school in a nearby town or city. Accepting Jesus's call to join him on his itinerant mission meant a range of worrying uncertainties and awkward implications. It was an open-ended commitment with no clear timeframe attached. There was also the geographical dislocation of radical itinerancy.[43] Unlike the eventual monastic residences of early Buddhism, there was no centre of operations or semi-permanent base, reflected in Jesus's words: "Foxes have holes, and birds of the air have nests; but the Son of Man has nowhere to lay his head".[44]

In fact, Jesus and his companions did not always sleep in the open or on the street and this was because not all of his followers took to the road with him. The gospels hint at a substantial network of supporters who remained in their homes and offered Jesus and his companions food and shelter. Moreover, many of them were quite affluent. In Capernaum, Jesus enjoyed a "banquet" at the home of Levi the tax collector. In Jericho, Jesus invited himself to the house of the diminutive, chief tax collector, Zacchaeus, who was willing to give away half of his wealth to the poor. In Bethany, Jesus dined at the house of Simon the Pharisee. In the same town, Jesus frequently visited his close friends Martha, Mary and Lazarus. In Jerusalem, an anonymous house-owner made available a large upstairs room where Jesus ate his last meal.[45] Jesus and his companions were often guests in the homes of sympathizers and supporters and it was through their generous hospitality that he was able to meet his basic physical needs. Moreover, Jesus often used these meals as a pedagogical vehicle for reinforcing some of his most radical teachings. What is striking about Jesus's dining habits is his tendency to challenge traditional social-religious protocols. Jesus certainly ate in the homes of upright persons, including Pharisees, many of whom enjoyed his company and conversation.[46] However, he was also guest at the table of "tax collectors and sinners", such as Levi and Zacchaeus – a provocative act that understandably generated protests of inappropriateness.[47]

The third criterion for being a disciple of Jesus was readiness to face inevitable hardships, dangers and hostility. One prominent theme in the gospel accounts of Jesus's private instructions to his closest followers is the heavy price of discipleship. He clearly anticipated that criticism and opposition would arise as a consequence of his provocative message and actions, and this would not only be directed at himself but also at anyone who intimately associated with him. The gospels record various sayings on this theme, all of which contain the same essential lesson: anyone who wishes to save his life will lose it and anyone who loses his life will save it.[48] The frightening image chosen by Jesus to drive home his point is the common form of execution used throughout the Roman Empire at the time: "If any want to become my followers, let them deny themselves and take up their cross and follow me".[49]

This is not a pretty picture. The excitement of the miracles and the joyous proclamation of a new world built on God's mercy and forgiveness are here tempered by a darker side to the story. The Kingdom will not come easily into this sinful world and its messengers will not have it easy.

One of the most personal and distressing ways in which the "cross" of discipleship was felt was the negative reaction by family members. Jesus's radical call for certain persons to follow him meant abandoning their kinsfolk for an indefinite period of time and for an uncertain future. Risking the loss of vital emotional and financial support would not have been an easy decision for the ordinary Jewish peasant. Moreover, not all of those called by Jesus were young and single, and the implications of leaving home for a parent or spouse, such as Peter, were even more scandalous. Yet this is what Jesus demanded – a complete break with family ties if necessary, sweetened by the promised compensation of a completely new type of family.[50] Luke's gospel records even stronger language used by Jesus to describe the wrenching divisions within families that following him might entail: households split and family members set against each other.[51] Given that the fifth commandment (in the Jewish ordering) explicitly decrees that Jews should always honor their parents, such language would have seemed not only disrespectful but verging on the sinful. Yet Jesus boldly announced that "whoever comes to me and does not hate father and mother, wife and children, brothers and sisters, yes and even life itself, cannot be my disciple".[52]

Jesus's revolutionary stance on the subordination of blood relations to his mission is not something that he imposed on his disciples without undergoing the same personal loss himself. There is evidence in the gospels that Jesus's own kin did not accept his claims or his message, at least initially. John's gospel includes the pithy, yet significant, authorial note: "his brothers did not believe in him".[53] In addition, Mark records that soon after Jesus commenced his public ministry, his own family concluded that he had gone insane and went looking for him in order to bring him home so that their embarrassment could end.[54] Upon arriving at the house, the relatives, including his mother, remained outside while Jesus stayed inside with his disciples and boldly declared that his true family was in the room with him.[55]

Mention of Jesus's mother raises the question whether there were women among the circle of disciples. There are no scenes in the gospels where Jesus explicitly calls a woman to be his disciple, as he does with several men.[56] However, there were women who offered him hospitality, including the sisters Martha and Mary in Bethany. Luke also notes that many women – including Mary Magdalene, Joanna and Susanna – provided for Jesus and his male disciples out of their resources.[57] If the idea of abandoning one's family and career to follow an itinerant prophet was not shocking enough, the thought of a group of women, possibly without their own husbands or kinsmen, travelling about with Jesus and his male companions, would have been considered by many as outrageous, even if the interrelationships within the group were proper.

At the centre of this larger group of followers, some itinerant and some residential, there was a small, elite circle that carried enormous symbolic significance. At some point during his ministry, Jesus personally selected twelve of his disciples and set them apart with a special role. It is surprising that the institution of the Twelve did not survive long after Jesus's death. The number was initially maintained when Matthias was appointed to take Judas's place, but there is no further replacement process mentioned when James was martyred soon afterwards.[58] Yet the establishment of the group and the careful selection of its membership were a vital part of Jesus's religious mission. It was another powerful symbolic action and the key to its meaning lies in the number itself. In the context of Judaism, 12 is the number of ancient tribes that together formed the entire nation, which the narrative links etiologically to the 12 sons of Jacob, the grandson of Abraham.[59] In other words, twelve was Israel's constitutional number. Given that most Jews would have been acutely aware of the significance of the number and the general hope of a gathering of the scattered tribes in the end days, the explicit appointment of 12 men at the heart of his community would have meant only one thing: Jesus saw himself as setting in motion the eschatological process of Israel's reunification.[60]

This grand religious vision centered on a reunified Israel is reflected in a saying of Jesus that speaks of the Twelve sitting on thrones of judgment in the coming Kingdom – an image that is unique in Jewish literature.[61] It is also reflected in the geographical pattern of Jesus's own missionary itinerary. In the main, Jesus confined his travelling within the borders of Israel, although there are a few short forays into Gentile territory, such as the Decapolis and the district of Tyre and Sidon where he healed a demoniac and the daughter of a Canaanite woman, respectively.[62] The latter is an interesting case in point since the healing only occurred as a result of the woman's persistence and wit. When Jesus bluntly told her that it was not fitting to "take the children's food and throw it to the dogs", she pointed out that dogs enjoy the crumbs that fall from the master's table. Matthew softens the potential rudeness in Jesus's tone by having him explain that he was sent only to "the lost sheep of the house of Israel".[63]

Although the term "apostle" later came to mean a missionary within the early Church,[64] Mark applies it to the Twelve during Jesus's public ministry, indicating that they were not just followers but also messengers.[65] They not only formed an intimate inner circle around Jesus but also shared in his preaching and healing work. The Synoptic gospels describe how Jesus bestowed on them authority to cast out demons and to cure diseases.[66] One passage in Mark conveniently summarizes their mandate:

> Then he went about among the villages teaching. He called the twelve and began to send them out two by two, and gave them authority over the unclean spirits. He ordered them to take nothing for their journey except a staff; no bread, no bag, no money in their belts; but to wear sandals and not to put on two tunics. He said to them, "Wherever you enter a house, stay there until you leave the place. If any place will not welcome you and they refuse to hear you, as you leave, shake off the dust that is on your feet as a testimony against them." So they went out and proclaimed that all should repent.[67]

The set of instructions for conduct on the road involved a strict prohibition on ordinary provisions: bread, bag, money, spare tunic. The missionaries were required to stay in a single, safe house in each location and perform the graphic gesture of shaking the village's dust off their feet if they were not received. Luke's version is even stricter, banning not only the staff and tunic but also stopping to greet people on the way.[68] Apart from the radical dependence on the hospitality of the household in which they were to stay, there was also an underlying sense of serious urgency. The Kingdom was coming and there was only time for a brief outreach. The Twelve not only symbolized Jesus's message that God was about to reconstitute Israel in her entirety but also that Jesus's plan was to bring this about quickly with their assistance.

So, who exactly were the members of the Twelve? A list of their names appears four times in the New Testament: in Mark, Matthew, Luke and Acts.[69] In general, the four lists agree on both the individual names and the basic ordering. There are typically three blocks of four names: Simon, Andrew, James and John; Philip, Bartholomew, Matthew and Thomas; James son of Alphaeus, Simon the Cananaean, Thaddeus and Judas Iscariot. Luke's lists have Judas son of James in the place of Thaddeus. While tradition understands these to be the same person, it is also possible that they are two different persons, thus suggesting that one member may have been replaced by another, for some unknown reason, during Jesus's ministry.[70] Similarly, the first gospel changes the name of the tax collector called by Jesus from Levi to Matthew. Again, tradition states that this was the same person with two names, but scholars see this as a device by the first evangelist to ensure that everyone explicitly called by Jesus is included in the Twelve.

In most cases, the canonical gospels provide frustratingly little biographical information about most of the members, although later tradition produced fuller accounts of their personalities and travels. Judas Iscariot is always listed last, which is understandable given that his betrayal of Jesus's whereabouts in Jerusalem directly led to his master's arrest and execution. The shocking fact that the traitor came from within the Twelve has made the name Judas synonymous with treachery and betrayal. His other name, Iscariot, has been the subject of scholarly speculation for some time with no real consensus emerging. The possibilities include fruit-grower, red-dyer, red-haired, hailing from the town of Kerioth or member of the Sicarii (dagger-men). This last item refers to nationalist extremists who assassinated Jews caught collaborating with the Roman authorities. A similar trace of anti-Roman political activism is found in the name of another member of the Twelve: Simon the Cananaean, whom Luke describes as Simon "the Zealot". On one hand, the epithet may refer to Simon's former association with radical Jewish groups that were fiercely opposed to foreign occupation and anyone who cooperated with the regime.[71] On the other hand, Simon's "zealotry" may have been more religious than political, resembling the Pharisees' passionate love of the Torah and their propensity for moral rigor. In either case, Simon would not have felt particularly comfortable with those who colluded with the Roman occupiers such as Matthew (or Levi) the tax-collector.[72]

The same shortage of data hovers over most of the other names. Thomas is best remembered for his initial disbelief that Jesus had risen from the dead – caused by his absence from a resurrection appearance. The result is the common English title "doubting Thomas" for those who display skepticism.[73] Like Thomas, Philip is also more prominent in John's gospel, often being paired with Andrew.[74] Andrew is also linked with his brother Simon as well as the two sons of Zebedee, James and

John, but there are a number of key gospel scenes that feature these three – Simon, James and John – to the exclusion of Andrew.[75]

James, son of Zebedee, was executed by Herod Antipas and should not to be confused with James the brother of the Lord, who was not a member of the Twelve but rose to prominence in the early church.[76] The other son of Zebedee, John, is a more complex identity and is commonly linked to four other New Testament per-sonalities: the anonymous "beloved disciple" of the fourth gospel; the anonymous author of the fourth gospel; the anonymous author of the three Johannine letters of the New Testament; and the author of the book of Revelation who identifies himself as "John". The gospel of Mark states that James and John were fishermen by trade and, with their father, owned a relatively prosperous business in Capernaum, since they had "hired men". Luke adds that they were commercial partners with Simon.[77] Jesus called them "Boanerges" ("Sons of Thunder") – an enigmatic phrase that prob-ably meant hot-tempered, impetuous or loud-voiced.[78] John is described as one of the three "pillars" of the early Church along with James, the brother of the Lord, and the person who is always listed first among the Twelve: Simon, also known as Peter.

Like the sons of Zebedee, Simon and Andrew were Galilean fishermen based in Capernaum. In Mark's and Matthew's gospels, they were the first to be called, abandoning their nets on the spot.[79] In Luke's account, Jesus healed Simon's mother-in-law and, at some point later, he used Simon's boat to preach to the crowds. At the end of his teaching, he asked Simon to put out into the deep where they caught an enormous shoal of fish. Jesus then called an astonished Simon, along with his partners James and John, to become "fishers of men".[80] The gospel of John has another version where Andrew, who had already been directed to Jesus by John the Baptist, then introduced Simon to him. According to John, Jesus instantly renamed him "Cephas", which is Aramaic for rock or crag, and which is translated into Greek as Petros (Peter).[81] Unlike the nickname given to James and John, this one stuck.

The renaming of Simon as Peter is also mentioned in the Synoptic gospels but the timing is not clear in Mark or Luke. In Matthew's gospel, it is linked with one of the most important incidents in Peter's career and possibly the reason for his prominence among the Twelve. All four gospels speak of a striking confession of faith uttered by Peter at some pivotal moment. In the Synoptic version, Jesus explicitly asks his disciples the searching question: "who do you say I am?" and it is Peter who boldly speaks out, identifying him as the Messiah (Christ). In the Markan and Lukan accounts, Jesus neither confirms nor denies the correctness of the answer but warns his disciples not to tell anyone about this.[82] However, Matthew's version contains a much more positive response that includes not only the renaming of Simon but also the conferral of authority that has become a storm center of controversy within Christianity ever since.

> Blessed are you, Simon Bar-Jona. For flesh and blood has not revealed this to you, but my Father who is in heaven. And I tell you, you are Peter, and on this rock I will build my church, and the powers of death shall not prevail against it. I will give you the keys of the kingdom of heaven, and whatever you bind on earth shall be bound in heaven, and whatever you loose on earth shall be loosed in heaven.[83]

There is no time here to venture into the protracted and complex ecclesiological debates about Church authority and the papacy that stem from this passage. Scholars often point out that it is highly unlikely that Jesus would have used the theological term "church" (Greek: ekklesia), which appears nowhere else in the gospels, although he may have used the Hebrew term "qahal", meaning the assembly of Israel in the coming Kingdom. On another occasion, in the same gospel, Jesus conferred the authority to bind and loose on the whole group of disciples and, thus, it is strictly not Peter's privilege alone.[84] The "rock" imagery is a play on Simon's nickname and may refer to the cosmic rock on which the Temple was built and which defended the holy city against the powers of the underworld. The "key" imagery echoes the role of Eliakim, the majordomo of King Hezekiah's palace, who had control over who could or could not enter.[85]

Peter is also singled out in John's gospel as the one who makes a remarkable profession of faith in Jesus at a critical juncture although it is not connected to his renaming. For John, the setting is the synagogue at Capernaum after the miracle of the loaves and fishes. As many of his disciples quit on the pretext that Jesus's teaching was too difficult to accept, it was Peter who declared his undying loyalty: "Lord, to whom shall we go? You have the words of eternal life; and we have believed, and have come to know, that you are the Holy One of God".[86] Furthermore, the Johannine equivalent to Matthew's conferral of special authority on Peter is a moving postresurrection scene where Jesus asks Peter three times if he loves him. As Peter responds in the affirmative each time, the third occasion causing him some grief, Jesus instructs him to feed his lambs, tend his sheep and feed his sheep. He then proceeds to warn Peter of the martyr's fate that he will suffer.[87] The threefold interrogation is usually seen as atonement for Peter's threefold denial of his association with Jesus during the arrest and trial.

It is a sobering fact that not only is the last name on the list of the Twelve linked to betrayal but also the first. Both Judas and Peter failed at critical moments, and they were not alone. The entire group of the Twelve is frequently portrayed in the gospels, especially in Mark, as struggling to understand the full truth of Jesus's identity and message. Jesus's inner circle of a dozen disciples, the group that powerfully symbolized the restoration of the whole of Israel, who had been promised thrones of judgment in the Kingdom, and who were his most intimate companions and fellow missionaries for two or three years, still had a long way to go when their master's life was cut short. Moreover, echoes of Peter's implicit or explicit appointment as the head of the Twelve during Jesus's lifetime are instructive. It highlights the interesting fact that Jesus did not count himself as part of the Twelve. Rather, he stood over and above this symbol of the new Israel, raising questions about his self-understanding and where he fitted into the entire symbolic scheme.[88]

Companions

The beginning of Muhammad's career as prophet and preacher stands in striking contrast to the sudden, spectacular entry of Jesus onto the public stage in Galilee. The initial revelatory experience in the cave on Mount Hira had been traumatic and frightening. The bewildered middle-aged merchant was profoundly shaken, afraid that he was losing his sanity or was a victim of a capricious jinni. It took some time for him to settle down and gain personal assurance that the elusive voice that spoke to him at unpredictable moments was truly God's angelic messenger. There had been a worrying pause in communication but once the messages recommenced and continued over time, Muhammad became convinced of their veracity and the seriousness of his vocation. However, rather than rush headlong into the Meccan spotlight, he began to communicate his experiences with discretion and caution to a small, select group of family and friends.

The initial believers were his wife, Khadija, and his Christian cousin, Waraqa, who died soon after the revelations began. Khadija's support had been critical during the first few months of doubt and confusion and she is usually acknowledged as the first of Muhammad's followers. The circle of discipleship soon expanded to include other members of the household: Baraka, his mother's Abyssinian maid who had stayed with the family; Muhammad's four daughters, Zaynab, Ruqayya, Umm Kulthum and Fatima; his former slave and now adopted son, Zayd ibn Haritha; and his young cousin, Ali, the son of Abu Talib.[89] Ali is identified by Ibn Ishaq as the first male believer and this is seen by Shi'ites as confirmation of his special vocation.[90] Ali's loyalty and courage were proven on many occasions, such as the night he risked his life by sleeping in Muhammad's bed to foil an assassination plot. He also emerged as a powerful warrior in military situations and was nicknamed Asadullah ("Lion of God") by Muhammad.

However, Ali's enthusiastic faith in Muhammad was not shared by all members of the family. Conspicuously, few of the older generation were sympathetic, including Muhammad's uncles. Abu Talib showed no interest at all, although he would remain a faithful protector of his nephew through turbulent times to come. Yet he was concerned that Muhammad seemed to be undermining traditional ancestor-based authority and was worried that it would split the family. Hamza and 'Abbas were indifferent in the early days, although both would eventually convert in their own way. The most negative response came from Abu Lahab, who considered his nephew to be either a fraud or a madman and remained an obdurate opponent to the very end.[91]

Debates have surrounded the identity of the first nonfamily members, but the honor is usually conferred upon Abu Bakr.[92] He was two or three years younger than Muhammad and a prosperous cloth merchant. Known for his unconditional loyalty and nicknamed al-Siddiq ("the truthful one"), he would become Muhammad's closest friend, advisor and deputy, often exerting a moderating influence on major decisions. In the early years, he actively recruited new members for the nascent community and purchased freedom for at least eight slaves, including four women.[93] He was Muhammad's companion on the dangerous migration to Medina, and their relationship was further reinforced when the Prophet married his young daughter 'A'isha.

During the first few years, the group of believers met in each others' homes, gaining instruction from the Prophet as the contents of the new faith were gradually revealed. Apart from the theological principles of monotheism and a revised set of moral norms, one of the distinctive features of the group was a daily prayer ritual that involved ablutions followed by a set of bodily gestures, including standing, bowing and prostrating in unison. Most commentators estimate that there were about 30–40 believers at that time. Although there were no restrictions based on gender, race, religion or clan, the socioeconomic background of the first members is instructive. First, there were young men from influential Meccan families, such as Khalid ibn Sa'id and 'Uthman ibn Affan. Second, there were other men belonging to less aristocratic clans, such as Abu Bakr. The third subset consisted of Meccans who were not Qurayshites by birth but confederates by affiliation and, thus, possessed little social, political and financial influence. This group also included slaves, the most famous of whom was the black Abyssinian, Bilal – a tall, thin man with a stentorian voice.[94] In other words, most of those initially attracted to Muhammad and his message were a mix of persons from lower social classes and the sons and daughters of influential families. Apart from personal religious motivations, they were younger, independent-minded individuals attracted to new ideas and not tied to the Meccan status quo.[95]

The Meccan leadership was another story. Approximately three years after the first revelation, Muhammad was given the signal to move beyond the cohort of his close family and friends and to take his message to the general public. The community finally emerged from its secretive lifestyle. Prayers were held in the vicinity of the Ka'ba and Muhammad began to preach to a broader audience, including the all-important clan chiefs. One tradition relates how Muhammad invited the leaders to Mount Safa, a small hill outside the town, where he asked hypothetically how they would react if armed horsemen were attacking the valley behind them. It was a baf-fling statement from a man considered to be reliable and balanced. Muhammad clarified that there was a real threat – not horsemen but the pending divine punish-ment for all who refused to accept monotheism. Abu Lahab expressed his disdain and walked away in disgust, taking most of the others with him.[96] It was not a good start, but Muhammad was so keen to woo the top layer of Meccan society that, on another occasion, he ignored a blind man's sincere questions because of his preoc-cupation with recruiting a group of tribal elders. Consequently, the Qur'an chastised the Prophet for his misplaced priorities.[97] A similar concern is behind the incident concerning the Satanic Verses, discussed earlier in Chapter 5. A modified theological position that allowed for a popular element of the Meccan religion must have seemed a shrewd strategy to entice the town's leadership into accepting the message. However, the subsequent Qur'anic reprimand reminded Muhammad that the truth should not be altered merely to win more converts, albeit high-ranking, influential ones.

Despite Muhammad's enthusiasm to win over the leadership, his message fell on deaf ears. The initial reaction of the Qurayshite majority was an amused tolerance directed toward what seemed to be a fringe group of harmless visionaries.[98] However, as time passed, cold indifference changed into suspicious concern. On the surface, there was a range of theological objections. Muhammad's claim to be an authentic prophet was questioned and he seemed unable to support his claims with a show of miraculous power. Moreover, a supercilious Meccan aristocracy could not believe that a genuinely divine message would be entrusted to someone like Muhammad and be accepted first by commoners.[99] There were also certain aspects of Muhammad's message that were foreign and repugnant. The concept of the resurrection of the body was singled out for particular derision. The idea of prostrating before Allah was diametrically opposed to the Meccan sense of self-importance and independence. The confirmation that all polytheists, including their ancestors, were in Hell was downright inflammatory. Yet behind the theological issues, there were also serious economic and political ramifications, which would make acceptance of the new faith a very costly one for those in power. First, the demotion of the tribal gods to mere creaturely spirits under the one supreme deity could spell disaster for the lucrative pilgrimage industry centered on the Ka'ba with its multiple statuettes. Second, the chiefs could see far-reaching political problems for themselves arising out of Muhammad's claim to speak for God. Where would the line be drawn between earthly and heavenly authorities?[100]

The consequence of such considerations was not totally unexpected: a deliberate campaign of ridicule and harassment that placed enormous pressure on the fledgling community. There was antagonistic mockery, verbal insults and threats of physical violence that were occasionally carried out. The key persecutors were Abu Lahab and Abu Jahl.[101] The extent of the persecution was limited by Arabia's entrenched tribal law, which guaranteed the protection of any member of the clan. Thus, even though Abu Talib did not convert, he continued to afford his nephew the full protection of the Banu Hashim. Yet the situation was still serious enough to warrant sending a group of believers in 615 CE to seek safe haven in Abyssinia. It was only a small band of emigrants – perhaps a dozen men and four women[102] – but the choice of destination is fascinating given that Abyssinia was a Christian kingdom. The first exiles probably stayed about three months and then returned home when they heard rumors that the Quraysh were thinking of converting. When they discovered that the situation was unchanged, a second group of about 100 persons returned to Abyssinia.[103]

Fortunes improved for the community in 616 CE with two unexpected conversions. Hamza, Muhammad's strong, quick-tempered uncle, had shown little interest in his nephew's preaching until one day, upon returning from a hunting trip, he discovered that Abu Jahl had personally insulted Muhammad. Incensed, he struck Abu Jahl with his bow and converted on the spot.[104] The second conversion had much greater significance in terms of outstanding leadership potential. 'Umar ibn al-Khattab was in his early thirties at the time. Like Hamza, he was prone to anger but he also possessed an iron will, extraordinary energy and a commanding presence. He had been a vowed enemy of this dangerous new development within Meccan society. When he discovered that his sister, Fatima, and her husband, Sa'id, had joined Muhammad's community, his rage exploded. He raced home and struck his frightened sister who had feigned ignorance. A remorseful 'Umar then settled down and demanded to know what the "noise" was that he had heard them reciting. When they began to read the Qur'an to him, 'Umar was overwhelmed at the beauty of the sacred text. He sheathed his sword and officially converted. Such an extraordinary pendulum swing has been likened to the conversion of Saint Paul in Christianity – another fanatical enemy of the faith who experienced a complete volte-face to become one of its most passionate champions.[105] Despite the risks, 'Umar would brazenly pray at the Ka'ba and, at the time of the Hijra, he audaciously migrated to Medina in broad daylight rather than under cover of darkness. Along with Abu Bakr, Zayd and Khalid ibn Sa'id, 'Umar quickly joined the inner circle of key advisors to Muhammad. As he had done with Abu Bakr, Muhammad later consolidated his relationship with 'Umar by marrying his widowed daughter Hafsa. The addition of Hamza and 'Umar gave the group of believers a greater sense of confidence. They began to call themselves "mu'min" ("the faithful"), but in time the preferred self-designation was "Muslim" ("one who has surrendered to God").[106]

The situation took a turn for the worse in 617 CE, when the Meccan leadership imposed a boycott on all members of the Banu Hashim and their allies, the Banu Muttalib – the clans to which most converts belonged.[107] Meccans were forbidden to marry the Muslims or to carry out commercial transactions with them. The clan members retreated to the valley on the eastern side of the town. The supply of food was almost completely halted although provisions were smuggled in. After two years, the ban was lifted, partially because some realized that the exclusion of the Hashim was playing into the political aspirations of the Shams and Makhzum clans. Moreover, the boycott tended to draw attention to the Muslims and inadvertently generate more interest and sympathy.

Unfortunately, the good news of the lifting of the boycott was countered by tragedy in 619 CE, otherwise known as the Year of Sorrow. Without warning, Abu Talib and Khadija died within a few days of each other.[108] Muhammad was deeply affected by both deaths. His marriage to Khadija had been monogamous throughout. Although his senior in years, she was an indispensable part of Muhammad's personal life and the first to believe in his divine calling. If the loss of Khadija was a difficult psychological blow, the death of Abu Talib was a deadly political setback. As clan leader, Abu Talib had afforded crucial protection but when the clan leadership passed to Abu Lahab, Muhammad suddenly found himself exposed to grave danger. Without Abu Talib's backing, he could be assaulted or killed with impunity. Abu Lahab may have shown some initial sympathy, but when his nephew resolutely confirmed that Abu Talib, who had died a pagan, and all other polytheists were indeed in Hell, he withdrew his support. Thus, the insults and assaults recommenced and Muhammad began to realize that he and his small community of faithful could not remain in Mecca.

So Muhammad began to seek possible havens for his endangered community but to no avail. Overtures to other towns, such as Ta'if, failed to find a sympathetic ear as he and Zayd were pelted with rocks and evicted.[109] He later reminisced that this was the lowest point in his career. The situation was looking more and more desperate until an extraordinarily providential opportunity opened up for him and his followers. In the summer of 620 CE, six pilgrims from Yathrib, a rich oasis about 240 mi north of Mecca, were in town and happened to meet Muhammad whose habit was to strike up conversations with visitors. They had heard rumors of a prophet in Mecca who had received revelations from the one God and who had been a victim of unremitting Qurayshite persecution. However, their interest in Muhammad was not merely his religious claims. Yathrib was a community torn asunder by internecine feuds. The two dominant tribes, the Aws and the Khazraj, had been locked for years in a bitter conflict that was undermining the public peace and the local economy. They were looking for a neutral outsider with the diplomatic ability to arbitrate between disputing parties and broker a lasting peace. In their eyes,

Muhammad's reputation and credentials met the job description. It would be a win–win situation. On the one hand, Muhammad and his followers could practice their religion in Yathrib free of harassment and discrimination. On the other hand, all disputes would be referred to Muhammad for settlement and the spiral of tribal violence would hopefully end.

The offer must have seemed like a dream come true for Muhammad and the six visitors promised to further the discussions when they went home. The following summer, five of them returned to Mecca with another seven citizens of Yathrib and met Muhammad at 'Aqaba. The discussions went well and Muhammad sent Mus'ab ibn Umayr back with them in order to teach the details of the new religion to those who were converting in Yathrib. The community of Muslims now had a foothold in a second Arabian town and it would prove to be one of the most decisive developments in its history. A third meeting occurred in secrecy during the summer of 622 CE, again at 'Aqaba. Seventy-five converts and representatives from Yathrib attended, including two women. Muhammad's uncle 'Abbas, who was still a polytheist, accompanied his nephew for fear that the clandestine deal would be discovered by the Quraysh. The resultant Second Oath of 'Aqaba stated that Muhammad and his followers would be protected if they moved to Yathrib. Twelve delegates (nine from the Khazraj and three from the Aws) were appointed to supervise the pact. The deal had been struck. All that was left now was to organize the relocation.[110] After a decade of opposition and suffering it must have seemed that Allah was opening up a wonderful future in a new home where the faith could flourish and grow. Yet the price was a hefty one. The followers would have to leave behind their homes, their properties, their kinsmen – in short their entire past – and live among strangers who, apparently, shared their commitment to the Prophet and his vision.

From July to September in 622 CE, about 70 Muslim families migrated to Yathrib in small, discreet groups. Apart from Ali, Muhammad and Abu Bakr were the last to leave and after ten days of travelling, they arrived exhausted at Quba' on the outskirts of Yathrib. Tradition states that it was 12 Rabi al-awwal (24 September) 622 CE. The year is significant because it was later chosen as the first year of a new Islamic calendar. Time would now be counted from the migration from Mecca to Yathrib: the Year of the Hijra. It was not just a change of address but a foundational moment and a new beginning, akin to the Exodus of the Israelites from Egypt. The powerful sense that a new chapter was commencing is also captured in the subsequent renaming of Yathrib to al-Madina al-Nabi (the town of the Prophet), which is usually abbreviated as Medina.

Muhammad decided that Allah should choose the site of his new residence and, thus, he allowed his camel to wander through the town until it stopped at a vacant lot owned by two orphaned brothers. Muhammad insisted on purchasing the land rather than receive it as a gift, and construction started on his home, which functioned not only as a space for public prayer and sermons, but also meetings, social gatherings, appointments, tending the sick and a range of other activities. It was truly the centre of community life for the believers. Within that community there were now two distinct groups: the exiles from Mecca (muhajirun) and the new converts from Medina who were named "helpers" (ansar). Most of the migrants were economically poor since they had been forced to leave behind much of their property and assets.

Thus, a brotherhood system was set up whereby each migrant was assigned to a helper for assistance, including employment.[111] However, there were problems since most of the migrants had little experience in agriculture, the main source of income in Medina, and, thus, many were forced to perform menial tasks initially although eventually they established commercial businesses.

As time passed and Muhammad confirmed his mediation skills in the eyes of the population, more and more polytheistic Arabs converted, especially members of weaker clans who had suffered under the bellicose main tribes. Apart from genuine religious reasons, the situation was now more conducive as well. In Mecca, where the believers were a persecuted minority, conversion was hardly an attractive option. In Medina, where the Prophet enjoyed growing religious and political authority, and where social momentum was in favor of the new faith, conversion had its benefits. Among the converts were those whom the Qur'an describes as hypocrites (munafiqun), feigning belief in the public eye for more selfish, ulterior motives.[112] The most notorious was 'Abdallah ibn Ubayy, a Khazraj clan leader, who was poised to take control over the town had Muhammad not appeared on the scene. He and his clan overtly became Muslim but there was a simmering resentment just below the surface.[113]

The burning theological issue that arose in Medina was the nature of the relationship between the believers and the Jews. In contrast to the low numbers in Mecca, the Jewish community in Medina was a considerable size and wielded much greater influence. There were three main Jewish tribes – Qurayza, Nadir and Qaynuqa – and all were Arabic in language and custom. The Jews had sided with the Aws tribe to defeat the Khazraj in 617 CE. Despite their earlier, cool attitude toward Muhammad from a distance, he hoped that the Jews of Medina would accept him as true prophet of the one God, now that he was in their midst. In this context, Muhammad adopted a number of features that were aimed at attracting Jewish interest. The tenth day of the first month, known as 'Ashura (tenth), was set aside as a 24-hour fast in imitation of the Jewish Yom Kippur.[114] Men were obliged to attend a communal prayer and sermon at noon on Fridays, the day before the Sabbath. The original direction of prayer (qibla) was set toward Jerusalem, and Muslims were allowed to eat Jewish food and marry Jewish (and Christian) women.

However, like the Quraysh in Mecca, the Jews of Medina were not convinced and very few joined the Muslim community.[115] As with the Meccans, it was probably a mix of theological and political obstacles. On the theological side, the Jews simply did not believe that Muhammad was a prophet of the one, true God in the same line as Noah, Abraham, Moses, Elijah and other key figures. Moreover, for Jewish intellectuals, the Qur'an distorted the biblical stories and contained errors and anachronisms. On the political side, some Jews were concerned that if the Aws and Khazraj rivalries were overcome, then the Jewish minority would be rendered more vulnerable.[116] The rejection of his religious claims led Muhammad to revise his original plans, which included hopes for the large-scale conversion of the Jews. They would still remain fellow monotheists and thus, along with Christians, formed the People of the Book. But they had declined to be an integral part of his community of faith.

The response to this disappointing development was reflected at both the theoretical and practical levels. The Qur'an began to focus on the primogenitor of the Jews, Abraham, recasting him as the first true Muslim rather than the first Jew.

Muhammad's role was not to create a new religion but to restore the original mono-theistic faith of Abraham, who predated both the Torah and the Gospel. Abraham's firstborn son, Ishmael, considered to be the ancestor of the Arabic peoples, was also given more prominence in Qur'anic messages. Ishmael helped Abraham rebuild the Ka'ba in Mecca; he is listed with Abraham as a patriarch who received revelations; and Islamic tradition claims that it was Ishmael, and not Isaac, whom Abraham was about to sacrifice in response to God's command.[117] Moreover, the Jewish accusation that Muhammad had distorted the truth of their scriptures was turned around. It was the Torah that was incomplete, containing only a portion of the heavenly book, which is most perfectly captured in the Qur'an.[118] On the practical level, the fast day of 'Ashura, whose timing was based on the Jewish holy day of Yom Kippur, was superseded by a new fasting practice that was set during Ramadan, the ninth month of the year. Moreover, the Muslims were required to avoid pork, blood and carrion but not the complete set of kosher laws that were imposed on Israel as punishment for their sinfulness.[119]

Perhaps the most striking symptom of the shift away from Judaism, was the deci-sion to change the qibla from the Temple site in Jerusalem to the Ka'ba in Mecca.[120] The connection with Abraham was maintained since it was thought that he had rebuilt the Ka'ba, but the 180-degree turn implied that the spiritual focal point of the young Muslim community was not in the distant land of Israel but right at home in Arabia. It implied that the greatest potential for expansion of members was not the conversion of the monotheistic Jews but the conversion of the polytheistic Arabs. It implied that Muhammad's movement was not a strange sect of Judaism, but an independent Arabian religion, with its own prophet, its own scripture, its own evolv-ing set of rules, its own character and its own God-given destiny.[121] The Hijra had taken the followers from Mecca to Medina, providing safe haven for a persecuted minority and the opportunity for significant consolidation and growth. The change of the qibla just two years later reflected the sad resignation that, although they shared many similar beliefs and practices, most Jews were not going to join this new com-munity of Arabian monotheists who placed their faith in God and his Prophet above deeply engrained tribal loyalties. It also underlined the ongoing relevance of the sacred shrine back in Mecca – a shrine still under polytheistic control but one that remained a vital piece in Muhammad's longer-term plans.

Observations

This chapter has concentrated on those who committed themselves to the Buddha, Jesus or Muhammad during their lifetimes and, thus, formed the foundational com-munity of faith within each tradition. As the first generation of believers, they played a critical role in the original establishment and eventual success of three major world religions. Once again, it is possible to discern areas of intersection and difference between each story. Looking first at the manner in which each founder entered the public sphere and began to gather followers around him, there is a distinct element of hesitation in the case of the Buddha. This reluctance stemmed from his honest concern that others would not be capable of comprehending the dhamma, thus rendering the entire exercise of instructing pupils futile. However, as a result of inner compassion and some external prompting by the Hindu deities, the Buddha decided to share his truth with others. There is a similar reluctance on the part of Muhammad to preach openly in Mecca, but this is not based on any apprehension about the intellectual capacity of the audience. The initial obstacle was Muhammad's fears that the Qur'anic voice may have been a jinni or his own imagination. Even when he gained confidence in the authenticity of his calling, helped by the vital support of Khadija, he still exercised prudent caution in a potentially hostile Meccan environment and confided only in a small circle of trustworthy family and friends for the first three years. In complete contrast to the Buddha's ambivalence and Muhammad's wariness, Jesus's entrance onto the public stage verges on the sensational. He burst onto the Galilean scene as miraculous healer and quickly captured the attention of large crowds who thronged to see this new religious celebrity.

The identity of the first followers was determined by a number of key factors in each case. Once the Buddha had decided to teach, his first instinct was to find potential listeners who could cope with his message. The natural choice was his former ascetical colleagues who had shared with him a similar quest for higher truth, and it is they who were the recipients of the First Sermon. As a result, all five committed themselves to the Buddha but some were quicker than others at grasping the truth. Even then it was only the first stage (stream enterer) of a longer process that led to full arhantship. The Buddha's preference for veteran ascetics as his main target audience continued with the mass conversion of the Kassapa brothers and their communities, but there were also conversions that arose out of chance meetings, such as Yasa and the 30 wealthy youths. Not all of these conversations were successful, such as the encounter with Upaka, who declined and went on his way. When a person did accept the dhamma, the next step was typically an explicit invitation by the Buddha to join his company with the words "Come, monk". There was also the domino effect in which a new convert brought along colleagues as fresh recruits, such as the friends of Yasa.

The crowds who thronged to witness Jesus were hardly followers in any real sense since they were motivated more by curiosity than commitment. Yet many among them were moved by his message and were beneficiaries of his healing powers, such as Bartimaeus and Mary Magdalene. Thus, an undefined group of sympathizers began to form as Jesus moved around Galilee but there was also a more defined group of individuals who were singled out by Jesus and issued the unusual invitation: "Follow me". This style of recruitment was unheard of in rabbinical schools and is more reminiscent of Elijah's call of his pupil Elisha. It echoes the imperative in the Buddha's invitation but places greater emphasis on the founder himself rather than just the teaching. As with Upaka, this invitation was not always heeded such as the case of the rich, young man but in the Synoptic tradition Jesus gains his first four disciples in this manner. However, there is also evidence that some of his earliest followers were already associated with him from his time with John the Baptist or were recruited by existing disciples such as Andrew and Philip, in a manner similar to Yasa and his friends.

In contrast to the Buddha's and Jesus's first disciples, who were a mix of former spiritual colleagues and strangers that they encountered on the road, Muhammad's earliest followers were close family members and friends in his hometown. His wife, Khadija, his four daughters, his young cousin, Ali, his freed slave, Zayd, his friend, Abu Bakr, and others comprised an intimate, semi-clandestine circle around him for several years. Unlike Buddhism and Christianity, the seed of Islam was first germinated with gentle feelers and measured instruction behind closed doors. In time, the group began to attract interest from the broader community and, similar to Yasa, Andrew and Philip, there was recruitment by the recruited, especially Abu Bakr who was responsible for discreetly bringing many fellow Meccans to the faith. Muhammad issued no call to come forth and be ordained, and no explicit command to "follow" him. Yet like the Buddha and Jesus, he also inspired deep, lifelong commitments on the part of those first believers.

In terms of demographic background and membership criteria, all three groups of disciples are characterized by broad inclusiveness. The Buddha's first converts were veteran ascetics already well advanced in the spiritual quest but there were also many restless sons of wealthy families who, like the Buddha himself years earlier, felt the superficiality of their lifestyles. Hindu cultural considerations should have meant restrictions concerning caste, life stage and gender, but the early stories suggest that these factors were of little relevance. The low caste convert Upali was accepted and promoted before princely co-novices; candidates as young as 20 years old were admitted to ordination; and an order of nuns, parallel to the monks, was established early on as a result of the insistence of Mahapajapati and Ananda, even though the Buddha had his own personal reservations. While there were some categories that precluded entry, such as criminal record or physical disability, just about anyone could join. Moreover, such an open admissions policy to the monastic order was complemented by the "skilful means" pedagogical policy that acknowledged different levels of understanding and tailored instructions accordingly.

In similar fashion, Jesus offered his good news to whoever had ears to hear, although it was particularly attractive to those who found themselves on the wrong side of the religious law and were in serious need of divine mercy. Like the Buddha, Jesus's down-to-earth teaching style based on commonplace parables, made his message accessible to all. Moreover, he gladly enjoyed table fellowship with all levels on the socio-religious ladder: wealthy and poor; righteous and sinful. The highly symbolic act of setting aside twelve male disciples also represents an agenda of restoring all, and not just some, of the twelve ancient tribes of Israel. Even the heterogeneous membership of the Twelve, which included commercial fishermen, a tax collector and a religious zealot, reflects a broad, inclusive vision. Although the gospels do not record the explicit calling of a female disciple, women, both named and unnamed, were among his itinerant entourage, as well as those who offered him hospitality in their homes.

Strikingly, it is a woman who enjoys the honor of being the first to believe in Muhammad's message. His wife Khadija was soon joined by other females from the household, including the Prophet's daughters and his late mother's servant. As with the Buddha, many of the earliest converts were young persons from influential families who had become disenchanted with Meccan social values and were seeking a new vision for the future. Others were from lower socioeconomic backgrounds, including a number of slaves who gained their freedom within the new movement. As with the

Buddha and Jesus, Muhammad's religious community was neither elitist nor exclusiv-ist: all genders, all ages, all incomes and all tribes were welcome to join.

While many of Muhammad's family members accepted his message at an early stage, not all did, including several important uncles. There was Hamza who took considerable time to be convinced; there was Abu Talib who continued to offer Muhammad protection but expressed serious concern at his actions and died a pagan; and there was Abu Lahab, who vehemently opposed Muhammad to the bitter end. Such family division was the price of the new religious faith, which placed fidelity to God and his Prophet above the deeply entrenched loyalty to clan. Similar tensions occurred in the story of Jesus and the Buddha. Jesus's family diagnosed him as insane and came to collect him in order to end their public embarrassment. While his mother, Mary, and brother, James, eventually emerge as leading members of the early Christian community, the memory persisted that Jesus's relatives did not believe in him and he was not accepted in his hometown. Like Muhammad, Jesus's experience echoes his teaching that the price of discipleship can include loss of family harmony. Jesus had brought a sword that split families down the middle. Moreover, his true mother, brothers and sisters were those who accepted his teaching and committed themselves to his cause. Once again, faith in the founder takes priority even over the sacrosanct obligations to kin. Similarly, the Buddha had already severed ties with his family on the night that he left the palace for the forest. However, the tradition recalls his return to Kapilavatthu and the poignant declaration to his father that his lineage was no longer that of Sakyan royalty but the line of the Buddhas. Furthermore, when his son, Rahula, requested his inheritance, the Buddha offered him the dhamma. The pain was lessened when, according to the stories, most of the Buddha's family con-verted, including his father, stepmother, son and most of his cousins. Yet the same underlying principle appears again: faith is thicker than blood.

In some cases, opposition came not only from family circles. Jesus warned his followers that the price of discipleship would be suffering and death. The imagery used was often graphic: drinking his cup, sharing his baptism, carrying one's cross, losing one's life. Although none of this occurred during his public ministry, Jesus's terrible predictions came true in his own case, and the first generations of Christians would have to endure three hundred years of sporadic persecution and martyrdom. The situation was quite the reverse in the case of Muhammad and his followers. They underwent systematic discrimination, harassment and maltreatment for over 10 years, including some cases of martyrdom, exile in Abyssinia and a prolonged boycott. It was only the Hijra that turned the tide and opened up a safe haven for the victimized and beleaguered faithful in Medina. By the time of Muhammad's death, Islam had become the unifying faith of the region, and the Islamic community ('umma) had grown to include most of the Arabian tribes. Just over one hundred years later, it had become a world empire. In contrast, the Buddha and his first fol-lowers managed to avoid serious involvement in the political scene, and the main opposition to his movement came not from kings or rulers but from rival religious groups in the fierce competition for souls.

Although all three religious traditions eventually reached global status, it is difficult to know precisely how far each founder imagined that their newly established faith communities would stretch in geographic terms. The Buddha limited his travels to the Ganges Plain but there is no explicit statement that the missionary monks who carried his message were to confine themselves to northern India or the Hindu sphere of influence. Of its very nature, the dhamma was for everyone and, thus, the sangha was potentially universal. In contrast, Jesus implied a number of times that his sole focus was his fellow Jews and the institution of the Twelve and their missionary mandate reflects this quite defined scope. He restricted his movements more or less to Israel, crossing over into pagan borderlands on a few exceptional occasions, although he did not refuse healing to non-Jews when they asked. The extraordinary Christian missionary thrust into the Gentile communities of the Roman Empire was something that only occurred after his death. Like Jesus, Muhammad's initial mission was essentially focused on his native cultural group: the polytheists of Mecca. However, the Hijra drastically broadened those horizons. Unlike Jesus, who took little interest in the pagan world beyond his Jewish context, Muhammad firstly extended a missionary interest in his fellow monotheists, the Jewish minority in Arabia. However it soon became crystal clear that they would not accept him as a genuine prophet, and the subsequent shift in focus is aptly symbolized by the changing of the qibla from the Temple in Jerusalem to the Ka'ba in Mecca. With or without the Jews, and as a result of historical circumstances, the recruitment of new converts quickly extended beyond Mecca and Medina to embrace all of Arabia and, in time, even further afield.

In all three cases, following the founder entailed not only a change in worldview, but also a change in practical lifestyle. The most serious disciples of the Buddha shaved their heads, donned simple robes and assumed a celibate, itinerant way of life. For most of the year, this meant travelling from village to village, either alone or in pairs, and teaching the dhamma to whoever showed interest. During the monsoons, monks and nuns would remain in their residences and use the wet season as a time of spiritual retreat and renewal. The monks lived according to the 10 precepts and carried with them just five basic possessions. It was a life of radical detachment and, in time, over 200 regulations, adding structure to the underlying values, were defined and collected in the Vinaya Pitaka (Basket of Discipline). Accepting Jesus's call to become his disciple involved a very similar commitment. As "fishers of men", they left home, family and career to join him on a circuit of towns and villages around Israel. Like the Buddha's monks, the disciples were also sent out to extend Jesus's work of teaching and healing. The missionaries were instructed to travel in pairs and to carry minimal provisions. It was a brief, urgent outreach with no clearly defined end, except the unpredictable coming of the Kingdom itself.

In stark contrast, joining Muhammad's circle of faith did not require radical abandonment of home, marriage or career, although the Hijra effectively meant that most Meccan believers had to forsake their native city, their tribal affiliation and their property. There were no priestly or monastic ordinations and, thus, no two-layered structures like the Buddhist monks–laity relationship or the Twelve within the larger group of disciples. Yet they were differentiated from their pagan neighbors by a set of rules and practices that were gradually revealed to Muhammad. The five "pillars" of Islam all date back to his lifetime: the declaration of the one God and his Prophet (shahada); the five daily prayers (salat); the annual monetary donation for the poor (zakat); the annual fast during Ramadan (sawm); and the pilgrimage to Mecca (hajj).

There were also food laws (including a total ban on alcohol), clothing restrictions (especially on women), rules regarding marriage and divorce, and so on. The Muslim community was essentially a group of dedicated laity gathered around their prophet leader.

There was also an important network of ordinary folk who provided much needed support for the Buddha's bhikkhus and Jesus's Twelve. While he was still enjoying the bliss of enlightenment, the Buddha was offered food by two strangers who are considered to be the first lay disciples. As the monks grew in number, more and more laity would donate material goods such as food, clothing, money and even land in return for spiritual goods such as wisdom and positive karma. The term 'bhikkhu' itself means beggar, and the daily alms routine epitomizes the symbiotic relationship between the two groups. Jesus and his fellow wanderers also benefited from the generosity of a group of disciples who did not take to the road but stayed and home, opening their doors in hospitality. There was also a group of women who travelled about with Jesus and his entourage, caring for them out of their own resources.

Finally, in all three cases, there is an inner circle of followers who are granted greater access to the founder, which brought with it a certain degree of privilege and authority. Tradition identifies Sariputta and Moggallana as the two "great" disciples who may have succeeded the Buddha as leaders had they not died before him. They head the traditional list of the ten most esteemed monks, several of whom assumed key roles at the First Council, including Maha-Kassapa, Ananda and Upali. The Twelve play a highly symbolic role at the centre of Jesus's group of disciples, sharing in his mission and being promised seats of judgment in the Kingdom. Among the Twelve, there was a smaller, intimate core of three disciples (Simon, James and John) who alone were invited to be present at certain key moments in Jesus's life. Among them, Simon emerges as the natural spokesperson for the entire group. Renamed Peter (rock) by Jesus, he was given some sort of leadership role among the Twelve, probably as a result of a notable confession of faith that he made at some point. To an even greater extent than the Buddha or Jesus, Muhammad often sought the confidence and advice of his closest companions, such as Abu Bakr, 'Umar, Khalid, Uthman and Ali. Although there was no questioning the Qur'anic revelations, these men provided him with valuable guidance at critical moments of decision-making. Moreover, it was not only men who provided Muhammad with wise counsel; the Prophet often discussed issues with a group of female disciples who shared a special type of intimate, personal relationship with him: his wives.

Notes

1 Mahavagga 1.4.1–5.
2 Mahavagga 1.15.3–13; Lalitavistara (Foucaux) 365–366; Buddhacarita XIV.98.
3 Mahavagga 1.6.7–9.
4 Nakamura I 242. See Mahavagga 1.6.10; Mahavastu (Jones) III 311, 323.
5 The four stages to liberation are stream-enterer, once-returner, nonreturner and arhant.
6 Mahavagga 1.6.32.
7 Mahavagga 1.7–8.
8 Mahavagga 1.9.

9   Mahavagga 1.15–20.
10 Foucher 161.
11 Nakamura I 319–327.
12 Nakamura I 326; Foucher 164–170.
13 The other five key disciples are Upali, Subhuti, Rahula, Mahakaccana and Punna.
14 Armstrong, Buddha 110; Blomfield 177–179.
15 Mahavagga 1.54; Nakamura I 339–343; Foucher 175–176.
16 Mahavagga 1.54.2.
17 Foucher 171.
18 Nakamura I 331; Foucher 178; Cullavagga 7.1.4.
19 Mahavagga 1.54.5.
20 There was also a general sense of annoyance that the movement was stealing away the flower of Kapilavatthu's youth and, thus, creating serious social disruption. Foucher 171; Mizuno 99.
21 Mahavagga 1.8.3.
22 Khandhaka 23; Cullavagga 10.1.
23 Mahavagga 1.12.3.
24 Foucher 184.
25 Digha Nikaya 1; Mahavagga 1.56.1. Another version has only eight precepts, effectively combining numbers 7 and 8 and ignoring 10: Anguttara Nikaya 8.41.
26 Nakamura I 270; Cohen 178; Armstrong, Buddha 127; Blomfield 204–206.
27 Armstrong, Buddha 118, footnote 13; Blomfield 204–205.
28 Samyutta Nikaya 10.8; Cullavagga 6.4.1–4; Nakamura I 345–352; Foucher 179.
29 Thomas 97, footnote 1. For traditional lists of where the Buddha spent each rainy season see Nakamura I 270–276.
30 Cohen 150–151.
31 Mark 2:4; 3:9, 20; 4:1; 5:24, 31; 6:34, 44.
32 Antiquities 18.3.3.
33 John 6:66; Meier III 21.
34 The Aramaic equivalent "talmida" appears as a technical term for the followers of a particular rabbi only from the second century CE. The arrangement was like joining a new family since the pupil would typically eat, sleep and travel with the rabbi. Meier III 48.
35 Meier III 42.
36 Prominent examples included the Pythagoreans, Platonists, Aristotelians, Epicureans, Stoics, the Qumran community, the house of Hillel and the school of Philo. Meier III 47.
37 Mark 1:16–20.
38 Mark 10:17–22.
39 Mark 5:18–20.
40 John 1:35–51; Meier III 51.
41 1 Kings 19:19–21.
42 Luke 9:59–62; Matthew 8:21–22; McClymond 412.
43 McClymond 409.
44 Matthew 8:20; Luke 9:58.
45 Mark 2:13–15; Luke 19:1–10; Mark 14:3–9; Luke 7:36–50; John 12:1–8; 11:1–45; Luke 10:38–42; Mark 14:13–16.
46 Luke 11:37–53; Luke 14:1–24.
47 Mark 2:15–17.
48 Mark 8:35; Luke 17:33; Matthew 10:39; John 12:25.

49   Mark 8:34–36. Luke's version adds two images strongly suggesting that potential disciples consider the cost beforehand, such as a tower builder or a king facing battle: Luke 14: 28–33.
50   Mark 10:28–30; Matthew 19:29–30.
51   Luke 12:51–53. Matthew's version refers to a sword that symbolizes the deep familial ruptures expected at the end of days: Matthew 10:34–39.
52   Luke 14:26; Matthew 10:37.
53   John 7:5.
54   Mark 3:21.
55   Mark 3:31–35; Matthew 12:46–50; Luke 8:19–21.
56   Meier III 73–75.
57   Luke 8:1–3; Mark 15:40–41.
58   Acts 1:15–26; 12:2; Revelation 21:14.
59   The link is complex since the twelve tribal territories within Israel include Ephraim and Manasseh, two grandsons of Jacob via his son Joseph (who is not listed). The number twelve is maintained since the tribe of Levi was not allocated land on the basis of its priestly role.
60   Micah 2:12; Isaiah 11:10–16; Jeremiah 31:1–14; Baruch 4:21–5:9; Sirach 36:1–17; 2 Maccabees 1:24–29; Psalms of Solomon 11:2–7; 17:26–32; Qumran War Scroll and Temple Scroll 1QM 2:1–3; 1QM 3:13–14. See Meier III 137.
61   Meier III 137, 141; Luke 22:28–30; Matthew 19:27–30.
62   Mark 5:1–20; 7:24–30. See also the cure of the centurion's son in Matthew 8:5–13; Luke 7:1–10.
63   Matthew 15:24.
64   1 Corinthians 15:7–11; Romans 16:7; Galatians 1:17, 2:8; 1 Corinthians 9:1–2, 15:9.
65   Mark 3:14–15.
66   Mark 3:15; Matthew 10:1; Luke 9:1.
67   Mark 6:6–12; Matthew 10:5–15.
68   Luke 9:1–6.
69   Mark 3:16–19; Matthew 10:2–4; Luke 6:14–16; Acts 1:13. The gospel of John mentions the Twelve on a number of occasions but never names the members and often focuses on other key disciples such as Nathanael, Lazarus and the anonymous 'beloved disciple'.
70   Meier III 131.
71   Meier III 205–208.
72   Mark 2:14. James and Levi are both described as sons of Alphaeus and may have been brothers.
73   John 11:16; 20:24; 21:2.
74   John 1:35–44. Andrew and Philip are the only members that have Greek names.
75   Mark 5:37; 9:2; 14:33.
76   Acts 12:2.
77   Mark 1:18–20; Luke 5:10.
78   Mark 3:17; Mark 9:38; Luke 9:52–56; Mark 10:35–40.
79   Mark 1:16–20; Matthew 4:18–22.
80   Luke 5:1–11. The term "fishers of men" is not used elsewhere in the Jewish scriptures but does appear in Greco-Roman writing where it has the negative connotation of gods snaring men for play. Jesus's positive use is probably original. See Meier III 160–162.
81   John 1:40–42.
82   Mark 8:29–30; Luke 9:20–22.
83   Matthew 16:17–19. Peter also walks on water in Matthew 14:28–32.

84   Matthew 18:18.

85   Isaiah 22:20–25; Meier III 230–231.

86   John 6:67–69.

87   John 21:15–19.

88   Meier III 250.

89   Emerick 63–64; Rodinson 98–99; Peterson 63; Ramadan 37.

90   Ibn Ishaq (Guillaume) 114; Shi'ites believe that Muhammad declared Ali to be his "brother, inheritor and vice-regent". They also believe that Muhammad designated Ali as his successor at Ghadir al-Khumm on the return journey from his final pilgrimage to Mecca.

91   Qur'an 111:1–5.

92   Ibn Ishaq (Guillaume) 114–115.

93   Ibn Ishaq (Guillaume) 115–117.

94   Rodinson 100; Emerick 63; Peterson 63; Armstrong, Muhammad 53.

95   Rodinson 102; Peterson 65.

96   Armstrong, Muhammad 65; Rodinson 102; Peterson 65; Emerick 67.

97   Qur'an 80:1–12.

98   Rodinson 102.

99   Qur'an 6:52–53.

100   Rodinson 104–105.

101   Ibn Ishaq (Guillaume) 145. On one occasion the slave Bilal was pinned down in the scorching noonday sun by a huge rock placed on his chest. The incident prompted Abu Bakr to purchase his freedom and organize the emancipation of other slaves within the faith community. Rodinson 110.

102   Ibn Ishaq (Guillaume) 146–155; Rodinson 116.

103   Ibn Hisham relates how the Negus was moved by the 19th chapter of the Qur'an, which speaks of the mother of Jesus, and concluded that this new religion was essentially consistent with Christianity. Rodinson 113–114.

104   Ibn Ishaq (Guillaume) 131–132.

105   Ibn Ishaq (Guillaume) 155–159; Armstrong, Muhammad 82; Emerick 84.

106   Rodinson 129.

107   Ibn Ishaq (Guillaume) 159.

108   Ibn Ishaq (Guillaume) 191.

109   Ibn Ishaq (Guillaume) 192; Emerick 94; Rodinson 138.

110   Ibn Ishaq (Guillaume) 197–212; Ramadan 75; Rodinson 144.

111   Qur'an 9:100; Ibn Ishaq (Guillaume) 234.

112   Qur'an 9:101.

113   Armstrong, Muhammad 119; Ramadan 91; Emerick 131.

114   Welch 367–369; Bukhari 31.222; 60.202.

115   Rodinson 185. One important convert was the rabbi 'Abdullah ibn Salam.

116   Rodinson 160.

117   Qur'an 2:127–129; 37:100–107. See also Genesis 17:20–21; 25:12–18; Judith 2:23.

118   Qur'an 4:44; 3:23; 10:37.

119   Qur'an 4:160.

120   The Qur'an does not contain an explicit command to change the qibla but there are verses that record advice to Muhammad on how to deal with reactions to the decision. See Qur'an 2:142–145. Ibn Ishaq mentions it in passing: Ibn Ishaq (Guillaume) 289.

121   Rodinson 187–188; 237.

Chapter 8

WOMEN

The last chapter focused on the family of believers that formed around each of the founders during their lifetime and were ultimately responsible for their far-reaching impact on history. Those circles of relatives, friends and associates consisted of both men and women, and this chapter turns its specific attention to the latter. Who were the female figures in their lives and what roles did they play in the unfolding of their stories? What sort or relationships did the Buddha, Jesus and Muhammad have with their female kin? As men, what sort of special relationships did they enjoy with particular women such as wives and friends? What was their attitude to marriage and celibacy? What can we glean from their teachings and actions concerning their view of women in general and the place that women occupied in their religious worldview?

The Renunciation

The first principal female character in the story of the Buddha is his mother. Known by various names in the scriptures (Mahamaya, Maya, Mayadevi and Gyutrulma), she was Suddhodana's cousin and the daughter of a local king. Their marriage was an arranged union for political purposes, but the tradition also speaks of the future Buddha selecting her from his penultimate reincarnation in Tusita Heaven.[1] While the spotlight of the birth narratives is squarely on the amazing child, the Buddha's mother is always there in the background, playing a vital role in the unfolding of events. Then, suddenly and unexpectedly, she is removed from the drama, passing away just seven days after giving birth to her celebrated son. The Nidanakatha explains that this was necessary because "the womb that holds a Bodhisattva is like the inner precincts of a temple and, therefore, cannot be occupied or used again by others".[2] However, it is not the last that we hear of Mahamaya, who reappears in the

Buddha, Jesus and Muhammad: A Comparative Study, First Edition. Paul Gwynne.
© 2014 John Wiley & Sons, Ltd. Published 2014 by John Wiley & Sons, Ltd.

narrative when the Buddha sojourned in Tavatimsa Heaven soon after the Twin Miracle. The purpose of his visit was to preach to its occupants, including his mother, who had been reincarnated in that celestial world. According to some texts, establishing his parents in the true teaching is one of the 10 acts that a Buddha must perform before entering nibbana.[3]

The task of raising the young child fell to Mahamaya's sister, Mahapajapati, who married Siddhattha's widowed father. The sources provide little information about those years, but the impression is that his aunt-stepmother was a loving person who cared for him as much as her own children, Nanda and Sundari. Suddhodana spared no expense to ensure that his son enjoyed the most sumptuous lifestyle possible, in the hope that he would gladly accept succession to the throne when the time came. Such unmitigated opulence meant the finest food, clothing, shelter, entertainment and possibly, once the young prince had come of age, a harem. Concubines were common in the ancient world, and the sources mention women among the sensual pleasures of the rich and powerful.[4] The Lalitavistara recounts how the young Siddhattha was surrounded by thousands of voluptuous beauties although the author declares that the main form of entertainment was musical rather than sexual.[5] Yet as one commentator states: "we cannot contest that the Buddha humanly enjoyed for a few years the pleasures of life made available to him by his fortune".[6]

Apart from the physical enjoyment of palace life, it was also a sacred Hindu duty to marry and have children – a fortiori for an heir to the throne. Typically, a Kshatria class prince would have had multiple wives to increase the odds, but the tradition speaks of a monogamous marriage in Siddhattha's case. When he was approximately 16 years old, a union was organized. In some versions, the proposed matrimony was against Siddhattha's will, but this looks suspiciously like the hand of later monastic authors keen to demonstrate their founder's lifelong aversion to physical craving. Indeed, there are stories of a sporting contest to win his future bride's hand in which a motivated Siddhattha vanquished all contenders. Similarly, there is a touching tale of how Siddhattha was presented with a string of hopeful female candidates only to fall in love with his future bride at first sight. The chosen girl was the daughter of the Koliyan king, Suppabuddha, whose own wife, Pamita, was Suddhodana's sister. Like his mother, the ancient texts are not clear as to the name of Siddhattha's wife. The traditional form is Yasodhara ("bearer of glory"), but the Pali Canon simply, and rather impersonally, refers to her as Rahulamata ("mother of Rahula"). Other variations of the name include Bimba, Bimbadevi, Bhaddakaccana and Gopa.[7] The wedding ceremony rarely figures in written text or visual artworks, although there is brief mention of the joining of hands and the customary Hindu circumambulation of the holy fire.[8]

Despite considerable religious and political pressure on the young couple to produce children, it was more than a decade before Yasodhara fell pregnant and gave birth to a son named Rahula. Given that the word literally means "shackle" or "chain", it is highly likely that this is also the editorial work of the later monastic redactors. Sadly, it seems that we may never know the real name of Siddhattha's son. What is clear is that very soon after the birth of Rahula, the young prince took the dramatic decision to leave home and follow another career path. It is possible that he may have been deliberately waiting to fulfill his sacred duty to become a father before taking such a radical step. Tradition confirms that he had been wrestling with the idea of a higher spiritual path for some time, perhaps since his mystical experience under the rose-apple tree as a young boy. The immediate cause is usually identified as the four sights. That first-hand encounter with sickness, old age, death and the holy ascetic profoundly shook Siddhattha's worldview, so much that in the end he opted to abandon family life and assume the vocation of an itinerant celibate. The moment is known as his Renunciation, and it is powerfully symbolized by the cutting of his long, princely hair and the donning of a pauper's yellow robes. No longer would Siddhattha enjoy the pleasure of the palace women or the caring love of his spouse. Instead, he would embrace abstinence in the solitude of the forest in a bid to discover a truth more sublime and permanent than the fleeting pleasures of the sexual act and the transient comfort of conjugal affection.

At first glance, the Renunciation may seem to endorse the irresponsible abandonment of one's marital duties but Buddhism sees the episode as the difficult choice of a greater good. There is nothing inherently evil or unskilful about marriage, including a healthy sexual life with one's partner and the sincere hope for the gift of children. The Sigalovada Sutta outlines the respect that husbands and wives should have for each other and the relationship between Siddhattha and Yasodhara is often held up as a worthy model of connubial love.[9] Yet there is no mistaking the lesson of Siddhattha's own experience. Marriage is good but celibacy is better.

The notion that religious celibacy is a more advanced path to spiritual enlightenment was not new. The restless prince was not the first young person to renounce the life of the settled, married householder for that of the peripatetic, celibate forest dweller. The shramana lifestyle was already a well-established tradition within Indian society by the time of the Buddha. A shramana (Pali: sammana) was a "striver" who rejected the authority of the sacred Vedas and protested against the ritualism of the dominant Brahmanic culture.[10] One key shramanic principle was that celibacy enabled one to channel sexual energy through the spine and into the mind where it enhanced the capacity to meditate. Abstinence from sex led to clarity of perception. The Buddha embraced this principle but added that sexual desire, while very common, is ultimately a form of ignorant craving that binds us to the wheel of rebirth. Although sexual activity brings pleasure, it is always ephemeral and holds one back from nibbana. Thus, although there were many married lay persons who accepted the Buddha's teaching, the superior form of discipleship was that of the ordained monk who not only adopted a life of material simplicity, but also one of sexual renunciation. It is no coincidence that many of the 227 rules for monks in the Vinaya Pitaka concern breaches of the spirit of celibacy. The first of the four gravest offences (Parajikas), which entail automatic expulsion from the community, is to engage in sexual intercourse.[11] The Samyutta Nikaya suggests some practical strategies to assist monks in dealing with inevitable temptations. They are encouraged to avoid occasions that might give rise to sexual thoughts, to imagine that the woman is their mother or sister, to think of unpleasant aspects of the body or even to visualize a decaying corpse.[12] One often quoted passage contains a conversation between the Buddha and Ananda in which the master suggests that monks not even look at females; if they must look, then they should not speak to them; if they must speak, then they must remain alert.[13]

There were also false accusations of sexual impropriety against the Buddha and his earliest companions by jealous rivals. One such incident involved a female ascetic known as Cinycamanavika who would dress in red and arrive at the Jetavana monastery in the evening as all visitors were leaving. The next morning she would pretend to exit the residence implying that she had spent the night with the Buddha. She then feigned pregnancy by placing a piece of wood under her garments. Tired of her ruse, the Buddha sternly confronted her one day and, at that precise moment, her belt mysteriously loosened and the wooden block fell out, thus exposing her wicked calumny.[14] A second story involves another female shramana known as Sundari. She was also persuaded by enemies to pretend to be the Buddha's secret lover, but in her case, tragically, the instigators killed her and left the body in the monastery grounds, suggesting that she had been raped and murdered by the monks. The case shocked the locals, but the Buddha calmly predicted that the resultant "noise" would pass and indeed the conspiracy was exposed within a week.[15]

The reference to female shramanas raises the important question of the role of women in the Buddha's new religious movement. The ranks of the first Buddhist monks were filled with men irrespective of their caste or age, in defiance of deeply entrenched Brahmanic attitudes. But was there a place for nuns in the sangha? The first test case arose just five years after the establishment of the order, and it came from within the Buddha's own immediate family.[16] Soon after the death of Suddhodana, the Buddha's aunt and stepmother, Mahapajapati, approached him while he was on a visit to Kapilavatthu and requested that she be admitted to the monastic order. The Buddha's instinctive reply was to decline, simply stating "please do not ask so" but not proffering any explicit reason for his stance. Mahapajapati must have been disappointed, but she was by no means unshaken in her conviction. According to the story, she and 500 other Sakyan women followed the Buddha all the way to Vesali. It was a long, debilitating journey and they arrived at the door with shaved heads and yellow robes. This time they had an intermediary in the person of Ananda, who resubmitted the request to the Buddha on their behalf. However, the Buddha gave the same reply as he had given personally to Mahapajapati earlier: "Please Ananda, do not ask this". The response is surprising given the Buddha's critical approach to discriminatory aspects of the Brahmanic religion such as caste and age. Indeed, Buddhist commentators have speculated on what hidden reasons may have prevented the Buddha from agreeing to women's admission, such as the strain on resources or concerns about the mix of men and women. In the end, it was Ananda's perseverance that finally shed light on the issue. He went to the heart of the matter and bravely asked his master if women were capable of achieving spiritual enlightenment to which the Buddha replied in the affirmative. It is a rare example of the pupil apparently outmaneuvering the teacher. Once it was clarified that the capacity to understand and to apply his truth was not gender based, the grounds for prohibiting females from entering the sangha evaporated, and the Buddha was broadminded enough to admit it. Subsequently, he relented and took the monumental decision to allow Mahapajapati and her colleagues to become nuns (bhikkhunis).

However, there are hints that the Buddha clearly had some ongoing concerns. First, he gloomily forecast that the decision would mean that his teaching would now only last 500 years rather than the 1000 years it should have otherwise.[17] It is difficult to know whether such negative sentiments actually did originate with the Buddha himself or whether they have been added later by the pen of disgruntled monks but, at face value, it seems that the Buddha had only begrudgingly accepted the presence of women in his order. Second, the Vinaya Pitaka contains a list of eight "garudham-mas" ("heavy rules") that the Buddha imposed upon the bhikkhunis as condition of their admission:

1. A nun must salute a monk even if she has been in the order for 100 years and he has only been in the order for one day.
2. A nun must reside within six hours' traveling distance from a monastery of monks for advice.
3. A nun must consult with monks on the fortnightly observance days.
4. A nun must spend the rains retreat under the orders of both monks and nuns.
5. A nun's offences must be dealt with by both monks and nuns.
6. A nun can only obtain ordination by both monks and nuns.
7. A nun cannot rebuke a monk.
8. A nun cannot advise a monk but the converse should be the case.[18]

The unmistakeable principle behind the garudhammas is the superiority of the bhikkhu over the bhikkhuni. Such an underlying bias seems to be reinforced by the fact that, in the Vinaya, there are 227 rules for monks whereas there are 311 rules for nuns. It has been argued that most of the extra rules are designed to protect the nuns rather than repress them. One example is the ban on nuns performing mundane chores for monks, such as sewing and washing, thus undermining their special monastic status. Others are aimed at ensuring decorum and avoiding situations that could easily lead to the compromise of their celibacy.

Clearly, it is inaccurate to portray the Buddha as an uncompromising champion of women's rights, two and a half thousand years ahead of his time. The initial reluc-tance, the caveat about the duration of the dhamma and the additional rules all suggest that he was still a man of his age, sharing the general belief that men and women were not absolutely on a par. Nor was the decision to admit women an absolutely original one given that there were some female shramanas already in exist-ence.[19] He had also stated that it was impossible for a woman to become a universal monarch or a Buddha.[20] However, the Buddha did affirm that women were as capable as men of understanding his teaching and he was courageous enough to put that principle into practice by allowing Mahapajapati and her colleagues to form the order of bhikkhunis. This was certainly a more positive religious attitude to women com-pared with their vastly inferior status in the Brahmanic system. In that world, a woman, along with lower caste members, were banned from reading the Vedas and could only find spiritual salvation through devotion and service to her husband. They were considered to be utterly dependent on men at every stage of their life: on their fathers when young, on their husbands when adult and on their sons when old. A widow was not allowed to remarry and, in extreme cases, was expected to practice sati in which she would lie down on her husband's funeral pyre and join him in death. Given that a girl was generally considered to be a burden on the family, it is not surprising that female infanticide was a widespread problem as it occasionally still is today in parts of India. In contrast, the Buddha abandoned the Brahmanic funeral ritual where only a son can ensure safe passage to the next life, and assured King Pasenadi that the recent birth of his daughter was not a curse but a genuine blessing: "A female offspring, O king, may prove even nobler than a male".[21]

The Buddha's prophetic decision to admit women into the sangha went against his natural instinct as a son of the Brahmanic system but, in the end, it was vindicated by the actual lives of outstanding bhikkhunis. The theory that women were capable of understanding and following the dhamma was confirmed in practice, and several of these exceptional women were the Buddha's closest female relatives. His stepmother, his wife and his half-sister not only shaved their heads and put on the yellow robes, but all three were said to have mastered the teaching and became arhants – those on the verge of nibbana.[22] Other examples of saintly nuns are recorded in the poems of the Therigatha (Verses of the Elder Nuns), which forms part of the Khuddaka Nikaya and complements the Theragatha (Verses of the Elder Monks). Moreover, just as the Buddha identified his two foremost male disciples as Sariputta and Moggallana, he also singled out two extraordinary nuns: Uppalavanna and Khema. Uppalavanna was the daughter of a merchant from Savatthi who suggested that she become a nun rather than have to choose between the many suitors who had asked for her hand in marriage. Like Moggallana, she developed iddhi powers as described in the Uppalavanna Sutta, which is dedicated to her.[23] Khema, a consort of King Bimbisara, was exceedingly beautiful but also exceedingly preoccupied with her beauty. One day, the Buddha took the opportunity to confront her with the transitory nature of the physical body. He conjured up an image of an attractive woman who rapidly aged and died before Khema's eyes. The technique of focusing on the transience of youth was a common one among the celibate monks, and the experience generated the same eye-opening effect in Khema. She asked permission of the king to join the sangha and went on to become one of the wisest of the Buddha's female disciples, mirroring Sariputta's brilliant ability to explain the dhamma.[24]

Khema's conversion from royal concubine to dedicated bhikkhuni is reflected in the story of Ambapali of Vesali, who was one of the most beautiful of Bimbisara's courtesans. Rather than shun a woman whose career was essentially to bring sexual pleasure to the king, the Buddha made a point of declining an invitation from the princes of Licchavi in order to keep a prior appointment with Ambapali. In gratitude, she donated a mango grove to the sangha and, in some traditions, she is said to have become a nun and eventually an arhant. Once again, the Buddha displayed the ability to transcend traditional prejudices, in this case, that tricky mixture of gender and occupation, in order to welcome into his spiritual company a woman of tainted means.

Eunuch for the Kingdom

The canonical gospels provide us with scant information concerning Jesus's female siblings, who are not named in the account of his visit to Nazareth.[25] Similarly in Acts, where James features as a key leader of the early Christian community, the other brothers and sisters are only mentioned in passing.[26] However, the situation is very different for Jesus's mother, Mary (Aramaic: Mariam), who plays a much more prominent role in the story. In contrast to the Buddha, whose mother passed away immediately after his birth, Mary appears on a number of occasions during Jesus's adult ministry, whereas it is Jesus's stepfather, Joseph, who is absent from the plot, presumably having died at an earlier stage.

The New Testament portrait of Mary is complex and not entirely consistent. Mark's gospel, which contains no infancy narrative, mentions her only once and in a distinctly negative light. Apparently concerned that he had lost his mind, his mother and brethren (adelphoi) arrived at the house in which Jesus was teaching his followers. Either unable or unwilling to enter, they remained outside at which point Jesus made the provocative claim that his real family was inside with him.[27] Similarly, Matthew only refers to this one incident concerning Mary during the public ministry. Furthermore, although Matthew includes two chapters describing Jesus's conception and birth, the key protagonist in these scenes is Joseph rather than the mother who remains in the backgound. It is Joseph who receives the revelatory dreams about the virginal conception and the need to flee to Egypt to avoid Herod's murderous intentions.

In contrast, Luke and John have more positive portraits of Jesus's mother. In John's gospel, Mary features at the beginning and the end of the public ministry. At the wedding feast of Cana she astutely notices that the wine supply has been exhausted, thus precipitating Jesus's first public miracle.[28] Commentators have noted the apparently curt manner in which Jesus speaks to her, using the term "woman" rather than "mother". It is the standard form of address that Jesus uses with other women, and it is the same term that he uses when she is standing at the foot of his cross.[29] According to John, the dying Jesus entrusted his mother into the care of the anonymous beloved disciple, who took Mary into his home from that moment, once again implying that she was a woman of true faith.[30]

Luke is even more explicit in his glowing admiration for Mary, not simply because she is the biological mother but, more importantly, because she is a model disciple. In contrast to Matthew, Mary occupies centerstage in the Lukan infancy narratives. It is she, not Joseph, who is visited by the angel announcing her pending, miraculous pregnancy. Gabriel addresses her as "highly favored" (traditionally translated "full of grace") and Mary's classical response to the unsettling angelic message is the epitome of trusting faith: "Here am I, the servant of the Lord; let it be with me according to your word". In one scene peculiar to Luke, the evangelist reinforces the sharp distinction between Jesus's blood family and the family of his followers:

> A woman in the crowd cried out "Blessed is the womb that bore you and the breasts that nursed you", but Jesus replied "Blessed rather are those who hear the word of God and obey it!"[31]

This is precisely what Mary does, since twice we are told by Luke that she treasured and pondered events in her heart like a true disciple.[32] The last we hear of her in the New Testament is as a member of the nascent Christian community in Jerusalem.[33] In time, some Christian traditions would elevate her as the Ever-Virgin Mary, Queen of Heaven, preeminent among the saints, at times assuming a quasi-divine role alongside her son as heavenly intercessor and benefactor.

One reason for the dominant role that Jesus's mother eventually played in Christian theology and spirituality is the conspicuous absence of a spouse for her son. Despite the occasional claim by scholars and popular writers that Jesus must have been married, there is no reference to a wife or children in the canonical gospels or in any other early Christian writing.[34] Jesus's siblings are explicitly mentioned, and the sources admit that Peter was married since his mother-in-law was the recipient of an early healing. Moreover, Paul notes that Cephas (Peter) and Jesus's brothers were accompanied by their "women" (presumably wives or sisters) on apostolic journeys.[35] Yet in situations where it would have been natural to mention Jesus's wife and children, if they existed, there is absolute silence, and the most likely explanation is that Jesus did not marry or have a family.[36]

The popular speculation that Jesus may have had an intimate relationship with Mary Magdalene is based on a few enigmatic references to her in later Gnostic writings where she is seen as the foremost of Jesus's disciples, almost in direct competition with Peter. In the Gospel of Mary, a jealous Peter confesses to her that "the Savior loved you more than the rest of women".[37] A similar theme is found in the Gospel of Philip, which contains one passage that possibly suggests that Jesus expressed his fondness for Mary with kisses on her lips:

> As for the Wisdom who is called "the barren", she is the mother of the angels. And the companion of [the savior was Mar]y Ma[gda]lene. [Christ loved] M[ary] more than [all] the disci[ples, and used to] kiss her [often] on her [mouth]. The rest of [the disciples were offended by it and expressed disapproval]. They said to him "Why do you love her more than all of us?" The Savior answered and said to them, "Why do I not love you like her? When a blind man and one who sees are both together in darkness, they are no different from one another. When the light comes, then he who sees will see the light, and he who is blind will remain in darkness".[38]

The brackets indicate words missing from the manuscript, thus making a definitive interpretation difficult. Moreover, the sexual tone of the kissing is contradicted by the description of Mary as "barren" and "angelic". The same gospel also refers to the three women named Mary who "always walked with the Lord": his mother, his mother's sister and Mary Magdalene who is described as Jesus's companion (koinonos).[39] The term could mean partner or consort, but it could also simply mean friend or associate.

The deliberate adoption of the celibate lifestyle would have been, and still is, extremely unusual within Judaism, since it is seen as a violation of the divine command to procreate.[40] The High Priest was required to have a wife, suggesting that celibacy was not seen as a means to sanctification and even the ascetical Nazirites married.[41] Consequently, there are very few cases of religious celibacy in the Hebrew Scriptures, one rare exception being the prophet Jeremiah, who was commanded by God to refrain from marrying, but this was because of the pending disaster of invasion.[42] A similar stress on the imminent end of the world as a motivation for the single life is found among the Essene community and in the writings of a celibate Paul, who declared: "I mean, brothers and sisters, the appointed time has grown short; from now on, let even those who have wives be as though they had none".[43]

The same eschatological principle seems to have been the key motivation for Jesus's deliberate decision to remain unmarried, even though it cut against the grain of the prevailing religious culture. The most revealing passage is a short statement by Jesus recorded in Matthew's gospel:

> There are eunuchs who have been so from birth, and there are eunuchs who have been made eunuchs by others, and there are eunuchs who have made themselves eunuchs for the sake of the kingdom of heaven. Let anyone accept this who can.[44]

Jesus specifies three types of eunuch: those born impotent, those who have been castrated for some purpose and those who voluntarily embrace the celibate life because of the Kingdom of God. The strong implication is that Jesus was speaking of his own radical choice to forego marriage and children because of the absolute priority given to the forthcoming reign of God. The crude imagery may reflect the fact the Jesus had been ridiculed by his opponents as a useless eunuch – a spiritually castrated half-man in the eyes of the Law. Yet the choice of celibacy to highlight the unrivalled importance of the Kingdom is consistent with his parables, such as the pearl of great price and the hidden treasure whose acquisition requires one to surrender all things.[45]

The notion that Jesus considered celibacy closer to the lifestyle of the Kingdom than marriage is also implied in the debate between Jesus and some Sadducees about the resurrection of the dead. Their probing question concerned the true husband, in heaven, of a woman who had married seven times on earth. Jesus's answer is that none of them are. The resurrected life utterly transcends our current physical existence and that it is more properly compared to an angelic existence. In such a state, marriage ceases to exist. The implication is that voluntary religious celibacy here and now is a more powerful symbol and a more accurate anticipation of the Kingdom to come.

A related episode is when Jesus visited the sisters, Martha and Mary. While the former was busy organizing food for their guest, the latter sat down with Jesus and listened to his words of wisdom. When Martha complained that her sister was neglecting practical matters, Jesus pointed out that Mary had "chosen the better part". The scene is only recorded in Luke and fits in with his emphasis on pondering the words of Jesus as a sign of true discipleship. However, some Christian traditions subsequently interpreted the two sisters' roles as a metaphor of the superiority of monastic over married life.[46]

Although Jesus personally practiced celibacy and taught that it was more intrinsically linked to the afterlife, his teachings reveal that he remained firmly within the Jewish tradition that understood marriage as a sacred institution. In fact, Jesus not only endorsed the importance of marriage, but adopted an unusually strict interpretation of its indissolubility. The eunuch saying quoted above comes at the end of a long discussion in which Jesus challenged his Jewish audience to look beyond the concessions of the Mosaic Law and to recall the Creator's original intention as expressed in the book of Genesis. What God has joined man should not divide. Such an idealistic position shocked not only his opponents but also his own disciples, who explicitly questioned it when they were in private. Jesus confirmed his stance and essentially declared that those who divorce and remarry are in an adulterous relationship.[47]

For some, Jesus's exacting teaching favors the wife who was not able to initiate divorce proceedings according to Jewish law. This mix of ethical idealism and compassion for victims of the law is evident in other episodes involving women. One of the most telling examples is the moving scene where an unnamed woman was brought before Jesus and accused of being caught in the very act of adultery. One can only wonder why her male sexual partner was absent. Instead of confirming the Mosaic Law, which demanded the death of both persons, traditionally by stoning,[48] Jesus gave his famous response: "Let anyone among you who is without sin throw the first stone". Utterly disarmed, the accusers slowly moved away, commencing with the eldest, presumably since they were more acutely aware of their lack of moral perfection.[49] Jesus did not condone the act of adultery and warned the woman not to sin any more, but he had essentially saved her life. Another prominent example of Jesus's compassion for women who were on the wrong side of the law is the "sinful" woman who bathed Jesus's feet with her tears, wiped them with her hair and anointed them with expensive ointment. Understandably, the Pharisee who was hosting Jesus objected that a true prophet would not allow a woman of ill repute to touch him. Jesus replied with a parable that demonstrated the direct relationship between the degree of guilt and the degree of gratitude when that guilt is removed.[50]

The story appears in all four gospels with interesting variations. Only Luke describes the woman as a "sinner", with the probable implication of prostitution. In Mark and Matthew, the issue is not the woman's impurity but the scandalous waste of money involved.[51] In John's gospel, the exorbitant cost of the ointment is also the issue, and it is Judas who hypocritically objects to its waste. The setting is also Bethany, but the host is now Lazarus. As in Luke's equivalent scene, Martha is in the background doing the serving but the person who anoints Jesus's feet is no longer an anonymous woman of the night but Mary, her sister.[52] It is not the only time that Martha and Mary feature in John's gospel. While Mary anticipates Jesus's imminent death by anointing his feet at Bethany, in an earlier scene, Martha is the one who recognizes Jesus as the Messiah, paralleling Peter's striking declaration in the Synoptic tradition. Her faith statement is similar to that of Jesus's mother at Cana and, likewise, it leads to a miracle – in this case the raising of Lazarus from the tomb.[53] For John, it is often women who utter incisive declarations about Jesus's true status and enable him to perform his signs.

There is another Mary who has been traditionally linked to the anonymous sinful woman in Luke's version of the anointing at Bethany. In 591 CE, Pope Gregory I suggested that the woman in question was Mary Magdalene, which led to the widespread and deeply entrenched concept in many Christians' minds that she was a reformed prostitute. Subsequently, Christian art often portrayed Mary Magdalene in scarlet gowns and long red hair, suggestive of her unsavory, former occupation.[54] Mary Magdalene was even declared the patron saint of wayward women. Yet there is no basis for this association in the canonical gospels. What the gospels do say is that she hailed from the small village of Magdala on the west side of the Sea of Galilee and that Jesus had freed her from seven demons.[55] Unlike the sisters Mary and

Martha, Mary Magdalene was one of the women, along with Joanna and Susanna, who accompanied Jesus and his disciples on his travels, providing for their practical needs out of their own means.[56] These women formed a vital support system behind the entire enterprise. If Jesus could confidently preach about birds not needing to reap and lilies not needing to spin, it was because his food, clothing and housing were quietly being looked after by that quasi-anonymous group.[57] Finally, and perhaps most importantly, the Magdalene was one of the key witnesses to Jesus's crucifixion, burial and resurrection (see Chapter 10).[58] According to Mark, Matthew and John, the risen Jesus first appeared to her, even though the official list, cited by Paul, names Cephas (Peter) as the initial recipient of an appearance.[59] The tradition that the Magdalene's vision preceded Peter and the Twelve gave rise to her traditional title as "apostola apostolorum" ("apostle to the apostles") and raises interesting questions about her status and authority within the early community given her first-hand experience of the most important events in the entire story.

The fact that Jesus allowed a sizeable group of women to accompany him and his male disciples on their missionary travels would have raised eyebrows. It also reveals something about Jesus's attitude to women and their role in the Kingdom as he envisioned it. Jesus was not one to be perturbed by the censorious attitudes of the morally righteous, and this extended to his willingness to allow females into his company. It is also evident across a range of other examples where Jesus was willing to bend the traditional rules in order to accommodate a woman who displayed genuine faith in his message. He ignored ritual impurity laws when a woman, suffering from long-term menstrual bleeding, touched his garments. Instead of issuing a reprimand for her audacity, he confirmed her cure.[60] Jesus contravened a series of taboos when he struck up a conversation in broad daylight with a Samaritan woman at Jacob's well – a sight that caused considerable consternation for his disciples. She was not only the wrong gender and the wrong ethnicity but also in an adulterous relationship. Yet Jesus spoke with her at length and took water from her bucket.[61] On another occasion, Jesus used the unconventional phrase "daughter of Abraham" to address a crippled woman whom he cured on a Sabbath day, thus emphasizing that the family of the one God is not solely comprised of males.[62] Moreover, Jesus's teaching also complements his actions on the issue of women. He frequently used female characters in his sayings such as the widow of Zarephath, the 10 wise virgins, the persistent widow and the generous widow.[63]

Like the Buddha, it is inaccurate to portray Jesus as a feminist in the modern sense of the term and his position concerning women's equality is conditioned by his historical context. The most often cited example is the fact that there were no women selected as members of the Twelve. The gospels do not provide any explicit reason for this exclusion, but the answer probably lies in its inherent symbolic meaning. Because the Twelve represented the reunification of the tribes of Israel, the natural choice was 12 men since each tribe traced its origins back to a son of Jacob. In that sense, Jesus probably had little choice but to select only males. The all-male membership of the Twelve has been interpreted by many Christian denominations throughout the ages as the basis for excluding women from certain ecclesiastical roles, but Jesus himself left few, if any, explicit instructions regarding the role of women in future church organizations. What is clear from the gospel accounts is that he was remarkably open to women within the context of his Jewish background, even to the point of bending long-standing rules and risking serious scandal.

Mothers of the Faithful

Like the Buddha, Muhammad suffered the loss of his mother at a very young age. His father had already passed away prior to his birth and, although he was about five years old when Amina unexpectedly died, he had spent most of his infancy in the care of the Bedouin wet nurse, Halima. Consequently, he had very little exposure to his natural mother and, as an only child, he had no immediate siblings. Raised by his uncle Abu Talib, his childhood playmates were his cousins but, even then, he spent much of his time alone tending sheep and goats. The first significant woman to influence the young Muhammad was Khadija bin Khuwaylid. She was a wealthy widow who first hired him as her caravan manager and then proposed marriage, which he accepted. It was an unusual union for several reasons: Khadija was about fifteen years senior to Muhammad, then in his mid-twenties;[64] she was his employer; and the 25 year long marriage was monogamous throughout, even though polygamy was widespread in Arabian society. According to Sunni Islam, Khadija bore Muhammad four daughters (Zaynab, Ruqayya, Umm Kulthum and Fatima) and two sons ('Abdallah and Qasim).[65] Sadly, both boys died in their early childhood. Khadija's consolation and support were a crucial factor that enabled Muhammad to cope with his anxieties and doubts soon after his first revelatory experiences. She is considered to be the first convert to his cause and 619 CE, when she and Abu Talib both died, is aptly called the Year of Sorrow.[66] Muhammad's later wives were often amazed and somewhat jealous at how keenly and affectionately he remembered her despite the passage of time.[67]

By the time of Khadija's death, their four daughters had grown into adults, but only one would survive Muhammad. The eldest, Zaynab, had married her cousin Abu al-'As. He never converted to Islam and, thus, Zaynab remained in Mecca with him at the time of the Hijra. In fact, her husband fought against the Muslims and was captured at the Battle of Badr. Zaynab redeemed him with a necklace she had inherited from Khadija, but the deal meant that he return to Mecca while she had to relocate to Medina, where she died. The second daughter, Ruqayya, married a son of Abu Lahab, one of Muhammad's uncles and a vehement enemy of the new religion. The political differences resulted in divorce, and Ruqayya then married Uthman, destined to become the third caliph. However, she contracted a disease, possibly measles, and died in Medina in 624 CE. The third daughter, Umm Kulthum, had been married to another son of Abu Lahab and that too ended in divorce. When her sister died, she married the widowed Uthman. As husband of two of Muhammad's daughters, Uthman is sometimes called "Possessor of Two Lights".[68] The fourth daughter, Fatima, married Ali, Muhammad's cousin, who eventually became the fourth caliph. The tradition states that Ali was too poor to afford Fatima's hand, but Muhammad was keen on the union and persuaded him to sell his shield to provide the bride's dowry. Fatima was very close to her father, although Muhammad was careful not to play favorites. Their two sons, Hasan and Husayn, were Muhammad's only grandchildren, and they would play a critical role in future conflicts concerning succession.

After Khadija's death, friends encouraged Muhammad, now in his 50s, to wed again quickly, and he soon took two wives, thus beginning the polygamous phase of his married life. As noted earlier, polygamy was the norm in Arabia,[69] but what was unusual about the two women is the striking difference in their ages. There is some dispute as to which wedding occurred first, but the usual order is Sawda and then 'A'isha.[70] Like Khadija, Sawda bint Zama was a widow and considerably older than Muhammad. She had emigrated to Abyssinia with her husband, who had converted to Christianity and died there. She was a plump, practical woman who acted more like a mother to the other wives and even surrendered her rostered conjugal visits to them.[71] In contrast, 'A'isha was the young daughter of Abu Bakr, so young in fact that the marriage is sometimes the subject of controversy involving claims of indecency and child abuse by non-Muslim sources. Several hadiths state that 'A'isha was six or seven years old when she was betrothed to Muhammad and nine years old when the marriage was consummated.[72] Apparently, she was playing on a swing just before her wedding day and was still using dolls and toys during the early years of their marital life. Given Muhammad's age, one can understand the sense of scandal evoked by such a scenario today. However, keeping in mind the historical context, commentators note that the three-year waiting period indicates that 'A'isha had presumably reached puberty when their sexual relationship commenced, something that would have been taken for granted. Arranged marriages of young girls were a common event, and there is no indication that this particular case was considered outrageous or inappropriate in its day.[73] Indeed, some modern scholars argue that she was older than the hadiths state, possibly in her late teens.[74] In fact, 'A'isha may have already been betrothed to another man, but the arrangement was cancelled by common consent to enable Muhammad to marry her instead. Such unions were often organized with the intention of strengthening the relationship between individuals, families or tribes, and the marriage to 'A'isha is clearly aimed at further cementing the already strong bond between the Prophet and one of his key right hand men.

'A'isha grew to become a strong, intelligent woman and the source of over 2,000 hadith sayings. She was also Muhammad's favorite wife, although he endeavored to spread his attention as evenly as possible across all of his spouses. In turn, she was utterly dedicated to her husband and his cause, although her fidelity was called into question on one terrible occasion. Women often accompanied their men on military expeditions, and 'A'isha had joined Muhammad on a raid against the Jewish Mustaliq tribe. On the return journey during the evening, she had dismounted from her camel to relieve herself in the desert and discovered that she had lost her necklace. By the time she had returned to the convoy it had departed, mistakenly thinking that she was in her covered compartment. Fortunately, a Muslim soldier named Safwan happened to pass some time later and brought her back to Medina the next morning on his camel. The sight of the couple emerging alone from the desert raised suspicion and soon rumors had spread that 'A'isha had indulged in a nocturnal affair with the young man. Several colleagues, including Ali, suggested that Muhammad divorce her immediately. Muhammad himself was deeply upset and unsure of what to believe even though 'A'isha had desperately pleaded her innocence. It was a serious matter since, as in Judaism, adultery attracted capital punishment, and there are several hadiths confirming that Muhammad approved the stoning of guilty parties.[75] However, in this case, he suddenly received a revelation exonerating his young wife and announcing that accusations of adultery required the support of four witnesses.[76]

Soon after the Hijra, Muhammad married three relatively young women who had lost their husbands in the military conflicts between Medina and Mecca. Hafsa bint 'Umar and Zaynab bint Khuzayma were widowed in the Battle of Badr in 624 CE. As with 'A'isha, the marriage to Hafsa, 'Umar's daughter, reinforced Muhammad's relationship with a key supporter and advisor. Hafsa was a feisty, garrulous woman who did not shrink from arguing with Muhammad, which shocked 'Umar but simultaneously reveals Muhammad's willingness to allow his wives to speak their mind. Zaynab was a gentler soul with a deep concern for the poor and needy. Sadly, she passed away only a few months after the marriage. The third war widow from this period was Umm Salama, who lost her husband in the Battle of Uhud in 625CE. She already had three children and was pregnant at the time with her fourth. Her physical beauty, incisive mind and aristocratic pedigree caused some tensions in the household, especially with 'A'isha and Hafsa.

If the marriage to 'A'isha was relatively uncontroversial at the time, despite profound misgivings today, Muhammad's seventh marriage certainly stirred up considerable controversy. Zaynab bint Jahsh was Muhammad's first cousin and had married his adopted son, Zayd, on the arrangement of Muhammad. Apparently neither person was particularly happy in the relationship, probably as a result of Zayd's former slave status, and possibly because Zaynab had actually been hoping to marry Muhammad. According to al-Tabari, Muhammad visited Zaynab's home one day and, unintentionally, saw her scantily dressed. The encounter apparently stirred deep feelings of attraction in him.[77] Zaynab related the incident to her husband who immediately offered to divorce her so that she would be free to marry the Prophet. Muhammad insisted that they persevere with their relationship, but it became clear within a year that it would not last and they divorced.[78] However, a serious obstacle remained. Marriage between Muhammad and Zaynab would be problematic since Zayd was Muhammad's legally adopted son. It was then that a new revelation came to Muhammad concerning the status of adopted children. It declared that a man could marry the former wife of his adopted son.[79] Thus, after the stipulated waiting period, Muhammad wedded Zaynab. The divine message had fundamentally changed the existing concept of adoption and redefined it for future Islam, but it is also often quoted by critics as an example of heavenly communications that seem suspiciously convenient from Muhammad's standpoint.

'A'isha later commented that if there was any revelation that Muhammad would have hidden, it was this one, which brought him a degree of embarrassment. A similar sentiment was expressed by 'A'isha on another occasion when the Qur'an gave Muhammad permission to change the order and frequency of conjugal visits to his wives. She is quoted as saying: "It seems to me that your Lord hastens to satisfy your desire".[80] Moreover, there are hints that Zaynab used the revelation to boast of her special status among the wives: "You were given in marriage by your families, while I was married (to the Prophet) by Allah from over seven Heavens".[81]

Muhammad's next four marriages were with daughters of key political and civil leaders, thus bringing significant strategic benefits as the Muslim community began to expand rapidly across southern Arabia. Two of the women were from enemy ranks: one a Meccan ally and the other Jewish. Juwayriyya bint al-Harith was among the female prisoners captured in a raid on the Mustaliq tribe near Medina in either 627 or 628 CE. Like many others, her husband was killed in the skirmish but, more importantly, her father was the tribal chieftain who attempted to negotiate her ransom. Instead, Muhammad proposed marriage, with the idea of sealing an alliance with the vanquished enemy and precluding future insurrection. According to al-Tabari, both the father and daughter agreed, and she became Muhammad's eighth wife. Consequently, all booty and captives were returned.[82] In 629 CE, the Muslim army had defeated the Jewish Nadir tribe at the battle of Khaybar and, once again, the daughter of their leader, Safiyya bint Huyayy, was taken captive with many others. It is not clear whether her husband had been killed in the fighting or executed afterwards, but it is reported that Muhammad rebuked Bilal for lacking compassion when he brought several of the women prisoners to him by passing their slain spouses.[83] Safiyya was given to a Muslim soldier named Dihya when Muhammad was advised of the identity of her father, who had also been killed. Upon hearing this information, Muhammad claimed Safiyya for himself and wedded her immediately, consummating the marriage on the journey home while a guard stood by the tent with a drawn sword for fear of reprisal.[84] The fact that Safiyya was reputedly beautiful and that the circumstances of the marriage were politically messy, has meant that this marriage, like that of 'A'isha and Zaynab bint Jahsh, is often the target of criticism today. Yet it is also claimed that Muhammad, as well as 'A'isha and Hafsa, protected Safiyya from the judgmental attitudes of the other wives who were suspicious of her Jewish background.

Muhammad also entered into two other strategic marriages with the daughters of key Meccan figures. Abu Sufyan was the chief of the Quraysh tribe and a long-standing opponent of Muhammad from the earliest days. His daughter, Ramla, had converted and emigrated to Abyssinia where her husband turned to Christianity and died. Once again perceiving a strategic opportunity, Muhammad married Ramla by proxy while she was still in Abyssinia, but she eventually took up residence with him in Medina around the year 629 CE.[85] The marriage significantly softened Abu Sufyan's attitudes toward Muhammad and Islam. Similarly, Maymuna bint al-Harith was the sister-in-law of Muhammad's paternal uncle, 'Abbas, another influential person in Meccan society who delayed conversion to the new movement until his capture at the battle of Badr. Significantly, the wedding took place in Mecca during Muhammad's emotionally charged return under the peace treaty that was signed in 628 CE. The event caused a stir among the wary Meccans, but it was another important bridge erected between the warring communities and it led to many conversions from Maymuna's clan.[86]

Finally, there were two women who are sometimes described as wives and sometimes as concubines. Maria al-Qibtiyya was a Christian slave girl who was sent with her sister as gifts to Muhammad by Muqawqis, the Byzantine ruler of Egypt. According to al-Tabari, Muhammad took charge of Maria and married her, although other sources suggest that she remained a concubine.[87] Maria gave birth to a son named

Ibrahim but, like Khadija's two boys, he also died in infancy, causing Muhammad profound grief. The other woman, sometimes listed as the thirteenth wife of Muhammad, was Rayhana, spouse of one of the executed Qurayza Jews. Ibn Ishaq reports that she was Muhammad's maiden slave and that he proposed marriage to her which she declined. There are hints in the hadith tradition that Muhammad may have had other concubines, which was normal practice for victorious tribes in the numerous internecine wars that plagued Arabia.[88]

Thus one can identify two very distinctive phases in Muhammad's married life: a long monogamous relationship with Khadija that resulted in four daughters; and a decade-long polygamous period involving another 11 or 12 wives but no surviving children. These phases also roughly correspond to the Meccan and Medinan phases of his life. Most of his wives were already Muslim but there were at least two from Jewish and Christian backgrounds, even though both converted to Islam. Muhammad's wives are collectively known as "Mothers of the Faithful", based on a verse in the Qur'an.[89] Many were widows for whom remarriage meant economic and social security. Many of the marriages carried important sociopolitical ramifications and helped to consolidate relationships with established allies or vanquished enemies. It is difficult to know what transpired between Muhammad and each wife in private moments of intimacy, but there are reports that Muhammad was an affectionate and tender husband. Despite his incredibly successful political career and elevated authority, Muhammad was not above helping out with the housework, including sewing clothes and repairing shoes.[90] Moreover, the wives felt free enough to offer him advice and even argue with him at times. Occasionally, there were moments of jealous tension between them, and on one occasion, when the wives demanded improvements to their austere household conditions, Muhammad separated from them for a month, threatening to divorce them all.[91] Yet there are no reports of him ever physically harming any of them. He openly admitted his love of women and perfume. He enjoyed an active sexual life and he expected his followers to do the same, once stating: "There is no celibacy in Islam".

Such was Muhammad's personal experience, but what did he teach about the status of women in the new religious community that he had established? His wife Umm Salama once asked him why women were so seldom mentioned in the Qur'an, and soon afterwards a new revelation came that confirmed that both men and women were part of the religious community with the same fundamental rights and duties on earth and the same ultimate destiny in heaven.[92] Despite this general statement of principle, critics often point out that there are other verses in the Qur'an and the hadith collections that either state or imply women's inferior status. One of the most controversial is the thirty-fourth verse of chapter 4, which is often interpreted to mean that men are superior (qawwam) to women and that they have the right to confine them to their bedrooms and beat (adribu) them if they are disobedient (nushouz). However, the term "qawwam" can also be translated as "maintainer", especially since the same verse speaks of the husband owning more property and, thus, carrying the greater responsibility to care for his wife and family. The term "adribu" can mean "to strike physically", but it can also mean "to forsake" or "to abandon", and some argue that this is the real intention of the verse: separate bedrooms initially and, if that failed, complete separation as a last resort. Moreover "nushouz" can also mean "unfaithful". Another commonly cited issue is the Qur'anic requirement that Islamic women wear the head veil. The actual Qur'anic verses suggest that Muhammad's wives and the believing women pull their head scarves over their breasts and conceal their ornaments in public, but there is no mention of covering the eyes or the face.[93] Muhammad indicated on one occasion that this sartorial modesty did not include the face, but apparently some women themselves decided to cover their faces.[94] The immediate context of the revelation seems to have been the increasing number of visitors to Muhammad's house and the consequent concern that his wives' privacy be protected.[95] A third example of an apparently negative attitude is the ruling that a woman was legally considered to be only half a witness.[96] Others point out that the requirement for two female witnesses concerns commercial contracts and is basically aimed at protecting them from harassment. This is supported by the fact that single-woman witness to a hadith narration is accepted as valid. There are also some hadith reports that Muhammad justified this inferior legal status because he believed women to be mentally weak and that they constituted the majority of the inhabitants in Hell.[97] Yet the intent of these sayings may be rhetorical since the original context seems to have been Muhammad's attempt to convince certain women to be more generous toward the poor.

There were also many elements of Muhammad's new religious movement that improved the lot of Arabian women. The Qur'an condemned the longstanding practice of female infanticide.[98] Although it did not ban the practice of concubinage, it forbade a man to sleep with anyone else's slave girl, including his own wife's servants. A concubine would become a permanent part of the man's family if she gave birth to a child and the Qur'an encouraged masters to free their slaves so that they may receive a higher reward.[99] The Qur'an also gave women partial inheritance rights whereas previously they had none.[100] It replaced the Arabian bride price with a dowry that the husband was required to pay directly to his wife and which became her personal property.[101] It imposed a limit on unrestricted polygamy by declaring that a man could have no more than four concurrent wives and insisted that he must treat them with equality in all aspects of their relationship.[102] It also warned husbands that such equality would not be easy to achieve, possibly implying that polygamy should not be the norm and that it was more appropriate in times of conflict when widowhood was rife.[103] The limit on polygamy had direct implications for Muhammad, who had up to 10 wives concurrently, but the Qur'an acknowledged the special case of the Prophet.[104] Tradition also suggests that, after the revelation, he did not add to the number of wives. Yet he did not divorce any of his existing wives to reduce the number since the Qur'an also forbad the wives of the Prophet to marry another man.[105] Such a world is still a far cry from today's society, but it should be admitted that, for its time, Muhammad's new religious vision was progressive and instituted a considerable number of key reforms in terms of women's rights.

Observations

Despite the dominance of male characters in the narratives, women also played significant roles in the lives of the three founders, but the circumstances and the women

in question vary considerably in each case. The Buddha and Muhammad both suffered the loss of their natural mother at an early age. Mahamaya passed from this
world just one week after her son's birth, which is understood by tradition to be the
appropriate fate of all mothers of Buddhas. Subsequently, Siddhattha was raised by
his father and his aunt-stepmother. The mother and son were reunited when the
Buddha visited her, in reincarnated form, in Tavatimsa Heaven. Although Muhammad was about six years old when Amina died, he had spent most of his infancy with
his Bedouin wet nurse and so, like the Buddha, hardly knew his natural mother. In
Jesus's case it is his father who disappeared from the story early on, whilst his mother
was still alive during his public career and ultimately survived him. The picture of
Mary varies considerably across the four gospels. In Mark and Matthew, she is named
among Jesus's kinsmen who came to bring him home because they believed that he
has lost his mind. However, Luke portrays her as a true believer, who pondered God's
mysterious workings in her life, and a member of the first Christian community. John
links Mary to the start of Jesus's ministry, where she initiated his first miraculous
sign, and the end of that ministry where a dying Jesus gave her as mother to his
dearest disciple. Christian tradition would later elevate her to quasi-divine status as
the ever-virgin Mother of God and Queen of Heaven.

Female siblings of sorts appear in all three stories, but their roles are utterly peripheral. Muhammad was an orphaned, only child and grew up in the company of his
first cousins, the sons and daughters of Abu Talib. Siddhattha had a stepbrother,
Nanda, and a stepsister, Sundari, who were the children of his widowed father and
his aunt. Tradition states that Sundari became a nun like many other members of the
family. There is a passing reference to Jesus's sisters living in Nazareth and these are
interpreted variously by Christians as his blood sisters (Mary's other children), his
cousins or his stepsisters from an earlier marriage of Joseph. They are not named and
are never mentioned again in the New Testament.

On the critical question of marriage and celibacy as a chosen lifestyle, there are
striking contrasts between the experiences of the three men. At one end of the spectrum is Muhammad who was married for almost all of his adult life but in two quite
distinct phases. The first phase involved his (approximately) 25-year monogamous
relationship with Khadija in Mecca. The second phase, following her death, involved
polygamous marriages to 11 or 12 women in Medina. Many of Muhammad's wives
were widows, several of them having lost their husbands in military campaigns. Many
of his marriages also carried political significance, cementing relationships with his
closest supporters such as Abu Bakr and 'Umar, and other tribal leaders including
defeated enemies. Several of these unions involve some degree of controversy:
'A'isha's age, Zaynab's previous marriage to Muhammad's adopted son and the
hurried consummation with the Jewish Safiyya, whose husband had just been killed.
Yet the tradition describes Muhammad as a caring husband who engaged in domestic
chores and sought his wives' opinions. Muhammad enjoyed an active sexual life,
understood as part of God's plan for humankind, and allegedly declared that there
was no place for celibacy in Islam. For Muhammad, marriage constitutes "half" of
one's religious duties and is particularly pleasing to God. The marriage to Khadija
produced four daughters and two sons, but only the girls survived to adulthood. The
final marriage to Maria also resulted in a boy but, like his brothers, he also died in
infancy. Three of Muhammad's daughters encountered problems with nonbelieving

husbands, and two of them remarried a key supporter and future leader, Uthman. The fourth daughter, Fatima, also married another prominent follower and future leader in Ali.

At the other end of the spectrum is Jesus who, as far as the evidence suggests, never married or had a family. This would have been highly unusual given his Jewish background and his informal status as religious teacher. As in Islam, voluntary celibacy had, and still has, no real spiritual value in Judaism, and he probably suffered ridicule as a result. Jesus described himself as a "eunuch" for the Kingdom, indicating that he saw no reason to marry and start a family given the overriding priority of the imminent reign of God. Like the early Christians who followed him, Jesus sensed that he was in the end-times and a new cosmic order was already breaking into the world. He chose an itinerant, detached lifestyle to announce his message in word and deed, and it left no room for wife or child. This does not mean that Jesus considered marriage and procreation as evil. Although he chose celibacy for the sake of the Kingdom, many of his parables draw on the image of the wedding banquet. Furthermore, his teachings on marriage confirm its sacred status and his strict, almost uncharacteristic, rejection of divorce reflects the seriousness with which he viewed the God-willed permanence of the marriage bond.

Somewhere in the middle of the spectrum lies the Buddha, who experienced both states of life. Like Muhammad, a young Siddhattha married but, in his case, it was an arranged union with his royal cousin for political purposes. Yet he and Yasodhara seem to have enjoyed a happy relationship, and they eventually had one son. The traditional name of the boy, Rahula (chain) suggests the hand of a later editor who saw the wife and child as an impediment rather than a blessing. Soon after Rahula's birth, Siddhattha made the monumental decision to leave his family and seek a higher spiritual truth. Like Jesus, he chose the path of the wandering, celibate teacher. Although it seems a dereliction of his marital and parental duties, in the eyes of Buddhism, his Renunciation was for a higher good, since it led to his eventual Enlightenment and the gift of the dhamma to our age. The implication of Siddhattha's life-changing decision is that, while marriage is not necessarily a bad thing, total renunciation of romantic love and sexual desire is the more advanced pathway to liberation.

In terms of the role of women in their respective religious worldviews, it would be inaccurate to portray the three as groundbreaking champions of women's rights in the full modern sense. There were many deeply embedded cultural inequalities and prejudices concerning women that they did not address or reform. The Buddha displayed a real reluctance to admit women to the monastic order and ultimately only did so as a result of the insistence of Mahapajapati and Ananda. Even when he conceded to admit nuns, he imposed a series of extra regulations on them and gloomily predicted that his truth would now only last 500 years instead of 1,000. Jesus did not appoint a woman as a member of the inner circle of the Twelve and seemed happy to have a group of women provide for their material needs. Muhammad did not ban concubinage or polygamy and there are some hadiths that seem to imply that women were considered intellectually and morally weak.

Yet there is also evidence that all three founders were sensitive to the needs of women and proposed or implemented genuine advancements within the context of their social worlds. The Buddha explicitly acknowledged that women were as capable as men of attaining nibbana. Moreover, despite initial hesitation, he did take the courageous step of admitting nuns into the sangha and later recognized outstanding examples of wisdom and virtue among his female followers. Given that the Twelve represented a reunited Israel, Jesus probably had no choice but to limit that symbolic group to males, but it was a radical, even scandalous, move to allow women disciples to accompany him and the Twelve on their missionary travels. Jesus also pushed against religious and cultural taboos in his encounters with various women, including close friends and perfect strangers. Muhammad may have retained the existing custom of polygamy, but the Qur'an introduced an upper limit of four concurrent wives and insisted on their equal treatment. It also banned the widespread practice of female infanticide, created rules regarding the treatment of female prisoners of war, established a personal dowry for the wife and endorsed inheritance rights for female relatives. In the end, the Buddha, Jesus and Muhammad were men of their day, hardly immune from the influence and limitations of their surrounding culture. There are elements in their teaching and behavior that suggest they forged some new ground on women's rights for their times, but their times are vastly removed from our present world, and it is quite another matter to argue that they can be taken out of their original context and held up in every respect as absolute, immutable standards for the treatment of women now and for all ages to come.

Notes

1   Nakamura I 54.
2   Nakamura I 68.
3   Cohen 144, 170–177.
4   Murcott, 34; Foucher 65.
5   Lalitavistara (Foucaux) 155–180.
6   Foucher 65.
7   Sumangala Vilasini 2.422; Buddhavamsa 26.15; Mahavamsa 2.24.
8   Foucher refers to the "timid" representations of the ritual in Gandhara art. Foucher 63.
9   Digha Nikaya 31 (Sigalovada Sutta).
10   The shramana ideal was absorbed into Brahmanic Hinduism in the form of the four ideal life-stages (ashramas).
11   The other three are theft, murder, and boasting about miraculous powers.
12   Samyutta Nikaya 35.127.
13   Foucher 198; Drummond 188.
14   Nakamura I 365.
15   Nakamura I 366; Khuddaka Nikaya 3, Udana 4.8.
16   Thomas notes a problem with the claim that the event took place in the fifth year of the order since Ananda was not the Buddha's assistant until the twentieth year and this is too late for Suddhodana's death.
17   Thomas 109.
18   Khandhaka 23.
19   Thomas 111.
20   Bahudhatuka Sutta, Majjhima Nikaya 115.
21   Drummond 189.
22   Therigatha 82–86. See Murcott 90.

23 Uppalavanna Sutta, Samyutta Nikaya 5.5.
24 Dipavamsa 18.9.
25 Mark 6:3. While the Protestant tradition accepts that these are Mary's children, Catholic and Orthodox traditions uphold her perpetual virginity and, thus, regard them either as cousins or as Joseph's children from an earlier marriage. The Orthodox Church identifies one of Jesus's half-sisters as Salome, who witnessed Jesus's crucifixion and burial. Mark 15:40.
26 Acts 1:14.
27 Mark 3:21, 31–35.
28 John 2:1–11.
29 John 4:21; 8:10; 20:15.
30 John 19:25–27.
31 Luke 11:27–28.
32 Luke 2:19, 51; 8:21.
33 Acts 1:14.
34 A recent case is *The Da Vinci Code* (2003) by Dan Brown, which drew heavily on Michael Baigent, Richard Leigh and Henry Lincoln (1982) *The Holy Blood and the Holy Grail*.
35 Mark 1:29–31; 1 Corinthians 9:5.
36 Meier I 342.
37 Papyrus Berolinensis 9–10. The Gnostic idea that Mary Magdalene was loved by Jesus more than the others led to the theory that she was the "beloved disciple" of the Fourth Gospel.
38 Gospel of Philip 63.33–38.
39 Gospel of Philip 59.6–11.
40 Genesis 1:28.
41 Leviticus 21:13–15; Numbers 6:1–21. The Talmud bans unmarried people from holding certain public and religious offices, such as judges in capital cases (Sanhedrin 36b).
42 Jeremiah 16:2.
43 Antiquities 18.1.5; Jewish War 2.8.2; Philo, Hypothetica 11.14–18; 1 Corinthians 7:29–31.
44 Matthew 19:12.
45 Matthew 13:44–46.
46 Luke 10:38–42.
47 Mark 10:2–12. Matthew's version adds the enigmatic phrase "except for unchastity": Matthew 19:1–8.
48 Leviticus 20:10; Deuteronomy 22:22–24.
49 John 8:1–11.
50 Luke 7:36–50.
51 Mark 14:3–9; Matthew 26:6–13.
52 John 12:1–8.
53 John 11:1–54.
54 Examples include Martin Scorsese's film adaptation of Nikos Kazantzakis's novel *The Last Temptation of Christ*, José Saramago's *The Gospel according to Jesus Christ*, Andrew Lloyd Webber's musical *Jesus Christ Superstar* and Mel Gibson's film *The Passion of the Christ*.
55 Luke 8:2; Mark 16:9.
56 Mark 15:40–41; Luke 8:1–3.
57 Matthew 6:25–33.
58 Matthew 27:55–56, 61; Mark 15:40, 47; Luke 23:49, 55; John 19:25.
59 1 Corinthians 15:3–7.

60 Mark 5:25–34.
61 John 4:1–42.
62 Luke 13:10–17.
63 Luke 4:24–25; 18:1–8; 21:1–4; Mark 12:41–43; Matthew 25:1–13.
64 Al-Tabari IX 127.
65 Shi'ite Muslims hold that only Fatima was Muhammad's daughter and that her three stepsisters were Khadija's children from an earlier marriage.
66 Muslim 5971.
67 Bukhari 58.168; Muslim 5972.
68 Emerick 180.
69 Armstrong, Muhammad 104.
70 Al-Tabari IX 128–129.
71 Al-Tabari IX 128; Muslim 3451; Bukhari 47.766.
72 Al-Tabari IX 129–131; Muslim 3309–3311.
73 Armstrong, Muhammad 104; Rodinson 135; Qur'an 65:4.
74 See Resit Haylamaz, "At what age did Aisha marry the Prophet?" *The Fountain* 69 (May–June 2009).
75 Muslim 4196–4223.
76 Qur'an 24:11–17.
77 Al-Tabari VIII 4.
78 Qur'an 33:37.
79 Qur'an 33:37–40.
80 Muslim 3453–3454; Qur'an 33:51.
81 Bukhari 93.516–518.
82 Bukhari 46.717; Muslim 4292.
83 Ibn Ishaq (Guillaume) 515.
84 Bukhari 14.68; 52.143.
85 Al-Tabari IX 133.
86 Emerick 242.
87 Al-Tabari IX 141. Ibn Ishaq does not list her among the wives of Muhammad. See Ibn Ishaq (Guillaume) 792; Rodinson 279.
88 Bukhari 64.274.
89 Qur'an 33:6.
90 Ramadan 119, 168.
91 Ramadan 168; Qur'an 33:28–29; 66:1–4.
92 Qur'an 33:35; 4:124.
93 Qur'an 33:59; 24:31.
94 Bukhari 60.282.
95 Emerick 135; Ramadan 119; Bukhari 60.317.
96 Qur'an 2:282.
97 Bukhari 76.456, 554–555.
98 Qur'an 6:137; 81:8–9; 17:31; 16:58–60.
99 Abu Dawud 4443–4445.
100 Qur'an 4:7.
101 Qur'an 4:4; 2:237.
102 Qur'an 4:3.
103 Qur'an 4:129.
104 Qur'an 33:50.
105 Qur'an 33:52–53.

Chapter 9

POLITICS

As the founders' public careers unfolded and their followers grew in number, questions of authority and power inevitably surfaced, not only within their movements but also at the external interface with contemporary political structures. It was only a matter of time before their popularity and influence caught the attention of those who reigned over various parts of society. This penultimate chapter explores the political dimension of their teachings and their actions. To what extent did their messages carry political implications and generate political responses? What was the nature of their relationship with the rulers of the day? Who were their chief allies and enemies? What was their attitude to the use of political means, including force, to further their cause?

The Enemy Within

The circumstances that characterize the early life of Siddhattha Gotama are highly political in nature. He was not only born into the Kshatria (warrior) class but, more specifically, he was the first son of the ruler of a small vassal state on the periphery of the kingdom of Kosala. Although scholars suggest that the Sakyans were governed by a council of appointed elders rather than hereditary monarchs, the traditional biography describes how his father was profoundly concerned about the smooth succession to the throne by his male heir. In his father's eyes at least, Siddhattha's vocation was mapped out, but it was also articulated by the sages that gathered at his birth and noticed the strange markings on the child's body. For the majority of the wise men, the ambiguous signs meant that the boy would either become a great political leader or a great religious teacher: a cakkavatti or a Buddha. The former term refers not just to a modest, local raja like Siddhattha's father, but the virtuous and just ruler of the entire world.[1] Suddhodana was delighted with such a glorious prospect for his boy but it was the second possible meaning of the marks that

Buddha, Jesus and Muhammad: A Comparative Study, First Edition. Paul Gwynne.
© 2014 John Wiley & Sons, Ltd. Published 2014 by John Wiley & Sons, Ltd.

disturbed him. Consequently, he lavished every luxury upon the young Siddhattha in a carefully constructed strategy to avoid anything that might distract him from his calling and tempt him away from the role for which he was being groomed.

Despite the extraordinary investment of time and money aimed at keeping Siddhattha on the political road, fate led him in a completely different direction. Indeed, most of the standard biographies of the Buddha focus heavily on this early stage of his career during which he made the critical decision to abandon the palace in favor of the forest. On the night of the Renunciation, Siddhattha symbolically cut his long princely hair and exchanged his royal garments for the rags of a beggar. In that moment, he relinquished the political control associated with crown and throne for that more elusive, spiritual control over mind and body.

The inner struggle between the two roles did not end there. One of the constant temptations of Mara was to remind Siddhattha of his regal background, enticing him to return to the earthly delights and privileges of Kapilavatthu. Even on the very night of his Enlightenment, Mara wooed him with memories of palace pleasures and power. The temptation to accept a political role surfaced again when King Bimbisara recognized Siddhattha's aristocratic demeanor and initially offered him command of a military regiment, followed by rule over a substantial portion of his kingdom.[2] Siddhattha resisted in both instances, thus reinforcing his earlier decision to renounce political office. By the time he returned to Kapilavatthu years later, it was clear in his own mind that his true lineage was not the Sakyan royal family but the line of Buddhas, which he had now joined.[3]

The fundamental vocational choice of spiritual over political paths is reflected in the essential thrust of the Buddha's message. The Four Noble Truths are concerned with overcoming enslaving forces that operate at the most personal level, within the individual psyche. While there are ethical ramifications that affect external behavior and social relationships, the Buddha's main interest is the deep-seated mental attitudes that can either bind us to the wheel of reincarnation or liberate us from its chains. The dhamma is not particularly concerned with political issues or processes per se, although its advocacy of moral virtues, such as respect for life, honesty, compassion and self-control, has implications in the social, economic and political spheres. For this reason, the Buddha's new religious movement was not regarded as a direct political threat to those who held power at the time, and this fundamental political neutrality facilitated its gradual expansion across the borders of kingdoms and states.[4]

This does not mean that the Buddha had nothing to do with politics whatsoever. There are sections of the scriptures that deal with the responsibilities of rulers, the most well-known example being the Dasa-raja-dhamma found in the Jataka Tales. As the name suggests, these are ten fundamental principles that should be practiced by a wise and just king:

1. Be liberal and avoid selfishness.
2. Maintain a high moral character.
3. Be prepared to sacrifice one's own pleasure for the well-being of the subjects.
4. Be honest and maintain absolute integrity.
5. Be kind and gentle.
6. Lead a simple life for the subjects to emulate.

7. Be free from hatred of any kind.
8. Exercise nonviolence.
9. Practice patience.
10. Respect public opinion to promote peace and harmony.[5]

Elsewhere, the dhamma teaches that crime and immorality are best eradicated via education rather than force, and that such means provide a greater guarantee of economic development.[6] Perhaps the most striking aspect of the Buddha's teaching, reflected in the eighth principle of the Dasa-raja-dhamma, is the stress on nonviolence, even in the case of the political ruler. While the Hindu religious framework allowed a place for legitimate killing by the warrior class, the Buddha's stance was much more radical:

> When a professional warrior exerts himself in battle, his mind is already debased and misdirected by the thought: "May these men be slaughtered, annihilated, destroyed." If others slay him while he is exerting himself in battle, after death, he will be reborn in the hell of those slain in battle.[7]

In the eyes of the Buddha, the taking of life generated so much negative karma that it was never justified, even in the act of self-defense. At the personal level, a monk was allowed to protect himself from physical attack but only to the extent that the aggressor was neutralized with minimal injury. At the national level, a just king, inspired by the Buddha's teaching, should never wage an offensive war and would endeavor to avoid military conflicts at all costs. Such pacifism was not merely a theory that the Buddha espoused. When occasions presented themselves, he was also willing to intervene in disputes, such as the argument between the Sakyan and Koliyan kingdoms over ownership of the Rohini River. The Buddha fearlessly placed himself between the combatants and reminded the two kings that blood was more precious than water. As a result, both sides laid down their arms and a peaceful settlement was negotiated.[8]

The story may have a historical basis, but it is difficult to ascertain exactly how much diplomatic influence the Buddha exerted over the political rulers of his day. Certainly, the scriptures speak of the close friendship between the Buddha and King Bimbisara of Magadha. According to the texts, the monarch would often visit the Buddha, removing his royal insignia and respectfully prostrating.[9] Such deference to a religious figure was not unheard of in ancient India where Kshatria kings would often seek the advice and blessing of Brahmin priests, especially before crucial decisions or military operations. Yet the Buddha's influence was limited since Bimbisara had no compunction about pursuing a successful strategy of expansionism. Nor could the Buddha prevent the son of Bimbisara, Ajatasattu, orchestrating the death of his own father by starvation. The Buddhist texts speak of Ajatasattu's repentance many years later, which the Buddha accepted provided he undertook a purification rite. The Buddha also pointed out that a remorseful Ajatasattu could not become an arhant because of the patricide that he had committed. There is one oft-quoted incident toward the end of the Buddha's life concerning his indirect political advice to Ajatasattu. The king had sent an emissary to the Buddha inquiring whether his plan to attack the Vajjis would be successful. In response, the Buddha remarked to Ananda, within earshot of the emissary, that the Vajjis held regular and frequent assemblies, practiced internal harmony and respected holy men and women in their midst. He continued: "As long as they do these things, the Vajjis may be expected to prosper and not decline".[10] Some interpret his astute observation as a deliberate attempt to prevent a Magadhan invasion. Other commentators argue that Ajatasattu took the hint and sent spies into Vajji territory with the specific aim of disrupting their meetings, thus undermining the inner unity that was their primary defense.

The Buddha's relationship with King Pasenadi of Kosala was not as intimate as his friendship with Bimbisara. Pasenadi was reputedly less cultivated and less sympathetic to the Buddha's cause. As a result, it was nearly two decades before the Buddha established a significant presence in Kosalan territory. Moreover, his homeland, the Sakyan kingdom, was a vassal state under Kosala. Nevertheless, the texts relate how Pasenadi eventually embraced the Buddha's teaching. The king once asked why he should consider the dhamma as superior since the Buddha was younger than most other teachers. The Buddha's insightful reply was that there are four things that one should not despise merely because they are young: a mighty prince, a serpent, fire and a Buddhist monk.[11] Like Bimbisara, Pasenadi was also a victim of the machinations of his heir. While he was away from his capital, Savatthi, his chief minister placed his son, Vidudabha, on the throne. Pasenadi fled to Magadha, seeking help from Ajatasattu, but the tradition claims that he died of exposure during the night at the city gates.

The ascent of Vidudabha generated a serious problem for the Buddha's homeland of Sakya. Years earlier, Pasenadi had sought a wife from the Sakyan people but, as a vassal state, they were extremely averse to his request. Consequently, they had sent the daughter of a slave girl to Pasenadi, claiming that she was Sakyan aristocracy. Pasenadi took her as his second queen and she became the mother of Vidudabha. When Vidudabha discovered the true pedigree of his mother and the deceitful insult perpetrated by the Sakyans, he vowed revenge on them. On several occasions, the angry king threatened to attack Kapilavatthu, but the Buddha intervened each time and persuaded him to turn back. Soon after the Buddha's death, Vidudabha took his vengeance, destroying the capital and massacring many of the Sakyan populace. Yet karma played its part, and the texts go on to state that most of Vidudabha's army was drowned in a flooding river on the return journey.[12]

Thus, apart from the occasional provision of advice or direct intervention on behalf of peace, the Buddha resisted being drawn into the world of politics. By and large, he operated at a different level. Conversely, the political leaders of his day kept their respectful distance as well. They allowed his monks to move about freely, they permitted his movement to expand alongside other religious groups without opposition, and they even provided substantial material support in the form of land and monetary donations from time to time. In fact, the most serious threat to the Buddha's authority, and indeed his life, did not come from an external political figure, but from someone within his very own monastic community.

Devadatta, Siddhattha's first cousin and brother-in-law, is portrayed in the Maha-vastu as a strong but petulant young man with a malicious inclination.[13] On one occasion, he injured the wing of a royal goose with an arrow. The hapless bird fell at Siddhattha's feet and Devadatta would have happily killed it on the spot had the compassionate prince not refused to hand it over, binding its wound instead.[14] A similar disregard for life was displayed during the archery contest for Yasodhara's hand. Devadatta encountered the white elephant that was meant to carry the prince to the games and, in a fit of rage, killed it, leaving the carcass blocking the city gate. Siddhattha arrived and tossed the body over the ramparts to clear the way.[15] The Pali Canon does not contain these stories, which may have been composed at a later stage when Devadatta's name had already been tarnished. The Vinaya Pitaka describes how Devadatta, along with other members of the family, joined the monastic movement when the Buddha visited Kapilavatthu. Soon afterwards, he mastered the iddhi powers and is listed among the elders of the community.[16] In the final decade of the Buddha's life, there is evidence that Devadatta, possibly motivated by impatience or jealousy, began to entertain thoughts of replacing the Buddha as head of the sangha.

It is reported that about eight years before the Buddha's death, Devadatta began to woo Ajatasattu for his support in a bid for greater benefits and recognition. Using his iddhi power, he so amazed and impressed the king that Ajatasattu built a monastery for him at Gayasisa and sent him copious amounts of fine food on a daily basis. Many monks made clandestine visits in order to share in the special treatment.[17] Buoyed by the royal backing, Devadatta audaciously approached the Buddha and suggested that the aged master should retire and allow Devadatta to assume the leadership. The texts claim that his blatant quest for earthly power and acclaim resulted in loss of his iddhi powers. The Buddha was already aware of Devadatta's ambitious intentions, having been alerted to them by Moggallana. The assertiveness of Devadatta sparked a sharp, candid reply from the Buddha, which reveals a great deal about his understanding of authority within the community: "Not even to Sariputta or Moggallana would I hand over the Order, and would I then to thee, vile one, to be vomited like spittle?"[18] Not only was Devadatta totally out of contention but even the two worthiest disciples would not be given such responsibility while the Buddha was alive. The leadership of the sangha intrinsically belonged to its founder.

Angry and disappointed at the dismissal of his brazen request, Devadatta orchestrated three attempts on the Buddha's life.[19] The first involved a group of royal archers who were provided by Ajatasattu. They were placed in hiding on various paths, but the Buddha's majestic appearance so overwhelmed the first assassin that he listened to a short sermon and converted. The master's iddhi powers also led the others to him, and they all eventually embraced the dhamma. In the second attempt, Devadatta decided to take matters into his own hands. According to the story, he waited for the Buddha on a steep hill and hurled an enormous rock as the master passed by. Miraculously, two peaks sprang up from the ground beside the Buddha and smashed the deadly rock, although a splinter lodged in the Buddha's foot. Alarmed by the incident, his followers urged the Buddha to travel with a bodyguard in future but he refused, confidently declaring that no one could deprive an enlightened being of his life. In his third attempt, Devadatta persuaded some elephant keepers to release their fiercest beast onto the road where the Buddha regularly walked. Again the assassination failed as the Buddha was able to subdue the wild animal and remove all danger.

According to the Pali Canon, Devadatta abandoned the idea of assassinating the Buddha, and turned instead to generating a schism within the ranks. The issue that resulted in a temporary split was Devadatta's insistence that the monastic life was too soft. In his view, more rigor and discipline were required of the bhikkhus.[20] Thus Devadatta persuaded several other monks to accompany him and submit a request to the Buddha that five more stringent rules be added to the Vinaya:

1. That monks should dwell all their lives in the forest
2. That they should accept no invitations to meals, but live entirely on alms obtained by begging
3. That they should wear only robes made of discarded rags and accept no robes from the laity
4. That they should dwell at the foot of a tree and not under a roof
5. That they should abstain completely from fish and flesh.

The Buddha conceded that monks would be allowed to follow such rigorist ideals if they so chose, except living in the forest during the monsoon season. However, he refused to impose them as obligations on all members. Subsequently, Devadatta began to accuse the Buddha of succumbing to luxury and called his own monthly uposatha meeting without the founder present. His idealistic model attracted several hundred monks who accompanied him to Gayasisa.[21] In response, the Buddha commissioned Sariputta and Moggallana to persuade them to return, and they successfully brought back the majority. As a result of his treacherous behavior, Devadatta had to withdraw from Magadha but soon afterwards he became gravely ill. We are told that he finally met his fate when the earth swallowed him alive. Sources claim that he was reborn in the lowest level of Buddhist Hell, where he was purged of his negative karma.[22] Despite Devadatta's defiance of his authority and violent acts against his person, the Buddha did not succumb to hateful thoughts of revenge. The founder kept his poise and expressed compassion for his wayward disciple.

It is difficult to know to what extent the legends about Devadatta are based on genuine historical events but it is quite possible that attempts were made on the Buddha's life and that he had to face a rigorist schism at some point.[23] We know that he survived both challenges, living well into his old age and remaining head of his religious movement to the end. Although he never became the Sakyan king after his father, he was the religious superior of a growing community whose members took refuge in his person and his teaching. His elevated status in the eyes of his followers might suggest that he functioned as a benevolent dictator, fashioning rules for the welfare of his monks in a gentle but autocratic manner. Indeed the Buddha did proclaim new regulations as situations arose that were not explicitly covered by existing precepts. The Vinaya Pitaka was not composed in a day but evolved out of the real experience of living the dhamma in community year after year. Yet the Buddha was not an autocrat. He encouraged discussion, allowed monks to vote and accepted the counsel of his most trusted companions.[24] The rebellion of Devadatta had been resolved successfully but the general question raised by the mutineer was a valid one. Although he would never step down from his leadership role during life, who among his chief monks would the dying Buddha appoint as his successor?

Messiah

Unlike Siddhattha, Jesus was not born into the household of a reigning monarch. The genealogies in Matthew and Luke identify him as a descendant of King David via his foster-father Joseph, but the sobering reality was that Jesus was raised in a peasant family in a peripheral village in remote Galilee – about as far away from the seat of political power as one could be.[25] There is no evidence that he had participated in local politics prior to his dramatic appearance on the public stage. Nor is it clear whether he partook in formal rabbinical training, although he was often called "rabbi" or "teacher" and displayed an impressive knowledge of the Hebrew scriptures.[26] However, his astonishing success as preacher and healer attracted large crowds, out of which a sizeable band of disciples evolved. Jesus was able to command the attention of curious onlookers and devoted followers not only because of his oratory skills, but also because his eloquent words were backed by convincing actions. His power over demons and diseases revealed an inner authority (exousia) that was observed and acknowledged by those present.[27] Thus, whether desired or not, the anonymous carpenter from Nazareth attracted widespread attention and with that came a mixed blessing. Among those sympathetic to his message, he enjoyed popularity and allegiance, but with those whose vested interests were threatened he would find suspicion and hostility.

According to the Synoptic gospels, Jesus met with opposition very early in his public ministry, and it initially came from religious opponents rather than political authorities. The main objections were voiced by persons described as "scribes and Pharisees", and they concern a number of sensitive issues. First, Jesus and his disciples were accused of breaking the Sabbath prohibition on work when he healed a man's withered hand and when his disciples were spotted plucking ears of corn in a field. Jesus's response was that saving life takes precedence even on the holiest of weekdays, adding that the Sabbath was made for man and not vice versa.[28] Second, his disciples were accused of failing to perform ritual washing prior to eating, thus defiling their food. However, Jesus argued that these were merely man-made laws and, thus, were subordinate to the core commandments that came from God. The same liberal approach to purity issues was applied to Jewish food laws when Jesus declared that nothing that a person consumes can render them impure.[29] Third, it was not only a question of washing before the meal and what food was allowed during the meal. It was also a question of one's company at table. The gospels record complaints by Pharisees that Jesus dined with "tax collectors and sinners". Such open commensality blurred the boundary between observant and nonobservant Jews, threatening to undermine deep-seated codes of honor and shame.[30] Behind these specific issues was a more fundamental questioning of Jesus's vision and, consequently, his authority. Jesus's propensity to bend traditional religious laws suggested to the conservative minded that he could not possibly speak for the God of Israel who had revealed them in the first place. Their conclusion was that his amazing power to heal must come from Beelzebul. Moreover, his pretentious claim to forgive the sins of the persons whom he healed verged on blasphemy.[31] In response, Jesus was scathingly critical of the scribes and Pharisees, who are portrayed in the Synoptic gospels as narrow-minded legalists with little concern for those outside the law. Indeed, the very term "Pharisee" has come to mean a hypocritical and arrogant person who places the letter of the law above its spirit.[32] The epitome of such condemnation is found in the "seven woes" of the Q source, where Jesus provides a litany of the Pharisees' shallow religious hypocrisy, bluntly denouncing them as whitewashed tombs, blind fools and vipers.[33]

Commentators have noted that such a negative, black-and-white portrait of the Pharisees is probably more caricature than accurate memory. It possibly reflects later tensions between Christian and Jewish communities after the destruction of the Temple when the Pharisee party became the dominant form of Judaism. In fact, rabbinical writings at the time suggest that the positions of Jesus and the Pharisees on certain issues may not have been that different. It was quite common to associate physical healing with spiritual forgiveness; divine mercy was seen as available to everyone including serious sinners; Sabbath rules could be overridden when life was at stake; and what defiled a person was not the food itself but the inner disregard for the divine commandment.[34] Jesus undoubtedly had debates with his religious rivals, including Pharisees, but there is also evidence in the gospels that he respected them, mixed with them and shared many of their fundamental theological principles. He dined with Simon the Pharisee; he sided with the Pharisees against the Sadducees regarding the resurrection of the body; his version of the greatest commandment is very close to the teaching of the Pharisee scholar, Hillel; and his position on divorce is close to that of another famous Pharisee teacher, Shammai.

The opposition in Galilee initially took the form of intellectual disapproval and public debate, but it also had a darker dimension. Mark describes how, after the cure of a crippled man on the Sabbath, some Pharisees and Herodians conspired on how to "destroy" Jesus.[35] Yet Luke reports that certain Pharisees also warned Jesus that Herod was planning to kill him, prompting Jesus to describe the king as a "fox", adding that the appropriate place for prophets to meet their fate is not in Galilee but in Jerusalem.[36] Indeed, it was in the capital city that Jesus met with a more disturbing form of opposition from a different group, namely the "chief priests and elders". The gospel of John recounts how Jesus visited Jerusalem during the pilgrim festivals each year and frequently met with hostility. On one occasion, Jesus healed a paralyzed man on the Sabbath, prompting "the Jews" to commence plotting his death.[37] During the festival of Sukkoth, "chief priests and Pharisees" asked the temple police why they failed to arrest him for claiming to be the Messiah despite his Galilean provenance. The police cited Jesus's eloquence, stating that they had never heard anyone speak like him.[38] Finally, as word spread that Jesus had raised Lazarus from the dead, John states that the chief priests called a meeting of the Sanhedrin, at which the High Priest, Caiaphas, expressed his grave fears that Jesus's popularity was sure to provoke a brutal reaction by the Roman forces. This is the context for his famous statement: "It is better for you to have one man die for the people than to have the whole nation destroyed".[39] However, the religious leadership in Jerusalem was also keenly aware that arresting Jesus could cause riots given his considerable following.[40]

The concerns of the priesthood went beyond those of the Pharisees. It was no longer a question about the minutiae of Jewish law but the challenge that Jesus directed at the very heart of their power and influence: the Temple ritual. That challenge was dramatically symbolized by a single act that was quite possibly the final straw for his religious enemies. All four gospels agree that it occurred during a Passover festival, but John's gospel places it at the very start of his public ministry while, the Synoptics state that it happened, not coincidentally, just before his death. Jesus had taught in the Temple precincts many times, but one day he entered the outer Court of the Gentiles where vendors sold cattle, sheep and pigeons to pilgrims for regular sacrifices, as well as lambs during the Passover festival. There were also money-changers seated at tables, converting pagan currency to Jewish shekels in order to pay the annual Temple tax. It was a lucrative trade since both types of merchants enjoyed an effective monopoly and charged accordingly. Jesus produced a whip of cords and began to drive the cattle and sheep, and possibly the animal vendors as well, out of the courtyard. He overturned the tables of the bankers and the seats of the pigeon sellers, paraphrasing the words of Isaiah and Jeremiah: "My house shall be called a house of prayer; but you make it a den of robbers".[41] It was a bold, provocative act in the tradition of Jeremiah whose outspokenness about corruption in the Temple had led to his arrest and persecution.[42] The tension and conflict that began in Galilee had escalated in Jerusalem. Jesus was on a collision course with the central religious authorities, and there would be no turning back or compromise on his part. Meanwhile, what were the implications of his actions in the eyes of the secular political leaders?

At one level, Jesus did not operate in the world of politics and his message did not involve an explicitly political agenda. Its focus was squarely on religious and ethical issues such as rethinking God as a loving father, opening one's heart to abundant divine mercy and recognizing both friend and enemy as one's neighbor. Nor did Jesus seek political office or use political power to achieve his ends. At the very start of his public career he had resisted Satan's temptation to assume lordship over all the kingdoms of the earth.[43] Later, faced with the enthusiastic adulation of those who had witnessed his miracles, he resisted the crowd's attempt to make him their king, instead withdrawing to a mountain by himself.[44] Nor was Jesus happy when his own disciples began to think that he might be the long-awaited Jewish Messiah. Mark's gospel is replete with incidents where Jesus rejects the title. Although "Christ" (Messiah) effectively became his surname in time, Jesus's preferred self-designation was the mysterious term "Son of Man". Furthermore, he commanded demons to be silent when they addressed him as Messiah, and he prohibited similar public statements from those he healed.[45] In the pivotal scene of Mark's gospel, when Simon Peter unequivocally declares him to be the Messiah, Jesus sternly ordered his followers not to tell anyone.[46] This is the enigmatic "messianic secret" of Mark, and it is generally explained by scholars in terms of Jesus's realization that the term had certain connotations that did not apply to him. The messianic hat, or rather crown, did not fit, and it would only confuse people to think that he would live up to the traditional expectations, especially the eviction of the Roman army and the establishment of an independent Jewish state. The "basileia" (Kingdom) that he spoke of was not territorial but spiritual. As the fourth evangelist succinctly states, it was "not from this world".[47]

The notion that the kingdoms of God and Rome existed on different planes is well articulated in the scene where Jesus was asked whether it was lawful to pay the unpopular imperial poll tax. The Pharisees and Herodians who posed the mischievous question were hoping to trap Jesus, since an affirmative answer would suggest that he was a Roman sympathizer, whereas a negative answer might incriminate him as a follower of Judas the Galilean who had led a revolt years earlier over the question of taxation. Jesus asked to see the Roman denarius used to pay the tax. It was a silver coin with "Tiberius Caesar, son of divine Augustus" on one side and "High Priest" on the other. Not only was the tax oppressive but the coins deeply offended the religious sensibilities of the monotheistic Jews. Jesus's disarming reply to the question was: "Give to Caesar the things that are Caesar's; and to God the things that are God's".[48] He avoided the antagonistic path of refusing to pay taxes, but his statement clearly implied that there was an authority higher and mightier than even the deified emperor in Rome whose blasphemous image appeared on the very coins collected in tax from his subjects.

Moreover, Jesus deliberately distanced himself from any military action against the Romans that many naturally associated with the long-awaited Messiah. Admittedly, there are enigmatic references to the Kingdom of God suffering violence and being taken or entered "by force", as well as the disturbing statement by Jesus that he has come "not to bring peace to the earth but a sword".[49] It would also seem that his disciples carried "swords" with them and, on one occasion, Peter used the weapon to cut off the ear of one of those attempting to arrest Jesus. However, commentators point out that these were probably small daggers commonly carried by travelers to protect themselves against thieves and wild animals.[50] Moreover, Jesus explicitly condemned Peter for resorting to violence even though it may have been justifiable self-defense: "Put your sword back into its place; for all who take the sword will perish by the sword".[51] This was consistent with his teaching on how to respond to physical aggression: "But if anyone strikes you on the right cheek, turn the other also".[52] Some commentators have suggested that he was referring to the highly insult-ing back-handed slap with the right hand. Thus, Jesus may not have been advocating radical, Gandhi-like pacifism but, rather, cunningly providing a way to preclude the insulter repeating the offensive gesture on the opposite cheek – a physical impossibil-ity.[53] Yet the saying sits with others that call on his disciples to offer a second cloak, walk an extra mile and to love one's enemies as fellow children of our common heavenly Father.[54] This sort of talk did not accord with groups like the Zealots and the Sicarii, who were convinced that well-planned violence was the only language that Rome would ever understand.

At another level, Jesus could not avoid becoming embroiled in the political caul-dron that was Roman Palestine. Although his primary focus was not the overthrow of the Romans or a reform of government structures and policies, his central message could not but raise political waves by virtue of its very language. When Jesus defined his mission in terms of God's Kingdom, even if was intended in a purely spiritual sense, it unavoidably evoked ideas and expectations in the minds of his followers and his opponents. Admittedly, God was the true king, but Jesus also drew on an image from the book of Daniel and spoke of the unpredictable, but imminent, coming of "the Son of Man" on the clouds of heaven in power and glory.[55] As noted above, Jesus frequently used that term to refer to himself, preferring it over "Messiah" (Christ) and, although it is not explicitly stated that Jesus is that future Son of

Man, he certainly saw an intimate link between himself and that mysterious heavenly figure:

> Those who are ashamed of me and of my words in this adulterous and sinful generation, of them the Son of Man will also be ashamed when he comes in the glory of his Father with the holy angels.[56]

Jesus may have been willing to pay Caesar's tax, but he seems to have believed that, in a short time, the political powers of the earth would be overturned by the coming of the Kingdom and the human-like figure who would be its celestial herald. Moreover, Jesus told his closest disciples that they would be seated on thrones to judge the 12 tribes of Israel in the coming new world.[57] James and John were clearly hoping for more than that when they asked if they could occupy seats on Jesus's right and left hand side in his glory, but Jesus pointed out that such allocations were not his to grant.[58] Even the exorcism of the Gerasene demoniac had some political connotations given that the demons are collectively called "Legion", and they are driven into the waters of the lake in a manner reminiscent of Pharaoh's army being drowned during the Exodus.[59]

Jesus may not have wanted anyone to think of him in political terms, but the language of the Kingdom and his central role in its advent made it almost impossible to avoid the title "Messiah" or to expunge it of all political elements. In John's gospel, characters such as Andrew, Nathanael, the Samaritan woman, Martha and even the evangelist himself all profess faith in Jesus as Messiah.[60] Even in Mark, where Jesus adamantly rejects the title, there are hints that Jesus did see himself as a Messiah of sorts. One of the most explicit declarations on his part is his dramatic entry into Jerusalem, riding from the Mount of Olives on a donkey and being hailed as a Davidic king by his branch-waving followers. The event, recorded in all four gospels and now commemorated by Christians on Palm Sunday each year, is replete with messianic imagery. Furthermore, it probably provoked a serious objection from Jesus's religious opponents and undoubtedly caught the eye of the city's overlords.[61] They would have noticed that he enjoyed undisputed authority within his religious movement, deliberately setting himself above the symbolic circle of the Twelve that represented all of Israel. Nor was Jesus so naïve to think that the political powers would not take any interest in a popular religious figure seen by many inside and outside of his circle as the long-expected Jewish Messiah. According to the Synoptic gospels, in the last months of his public career, he began to prepare his disciples for a darker scenario. Alongside the heavenly imagery of a glorious Son of Man, he began to speak about the real possibility of arrest, torture and execution.[62] In traditional thinking, the Messiah was not supposed to be defeated and killed, but Jesus was redefining the concept, and he knew very well what had happened to John the Baptist and the sons of Judas the Galilean. Within a few decades of Jesus's death, the Roman prefect would deal harshly with other messianic claimants and their followers, including an anonymous Samaritan in 36 CE, Theudas in 46 CE and the Egyptian Prophet a few years later. It was clear that Rome would not tolerate anyone who explicitly claimed or was popularly perceived to be the "King of the Jews".

Ruler of Arabia

Muhammad was born into the Hashim clan of the Quraysh tribe, which was the dominant group in Mecca. Although his clan had local aristocratic links, its members were far from wealthy or powerful. As an orphan, he was raised by his uncle, Abu Talib, who became a much respected leader, but who also struggled economically. Consequently, a young Muhammad had limited educational opportunity and spent much of his youth as a shepherd boy followed by work on the caravans. His economic lot improved dramatically when he married Khadija, who had initially hired him as caravan manager. By the time Muhammad was 40 years old, he was able to enjoy a relatively comfortable lifestyle. He was known as an honest man with a gift for successful arbitration as shown by his deft handling of the dispute over who would replace the Black Stone in the newly refurbished Ka'ba (see Chapter 3). However, he was not a tribal leader and was not directly involved in affairs of the state as such.

Things changed dramatically when Muhammad began to receive the divine revelations that required him to enter the public arena as God's prophet. His message of monotheism was initially seen by the Meccan leadership as innocuous and marginal but, as time progressed, attitudes hardened. The tribal chiefs became more concerned about the steadily growing movement. In particular, they were worried about the economic implications of his monotheistic message for the polytheistic pilgrimage business and the political implications of his claim to enjoy divinely sanctioned authority. Eventually, Muhammad and his followers were subject to a deliberate campaign of harassment, violence and a prolonged boycott. The Muslims were powerless to resist the attacks although Muhammad himself enjoyed the protection Abu Talib. However, Abu Talib's death in 619 CE placed Muhammad and his followers in a seriously precarious position, especially when Abu Lahab, a bitter opponent, took over leadership of the Banu Hashim. Faced with the prospect of more systematic persecution and possible death, Muhammad began to seek safe haven outside of Mecca. Abandoning one's hometown and clan was an extraordinary move, but there was no other realistic choice. His first preference was Ta'if, but the local chiefs rejected Muhammad's overtures and he was chased from the town with even children pelting him and Zayd with stones.[63] Suddenly, an unexpected opportunity presented itself and the chain of events that followed would not only save the nascent community from annihilation but drastically change the course of world history.

During the summer of 620 CE, Muhammad happened to meet six pilgrims from Yathrib – a rich oasis town about 250 mi north of Mecca. They had heard rumors of a Meccan prophet who had received revelations from the one God and had suffered unremitting persecution from the Qurayshite leadership. They were also aware that he had a reputation as a highly successful arbitrator in disputes and might be just the person they needed in Yathrib, where the two dominant tribes – the Aws and the Khazraj – had been locked in an intractable and costly blood feud for decades. Profoundly impressed by Muhammad, they promised to consult with their chiefs upon their return and report back in one year. True to their word, a second meeting occurred the following summer at 'Aqaba, this time involving 12 persons – five of the original party and seven others. Significantly there were representatives from both the Aws and Khazraj tribes. It was at this meeting that the delegates swore an oath of allegiance to Muhammad and accepted Islam. Muhammad then sent Mus'ab ibn Umayr back with them to Yathrib as religious instructor, and more conversions followed, including some chiefs.[64] Islam now had a foothold in a second location but, unlike Mecca, personal familiarity with Muhammad was not an obstacle to faith and no central polytheistic shrine was threatened by his message.

A third clandestine meeting was organized one year later in 622 CE when 75 citizens of Yathrib, most of whom were converts, met with Muhammad. The encounter was held at night, since fears were growing that the Quraysh might become suspicious of the negotiations. Muhammad was even accompanied by his uncle 'Abbas, to ensure his safety. The resultant "Second Oath of 'Aqaba" guaranteed the Muslims of Mecca full protection if they relocated to Yathrib. In return, Muhammad was to act as mediator and judge in intertribal disputes. Supervision of the agreement would be the responsibility of a body of 12 men from both Khazraj and Aws tribes – the number possibly inspired by Jesus's 12 disciples.[65] The pact was the perfect solution for the embattled Muslim community, and it had significant consequences and risks. The entire Muslim community would have to uproot itself and move to a town of strangers in the north, risking discovery and retaliation from the Qurayshite leaders. Moreover, Muhammad would not only be a figure of religious authority but would now be assuming a very real political–judicial office. There was no time to delay. During the same summer, 70 Muslim families made the journey in small discreet groups over a period of several months. The migration is known as the Hijra, and it is often compared with the Exodus experience of the ancient Hebrews from Egyptian slavery. Indeed, its extraordinary significance is reflected in the fact that the first year of the Islamic calendar is not the Prophet's birth or death or even the first revelation of the Qur'an but 622 CE – the year of the Hijra. Moreover, the name of the new home for Muslim faithful was soon changed from Yathrib to al-Medina al-Nabi ("the town of the prophet"), conventionally shortened to Medina.[66]

It was a dangerous time. The Meccan leaders began to realize what was happening and hatched a plot to assassinate Muhammad. The strategy to avoid tribal vendetta was to have a member of every clan participate in the killing. It was only foiled because Muhammad, who had been forewarned, asked Ali to impersonate him asleep in his bed so that he could escape the surrounded house.[67] Armed men were also patrolling the countryside, and so Muhammad and Abu Bakr had to take a circuitous route to Yathrib to avoid capture, including hiding in a cave, where they were saved by the spider's web and the pigeon's nest. After a 10-day journey, they arrived safely in Quba' on the outskirts of Medina and waited for Ali to join them. During that time, Muhammad laid the foundations of Islam's first public mosque and led the first Friday prayer. When Ali finally arrived, Muhammad entered the town and purchased the plot of land where his camel rested. He set about constructing a house for himself and his two new wives Sawda and 'A'isha. The building would not only be his domestic residence but also the gathering place for communal worship and the office for his new role as arbitrator of disputes.

According to Islamic tradition, one of the first initiatives that Muhammad took in his new judicial role was to conduct a census and draw up a document known as the Constitution of Medina. It specified the rights and duties of citizens, as well as the relationship between different communities, including the town's Jewish tribes.[68] For many commentators, it was a revolutionary document in that it envisaged a new multi-faith community ('umma) that transcended the deeply entrenched tribal boundaries. It meant that the Meccan and Medinan Muslims, who naturally hailed from different tribes, were now brothers and sisters while pagan relatives back in Mecca were the outsiders. Faith was thicker than blood. Indeed, the Medinan converts were known as helpers (ansar) who supported the Meccan migrants (muhajirun) in practical ways including providing board and lodging until they had established themselves in their new circumstances.

As neutral resolver of disputes, Muhammad was more akin to head judge than king or governor. Political power was still widely dispersed among the local Arabian and Jewish tribal leaders.[69] However, his decisions were widely accepted, and he was soon considered as a more natural, acceptable leader than the Khazraj chief, Ibn Ubayy, who clearly had ambitions beyond his own tribe. Many of the weaker clans in Medina began to join Islam, but there were also strategically important conversions, such as Sa'd ibn Mu'adh, one of the prominent chiefs. The Hijra meant much more than a change in location for the Muslims. It had opened up significant political opportunities for their prophet, whose leadership genius was about to be unleashed with the help of a cadre of talented and devoted individuals, such as Abu Bakr, 'Umar, Uthman and Ali. Muhammad's role was rapidly evolving from persecuted prophet to statesman-prophet, somewhat akin to the judges of early Judaism.[70] The post-Hijra shift in Muhammad's own role is also reflected in a shift in the tone and contents of the Qur'an. The terse, poetic, apocalyptic style of the Meccan period was replaced by more elaborate, prosaic, legal and organizational instructions in the Medinan years.[71]

As the number of Muslim converts increased Muhammad's religious and quasi-political authority in Medina, there were two groups that presented a domestic problem. The first group is referred to by the Qur'an as the hypocrites (munafiqun), who had publically professed faith in Islam but for dubious motives. As time progressed, being Muslim in Medina could have its advantages. Ibn Ubayy himself is portrayed as the arch-hypocrite who declared his loyalty to Muhammad but secretly plotted to undermine the Prophet and seize power.[72] The second group were the local Jewish tribes who, apart from a few conversions, did not accept Muhammad's claim to be a genuine prophet of the one God despite his considerable efforts to convince them otherwise. Many features of early Islam reflect Jewish belief and practice, such as facing Jerusalem for prayers, meeting on the eve of Sabbath (Friday), fasting on Yom Kippur (the tenth day of the first month), staggered daily prayer times and many of the kosher dietary laws. However, as the rejection of Muhammad's prophetic claim became clearer, the Qur'anic assessment of the Jews became more negative, and Islam began to differentiate itself more clearly.[73] The Torah was seen as a distortion of the true book of God, Ramadan became the month of fasting and the qibla was changed from The Temple in Jerusalem to the Ka'ba in Mecca.[74]

However, the graver political threat was still Mecca itself and the change of the qibla implied that the Muslim movement had long-term designs on the town.[75] Moreover, Muhammad was faced with a serious socioeconomic problem in that most of the Meccan migrants were having trouble reestablishing themselves in Medina.

The helpers were not expected to house and support them forever, but the migrants were mainly urban merchants with little agricultural experience, and most of the arable land around Medina was already taken. Furthermore, the migrants had paid a considerable financial price as a result of the Hijra, leaving behind most of their property and assets in Mecca, where they were immediately seized by the Quraysh. Consequently, most migrants were forced to take on demeaning tasks more fitting to servants and slaves. Some also established an alternative to the Jewish-dominated market in the city and began to engage in trade.[76] In the harsh Arabian world at the time, the solution was relatively obvious. Medina was very well positioned to engage in raids on the Meccan caravans travelling to and from Syria. All that was needed was divine approval and, soon after the relocation to Medina, Muhammad announced one of the most far-reaching and controversial revelations of the Qur'an:

> Permission to fight is given to those upon whom war is made because they are oppressed, and most surely Allah is well able to assist them; Those who have been expelled from their homes without a just cause except that they say: Our Lord is Allah. And had there not been Allah's repelling some people by others, certainly there would have been pulled down cloisters and churches and synagogues and mosques in which Allah's name is much remembered; and surely Allah will help him who helps His cause; most surely Allah is Strong, Mighty.[77]

After decades of passive resistance to continuous Meccan persecution, the Qur'an now issued a call to arms on the basis of justified resistance to oppression and compensation for property stolen. From their new base in Medina and with considerably more political and military resources at their disposal, the Muslim community was in a position to strike back. The revolutionary divine message gave Muhammad the green light to send out armed Muslim raiding parties on Meccan caravans. In the eyes of some Western critics, this was a fateful turn for the worse, tantamount to highway robbery or a deliberate action aimed at provoking armed conflict with Mecca.[78] For others, it was a legitimate attempt to restore justice for a community that had been wronged. Some point out that only Meccan muhajirun, and not Medinan ansar, were permitted to participate in these raids since only the former had been the direct victims of persecution, eviction and theft.[79] Some also point out that the raid (ghazu) was a widely accepted practice in Arabian culture, akin to a national sport and a crude means of distributing limited resources. The aim was to make off with goods from enemy tribes without taking human life, which would automatically trigger a vendetta.[80] Furthermore, such raids were never directed against tribes with whom an alliance had been signed.

The first series of excursions were useful in terms of gathering intelligence for defense purposes but they were not particularly successful in terms of commercial gain since the caravans were often difficult to locate. However, in January 624 CE, a raiding party led by 'Abdullah ibn Jahsh did discover its target at a place called Nakhla. It was the last day of the month of Rajab, one of the four sacred months in which armed conflict was taboo according to Arabian tradition. After some deliberation, 'Abdullah decided to attack the small caravan rather than wait for the morrow and risk losing the narrow opportunity. To complicate matters, one of the caravan personnel was killed in the operation. The violation of the sacred month was a scandalous act and Muhammad himself was deeply troubled, giving the raiders a cool reception upon their return and refusing to divide the booty.[81] Then, another controversial revelation came to him declaring that the act, while it broke pagan custom, was justified in the eyes of Allah:

> They ask you concerning the sacred month about fighting in it. Say: Fighting in it is a grave matter, and hindering (men) from Allah's way and denying Him, and (hindering men from) the Sacred Mosque and turning its people out of it, are still graver with Allah, and persecution is graver than killing.[82]

The divine message calmed the anxieties of the Medina citizens and encouraged Muhammad to expand the campaign. In Ramadan of the same year, 624 CE, Muhammad himself led a group of 300 men to attack a large caravan under Abu Sufyan, who had allegedly been selling former Muslim property in Mecca to raise funds for an eventual attack on Medina. The ambush point was a complex of wells at Badr, about 100 mi from Medina, but a perceptive Abu Sufyan noted from camel droppings that Medinan raiders were in the area. He requested aid from Mecca and safely diverted the caravan to the coast. The Meccans quickly sent a small army of about one thousand men and caught Muhammad's group off-guard. A Khazrajite suggested filling the wells with sand and so Muhammad began to prepare for the first major battle of his career.[83] As was the Arabian tradition, a series of single combats were initially fought, and all three Muslim warriors were victorious: Hamza, Ali and 'Ubayda, although the third was mortally wounded. Then, Muhammad threw some gravel in the direction of the enemy, arrows were released and the real battle commenced. Muhammad and Abu Bakr directed operations from a small hut outside the fighting zone. While tribal affiliation meant that the Meccans were instinctively reluctant to fight their own kin, the Muslims had been motivated by Muhammad's promise that martyrs who died in battle would enjoy the pleasures of Paradise in the next life. When their commander Jahl was killed, the Meccans began to panic and flee. Despite being outnumbered three to one, the Muslims amazingly won the day. The final casualty count was about 15 Muslims and 50 Meccans. 'Umar had recommended that all prisoners should be killed, but Abu Bakr convinced Muhammad to ransom them, which was organized during the following weeks. There were two exceptions. Muhammad ordered the execution of two Meccan poets who had been particularly vociferous critics. Unaccustomed to the spoils of war, the Muslim soldiers began to argue about the booty, but the Qur'an announced that Muhammad should oversee its equitable allocation and that one-fifth would be his to dispense with as head of the community.[84]

The victory at Badr was seen as a sign of divine support for Muhammad and his cause, and the Qur'an even suggests that angels fought alongside the Muslim soldiers.[85] Moreover, the tough, strategic decisions taken by Muhammad before, during and after the battle reveal his rapid and successful self-adaptation beyond religious leader into an emerging political and military commander. It was a career path that he apparently had no qualms in following, convinced as he was that Allah was guiding him along it. The success at Badr immeasurably strengthened his position in Medina and elevated his status, resulting in more waves of conversions. It also made a deep impression on surrounding Arabian tribes who began to take more notice of the rising political star who had inflicted such a humiliating defeat on the Quraysh.

Badr was only the first of three battles between Medina and Mecca. In 625 CE, the Quraysh sent an army of 3,000 men led by Abu Sufyan to avenge the ignomini-ous loss of the previous year. The Meccans camped at a small mountain named Uhud about 5 mi from Medina. Muhammad preferred to stay inside the town and withstand a siege, but a large number of younger Muslims, inspired by the glorious triumph at Badr and enthusiastic to become martyrs, convinced him to face the enemy head on.[86] Ibn Ubayy had promised support, but withdrew with his troops at the last minute, leaving the Muslim forces seriously depleted and outnumbered. Once again a series of single duels were held, with Ali and Hamza successful. In the ensuing fight, the Muslim archers prematurely sensed victory and abandoned their positions to collect booty. Seizing the opportunity, Khalid ibn al-Walid, the Meccan cavalry commander, charged around the hill and the Muslims were trapped in a pincer move-ment. Hamza was speared and Muhammad himself was wounded in the mouth by a rock.[87] Rumors quickly spread that the Prophet was dead but in reality he had desperately scrambled to safety. It was a deflating defeat for the Muslims who lost about 70 men, while the Meccans suffered about 20 casualties. One of the more gory details was that Hind, the sister of Abu Sufyan, mutilated the body of Hamza and ate his liver. However, the Meccans made the fatal decision not to press their advantage, choosing instead to withdraw with their limited victory, rather than risk a protracted siege. In contrast to Badr, the loss at Uhud seriously undermined Muslim confidence, but the Qur'an provided consolation, pointing out that Allah was testing their faith and stressing that even Muhammad was dispensable.[88] It was a close shave, but Muhammad and his community had survived its most serious setback.

Two years later, a third battle occurred, this time with even more troops. Abu Sufyan assembled a tribal coalition of 10,000 men, intending to wipe out Islam definitively. The Muslims had received early warning, and a Persian convert named Salman had suggested excavating a trench in front of the exposed city walls. Legends abound of Muhammad and his men confidently singing and chanting as they dug their defense for a week. The strategy worked brilliantly. Abu Sufyan's troops were unprepared for such fortifications and the prolonged siege that ensued. After a month of futile efforts to cross the trench, the Meccans began to run out of supplies and to lose motivation. As with many historical battles, the weather also played its part. A strong wind created havoc in the Meccan camp, and Abu Sufyan was forced to abandon the entire project in utter failure.[89] The encounter became known as the Battle of the Ditch, and it spelt the humiliating end of Mecca's dominance in central Arabia. The gods of Mecca had failed to eradicate the God of the Muslims. More tribes sided with Medina and alliances were drawn up. Islam was now inextricably on the rise.

During the period that Muhammad was engaged in conflict with Mecca, there were also three domestic incidents involving Jewish clans in Medina. The tradition states that soon after Badr, a Jewish goldsmith had insulted and assaulted a Muslim woman. A Muslim convert had intervened and killed the goldsmith but the con-vert himself was then killed by fellow Jews from the Qaynuqa clan. Although the

Constitution of Medina should have resolved the issue of blood money, the Qaynuqa Jews withdrew to their strongholds and expected Ibn Ubayy to protect them. After a fortnight blockade, the Jews surrendered and were expelled from Medina. Their vacated houses were allocated to Muslim migrants.[90] A second incident concerned the Jewish Nadir clan soon after the defeat at Uhud. According to Islamic sources, the trigger was an assassination attempt on Muhammad involving someone trying to throw a rock on him from a rooftop. The consequence was that the entire Nadir clan were given ten days to leave the town. Again Ibn Ubayy promised to help them and so they locked themselves in their fortresses and a three-week siege began. Against his usual policy, Muhammad ordered the destruction of their orchards and date palms, arguing that it was an unfortunate step required by a drastic situation. The Nadir Jews surrendered and, like their Qaynuqa colleagues, were evicted from Medina with whatever their camels could carry.[91]

The third confrontation with a Jewish clan in Medina was bloodier. The Jewish Qurayza clan were accused of assisting the Meccans during the Battle of the Ditch. Once again, the Jewish community surrendered after a siege of several weeks. However, this time, the crime was treason and the standard punishment was not expulsion but execution. Muhammad invited the accused to choose their own judge to decide their fate, and Sa'd ibn Mu'adh from the sympathetic Aws tribe was selected. It is difficult to know if they misjudged their choice or whether Sa'd, who was injured at the time, was simply in bad temper. When advised that the Torah imposes death in such a case, he ruled that all of the adult men be executed and that the women and children be sold into slavery. Muhammad accepted the ruling and hadith material describes what followed in gruesome detail. According to Ibn Ishaq, between 600 and 900 men were beheaded that day – only a handful accepting the offer to convert and save their lives.[92] For some commentators, it is evidence of a ruthless side of Muhammad's leadership and the low point of his career. For others, the executions were not based on religious or racial grounds but were a necessary act in the grim world of realpolitik. Moreover, some commentators question the historical accuracy of such high numbers.[93]

Just when the military conflict between Mecca and Medina seemed doomed to be long, bitter and bloody, Muhammad suddenly switched tactics. In early 628 CE he ordered his followers to prepare for the annual pilgrimage to the Ka'ba and set out with over 1,000 followers. They wore the simple pilgrim's robes (ihram) and carried no weapons. The extraordinary irenic gesture caught the Quraysh completely by surprise. They did not want the Muslims to enter their city but neither could they violate Arabian tradition and attack them. A small cavalry was commissioned to block the travelers but Muhammad evaded them and arrived on the outskirts of Mecca. What followed were essentially peace talks that resulted in the Treaty of Hudaybiyya.[94] There were some tricky moments, such as the false rumors that Uthman, who had been sent into Mecca as a delegate, had been killed. The Meccans also objected to a number of phrases in the document, including the description of Muhammad as "messenger of God". Rather than argue the point, Muhammad agreed to omit the phrase for the sake of diplomacy. The main points of the agreement were: a 10-year truce; the Muslims would not be allowed to visit the Ka'ba this time but could do so in the following year for a three-day period; Medina would return any new converts to Mecca but the Quraysh were not obliged to return the favor; all tribes were released from current alliances and could choose either town. The sense that the treaty unfairly favored Mecca was very strong among some of Muhammad's deputies, especially 'Umar, but the Qur'an described it as a "victory" and Muhammad agreed that there would be real gains.[95] Muhammad was recognized by the Meccan leaders as an equal, the military conflict had ended and the Meccan residents were pleased that the new religion incorporated some of their customs. Muhammad was hoping that the investment in Meccan goodwill would bring greater, more enduring, dividends than victory on the battlefield.

The pilgrimage of 629 CE went well, with over 2,000 participants. Under the terms of the agreement, the Quraysh had vacated the town and watched curiously from the surrounding hills as Muhammad and his followers shaved their heads, circum-ambulated the Ka'ba, walked seven times between the hills of Safa and Marwa, and performed the animal sacrifices.[96] At the end of the visit, Muhammad and his fellow pilgrims returned home peacefully without any attempt to repossess their lost properties. The entire episode impressed the Meccans and augured well. Key people, such as Khalid, converted and the new religion gained considerable ground in Mecca. Then suddenly another twist occurred. The truce had held firm for the first year, but in late 629 CE, a tribe allied to Mecca attacked a tribe allied to Medina. It meant a formal breach and when Mecca refused to compensate, declaring the treaty null and void, Muhammad responded. In early 630 CE, he marched on Mecca with 10,000 men gathered from Medina and the many tribes now allied with him. By now, many of the Meccan leaders had defected to Islam, including 'Abbas, Khalid and even Abu Sufyan, who had met with Muhammad in secret. Muhammad promised that no Meccan would be harmed provided they remained in their houses, and only one small group of armed men resisted. The tide had now irrevocably swung in favor of Muhammad. The triumphant prophet rode to the Ka'ba and cried "Allahu akbar", to which 10,000 soldiers enthusiastically responded. He then destroyed the hundreds of statues housed in it and painted over the pagan icons inside, except one fresco of Jesus and Mary.[97] The Ethiopian Bilal then climbed onto the roof of the Ka'ba and issued the haunting call for afternoon prayer. In defiance of Arabian custom, Muhammad issued a general amnesty and sought no vendetta against his enemies, except for a few outspoken critics who were executed. Even Hind, who had mutilated the body of Hamza, was pardoned.[98] All those who converted were allowed to retain their property and, understandably, many joined the ranks of Islam that day. There had been speculation that Muhammad would now resettle in his hometown and make that his headquarters, but he declined to do so and returned to Medina. After 10 years of exile, it was arguably Muhammad's most triumphant moment. The ancient shrine had been reclaimed in the name of the one God, his oldest political enemy had been subdued and Arabian tribal delegates came from all directions to convert and to transfer their allegiance to the new power in the land.[99]

Muhammad's conviction that a valid part of his prophetic role was the exercise of political and military leadership continued to shape his career after the surrender of Mecca. He had already sent troops to crush resistance at Khaybar, near Medina, marrying Safiyya, the daughter of their leader, and imposing a harvest tax on the defeated communities.[100] The final obstacle to undisputed command of central Arabia was Ta'if, where 20,000 men had been mobilized under Malik ibn Awf. Muhammad and his men rode out to meet them, but were ambushed in the valley of Hunayn. Once again, despite the odds, the Muslim forces prevailed. Muhammad displayed a brilliant mix of political canny and un-Arabian clemency, freeing 6000 prisoners and giving much of the booty to the newly converted Meccan leaders, such as Abu Sufyan. Many of the vanquished soldiers had fled to Ta'if, but within a year they too had surrendered. The foundations of an Islamic state had been laid, and Muhammad now began to look further north, beyond the boundaries of his homeland.

On the diplomatic level, Islamic tradition states that Muhammad sent out letters to rulers of neighboring states, including Heraclius (Emperor of Byzantium), Khosrau (Emperor of Persia), the Negus (King of Abyssinia), Muqawqis (Vice-Regent of Egypt), Mundhir (King of Bahrain) and Harith (the Ghassani ruler). Scholars are divided over the authenticity of the letters and the responses varied from courteous to dismissive, but the story suggests that Muhammad saw himself on par with the most powerful figures in the region.[101] On the military level, in response to reports that Byzantine troops were amassing in southern Syria and their tribal allies were attacking Muslim allies in northern Arabia, Muhammad sent a group of 3000 men to Mu'ta near the southern end of the Dead Sea in 629 CE. The battalion was under the command of Muhammad's adopted son, Zayd, along with his deputies Ja'far and Abd Allah. According to tradition, they encountered an enormous Byzantine force of 100,000 soldiers, and all three were slaughtered along with most of the men. It was the first military excursion beyond Arabia and it ended in utter defeat, compounded by the distressing, personal loss that Muhammad suffered with the death of Zayd. However, the memory of Mu'ta did not deter the Prophet and, in late 630 CE, Muhammad himself rode north with an army of 30,000 men. They reached Tabuk in northwest Arabia, but rumors of a large Byzantine presence proved false. This time there was no confrontation but Muhammad took the opportunity to secure further treaties with local tribal leaders. Tabuk was to be his last military campaign, but the confident, divinely sanctioned mission of expanding the Islamic state northward into Byzantine and Persian territory was passed on to Muhammad's immediate successors. With staggering speed, the armies of a new, united Arabia would transform world history, and within 100 years of Muhammad's death, an Islamic empire would stretch from the shores of Morocco to the mountains of Afghanistan.

Observations

The existence of a political dimension to the life of the Buddha, Jesus and Muhammad is an inevitable consequence of their respective claims to authority. Questions of leadership and control, support and opposition naturally arose both within their faith communities and externally in relation to religious and political powers. All three were unavoidably involved in politics to some degree, but the particular circumstances of that involvement and each founder's personal response reveals a fascinating mix of similarities and differences.

In terms of socioeconomic background, all three are portrayed as having some connection to royal or aristocratic pedigree. The most obvious case is Siddhattha, who was not only born into the Hindu Kshatria (warrior) caste but was also the firstborn son of a local king, even though his Sakyan kingdom was probably a modest vassal state and its political model may have been oligarchic council rather than hereditary monarchy. Siddhattha was trained and educated as a prince within the safety of palace walls. It was a formative lifestyle, more concentrated and sheltered than usual as a result of Suddhodana's preoccupation with ensuring a smooth succession to the throne. Siddhattha was royalty and should have become a king like his father.

The gospels of Matthew and Luke both claim that Jesus was a descendant of Israel's ancient kings, ostensibly because it was widely believed that the Jewish Messiah would have royal Davidic blood. Despite the lofty genealogical claim, Jesus was actually born into peasant stock in an inconsequential town in Galilee, at the northern end of Israel. In striking contrast to Siddhattha's luxurious palace upbringing, Jesus was raised as the son of a local village tradesman and there is no evidence that he played any role in local Galilean politics.

A similar mix of noble lineage in theory but low economic standing in actuality characterizes Muhammad's circumstances. Although it was an aristocratic connection rather than a royal one, Muhammad was born into the Hashim clan of the Quraysh tribe, which dominated the Meccan leadership. The Hashim clan was entrusted with the esteemed role of safeguarding the sacred waters of the Zamzam spring. However, its membership had experienced difficult times, and it was one of the weaker subgroups within the Quraysh. Moreover, the loss of both parents at a young age meant that an orphaned Muhammad was seriously disadvantaged. He was fortunate to have been raised by his grandfather and, then, his uncle, but he probably spent most of his youth as a marginalized shepherd boy with no education and very limited opportunities for advancement. His prospects were not particularly promising, but a critical break came when his managerial skills caught the business eye of Khadija and his charming personality won her heart. According to tradition, his diplomatic potential was revealed in his clever solution to the problem of replacing the Black Stone in the renovated Ka'ba. Despite such skills, Muhammad was essentially a well-respected and successful merchant with minimal involvement in Meccan politics.

Life is rarely predictable, and although one of the founders was born to be king, it was another who ended up as successful ruler on the political stage. The young prince Siddhattha had been groomed to assume his father's throne but the experience of the four sights so profoundly unsettled the young man that he made the momentous decision to abandon not only his wife and child but also his vocation and inheritance. It was a deliberate and explicit renunciation of the palace in favor of the forest; a renunciation of the political path in favor of the spiritual one. As predicted by the sole sage at his birth, Siddhattha would never be a cakkavatti; he would instead become a Buddha. Commitment to this path was not without its challenges and distractions. The tradition describes how Mara, the tempter, attempted to persuade him to return to the safety and comfort of his father's home on many occasions, not the least during the very night of his Enlightenment. The earth-touching hand gesture on Buddha statues symbolizes the master's firm resolve and his resistance to Mara's wiles on that night. Yet it was not only a troublesome spirit who put obstacles in his way. Struck by his regal demeanor, King Bimbisara offered Siddhattha command of an army battalion and possibly half of his kingdom. The gestures were politely declined. The Buddha did not wish to command an army or rule a nation. His message did not focus on political, economic or social issues so much as the individual's struggle to overcome ignorant craving and, thus, reach ultimate liberation from the wheel of rebirth.

The same explicit rejection of political office can be seen in the case of Jesus. Although he was not raised in a palace with weighty expectations of succession on his shoulders like Siddhattha, nevertheless, his sudden popularity as a miracle worker and preacher raised questions about his leadership potential and the possible acquisition of political power. At the very start of his public ministry, Jesus resisted Satan's offer of the kingdoms of the world in all of their splendor. Like Siddhattha, the lure of earthly power was presented not only by the spirit of temptation but also by those around Jesus. The crowds who witnessed the miracle of the loaves were on the verge of spontaneously declaring him their king but Jesus escaped to the hills. Similarly, his own disciples considered him to be the long-awaited Messiah who, for some, would evict the Roman occupiers and establish peace and justice in Israel. Yet Jesus cast aside such understandings of Messiahship and forbade his disciples (and demons) to refer to him by that title. Like Siddhattha, his message was not primarily about political or economic reform. Jesus was willing to pay the imperial tax but saw Caesar's authority as distinct from and inferior to God's authority. If Jesus must be called king, then it should be kept in mind that his kingdom was not of this world.

In striking contrast, Muhammad saw no problem in assuming political office when the opportunity arose. After years of harassment and persecution at the hands of the Quraysh in Mecca, he did not hesitate to accept the offer to act as a neutral arbitrator in Yathrib's crippling internecine disputes. It was a career-changing moment, and it enabled the beleaguered Muslim community to escape ongoing Meccan hostility and resettle in a town where they could consolidate and grow. What was initially a judicial, diplomatic role, quickly evolved into de facto political leadership as a result of Muhammad's formidable decision-making skills, uncanny sense of timing and an audacious willingness to take calculated risks. In Muslim eyes, his emergence as the undisputed ruler of Yathrib (aptly renamed Medina) was the result of divine providence. While his fundamental religious mission was the conversion of his fellow Arabs to monotheism, this quickly became linked to the establishment of an Islamic state. Being God's final prophet did not preclude him being God's earthly regent as well.

Within their own faith communities, the authority of the three founders was, in the main, undisputed. Jesus's teachings on leadership stressed service of others and concern for the weakest members of the flock, but the gospels also suggest that he made his decisions in spite of, rather than in consultation with, the inner circle of the Twelve. The fact that Jesus did not include himself in the Twelve – a number that symbolized Israel reunited and whole – implies that he saw himself occupying a special position outside and above them. He spoke with quasi-divine authority to both the crowds and his closest companions, who acknowledged his superior status. In a similar manner, Muhammad enjoyed the solid loyalty and obedience of his followers throughout the two decades of public life. Extraordinary levels of dedication are evident among the true faithful who acclaimed him as the peerless spokesperson for God in their midst. Yet unlike Jesus, there is evidence that Muhammad frequently sought counsel from his closest advisors, as well as his wives. Although he usually made the final decision, it was often shaped by the guidance of others. Similarly, the Buddha is portrayed as one who clearly stood head and shoulders above his monks. As with Muhammad, there is evidence that the Buddha encouraged his followers to discuss ideas and express their opinions on disputed matters but the final decision always rested with him.

Unlike Jesus and Muhammad, the Buddha had to face a serious act of rebellion within his own ranks. Such insubordination is probably not surprising given that the Buddha presided over his ever-growing community for more than four decades – an interval considerably longer than that of Muhammad and, especially, Jesus. Siddhattha's cousin and brother-in-law, Devadatta, had displayed a cruel disposition as a child but entered the monastic life and mastered the iddhi powers. At some stage, he suggested that an ageing Buddha step aside and allow him to assume the mantle. When that audacious request was denied, Devadatta instigated a rigorist schism that was only suppressed with the intervention of Sariputta and Moggallana. On a more sinister note, Devadatta is also accused of organizing at least three assassination attempts on the Buddha's life – all of which failed. The most serious threat to the Buddha's authority, and indeed his very life, came from an enemy within.

On the external front, the Buddha had to deal with other religious movements in what was a highly competitive market. It is difficult to know the details since the Buddhist texts usually depict their master as supremely victorious in contests of miraculous powers or persuasive oratory. The Buddha's itinerant monks eventually carried his message beyond the boundaries of the Ganges Valley in all directions across Asia. However, it was a slow, gradual expansion that was given significant impetus by the conversion of the emperor Ashoka in the third century BCE. What is significant is that the Buddha and his monks faced no real opposition or persecution from political authorities. In fact, the Buddha is depicted as a close friend and counsellor of King Bimbisara who, despite embracing the Buddha's teachings, nevertheless still pursued a policy of regional expansionism. The Buddha is also said to have eventually won over Bimbisara's rival, King Pasenadi. While his influence on their political decisions may have been limited, his monastic movement was allowed to flourish in their realms with their apparent blessing.

There is really no equivalent to the character of Devadatta in the stories of Jesus and Muhammad. Even the ambitious request of James and John only involved sitting at Jesus's right and left hand, not taking over completely. Unlike the Buddha, Jesus and Muhammad faced no mutiny within their communities. Rather, the most menacing threats were external. Jesus faced two forms of religious hostility. The first came from groups such as the Pharisees, who objected to his liberal interpretation of certain traditional laws, especially those pertaining to the Sabbath, purification and diet. The second came from more powerful groups based in Jerusalem who objected to his criticism of the Temple financial trade. The gospels claim that both groups not only disagreed with his theological agenda but actively plotted to have him killed. The situation was further compounded by the fact that Jesus's claims carried not only religious but also political implications. Even though he refused to accept the title "Messiah" in the way that it was broadly understood in his day, Jesus's declaration of an imminent Kingdom and his self-identification as the Son of Man who would usher it in, suggested the overthrow of worldly government structures in some manner. While the Buddha seemed to pose no direct threat to the reigning monarchs of his day, and is even portrayed as a welcome advisor to kings, Jesus was perceived in a very different way by those who ruled Palestine and every visit to Jerusalem was risky business.

The early public career of Muhammad in Mecca reflects a similar pattern. Muhammad proclaimed an unsettling message for the town's leadership. His uncompromising monotheism threatened to undermine the polytheistic shrine industry centred on the Ka'ba, and his claim to be the one God's definitive spokesperson naturally made tribal leaders wonder how his authority related to theirs. Initial, curious fascination soon gave way outright conflict, harassment and persecution. Were it not for the traditional clan protection afforded to his nephew by Abu Talib, Muhammad may well have suffered the same premature death that Jesus experienced. When his uncle and protector died, Muhammad realized that the only way to ensure personal and communal survival was to leave Mecca, which is precisely what happened.

If the experience of Muhammad in Mecca was very close to that of Jesus, then the Hijra radically sets them apart. By moving his community to Yathrib and accepting the role of arbitrator in that town, Muhammad simultaneously found a vital safe haven for his fledgling group and stepped into the world of political power. The latter brought with it the possibility of having military force at his disposal and, soon afterwards, the Qur'an gave him explicit permission to take up arms in the struggle with the enemy. It was a watershed moment with enormous consequences for not only Muhammad and his followers, but the entire Arabian peninsula and beyond. The Buddha had recoiled from all forms of violence, allowing his monks to use only minimal force in self-defense and advising monarchs that offensive war was never justified. Jesus had spoken of a metaphorical sword that he would bring to the earth and his followers carried small traveller daggers for self-defense, but his position on the use of force is very close to that of the Buddha. His advice to followers that they turn the other cheek to an aggressor was spelled out in practice by his passive resistance on the night of his arrest and his famous statement that one who lives by the sword will die by the sword.

In contrast, Muhammad accepted the role of army commander as a natural corollary of his decision to assume political leadership. In doing so, he revealed a hidden genius that would transform the region within a decade via a mix of diplomatic alliances, strategic marriages and military campaigns. Such a decision inevitably involved the spilling of blood: the slaying of soldiers on the battlefield and the execution of those convicted of treason. Muhammad himself was almost killed at Uhud and survived several assassination attempts. Yet there were also peaceful initiatives, un-Arabian displays of clemency, a revision of the rules of war and an austere lifestyle hardly typical of most earthly rulers. This is undoubtedly one of the most controversial and divisive aspects of Muhammad's life. For critics, his use of force is evidence of ambition and intolerance, indicating that he was not a true prophet. For sympathizers, these are justifiable acts based on principles of compensation, self-defense and harsh political reality. Indeed, there are two quite distinct phases in Muhammad's public career. While the powerless victim of persecution during the Meccan period strongly resembles Jesus, the prophet-warrior of the Medinan period is more reminiscent of figures such as Moses, Joshua and the judges of Israel. In a similar fashion, Muslims see Muhammad's unlikely political success against the odds as an unequivocal sign of divine support. In contrast, Christians must look elsewhere for divine endorsement of Jesus who, far from triumphing on the world's stage, was a tragic casualty of political interests.

Notes

1 Nakamura I 84–85.
2 Sutta Nipata 419–421; Nakamura I 123; Mizuno 20–22; Thomas 69.
3 Mahavagga 1.54; Nakamura I 339–343; Foucher 175–176.
4 Carrithers 96.
5 Rahula 84; Blomfield 243.
6 Kutadanta Sutta and Cakkavattisihanada Suttanta.
7 Samyutta Nikaya 42.3.
8 Dhammapada Atthakatha 25; Dhammika 37–38.
9 Foucher 190–191.
10 Mahaparinibbana Sutta 72–74.
11 Mizuno 142.
12 Thomas 139–140.
13 Thomas 131.
14 Foucher 62; Thomas 131.
15 Foucher 63; Thomas 131.
16 Foucher 212–214; Thomas 131–138.
17 Vinaya II.184ff.
18 Vinaya II.188; Abhaya Sutta, Majjhima Nikaya 58.
19 Thomas 133.
20 Cullavagga 7; Foucher 211; Blomfield 260.
21 Dhammapadatthakatha i.122.
22 Cullavagga 7; Dhammapadatthakatha i.147; Thomas 135.
23 Thomas 137.
24 Carrithers 96; Armstrong, Buddha 129.
25 See also Matthew 1:6; 2:2,5; Luke 1:33; 2:4.
26 For examples of the title "rabbi", see Mark 9:5; 11:21; 14:45; John 1:38, 49; 3:2; 4:31. For examples of the title "teacher" (didaskale) see Mark: 4:38; 9:17, 38; 10:17, 20, 51.
27 Mark 2:10–12.
28 Mark 2:23–28; 3:1–6.
29 Mark 7:1–8, 14–23. The issue arose in the early Church and is recorded in Acts 10 where Peter has a vision declaring all foods permissible.
30 Crossan 261–264.
31 Mark 2:7; 3:22; 11:27–28.
32 Luke 18:9–14.
33 Matthew 23:1–36.
34 Vermes, Changing 196.
35 Mark 3:6; Matthew 12:14; Luke 6:11.
36 Luke 13:31–35.
37 John 5:18.
38 John 7:40–52.
39 John 11:50.

40   Mark 11:18–19; 12:12; 14:1–2; Matthew 21:45–46; 26:3–5; Luke 20:19; 22:1–2.
41   Mark 11:15–17; Matthew 21:12–13; Luke 19:45–46; John 2:14–22; Isaiah 56:7; Jeremiah 7:11.
42   Jeremiah 7:3–12.
43   Matthew 4:8–10; Luke 4:5–8.
44   John 6:15.
45   Mark 1:24–25, 34, 43; 3:11–12; 5:6–8, 43; 7:36; 9:20.
46   Mark 8:30.
47   John 18:36.
48   Mark 12:17.
49   Matthew 11:12; 10:34; Luke 16:16.
50   Gabriel 132; Luke 22:38.
51   Matthew 26:52; Luke 22:49–51; John 18:11.
52   Matthew 5:39.
53   Amer 111; Breckenridge 100.
54   Matthew 5:38–46.
55   Mark 13:26; 14:62; Luke 12:40; Matthew 25:31.
56   Mark 8:38.
57   Matthew 19:28; Luke 22:30.
58   Mark 10:37.
59   Mark 5:9, 13.
60   John 1:41, 49; 4:25; 11:27; 20.31.
61   Matthew 21:1–11; Mark 11:1–10; Luke 19:28–44; John 12:12–19.
62   Mark 8.31; 9:12, 31; 10:33.
63   Ibn Ishaq (Guillaume) 192.
64   Ibn Ishaq (Guillaume) 198–199.
65   Ibn Ishaq (Guillaume) 201–204.
66   The name Medina is also linguistically linked to the word "medaniyyah", meaning "civilization".
67   Ibn Ishaq (Guillaume) 222.
68   Ibn Ishaq (Guillaume) 231–234.
69   Armstrong, Muhammad 110.
70   Emerick 133.
71   Emerick 134.
72   Qur'an 2:14; Armstrong, Muhammad 119.
73   Qur'an 5:82; 57:26; 3:110.
74   Ibn Ishaq (Guillaume) 289; Emerick 142–144; Peterson 98.
75   Ramadan 99.
76   Armstrong, Muhammad 126.
77   Qur'an 22:39–40; Ibn Ishaq (Guillaume) 212–213.
78   Andrae 140; Rodinson 162; Peterson 101.
79   Ramadan 96.
80   Armstrong, Muhammad 126.
81   Armstrong, Muhammad 129; Emerick 153, 157.
82   Qur'an 2:217; Ibn Ishaq (Guillaume) 286–289.
83   For details of the Battle of Badr see Ibn Ishaq (Guillaume) 289–314; Lings 138–159.
84   Qur'an 8:41.
85   Qur'an 3:123–125.
86   For details of the Battle of Uhud see Ibn Ishaq (Guillaume) 370–391; Lings170–197.
87   Ibn Ishaq (Guillaume) 380; Armstrong, Muhammad 141; Ramadan 122; Emerick 195.

88   Emerick 202; Qur'an 3:144, 165–169.
89   For details of the Battle of the Ditch see Ibn Ishaq (Guillaume) 456–461; Lings 215–230; Qur'an 33:9–27.
90   Ramadan 107; Armstrong, Muhammad 140. Lings points out that each Medinan tribe had its own fortified hamlet. Lings 105–111.
91   Qur'an 59:1–4; Ibn Ishaq (Guillaume) 437–439; Emerick 207; Armstrong, Muhammad 150.
92   Ibn Ishaq (Guillaume) 464; Bukhari 59.447; 52.280; 58.148.
93   Emerick 225. See also W.N.Arafat, "New Light on the Story of Banu Qurayza and the Jews of Medina", in *Journal of the Royal Asiatic Society of Great Britain and Ireland* (1976) 100–107.
94   Ibn Ishaq (Guillaume) 499–507.
95   Qur'an 48:1–4.
96   Armstrong, Muhammad 193; Emerick 242.
97   Ibn Ishaq (Guillaume) 552.
98   Ibn Ishaq (Guillaume) 553; Ramadan 177.
99   Ibn Ishaq (Guillaume) 627–628; Qur'an 110:1–3.
100 Ibn Ishaq (Guillaume) 515; Armstrong, Muhammad 190; Ramadan 162.
101 Armstrong, Muhammad 196; Emerick 243–244; Ramadan 171. The Topkapi Palace in Istanbul houses what is claimed to be the original letter from Muhammad to the Muqawqis.

Chapter 10

DEATH

As mortal beings, all three founders eventually experienced the inescapable reality of dying. Although religious faith regards each of them as a unique figure within human history, holding the key to life and death, nevertheless, there came a time when the Buddha, Jesus and Muhammad all passed from this world. This final chapter focuses on that crucial moment. What were the circumstances and manner of their deaths? What was the fate of their bodies? To what extent did each founder anticipate and prepare for his demise? What theological significance does each tradition ascribe to the event? What impact did the death have on their followers, and how did the bereaved community deal with the question of the succession of authority?

The Blacksmith's Meal

As noted in the first chapter, the Buddhist scriptures and the earliest biographies concentrate heavily on Siddhattha's journey to enlightenment and, in most cases, terminate at the First Sermon and the establishment of the religious order. Although there are snippets of information about the many decades that followed, these are often piecemeal and without a narrative framework. The one exception is the death of the Buddha, which is recounted in considerable detail in the sixteenth chapter of the Digha Nikaya, otherwise known as the Mahaparinibbana Sutta (The Discourse on the Great Passing into Nibbana). It is the longest single sutta in the Digha Nikaya and its general contents are mirrored in many other later versions of the basic story across various Buddhist schools. The length of the text reflects a heightened interest in the final phase of the Buddha's life, in contrast to the scant information concerning the many decades preceding it. It is as if the scriptural authors were seeking a concentrated wisdom from the last chapter of his long and esteemed career.

The setting of the Mahaparinibbana Sutta is an arduous journey undertaken by the 80-year old Buddha, from Vulture Peak, near Rajagaha, in the general direction

Buddha, Jesus and Muhammad: A Comparative Study, First Edition. Paul Gwynne.
© 2014 John Wiley & Sons, Ltd. Published 2014 by John Wiley & Sons, Ltd.

of his Sakyan birthplace in the north. Although the texts state that many disciples accompanied him, commentators suspect that only a few close companions were actually with him, including his personal attendant, Ananda. The itinerary took them away from the larger bustling cities into more obscure territory at the very edge of the civilized world. Essentially, he was retracing his original steps in reverse order.[1]

The Buddha left Magadha and entered Vajji country by miraculously crossing the flooded Ganges in the blink of an eye, whilst others looked vainly about for a boat or a raft.[2] As he moved through town and village, the Buddha took the opportunity to instruct his followers and recapitulate the main themes of his lifelong teaching. While the names of the places visited are the same in most versions, the content of the sermons varies, suggesting that they are later insertions into an ancient story. According to the Pali text, he gave a final exhortation to his lay disciples in Pataliputta; in Kotigama, he spoke about the Four Noble Truths; and in a brick house at Nadika, he spoke of the "mirror of the doctrine" that revealed whether certain deceased monks had attained nibbana.[3]

The Buddha was planning to stay in the village of Beluva for the rainy season, and it is here that the text first mentions the illness that suddenly overcame him. Although crippled with severe pain, the Buddha marshalled his formidable mental powers in order to endure the physical suffering and carry on. Seeing his recovery, yet simultaneously sensing that the end was approaching, Ananda expressed his gratitude that the master would not depart from this world without providing some final instructions for his followers. The remark prompted the Buddha to ask what more he could add given that he had spent his entire life communicating and explaining his doctrine. In his mind, there were no lingering, esoteric secrets to be revealed at the eleventh hour. When he departed, the monks should be like islands that remain above devastating floodwaters, drawing on the teaching that he had bequeathed rather than on his person.[4] Ananda's lack of understanding was exposed again in the following scene although the theme seems to contradict the earlier incident. While reflecting on his many years of teaching and meditating, the Buddha commented three times to Ananda that he could remain in the world indefinitely if someone requested it. However, Ananda remained silent on each occasion, failing to seize the opportunity to ask that the Buddha delay his death. Disappointed, the Buddha resignedly dismissed his loyal, but obtuse, attendant: "Go now Ananda, and do as seems fit to you".[5] Later when he realized his mistake, Ananda pleaded for the master to reconsider but it was too late. The story is an attempt to explain the Buddha's "premature" death after only 80 years and the author lays the blame squarely at Ananda's feet.[6]

The door was now open for the spirit-tempter, Mara, to reappear and declare to the Buddha that there was no point in him lingering any longer in this world. He had shared his teaching and established his community. It was now time to die. Somewhat surprisingly, the Buddha agreed: "Do not trouble yourself, Evil One. Before long the Parinibbana of the Tathagata will come about. Three months hence the Tathagata will utterly pass away".[7] According to the Pali text, the gravity of the announcement caused an earthquake, reminiscent of other key moments in his life story.[8] The Buddha then left Vesali, looking back with his "elephant gaze" for one last impression of the city in which he had spent much of his public life.[9] He passed through several villages and arrived in Pava, staying in a mango grove that belonged to a certain Cunda, the "son of a blacksmith".[10] Cunda invited the Buddha and his companions to his residence where he prepared a meal of hard and soft food, including a dish described as "sukara-maddava".[11] The Buddha told Cunda to serve the sukara-maddava only to him and bury any leftovers in a pit, since no other being would be able to digest it. Soon afterwards, the Buddha became gravely ill. Once again, he was able to use his superior mental discipline to control the pain, but the damage had been done, and this time the Buddha would not recover. Later tradition speculated that he may have been deliberately poisoned, but the Pali text does not state this and there is no indication that Cunda had any intention other than to be a polite host. Indeed, he is later exonerated of any wrong doing by the Buddha himself who stated that the two most important meals of his life were just prior to his Enlightenment and his death. Moreover, there is a ring of authenticity about the ancient account of the Buddha dying of dysentery aggravated by accidental food poisoning in an obscure village.[12] What has been extensively debated are the contents of that last supper. According to some, "sukara-maddava" means tender pork, which adds a certain irony to the story given the general Buddhist commitment to vegetarianism.[13] However, other commentators argue that the term more likely means mushrooms or truffles that are dug up by pigs.[14]

With just days to live, the Buddha and his companions headed for Kusinara, which was located even further off the beaten track in the territory of the Mallas. Ananda described it as an uncivilized township in the midst of the jungle – "a mere outpost of the province".[15] The fact that Kusinara was such an obscure and unbecoming location for the Buddha's death gives weight to its historicity and the authors of the Pali text have even inserted a dialogue in which the Buddha explains to a quizzical Ananda that Kusinara was once a resplendent capital under a mythical, universal monarch named King Mahasudassana.[16] The journey would have been exhausting for an old, sick man, and the Buddha was forced to rest at an unspecified spot along the way. Suffering from acute thirst, he asked Ananda to fetch some water from the local river but Ananda explained that a convoy of carts had recently passed and had churned up the water making it no longer potable. The Buddha persisted and when Ananda reached the stream he was amazed to discover that the water had miraculously become limpid.[17]

The Pali text mentions a second miraculous sign, this time involving the Buddha's body. A student of the Buddha's former teacher, Alara Kalama, happened to be walking by and began to acclaim Kalama's extraordinary powers of concentration, allegedly to the point of being able to ignore the distracting noise of 500 passing wagons. In response, the Buddha described how he could remain transfixed even during a violent thunderstorm, at which point the stranger, named Pukkusa, pledged his allegiance and converted on the spot. In gratitude, he presented the Buddha and Ananda each with a beautiful, golden robe, and Ananda noticed that it looked dim in comparison to the Buddha's skin. The text explains that, like the earthquakes, the skin of a Buddha becomes radiant not only at his Enlightenment but also as death approaches.[18]

Upon crossing the Hirannyavati River, the Buddha found a comfortable place between two sala trees and lay on his right side in the lion's posture. As with his birth, Enlightenment and the First Sermon, his death also occurred in the shade of trees, which were in bloom even though it was not springtime. The scene was now being set for the climax of the entire journey as the reclining Buddha serenely prepared to cast off his failing physical body for the last time and enter fully into nibbana. According to the text, the gods of the Hindu pantheon were keen to witness this momentous occasion, prompting the Buddha to command the monk Upavana, who was fanning him, to move aside and not impede their view. The Buddha then delivered some short discourses about the need for caution when dealing with women and a prediction of future pilgrimages to the four key sites of Lumbini, Bodhgaya, Sarnath and Kusinara.[19] It was not only the monks and the gods who were privy to the Buddha's Parinibbana. Ananda was sent into town to inform the Mallas that the Buddha was in their territory and was soon to pass away, thus affording them an opportunity to visit him. They accepted with gratitude, and so many came that Ananda had to organize them into manageable groups. The last person to meet the Buddha was a wandering ascetic named Subhadda who suddenly arrived on the scene. Three times he insisted and three times Ananda refused to allow him to disturb the Buddha who was now rapidly approaching the end. However, the dying master heard Subhadda's pleas and granted him the last audience. Even in those final moments, the Buddha is portrayed as someone who was always ready to share his wisdom with a genuine searcher for the truth. Subhadda was converted and took the monastic robes on the spot. He was the last monk to be ordained by the founder.

In his final exhortation, the Buddha reminded his monks that, although he would no longer be physically present, they now had his sermons and the monastic rule: "For that which I have proclaimed and made known as the Dhamma and the Discipline. That shall be your Master when I am gone".[20] There is no mention of a successor or a replacement; only the concept that the Buddha would live on in the doctrine and the rules that he had spent a lifetime expounding and developing. Then, in order to confirm that those doctrines and rules had been thoroughly communicated by the master and fully appropriated by the disciples, the Buddha asked his companions three times if any of them were "in doubt or perplexity". The silence that followed testified to the effectiveness of his mission. As Mara had stated earlier, he was now free to leave behind his legacy: a faithful community that had received his liberating wisdom. His final words were addressed to his beloved monks: "Behold now, bhikkhus, I exhort you: All compounded things are subject to vanish. Strive with earnestness!"[21] At this, Siddhattha Gotama's life came to an end and he died serenely, lying on his side under the sala trees at Kusinara. According to the Pali text, the Buddha passed through each of the four highest levels of meditation and then fully entered nibbana, definitively leaving behind the wheel of samsara, never to be reborn again. As with other important events in his life, his death was marked by a "dreadful and astounding" earthquake.[22] Theravadan Buddhism holds that he died on the same date as his birth and his Enlightenment: the full moon of the Hindu month Vesakha (April–May) although such a coincidence seems contrived and is not consistent with the claim that the trees bloomed out of season. Furthermore, an earlier tradition allocates different dates to the three events.[23]

The Pali version openly admits that many monks who were present grieved deeply, although they were admonished for displaying such a lack of detachment by a more impassive Anuruddha. There is one verse that records another, more troubling reason why at least one monk refrained from mourning. Subhadda, the Buddha's last convert, is said to have insolently remarked:

> Enough, friends! Do not grieve, do not lament! We are well rid of that great ascetic. Too long, friends, have we been oppressed by his saying: "This is fitting for you; that is not fitting for you." Now we shall be able to do as we wish, and what we do not wish, that we shall not do.[24]

Such a statement would hardly have been manufactured by later editors and reflects a genuine disloyal element and the potential for schism in the very earliest community.

The word of the Buddha's death soon reached the Mallas, who were also greatly upset and they gladly agreed to organize the funeral. The Buddha had earlier instructed Ananda that his body should be treated in the same way as a universal monarch. The corpse was to be wrapped in hundreds of layers of cotton and linen, and then burned on a funeral pyre. The ashes were then to be stored in a stupa at a crossroads.[25] After a week of mourning, including perfumes, garlands and music, the time came for the cremation but there were several hitches (and possibly disputes) about the direction of the procession and who should ignite the pyre. The Pali text relates how the eight chosen Malla nobles could not lift the bier because they had intended to use the south gate instead of the north and east gates that led to the Mallas' shrine and meeting hall.[26] Similarly, the story states that the Mallas were unable to light the wood possibly because this task properly belonged to the monk Maha-Kassapa, who had been delayed. Upon his arrival, we are told that the pyre burst into flame spontaneously.[27] A second miracle eventually saw the fires extinguished by rain and water from the surrounding trees, but the cremation was so effective that only the ashes remained. These were stored in the Mallas' council hall, surrounded by a lattice of spears and bows.

Although the Buddha died in Kusinara, it is not surprising that a number of neighboring kingdoms expressed their desire to erect the stupa that would contain his remains in their own territory. Seven tribes sent representatives: King Ajatasattu of Magadha, the Licchavis of Vesali, the Sakyans of Kapilavatthu, the Bulis of Allakappa, the Koliyas of Ramagama, a Brahmin from Vethadipa and the Mallas of Pava. Undoubtedly, their motives were a mix of respectful devotion and political-economic investment, but they all had a reasonable case. Initially, the Mallas of Kusinara were not keen to surrender the precious relics and a dispute quickly arose. It was only quelled when a Brahmin named Dona intervened and mediated a solution. The relics were then divided into eight equal shares and allocated to each of the claimants while Dona himself received the urn that had contained them. The Pali text describes how a delegate from the Moriyas of Pipphalivana arrived unexpectedly and was also given some of the ashes. The result was that ten stupas, containing physical remains of the Buddha's corpse and the urn that originally held them, were erected across northern India.[28] It is said that during the third century BCE these relics were further redistributed to 84,000 other locations by decree of the emperor Ashoka.

The desire to possess the Buddha's relics seems inconsistent with his constant insistence that the physical world is transient and must be abandoned in order to attain complete liberation. In one sense, the Hindu practice of scattering the ashes of the dead in a river or lake, thus consigning them back to nature, appears more in keeping with the emphasis on detachment. Moreover, the Buddha had frequently called himself Tathagata – the one who had come and gone – and his bereaved disciples were told not to seek his person any longer but to turn to the dhamma as their ongoing source of leadership and inspiration. Yet the earliest followers, especially the laity and their political leaders, clearly still desired some physical connection with the man who had shown them the way to ultimate fulfilment.[29]

At this point, the Mahaparinibbana Sutta ends. The first jewel – the Buddha – was gone. The teacher had shared his vision and moved on. He was truly Tathagata. Yet the other two jewels remained: the teaching itself (dhamma) and the community that lived by it (sangha). During the rainy season following the Buddha's death, over 500 monks gathered at Saptaparni Cave near Rajagaha for what was later called the First Council. There, with the help of the extraordinary memories of Ananda and Upali, they identified and ratified a collection of the Buddha's sermons and monastic guidelines, which would eventually be put down in writing and become the main contents of the Pali Canon. The Council was presided over by Maha-Kassapa, the monk who had lit the Buddha's funeral pyre. Tradition claims that he convened the gathering in response to the disrespectful remark made by Subhadda about how the Buddha's death was good news for monks who felt restricted by the many rules and regulations. Maha-Kassapa was not the Buddha's successor, nor was anyone else. The two outstanding disciples, Sariputta and Moggallana, who had been the most likely to lead the community after the Buddha's death, had already died. Yet, even while he was alive the Buddha had not designated them as heirs to his authority either. There was no universal head or leader. On the contrary, the structure of the monastic communities was highly decentralized, with local superiors based on age and experience.[30] Moreover, while the Council undoubtedly helped to establish a common position, it would not be long before disputes and schisms fragmented the sangha into many diverse schools and groups.

At one level, the story ends with Siddhattha's death and cremation in Kusinara but, at another level, it is only the first chapter of a greater story. With the vital imperial support of Ashoka, Siddhattha's missionary monks would eventually carry his message outside of his native India to the far corners of the Asian continent and beyond. The movement, in its myriad of forms, would become a global phenomenon known as Buddhism, and its founder would be remembered primarily as "the Buddha" – a title originally used for other enlightened teachers in his day. The former prince, who became a wandering ascetic, would be revered by hundreds of millions as the wisest and most sublime of all human beings: the very personification of an eternal truth. He would become a household name, and it is probable that no other human being boasts as many sculptured or painted portraits.[31] Yet his elevated status is, strictly speaking, not unique. As early as the Ashokan period, Buddhism also gave rise to the concept of other Buddhas: those who preceded the Buddha Gotama in past eons, such as Konagamana and Kassapa; those who inhabit celestial realms, such as Amitabha in his Western Pure Land; and those who are still to come, such as Metteya (Sanskrit: Maitreya), the future Buddha who awaits in Tusita Heaven for the appropriate time to descend and restore the fading truth.[32] Moreover, Siddhattha

Gotama is not necessarily the main subject of worship in different schools, which vary in their attribution of significance to each Buddha. The notion of multiple Buddhas reminds us that Buddhahood is not the monopoly of Siddhattha and that our empirical world may not be the only one in existence. Yet in the end, these other Buddhas are mythical. Only Siddhattha's story is actually grounded in human history, even though the times and places have been difficult to pin down with certainty. There may be many Buddhas, but Siddhattha Gotama will always be the Buddha of our time and space; the person who stands at the fountainhead of one of history's great religious traditions.

Cross and Tomb

Like the Mahaparinibbana Sutta, the canonical gospels also contain a significant amount of detail about the death of Jesus. In fact, scholars have long believed that a passion narrative already existed as an independent literary unit well before Mark's gospel was composed. As also evidenced by Paul's writings, the earliest form of Christian faith seems to have focused primarily on the end of the story, which is perhaps not surprising given its shocking and traumatic character. Unlike the Buddha, Jesus died a tragic, violent death in his early 30s. The religious and political opposition, which had been ominously building during his short public ministry, reached a terrible climax during his pilgrimage to Jerusalem for one particular Passover festival.

    Although there were hostile forces at play, it has to be admitted that Jesus himself contributed to the causes that brought about his premature death. Apart from his controversial message about God's Kingdom and his own central role in its imminent arrival, Jesus performed at least two highly provocative public acts in Jerusalem that week. First, his dramatic entry into the holy city, riding a donkey from the Mount of Olives and being hailed as Messiah by his palm-waving disciples, without doubt caught the suspicious eye of the Jewish and Roman leadership. Second, the physical eviction of moneylenders from the Temple precincts and his prophetic declaration, in the words of Jeremiah, that God's house had once again been turned into a robbers' den, was an unambiguous criticism of a corrupt priesthood. It was fuel to the fire and, in the tense atmosphere that characterized every Passover when hundreds of thousands of pilgrims were in town, the authorities acted quickly.

    Tradition suggests that Jesus was fully aware of the probable repercussions of his actions and that he intentionally prepared a final meal with his closest followers on a Thursday evening in an upper room somewhere in the city. However, the gospels disagree over the precise timing of the last supper. According to the Synoptics, it was a Passover meal, which is normally held on the eve of the principal day of the festival – 15 Nissan. In contrast, John states that the 15 Nissan fell on the Sabbath (Saturday) that year and thus simply speaks of a meal on the eve of Preparation Day.[33] Although the Last Supper is sometimes imagined as a cozy gathering of Jesus's most intimate companions, in fact the atmosphere was more likely filled with anxiety and alarm. During the meal, Jesus dramatically announced that one of the Twelve would soon betray him. In the Synoptic tradition, it is not clear who the culprit is, although each disciple worriedly asks if Jesus meant him.[34] Jesus adds that even Peter, despite his earnest protestations of loyalty, would deny him under pressure.[35] The sense of foreboding would only have been heightened by the unusual gesture that is recorded not only in the Synoptics but also in one of the oldest passages in the New Testament:

> For I received from the Lord what I also handed on to you, that the Lord Jesus on the night when he was betrayed took a loaf of bread, and when he had given thanks, he broke it and said, "This is my body that is for you. Do this in remembrance of me." In the same way he took the cup also, after supper, saying, "This cup is the new covenant in my blood. Do this, as often as you drink it, in remembrance of me".[36]

The unmistakeable message of this prophetic action was that the imminent, violent death that Jesus was seriously anticipating (a broken body and the shedding of blood) would not be in vain, but would somehow bring about a new covenant between God and Israel. Moreover, his followers should remember him every time they reenact the memorial meal of sharing bread and wine. In Christian thinking, the Last Supper was simultaneously the first Eucharist.

Jesus and his disciples then retired to garden named Gethsemane in the Kidron Valley, where they customarily met. Taking Peter, James and John aside, he entered into heartfelt, solitary prayer while they slept, exhausted and unaware of what was about to transpire. The scene of the "agony in the garden" is a rare, poignant moment in the gospels where the normally confident Jesus displays genuine human fear and begs his heavenly father to spare him the bitter cup of suffering that is to come. Then, suddenly, the garden was filled with armed members of the temple guard led by Judas Iscariot. The identity of the traitor was now made clear, and with his usual greeting kiss to the master, he also revealed the identity of Jesus to the soldiers. There was apparently some armed resistance. One of the disciples, identified as Peter by the fourth gospel, drew a sword and struck the High Priest's slave, cutting off his ear. But Jesus ordered him to desist and allowed himself to be taken away.[37] The clandestine arrest had been planned for the dead of night presumably to avoid any problems with crowds of sympathizers.

Mark provides no motive for Judas' treacherous act but Matthew suggests it was for money and explicitly mentions the payment of 30 silver pieces. John agrees, pointing out that, although Judas was the treasurer of the group, he was also a thief.[38] As for Judas's fate, the New Testament provides two versions. Matthew states that he repented, returned the money to the chief priests and hanged himself out of remorse and despair. The priests used the money to purchase a potter's field as a burial ground for strangers known as the Field of Blood.[39] In contrast, Acts claims that Judas himself purchased the plot, which was so named because "falling headlong he burst open in the middle and all of his bowels gushed out".[40] Although his name is now synonymous with traitor, Judas was not alone in his act of betrayal. The gospel of Mark tersely notes that all of the disciples fled in panic at Jesus's arrest, with one exception. Peter cautiously followed the cohort at a distance, right into the courtyard of the High Priest's house, but even he failed the test of fidelity.[41] When recognized by bystanders as one of Jesus's band, evidenced by his Galilean accent, he vehemently denied any association but, then, privately choked with shame as he heard the cock crow for dawn. The elite group of 12 men that Jesus had personally chosen to be a primary symbol of the forthcoming Kingdom was falling apart in utter disarray.

Jesus was brought to the house of Caiaphas, the High Priest, although John claims that he first met with Annas, Caiaphas' father-in-law. It was not a private appointment, since the entire Sanhedrin is alleged to have been summoned and a religious trial followed. The gospels vary on the details of the deliberations. John notes that the High Priest asked Jesus generally about his teaching, to which Jesus replied that it was all public knowledge. The Synoptics state that many witnesses made a range of accusations against Jesus but these were littered with inconsistencies. The one that is highlighted is Jesus's alleged claim that he would destroy the Temple and, in three days, build another not made of human hands.[42] At this point, the High Priest intervened and asked Jesus directly whether he was the Messiah. Although in Luke's version Jesus answers indirectly with the phrase "You say that I am", both Mark and Matthew record a more explicit affirmation: "I am; and you will see the Son of Man seated at the right hand of Power, and coming with the clouds of heaven".[43] At this response, the High Priest tore his garments – the traditional gesture of grief or scandal – and declared that Jesus had spoken blasphemy, for which the divinely ordained punishment was death.[44] There are references to physical and mental maltreatment of the prisoner, including spitting, slapping, blindfolding and teasing.[45] However, the High Priest and the Sanhedrin did not have jurisdictional power to apply capital punishment and so, as morning came, they took Jesus to the Roman prefect, Pontius Pilate.

According to John, Pilate met with Jesus alone in the Praetorium because the Jewish leaders would have been defiled if they had entered such profane space and, consequently, could not have eaten the Passover meal.[46] The charge brought against Jesus varies according to each evangelist. Luke has the most details, mentioning four elements: perverting the nation, stirring up the people, forbidding the payment of tribute to Caesar, and claiming to be king. There is no mention of threatening to destroy the Temple or blasphemy, indicating that this was now a political rather than a religious trial and the aim was to find a crime that Pilate would recognize as deserving execution.[47] Luke adds that when Pilate discovered that Jesus was from Galilee, he sent him to Herod who was in Jerusalem at the time, presumably for the Passover festival. Herod was keen to witness a miracle but Jesus refused to oblige and so the frustrated tetrarch sent him back to Pilate.[48] It is difficult to know if this is an authentic historical memory, but all gospels agree that the crucial decision was Pilate's and the crucial issue was the fourth item in Luke's list: Jesus's claim to be king. When Pilate emulated the High Priest's direct question, the Synoptics state that Jesus answered indirectly "You have said so" and then declined to make any further statements. In contrast, John has an extensive dialogue between the two men about kingship and truth.[49] Yet in all four gospels, Pilate is unconvinced that Jesus is guilty and is portrayed as being at pains to have him released. To that end, the gospels allege that Pilate drew on a custom (unsupported in any other ancient source) that the prefect would release one prisoner of the crowd's choice at Passover. As an alternative to Jesus he selected a certain Barabbas who is variously described as a robber, a murderer and a rebel involved in a recent insurrection. But Pilate's ploy backfired and the crowd, directed by the chief priests, chose Barabbas instead of Jesus.[50] Now cornered, the prefect was forced to make a decision, and it was one of the most fateful in human history. Sitting in the place known as Gabbatha (the Pavement), Pilate reluctantly handed Jesus over for crucifixion.[51]

Although the final call was Pilate's, the four canonical gospels squarely lay the blame on the Jewish leadership and the crowd who screamed for Jesus's execution. Matthew includes an anecdote about Pilate's wife who had been troubled by a dream that confirmed Jesus's innocence. In the same gospel, Pilate dramatically washed his hands of the entire affair while the crowds declare Jesus's blood to be on them and their children.[52] John goes further, referring to Pilate's fear and his attempt to placate the crowd by having Jesus's flogged and then brought out wearing a crown of thorns and a purple robe to mock his supposed kingship. In response, the crowd hypocritically insisted that they had no king except Caesar.[53] However, scholars have long noted the anti-Semitic tone of the passion narrative, written at a time when there may have been enmity between Christian and Jewish communities who were essentially parting ways, and when potential gentile converts needed convincing that the new religion was not seditious even though its founder had been executed as a political criminal. It has also been pointed out that the Sanhedrin would not have met during the night or on the eve of a major festival. Moreover, history remembers Pilate as a ruthless overseer who cared little for Jewish sensibilities and did not hesitate to execute protestors and rebel leaders.[54] If Jesus represented a threat to the civil order, the historical Pilate would not have needed a boisterous religious crowd to persuade him to act.

Crucifixion was a method of execution initiated by the Persians and adopted by the Carthaginians and the Romans who used it systematically for rebels and escaped slaves. It could involve individuals, small groups or even large numbers, such as the mass crucifixions of Spartacus and his followers during the Third Servile War (73–71 BCE), and many Jewish rebels after the destruction of Jerusalem in 70 CE. In Jesus's case, we are told that there were two others crucified with him on that day. It was a particularly gruesome and humiliating form of execution, intended not only to punish the offender but also to act as a brutal deterrent to all others. So shameful was it that condemned Roman citizens were usually exempt and the early Christians avoided the cross as a religious symbol for at least the first century.

The actual crucifixion was often preceded by scourging of the condemned, although only John records that Jesus was flogged.[55] However, Matthew and Mark agree with him that the soldiers mocked Jesus by dressing him in purple and placing a crown of thorns on his head and a reed in his right hand.[56] The condemned was usually forced to carry his own cross, or at least the cross-beam section, to the place of execution but the Synoptics note that a bystander named Simon of Cyrene was enlisted to assist, possibly because Jesus was so weak from the earlier scourging. Mark identifies the stranger as "the father of Alexander and Rufus", who were probably known members of the early Christian community.[57] The execution site was known in Hebrew as Golgotha ("place of the skull"), from which is derived its traditional Latin name Calvary (calvariae locus). There is no mention of a hill, but archaeologists believe that Golgotha was located just outside the old city gates, close enough for travelers to see the terrible sight and to read the scornful note placed on Jesus's cross and written in Hebrew, Greek and Latin: "Jesus the Nazarene, King of Jews".[58]

Victims of crucifixion were usually stripped naked and the four gospels mention the military guard dividing Jesus's clothing.[59] The condemned was then strapped or nailed to a cross-like structure and literally left to die in a slow, painful manner. Some survived for days until exhaustion, dehydration and asphyxiation finally overcame them. In contrast, Jesus lasted only a few hours although there is some discrepancy since Mark states that he was crucified at the third hour (about 9 a.m.), whereas John claims that the trial took place at about the sixth hour (noon).[60] In either case, all four gospels agree that Jesus passed away prior to sunset. The Synoptics stipulate the time of his death as the ninth hour (3 p.m.) and John notes that, since the Sabbath was about to begin at sundown, the Jewish leaders requested that the soldiers break the legs of the victims to hasten death. However, they discovered that Jesus had already died and reported back to Pilate who seemed surprised.[61]

The gospel accounts diverge considerably when they describe the final series of statements spoken by Jesus from the cross. According to John, Jesus commended his mother to the safe keeping of his beloved disciple, neither of whom is mentioned in the Synoptics as being present.[62] John also mentions that Jesus asked for a drink ("I thirst") and was given some vinegar on a stick, which he took.[63] Mark and Matthew agree but they also include an earlier offer of wine mixed with myrrh, presumably to reduce the pain, but Jesus did not accept it.[64] Luke describes how one of the thieves crucified with Jesus refused to join the other in criticizing Jesus for not using his miraculous powers to save them all. In reply Jesus promised that the "good thief" would be with him in Paradise that very day.[65] According to Matthew and Mark, both thieves joined the passers-by and the chief priests in general derision of Jesus's inability to save himself. Luke continues the theme of gracious mercy by describing how Jesus requested forgiveness for the soldiers because they did not know what they were doing.[66] The gospels do not agree on the very last words spoken by Jesus. According to John it is the regal statement "It is finished"; in Luke it is a trusting surrender: "Father into your hands I commend my spirit". However, Matthew and Mark have a more unnerving, enigmatic version in which Jesus cries out loudly: "Eloi, Eloi, lema sabachthani?" ("My God, my God, why have you forsaken me?").[67] Taken at face value, this heart-wrenching cry might suggest that Jesus's last moments were characterized by shocked disbelief that his Father had not intervened and his life's work of preparing for the Kingdom seemed to be coming to nought. Yet commentators have also noted that these words constitute the opening line of Psalm 22, which expresses the psalmist's desperate appeal to God in time of crisis but, importantly, ends on a note of hope and triumph. It is difficult to know with certainty what Jesus's final thoughts were, but the cowardly betrayal of his closest disciples, the horrific physical pain of his execution, the public shame of his fate, the ostensible triumph of his enemies and the inexplicable silence of his Father must have pushed his faith to the very edge.

The Synoptic gospels describe apocalyptic signs that announce Jesus's death, including darkness, the rending of the Temple curtain, an earthquake, the emergence of dead bodies from their graves, and a proclamation of faith by the centurion attending the execution, although John mentions none of these.[68] There is also some disagreement as to which disciples actually witnessed the crucifixion. The author of the fourth gospel implies that he was present to see a soldier pierce Jesus's side with a lance.[69] The same gospel also states that Jesus's mother was standing at the foot of the cross along with "his mother's sister, Mary the wife of Clopas, and Mary Magdalene" – it is not clear if the phrase refers to two or three women apart from his mother.[70] The Synoptics makes no mention of Jesus's mother or any male disciple near the cross, but they do speak of "many women" watching from afar, including three in particular: Mary Magdalene; Mary, the mother of James and Joses; and Salome (possibly the same person as "the mother of the sons of Zebedee" mentioned in Matthew).[71]

The bodies of the crucified were customarily left on the cross to decay or be devoured by wild animals, with the remains then buried in a shallow, mass grave. However, there has been at least one archeological discovery of a crucified man who was buried in a family tomb.[72] In similar fashion, the gospels relate how, as evening came, a certain Joseph of Arimathea gained permission from Pilate to take Jesus's body down from the cross and bury it in his own new tomb, which was nearby. There was a sense of urgency since sunset meant the commencement of the Sabbath (Saturday) and probably the Passover festival as well. According to Mark and Luke, Joseph was a respected member of the Sanhedrin but Matthew and John add that he was also a secret disciple of Jesus.[73] The corpse was wrapped in a linen shroud, laid in the tomb and the opening was sealed with a stone that was rolled into place. Jesus was literally dead and buried. His fledgling movement was in serious crisis. What happened next arguably constitutes the single, most important question for Christianity, in many ways eclipsing everything that Jesus had said and done during his public ministry and simultaneously placing incalculable consequence on claims about his ultimate fate.

According to all four gospels, some of the women went to the tomb at dawn on the first day of the week, once the Sabbath had passed. The Synoptics give the reason for their visit as the fact that Jesus's body had not yet been anointed with spices.[74] In contrast, John states that the anointing had already occurred before the burial but gives no explanation for the Sunday morning visit.[75] The names of the women vary across the four gospels but one name is common to all lists: Mary Magdalene. There are also variations as to what happened precisely but again the common element is that the women found the stone had been rolled away and the body was missing. Apart from the obvious initial shock, the first explanation that sprang to mind was that the body had been stolen and this is what Mary reports to Peter according to John's gospel. Peter and the beloved disciple then ran to the tomb and see for themselves, noticing that the linen cloths and head napkin were still there.[76] In contrast, the Synoptics speak of an angel who explains to the women that Jesus has been raised from the dead and that they must report this to his (male) disciples. Whether such an apparition actually occurred or whether it is a literary device, the story hints at the genuine bewilderment and disbelief that must have been associated with the discovery of an empty tomb. The earlier ending of Marks' gospel states that the women were so frightened that they failed to tell anyone.[77] Luke and Matthew have them convey the news, but Luke notes that a skeptical eleven did not believe them.[78]

Christian theologians have always pointed out that an empty tomb in itself is an ambiguous sign, for which there could be a natural explanation, such as theft of the body. What clarifies the meaning of the event for Christians is the subsequent series of alleged appearances by the risen Jesus. One of the oldest references to these events is found in a statement that Paul himself received from his teachers:

> For I handed on to you as of first importance what I in turn had received: that Christ died for our sins in accordance with the scriptures, and that he was buried, and that he was raised on the third day in accordance with the scriptures, and that he appeared to Cephas, then to the twelve. Then he appeared to more than five hundred brothers and sisters at one time, most of whom are still alive, though some have died. Then he appeared to James, then to all the apostles. Last of all, as to someone untimely born, he appeared also to me.[79]

This pithy statement lists, in deliberate order, the official witnesses who number more than five hundred, but it provides no further information. It is the gospels that spell out the details although, once again, there are significant variations between the four versions due to editorial influence.

Only Luke seems to agree with the pre-Pauline statement's claim that Jesus first appeared to Peter individually. In the other three gospels, it is Mary Magdalene who not only finds the tomb empty, but is the first to encounter the resurrected Jesus (although Matthew claims that the "other Mary" was also with her).[80] Her various reports of an empty tomb, angels and seeing Jesus alive are initially met with skepticism by the eleven, but that is dramatically overturned when Jesus himself appears to them while they were at supper in a locked room somewhere in the city. John adds that Thomas was not present and expressed a similar doubting attitude until a week later when Jesus appeared to them again, this time including him.[81] Luke and the longer ending of Mark also mention an appearance to two disciples who were travelling in the countryside (Luke specifies their destination as Emmaus).[82] Matthew situates the appearance to the eleven on a mountain in Galilee, where Jesus had prearranged to meet them. John agrees that there was an apparition in the north, but he locates it on the shore of the Sea of Galilee, suggesting that the disciples had returned to their old occupation of fishing.[83]

There is very limited information about the nature of these appearances, but there are a number of salient features that can be noted. Jesus only appeared to his disciples and not to his enemies or even to neutral observers. It could be argued that the one exception to this rule was Paul but his experience of the risen Jesus is much later and does not fit the normal pattern of resurrection appearances.[84] Something about Jesus had changed, since the disciples failed to recognize him at first, yet his body still bore the marks of crucifixion, which enabled his identity to be established.[85] He came and went like a ghostly figure, yet Luke and John speak of a real physical presence so that his body could be touched and he was able to cook breakfast and eat food.[86] All four gospels mention various conversations between Jesus and his disciples during which he deepened their understanding and gave them the initial instructions for what was soon to become an extraordinary missionary outreach across the Roman Empire.[87]

At some point, the appearances ended and the gospels express this critical transition in terms of Jesus's ascension to heaven. In John's gospel, the risen Jesus tells Mary Magdalene not to cling to him since he has not yet ascended to his Father. Luke describes Jesus's final departure occurring near Bethany. In contrast, Matthew does not mention an ascension and ends his gospel with Jesus's promise: "I am with you always to the end of the age".[88] The reference to the end of the age is pertinent here because the resurrection of the dead was already an element of Jewish belief, at least according to the school of the Pharisees. It was due to occur in the last days and the first Christians naturally presumed that the resurrection of Jesus meant that the end of the world had begun. The earliest New Testament writings still reveal the initial Christian belief that, although Jesus had departed, he would return again very soon in his "parousia" (second coming).[89] Several decades later, the early Church would have to deal with the obvious fact that Jesus was not going to return in glory as soon as expected and, indeed, Luke's gospel is a good example of a Christian community grappling with that difficult realization and adapting their faith accordingly.

More importantly, the claim that Jesus was the first to be raised from the dead cast a completely different light on his personal identity. It was not only clear divine vindication of his message, despite the shame and ignominy of the cross, but it also implied that Jesus himself was someone more than just another rabbi, prophet or miracle worker. For the first disciples, Jesus's resurrection meant that he was the long-awaited Davidic king, even though he had been rejected by the leadership and executed as a messianic pretender. In their eyes, he was (and is) truly the Messiah and the Greek version of that term quickly became not only his preeminent title but effectively his surname: Jesus Christ. Moreover, they themselves would use that same word to describe their own identity as followers of the crucified and risen one: Christians.

For his followers, all of this meant that Jesus's death must have been part of God's plan all along. At one level, it may have been the tragic destruction of an innocent man by murky political forces but, at another level, there was a concealed divine purpose. Inspired by a number of relevant passages in the Jewish scriptures, including the enigmatic Suffering Servant poems in the book of Isaiah, Christians began to develop a theology of the cross in which God's wisdom overcomes human folly and Jesus's violent death ransoms sinful humanity.[90] Jesus is seen as completing the supreme sacrifice that ends all Temple sacrifices. He is described as the true Passover lamb whose blood saves God's people from slavery and death. Moreover, the first Christians also began to pray to him with the title "Kyrios" (Lord), implicitly elevating him above the level of human. Exactly how far above became the most contentious and dominant theological question of the next 400 years. An official answer would eventually be provided by a series of councils that declared Jesus to be fully divine and fully human – the unique incarnation of the one transcendent God. Yet the kernel for this idea was already present in New Testament passages that refer to him as a preexistent being who descends into this world for its salvation.[91] In effect, the messenger had become the message. The focus had shifted from the Kingdom to the King. The son of the carpenter was now worshipped as Lord Jesus Christ, Son of God and Savior.

Unlike the Buddha and Muhammad, the end of the Jesus story involves an unexpected, dramatic double-twist to the plot. His brutal, premature death undermined the optimistic message of an imminent Kingdom of justice and mercy, sending his nascent community into disillusionment and disintegration. The crucifixion was nothing short of disastrous for the man, his message and his followers. His name should have been consigned to the dustbin of history along with hundreds of other religious innovators over the centuries. Yet somehow the group regathered, buoyed up by an unshakeable belief that their master had been raised from the dead and was still mysteriously present guiding his community. Prior to his untimely death, the founder had left very few explicit instructions or structures on how his followers were to live out their newborn faith and scores of issues quickly arose. Who should assume leadership in Jesus's absence: Peter, the Twelve or other designated persons? Should they adopt all or some or none of the many Jewish religious laws and customs? Was membership restricted to Jews only or should Gentiles be welcomed into the fold? And so on. The issues generated debates, deliberations, decisions and divisions as the movement grew and spread across the Mediterranean. Christianity had been born without a clear blueprint from its founder and, in a real sense, it had to find its own way forward.

In 'A'isha's arms

In contrast to the considerable amount of material available concerning the death of the Buddha and Jesus, the main sources of information for Muhammad's life display minimal interest in his passing. Ibn Ishaq dedicates only a few pages to the topic in his voluminous work, which ends abruptly with a few testimonies concerning Muhammad's burial and the crisis that his death generated in terms of succession. Similarly, while Vesak and Easter constitute the most important events in the Buddhist and Christian religious year, the Islamic calendar pays almost no attention whatsoever to the death of the Prophet, which is presumed to have occurred on the same date as his birthday. Although the latter is celebrated as Mawlid al-Nabi, even its importance is disputed by some Muslims and it is completely overshadowed by other more prominent commemorations, such as the Ramadan fast and the Feast of the Sacrifice, which marks the annual pilgrimage to Mecca.

In fact, the pilgrimage to Mecca was one of the final Islamic practices instituted by Muhammad just prior to his death. After the conquest of Mecca in 630 CE, many thought that Muhammad might relocate to his hometown, but he deliberately maintained his residence and headquarters in Medina. However, he was now free to make the Meccan pilgrimage a regular feature of his religion. Indeed, the Qur'an declared it to be an obligation on all Muslims who could afford to do so.[92] Muhammad had sent Abu Bakr to lead the pilgrimage in 631 CE and, from that time, all pagan forms of pilgrim to Mecca were banned.[93] The following year, Muhammad himself led the pilgrimage and defined the Islamic version with greater precision. He effectively combined two preexisting pagan practices – the 'umra and the hajj – and linked them to episodes in the life of Abraham. The former involved the circumambulation of the Ka'ba and the sevenfold circuit between the hills of Safa and Marwa. The latter consisted of a standing prayer at Arafat, throwing pebbles at the jamra and the sacrifice of an animal.[94] The fifth and final pillar of the new religion was now in place. It was his first official Islamic pilgrimage but, as it turned out, it was also to be his last.

The pilgrimage of 632 CE was a momentous occasion since Muhammad was accompanied by approximately 100,000 fellow believers. At Arafat, he addressed this enormous crowd at some length in what is known as his Farewell Sermon.[95] The key points of the discourse include respect for property, the ban on usury, the dangers of Satan, the rights of women, the rejection of racism, the five pillars and the finality of the Qur'an as divine revelation. Significantly, the sermon opens with a sombre note that Muhammad sensed that the end was near: "I do not know whether, after this year, I shall ever be amongst you again". Moreover, Muhammad then asked the crowd if they thought he had succeeded in his role as God's messenger, faithfully and accurately delivering the divine message, to which they replied with a resounding "Yes". After repeating this request three times and receiving the same answer, Muhammad pointed his finger to the sky and uttered "O God, be my witness". There is a strong sense here of summing up a life's work as if there was nothing more to be revealed and God had now perfected his religion.[96] There is also a hadith tradition that Gabriel would recite the entire revealed Qur'an to Muhammad each year as a sort of revision exercise. In that year (632 CE), the angel did so twice, indicating that his time was drawing to a close; after all, Muhammad was now a man in his early 60s.[97] However, there is also a sense that it was business as usual for Muhammad, who returned to Medina and continued with plans for a military expedition to Transjordania led by 19-year-old Usama ibn Zayd. Soon after this, he suddenly fell ill.

According to Ibn Ishaq, the sickness struck Muhammad one morning after he had spent the night praying in al-Gharqad cemetery.[98] When he entered the house, 'A'isha told him that she had a headache but Muhammad remarked that he was suffering from a worse one. He had contracted the desert fever, which meant severe head pain, high temperatures and physical debilitation. Muhammad's condition deteriorated over the next two or three weeks and eventually he collapsed in the apartment of his wife Maymuna.[99] In his disorientation, he was constantly asking which wife he would be with on the following day and his spouses realized that he wanted 'A'isha. So they agreed to waive their conjugal rights and allow Muhammad to stay with her. In no fit state to lead the daily prayers, Muhammad asked Abu Bakr to take his place, although 'A'isha remarked that he was not really suitable given his delicate disposition, weak voice and propensity to cry when he read the Qur'an. However, Muhammad insisted and his longstanding friend and companion accepted the important task.[100]

Suddenly, the fever broke and Muhammad felt strong enough to attend the daily prayers, which brought great joy and relief to all who were present. Sitting at the stand with a bandage on his head, he asked forgiveness from God for the slain men of Uhud and overruled those who had objected that Usama was too young to lead the military expedition, which had been delayed due to the Prophet's illness. Muhammad then made reference to an unnamed person who had been offered two options by God: either remain in this world with its pleasures or leave it now and enjoy the divine company. Abu Bakr realized that Muhammad was speaking about himself and began to weep.

Unfortunately, the recovery was short-lived and the fever returned within a few hours, intensifying to a critical level. Muhammad retired to 'A'isha's apartment and was lying in her lap when he uttered his last words: "Nay, rather the most exalted Companion in Paradise".[101] 'A'isha realized that he was choosing the company of God rather than remain in this world. The end had come; the Prophet was dead. According to most commentators it was Monday 8 June, 632 CE.[102] 'A'isha later recalled:

> The Apostle died in my bosom during my turn. I had wronged none in regard to him. It was due to my extreme youth that the apostle died in my arms. Then I laid his head on a pillow and got up beating my breast and slapping my face along with the other women.[103]

While 'A'isha and the other wives began to mourn his death, 'Umar uncharacteristically began acting as if in serious shock, apparently incapable of accepting what had just happened. He kept insisting that Muhammad was not really dead but that his spirit had simply left his body and "gone to his Lord like Moses did for forty days".[104] However, a more realistic Abu Bakr went into 'A'isha's room and kissed Muhammad's corpse, saying: "You are dearer than my father and mother. You have tasted the death that God has decreed; a second death will never overtake you".[105] He then tried to calm 'Umar but to no avail, so he declared loudly to all those present: "O men, if anyone worships Muhammad, then know that Muhammad is dead. If anyone worships God, then know that God is alive, immortal". It was a powerful statement of the obvious truth that Muhammad was merely the human agent of the one, true God and, like all prophets, his time had come.[106] The words dumbfounded 'Umar, whose legs almost collapsed under him when he finally realized the truth. After two decades of extraordinary leadership in the religious and political spheres, their inspirational commander was no longer with them.

Muhammad's body was washed and wrapped in two shrouds of Yemeni cloth and a striped mantle.[107] Some had suggested that he be buried with his dead companions in the cemetery, but Abu Bakr had heard him once say; "No prophet dies but he is buried where he died". So they took up 'A'isha's bed and made a grave in the dirt floor of her room. Muhammad was laid to rest there on the Wednesday night, and this is still the site of his tomb today, although it is now housed inside the splendid Masjid al-Nabi (Mosque of the Prophet). In the meantime, the question of who should succeed Muhammad as the leader of the Islamic state quickly became an issue. Muhammad's infant son Ibrahim, born of his last wife, Maria, had died earlier in the same year. The fact that he had no surviving male heir meant that direct hereditary succession was not an option. According to Ibn Ishaq, a group of Medinan helpers met immediately after Muhammad's death and proposed that Sa'd bin 'Ubada should take charge. They argued that Medina had offered protection for the oppressed Islamic community and had helped it to consolidate and to spread from its new centre. Meanwhile, Abu Bakr and 'Umar, who were with a group of Meccan migrants at the time, heard about the meeting and decided to join the discussion before matters progressed too far. Abu Bakr acknowledged the important role that the Medinan helpers had played but argued that the Islamic community now embraced almost all of Arabia and the tribes would realistically only accept a leader from the Quraysh of Mecca. He proposed 'Umar or Abu Ubayda but the former interjected and nominated Abu Bakr instead on the basis that he was "the second of the two who were in the cave".[108] At this, all of those assembled spontaneously acknowledged Abu Bakr as the new leader (caliph) and gave him their support.

However, not all Muslims agree that this was the appropriate process and herein lies the origin of the most fundamental division within the Islamic world: Sunni and Shi'ite. The latter believe that, on his way home from the conquest of Mecca, at a place known as Ghadir al-Khumm, Muhammad had stated: "Of whomsoever I am the mawla, Ali is his mawla".[109] For Shi'ites, this was an explicit and intentional identification of Ali, Muhammad's cousin and son-in-law, as his rightful successor. Moreover, Shi'ites argue that Ali deserved to be the first caliph since he was one of the earliest converts, a champion in battle and the leader of Medina while Muhammad was away at Tabuk. In contrast, Sunnis believe that Abu Bakr was the rightful successor to Muhammad in God's eyes. For them the term "mawla" simply means friend and not leader. Moreover, Abu Bakr was designated by Muhammad as the leader of prayer in his absence. Of course, the fact that Ali was not present at the crucial meeting adds to the complexity, as do Shi'ite claims that 'Umar and others burnt down the house of Fatima, Ali's wife and Muhammad's daughter, in the subsequent drive to obtain support for Abu Bakr. Ali would eventually become the fourth caliph, after Abu Bakr, 'Umar and Uthman, but for Shi'ites it was an improperly delayed appointment. The death of Muhammad had sparked a leadership issue at the very start of Islam's history and, although the leadership changed three times through various forms of election, the reign of the fourth caliph, Ali (656–661 CE), was marked by a series of bloody civil wars.

Muhammad already enjoyed great esteem from his followers during his lifetime. In his final years, he was treated with awesome respect and people had begun to collect souvenirs and relics that were associated with him, such as his hair, clothing and even the water that he had used for washing.[110] After his death, devotion to him became a central aspect of Islamic spirituality. He would be known by many titles, including Seal of the Prophets (Khatam al-Anbiya) – the final spokesperson for the one God in a long line stretching back to Abraham and earlier.[111] His name would be placed next to Allah in mosques, and it would be followed by the honorific phrase "Peace Be Upon Him" (PBUH) when spoken or written. Muslims would look to him as a paragon of virtue and the perfect model for moral life. Men would wear beards in imitation of him and routinely name their sons Muhammad in his honor. Insults against him would be considered as the equivalent of insulting God. He would rarely be depicted in art but, if so, it would be customary to cover his face with a veil to highlight his special status. Yet despite the devotional tendencies to maximize his honor, there is a theological counterforce that works in the opposite direction. Muhammad may be the final prophet and the greatest of human beings, but there is an abiding concern that ascribing excessive esteem to him can easily lead to idolatry (shirk), which is the gravest sin in Islam. Unlike the Buddha and Jesus, the apotheosis of Muhammad is a real danger for Muslims and, thus, Islamic theology has always felt the need to rein in Muhammad's glorification in order to avoid crossing the line into outright deification.

Observations

Like all human beings, all three founders had to face the grim reality of death at a certain point in their lives. That much at least they have in common, but there are also other fascinating similarities as well as striking differences in the timing, circumstances, manner and meaning of their deaths. In terms of longevity, their age at death varies considerably. The Buddha enjoyed the longest life, which is usually estimated to be approximately 80 years, although the tradition states that the normal lifespan for any Buddha is 100 years. Thus, despite the considerable length of his final reincarnation, there is a sense that it was still cut short and the Pali Canon tends to blame his personal assistant, Ananda, for missing the opportunity to request that the Buddha remain on earth for another two decades. Yet there is also an element in the story that suggests that the reason for the Buddha's death at 80 years of age is that he had accomplished his task. As Mara frankly declared, he had taught the dhamma and had established the sangha. There was no further need for him to linger in this transient world. A similar theme is found in the story of Muhammad who died in his early sixties. Given the harshness of the Arabian environment, the various assassination attempts on his life and his personal involvement in a number of military battles, reaching sixty could be considered very fortunate or a sign of divine protection. Like the Buddha, the tradition implies that he too had completed his prophetic mission. He had communicated the Qur'an, restored the Arabian tribes to monotheism and established the Islamic community with its five pillars. In his Farewell Sermon, Muhammad explicitly asked for and received confirmation from his followers that he had faithfully fulfilled the role entrusted to him by God. In contrast, Jesus died in his early thirties after a very brief public ministry of just two or three years. Although it was later seen by Christians as part of God's providential plan, by any normal measure his death was premature. Unlike the Buddha and Muhammad who were old men who died of natural causes, Jesus was a young man who was killed by human design. In contrast to them, he had very little time to establish a new religious system in great detail so that he could say that his life's work was accomplished and that he could depart this world in peace. At the time of Jesus's death there was not much in place that is obviously recognisable as later Christian belief or practice. In response, the Christian tradition reinterpreted Jesus's death itself as one of his principal tasks, in terms of a perfect self-sacrifice that redeems the world.

This last point brings out the obvious differences in the circumstances and manner of the death in each case. Jesus's torture and crucifixion is by far the most brutal and shocking of the three. For several hours, he would have endured excruciating physical pain, although the sheer cruelty of the flogging probably spared him days of agonizing asphyxiation on the cross. It was also the most humiliating. A naked Jesus would have been crucified in a prominent place near the city gates in full view of all, and he would have endured sarcastic mockery from the soldiers and his enemies below. Moreover, it was a lonely death. The gospels state that Jesus was betrayed, denied and abandoned by his closest male followers in those final hours, with only a handful of women disciples standing at a distance to witness his dreadful end. Although Luke and John portray Jesus's final utterances as statements of majestic command and profound trust, the plaintive cry of abandonment recorded in Mark and Matthew hints at genuine mental anguish and desolation in his last moments.

There was also significant physical suffering in the case of the Buddha and Muhammad as well, although not to the same degree as Jesus. The Buddha endured severe dysentery for several weeks, and the discomfort and pain would have been exacerbated by the fact that he was travelling at the time. Similarly, for two or three weeks, Muhammad was struck with acute fever that seriously debilitated and disorientated him. Yet both men were surrounded by loved ones and met their end with a degree of comfort and serenity. Muhammad died in his own home and in the arms of his favorite wife. His final words indicate peaceful acceptance that his time had come and that he would soon replace loved ones on earth with the ineffable joy of God's company in Paradise. The Buddha was more or less heading toward his hometown when death overtook him in Kusinara – an unlikely place that was so remote that it required some explanation in the later scriptures. However, he was accompanied by members of his monastic family as well as many other visitors. Despite the physical discomfort, he is depicted as being in full control, regally reclining under two trees – a common theme regarding the main events of his life. His final words are a brief summation of the heart of his message: the transience of this world and the constant need to strive for liberation. He was a teacher to the very end, and his actual death was itself the final practical lesson on how to transcend the wheel of reincarnation and achieve nibbana.

There is considerable difference concerning the fate of the body in each case, which not only affects the practicality of postmortem veneration but also reflects underlying theological considerations and conclusions. The Buddha's body was cremated in the tradition of Indian kings, according to his own explicit instructions. Indeed, cremation makes theological sense within the reincarnational framework that is characteristic of Hinduism and Buddhism. On the wheel of rebirth, a person will have many bodies and none of them carries any particular significance. In fact, the body must be discarded and destroyed each time in order to facilitate progress toward final liberation. Hindus are most consistent with this notion in that they scatter the ashes of the dead over water, thus freeing the spirit to move to its next reincarnational form. In contrast, the Buddha's ashes were distributed among eight kingdoms and stored in stupas. Several centuries after his death, the emperor Ashoka further redistributed the remains among thousands of monasteries. The desire for relics reflects a tension in Buddhism between the ideal of total detachment and the natural inclination to cling to some physical connection with the one called Tathagata – he who has come and gone.

In contrast, Muhammad's body was buried in the very spot where he died. Burial makes theological sense in a religion such as Islam, which professes a more linear view of human existence. A person only ever has one body, which is an essential part of their psychosomatic identity and which will play some part in the afterlife. Thus, preserving the body via ground burial is an expression of faith in the resurrection at the end of time. Today, the splendid Masjid al-Nabi houses Muhammad's tomb as well as those of Abu Bakr and 'Umar, and many pilgrims visit the site to pay respects to the Prophet and his first two caliphs. The ability to stand before the actual corpse of Muhammad is a powerful drawcard for Muslims who naturally wish to connect spiritually with the Prophet, but the challenge for Islam is to ensure that respectfully visiting his tomb in Medina does not eclipse the more important Meccan hajj or become a catalyst for Muhammad's idolatrous deification.

The fate of Jesus's body is much more controversial and carries much deeper and broader theological implications. Some scholars believe that his body, like other victims of crucifixion, would have been left on the cross to decay naturally or to be devoured by wild animals, with the remains eventually thrown into an unknown mass grave. However, the gospel tradition claims that his body was taken down at sunset and hurriedly buried in a nearby tomb provided by Joseph of Arimathea. The 1968 archeological find of a crucified man buried in a family tomb in Israel lends some credence to this version of events. The Church of the Holy Sepulchre in Jerusalem stands on what is claimed to be the site of Golgotha and the tomb of Jesus. However, unlike Muhammad's resting place, this tomb is empty. According to the gospels, some women disciples visited the grave on the first day of the week and discovered that the stone was rolled away and the corpse was missing. One possible explanation is that Jesus's body was stolen by some unknown persons. However, the gospels offer a different interpretation: God had raised Jesus from the dead. The empty tomb stories are complemented by a series of episodes in which the risen Jesus appears, partially recognizable and partially unrecognizable, to many of his followers. After a period of time, these appearances ceased, and the tradition speaks of Jesus ascending bodily to heaven from where he will come again at the end of time in his glorious parousia. While the Buddha's ashes are distributed across Asia and Muhammad's corpse lies in a grave in Medina, Christians believe that the body of Jesus has been transformed as the first fruits of the resurrection of the dead. Such a position is much more demanding in terms of faith and credibility, and it is simultaneously vulnerable to refutation, or at least reformulation, if the bodily remains of the crucified Jesus of Nazareth were ever uncovered in an archaeological dig.

Given the earlier discussion, it is clear that each religion attaches very different degrees of theological significance to the death of the founder. The least attention is given to Muhammad's death, which occupies only minimal space in the classical biographies and is not even commemorated on the Islamic calendar, although it is presumed that, like the Buddha, he died on the same date as his birth. Even Muhammad's birth, which is marked by the annual festival of Mawlid al-Nabi, is subordinated to more important occasions such as Ramadan and the Feast of the Sacrifice. The calendric focus is not so much on Muhammad but on the revelation of the Qur'an and the original monotheism of Abraham that he preached. Muhammad's real work was done well before his death, which was the natural end of his life and nothing more. In Islamic thinking, Muhammad was the last and greatest of the prophets, but he was still a prophet and all prophets must die – a truth of which Abu Bakr had to remind 'Umar in his distress. Only God is immortal and there is only one God.

In contrast, the Buddhist calendar marks the Buddha's death, and in the Theravadan tradition it is combined with his birth and Enlightenment to create a triple feast day known as Vesak. Although it is said that all three events occurred on the same lunar date, it is also theologically appropriate to link the Parinibbana with these other two key moments in his story. Death is always linked to rebirth in Buddhism, but the Buddha's death is particularly significant in that it was to be his final experience of the samsaric process. He had achieved the fullness of nibbana and would never be reborn again. For the Buddha, it was not just the end of this particular life as the former Prince Siddhattha. It was the end of an epic journey involving hundreds of previous existences. His death is also intrinsically linked to his Enlightenment because together they represent the attainment of nibbana in two steps. At Bodhgaya, he achieved ultimate liberation in his mind and could have quietly slipped away in utter peace. But he chose to remain and share his dhamma with others, thus delaying his own personal fulfilment as a result of compassion. His physical death was the completion of the transition to nibbana, achieved by the shedding of his last corporeal form, which was appropriately relegated to ashes.

While Muhammad's death is missing from the calendar, and the Buddha's death is celebrated conjointly with his birth and Enlightenment, the Easter commemoration of the death and resurrection of Jesus stands on its own and constitutes the most important feast on the Christian calendar – and for good reason. Unlike the stories of Muhammad and the Buddha, the end of the Jesus story holds the key to everything. Although the parables, the miracles and the formation of a nascent community during Jesus's ministry are vital ingredients, Christianity places an enormous amount of theological weight on the twin events at the close of Jesus's career. The initial disaster of the crucifixion, which threatened to end everything, is understood to be part of God's mysterious plan after all. Jesus's death is seen as the supreme self-sacrifice that renders all Temple sacrifices obsolete. For Christians, the crucified Jesus is the Lamb of God whose blood takes away the sins of the world, and he is the anonymous Servant of Isaiah whose suffering brings salvation to God's people. Such a positive interpretation of the cross is only possible due to the Christian belief that his death was not the end of the story. For Christians, Good Friday is followed by Easter Sunday, and this is the crucial element. If Jesus has been raised then everything changes, especially in terms of Jesus's identity and mission. For Christians, a raised Jesus means that he was not merely a rabbi, healer or prophet, but God's true Messiah, the Christ. In fact, faith in the resurrection led Christians to go even further and eventually proclaim Jesus as the incarnate Son of God – fully divine and fully human. Moreover, his apotheosis led to a rethinking of strict monotheism and the development of the distinctive Christian notion of a triune God – Father, Son and Holy Spirit.

The passing of any founder typically constitutes a crisis for the organization concerned, and one final, critical issue associated with the death of the Buddha, Jesus and Muhammad is the question of ongoing authority. In all three cases, there is an element of ambiguity that contributes to the inevitable fragmentation that followed. Jesus had no children and Muhammad's three sons had all died in infancy. Only the Buddha had a male heir, but neither his son nor other more senior monks were nominated. The Buddha's position was that the dhamma itself would be the new leader, which is a noble idealism but not particularly practical in times of real dispute when decisions have to be made by someone. Jesus's own intentions are unclear in that he invested the Twelve with authority but simultaneously gave Peter some sort

of special responsibility as well. The institution of the Twelve did not last, but Christianity would eventually be split between supporters of Petrine, conciliar, episcopal
and other forms of Church order. Finally, the most fundamental schism in Islam rests
on the question of who should have been appointed as the first caliph. Did Muhammad identify his cousin and son-in-law Ali as his successor at Ghadir al-Khumm as
claimed by the Shi'ites or was the appointment of his long-time companion and
occasional deputy Abu Bakr in accordance with God's will as asserted by the Sunnis?

By the time of their death, the Buddha, Jesus and Muhammad had created a community of followers that shared their worldview and was committed to taking it
forward into an unknown future. In time, those communities would expand and
become global religious movements but they would also be fractured by internal
dispute and division. While grounded in the story of their founders, Buddhism,
Christianity and Islam would each follow its own particular pathway through history.
Those pathways are unquestionably colorful and complex, and the extent to which
each remained faithful to the original vision of its founder is a fascinating question;
but that is another story.

Notes

1   Armstrong, Buddha 159, 163; Foucher 50–51.
2   For various allegorical interpretations of the crossing see Nakamura II 61–63.
3   Nakamura II 63; Digha Nikaya 16.2.1–11.
4   Nakamura II 89–94; Digha Nikaya 16.2.27–35.
5   Digha Nikaya 16.3.6.
6   Digha Nikaya 16.3.3–6. Some state that the Buddha's natural lifespan should have been
    one hundred years. Mizuno 181; Cohen 135.
7   Digha Nikaya 16.3.7–9.
8   Digha Nikaya 16.3.10–21. The eight causes of an earthquake are: natural forces; a
    shramana; the conception, birth, enlightenment, first sermon, renunciation and death
    of a Buddha.
9   Digha Nikaya 16.4.1.
10 Digha Nikaya 16.4.13. "Blacksmith" is the common translation although "metalworker"
    is more accurate. Nakamura II 119, 115.
11 Digha Nikaya 1.4.17.
12 Digha Nikaya 16.4.56–57; Foucher 230; Armstrong, Buddha 163.
13 There is evidence that the Buddha and his monks did occasionally eat meat provided
    that the animal was not killed specifically for them and that declining to eat it did not
    cause offence to the host or donor. The Buddha also refused to endorse Devadatta's
    rigorist position that meat must never be consumed.
14 A thorough discussion can be found in Nakamura II 122–124.
15 The site is thought to be near the present town of Kasia about thirty miles east of
    Gorakhpur in Uttar Pradesh; Foucher 234.
16 Digha Nikaya 16.5.41–44.
17 Digha Nikaya 16.4.24–32.
18 Digha Nikaya 16.4.33–51.
19 Digha Nikaya 16.5.16–31.

20 Digha Nikaya 16.6.1.
21 Digha Nikaya 16.6.8.
22 Digha Nikaya 16.6.9–12.
23 Nakamura II 158–161.
24 Digha Nikaya 16.6.28.
25 Digha Nikaya 16.5.26–31; 16.6.24.
26 Nakamura II 189.
27 Digha Nikaya 16.6.29–30.
28 Digha Nikaya 16.6.33–43. On the fate of the relics see Thomas 159–164.
29 Cohen 166–170.
30 Thomas 168.
31 Foucher 244.
32 Nakamura II 203–225; Cohen 131.
33 John 13:1; 19:31–37.
34 In the Synoptics, Jesus does not name the traitor, which causes consternation among the Twelve. In John he indicates Judas by handing him a piece of bread but the others are not sure what this means and why Judas subsequently left the room: John 13:26–30.
35 Luke 22:31–34; John 13:36–38; Mark 14:27–31; Matthew 26:33–35.
36 1 Corinthians 11:23–25. See also Mark 14:22–25; Matthew 26:26–29; Luke 22:15–20. In John, the "Eucharistic" words of Jesus are recorded earlier in 6:28–59.
37 Only Luke 22:51 mentions that Jesus healed the man's ear. John 18:10 identifies him as Malchus – possibly someone known to the early Christians.
38 Matthew 26:15; John 12:6; 13:28–30. Although Matthew claims that the payment fulfils a prophecy in Jeremiah, the reference to thirty silver pieces is actually found in Zechariah 11:12–13.
39 Matthew 27:3–10.
40 Acts 1:18–20.
41 John 18:15–17 adds a second disciple who was known to the High Priest and convinced the doormaid to let them enter the courtyard.
42 Matthew 26:59–62; Mark 14:55–61.
43 Mark 14:62; Matthew 26:64; Luke 22:67–71.
44 Leviticus 24:10–23.
45 Matthew 26:67–68; Mark 14:65; Luke 22:63–65.
46 John 18:28.
47 Luke 23:2.
48 Luke 23:8–12.
49 Matthew 27:11–14; Mark 15:2–5; Luke 23:3–5; John 18:33–38.
50 Matthew 27:15–18, 20–23; Mark 15:6–15; Luke 23:17–19; John 18:39–40.
51 John 19:13–16; Mark 15:15; Matthew 27:26; Luke 23:24–25.
52 Matthew 27:19, 24–25.
53 John 19:15.
54 Jewish War 2.9.4; Antiquities 18.3.2; 18.4.1, 2; Philo, On The Embassy of Gauis 38.299–305.
55 John19:1.
56 Mark 15:16–20; Matthew 27:27–31.
57 Mark 15:21; Matthew 27:32; Luke 23:26.
58 John 19:19–22; Mark 15:26; Matthew 27:37; Luke 23:38.
59 Mark 15:24; Matthew 27:35; Luke 23:34; John 19:23–24.

60   Mark 15:25; John 19:14.

61   John 19:31–37.

62   John 19:25–27.

63   John 19:28–30.

64   Mark 15:23, 36; Matthew 27:34, 48.

65   Luke 23:39–43.

66   Luke 23:34.

67   John 19:30; Luke 23:46; Mark 15:34–37; Matthew 27:46–50.

68   Mark 15:33, 38; Matthew 27:45, 51–53; Luke 23:44–45.

69   John 19:31–37.

70   John 19:25–27.

71   Mark 15:40–41; Matthew 27:55–56.

72   The bones of a crucified man named Jehohanan were found by archaeologists in a tomb near Jerusalem in 1968.

73   Mark 15:42–47; Matthew 27:57–60; Luke 23:50–53; John 19:38–42.

74   Mark 16:1–2; Matthew 28:1; Luke 24:1.

75   John 20:1.

76   John 20:1–10.

77   Mark 16:5–8.

78   Luke 24:4–12; Matthew 28:2–8.

79   1 Corinthians 15:3–8.

80   Mark 16:9–11; Matthew 28:8–10; John 20:11–18.

81   John 20:19–29.

82   Luke 24:13–35; Mark 16:12–13.

83   Matthew 28:16–17; John 21:1–23.

84   Acts 9:1–9.

85   Matthew 28:17; Luke 24:16, 31, 37–39; John 20:15–16, 27; 21:4.

86   Luke 24:39–43; John 20:27; 21:13.

87   Mark 16:14–18; Matthew 28:18–19; Luke 24:44–49; John 20:21–24; 21:15–23.

88   Luke 24:50–51; Mark 16:19; John 20:17. Although Luke's gospel describes Jesus's ascension occurring on the same day as his resurrection, Acts states that it was forty days later. See Acts 1:1–11.

89   1 Thessalonians 4:13–17; 2 Thessalonians 2:1–3; 1 Corinthians 7:29–31.

90   1 Corinthians 1:18–2:9; Acts 2:23–24; 3:17–19. The four "Servant Songs" are found in Isaiah 42:1–9; 49:1–6; 50:4–9; 52:13–53:12.

91   Philippians 2:6–11; Colossians 1:15–20; John 1:1–18.

92   Qur'an 3:97; 2:196–197.

93   Peters, Origins 243; Ibn Ishaq (Guillaume) 617.

94   Peters, Origins 247–253; Rodinson 285.

95   Bukhari 81.776.

96   Qur'an 5:3.

97   Ramadan 195. He quotes Bukhari in footnote 36 but provides no reference.

98   Ibn Ishaq (Guillaume) 678.

99   Ibn Ishaq (Guillaume) 679.

100 Ramadan 204; Ibn Ishaq (Guillaume) 680–681.

101 Ibn Ishaq (Guillaume) 682.

102 The Islamic date is usually given as 12 Rabi al-awwal 11AH.

103 Ibn Ishaq (Guillaume) 682.

104 Ibn Ishaq (Guillaume) 682–683.

105 Ibn Ishaq (Guillaume) 683.

106   Qur'an 3:144.
107   Ibn Ishaq (Guillaume) 688.
108   Ibn Ishaq (Guillaume) 683–687.
109   See Hadith of Ghadir al-Khumm. See also Qur'an 5:55, 67. Shi'ites believe that these verses refer to Ali and his family.
110   Hilliard 115; Phipps 191.
111   Qur'an 33:40.

CONCLUSION

The principal aim of this comparative study was to identify the major areas of similarity and dissimilarity between the traditional life stories of the Buddha, Jesus and Muhammad. After considering these three influential figures across 10 themes, it is now time to see what the juxtaposition has revealed. As one might have suspected from the outset, there are fascinating areas of both commonality and difference. Moreover, the elements of intersection sometimes involve all three and sometimes only two of the three, with the third figure set apart in striking contrast.

The first point to acknowledge is that the comparative method is always in danger of imposing a contrived level of similarity upon genuine uniqueness. There was only ever one Siddhattha Gotama, one Jesus of Nazareth and one Muhammad ibn 'Abdullah. They lived at very different points on the historical timeline, separated by approximately 500 years in each case. Their diverse geographical contexts were the lush fields and forests of the Ganges Plain, the pasturelands of Galilee, and the harsh desert of Arabia. Their political worlds were at very different stages of the empire building process: small republics being swallowed up by emerging kingdoms; a vast empire approaching its glorious zenith; and disunited tribes beyond the pale of two crumbling empires. In the same vein, their religious worlds greatly differed: traditional Vedic polytheism challenged by new monistic thinking; Hebrew monotheism with a heightened sense of apocalyptic expectation; and animistic polytheism sprinkled with marginal groups of monotheists.

Their individual backgrounds are also totally diverse: an unsettled prince willing to abandon his palatial home and family for the rigors of the forest in quest of personal enlightenment; an unknown village carpenter attracted to the preaching of a new prophetic voice in the land; a well-respected merchant who regularly retreated to the solitude of the nearby hills in meditation. Not surprisingly, their fundamental messages also appear to be utterly distinctive. The Kingdom of God is not identical with the "Straight Path" advocated by the Qur'an, and both of these are very dif-

Buddha, Jesus and Muhammad: A Comparative Study, First Edition. Paul Gwynne.
© 2014 John Wiley & Sons, Ltd. Published 2014 by John Wiley & Sons, Ltd.

ferent to the Four Noble Truths. One could continue with more specific biographical details that underpin the essential truth that we are dealing with three different figures from three different historical contexts, with three different personal stories, three different messages and, hence, three different religions that constitute their legacy.

Nevertheless, we cannot ignore the other side of the coin: namely, the very real points of similarity that exist between them as well. In terms of information, all three men are figures from the ancient world, unavoidably shrouded by the mists of time. In each case, the primary sources were composed by committed followers within the faith rather than disinterested writers outside it. Furthermore, there is a time gap between their deaths and the emergence of written texts – a considerable one in the case of the Buddha – although all three traditions claim a reliable link back to the original eye witnesses. There are also large sections of their lives absent from the earliest biographies, although this missing information varies in each case. We have scant information about the early years of Jesus and Muhammad and, conversely, little data about the Buddha's middle years.

All three were the firstborn and only son of their mother (if Jesus's siblings are indeed cousins or Joseph's sons from an earlier marriage), and all three were raised by a surrogate parent. Muhammad lost both parents as a child and he was placed in the care of his grandfather and uncle; the Buddha's mother died at birth and his aunt-stepmother replaced her as carer; and it is claimed that Jesus was not the bio-logical son of Joseph but was conceived without a human father. A virginal concep-tion is also an aspect of later stories of the Buddha's infancy. On that point, each infancy tradition includes miraculous events that establish the special, holy status of each child, and all three traditions include a narrative about a wise and perspicacious stranger (Asita, Simeon and Bahira) who recognizes the true identity of each child and foretells his future greatness.

The radical turning point that changed their careers occurred more or less in that period of life described as "thirty something". There are external stimuli in both human and divine form: the four sights, the dancing girls and the gods' constant prompting for Siddhattha; the theophany in the Jordan and the arrest of the Baptist for Jesus; the frightening appearance of Gabriel combined with the support of Khadija and Waraqa for Muhammad. There is also an inner predisposition: Siddhattha's restlessnes, Muhammad's regular retreat to Mount Hira and Jesus's interest in the Baptist's message. In their public career, all three present a message that addresses the fundamental questions about the meaning of human existence, yet all three are aware that not all listeners would respond favorably. The Buddha requires "right view" and "right intention"; Jesus knows that some seed will fall on rich soil and some on rocky ground; and al-Fatiha speaks of two possible paths that can be taken. All three messages also insist that moral behavior is a crucial element on the path to ultimate fulfilment: the Buddha calls for "right action"; Jesus inextricably links love of God and neighbor; and the five pillars of Islam include both regular worship of God (salat) and practical assistance for the poor (zakat).

The miraculous element of the infancy stories is carried over into the adult careers of each founder, although this element is conspicuously absent in the Qur'an. The ability to work amazing feats is not unique to the three founders since there is a preexisting miracle tradition in each case: the iddhi powers of yoga masters and the biblical figures of Moses, Elijah and Elisha. Yet the miracle narratives present each founder as superior within their tradition: the Buddha's victory via the Great Miracle and his descent from Tavatimsa Heaven accompanied by Hindu gods; Jesus's endorsement by Moses and Elijah at the Transfiguration; and Muhammad's priority over earlier prophets as reflected in the Night Journey. All three traditions also acknowledge the limitations of miracles. The Buddha banned his monks from displaying iddhi powers in public for vainglory; Jesus refused to work miracles for a cynical Herod; and Allah informed Muhammad that no miracle would ever have converted the hardhearted Meccans. The last point touches on another experience common to all three: skepticism in their home town. The Buddha's miraculous performance generated only shallow belief in Kapilavatthu; Jesus could not work many miracles in Nazareth because of their little faith in one so familiar; and the lack of a miraculous sign only exacerbated local Meccan hostility toward Muhammad.

All three men were successful in attracting a group of dedicated followers and, in each case, the membership was broadly inclusive, cutting across tribal, social and cultural divides. The Buddha's first converts were a mix of veteran ascetics and restless sons of wealthy families, and he soon began ordaining persons irrespective of caste, gender or age. Jesus practiced table fellowship with both the righteous and sinners, and the composition of the Twelve reflects a heterogeneous mix of personalities, backgrounds and occupations. Muhammad's first supporters were close relatives and friends, but the community also welcomed disenchanted youths from influential families alongside those from lower socioeconomic strata, including slaves. Sadly, the three founders also experienced rejection from their own kinsfolk, prompting a redefinition of family based on belief rather than blood. Siddhattha dramatically severed ties with his family on the night of the Renunciation and, on his return to Kapilavatthu, informed his father that his lineage was now that of the Buddhas. Jesus was considered insane by his family and spoke of his disciples as his true mother and brothers. Muhammad's uncles, Abu Talib and Abu Lahab, both died as pagans, while the Hijra meant complete abandonment of tribal affiliation for the new community grounded in a common faith.

None of the three founders can rightly be called pioneers of feminism, and all were clearly influenced by the cultural presuppositions of their day. The Buddha was initially reluctant to admit women to the monastic life and, even when he did relent, he imposed extra rules upon them and predicted that the dhamma would not last as long as a result. Jesus did not include a woman among the Twelve and did not explicitly call for reform of Jewish laws that were prejudiced against them. Muhammad did not ban concubinage or polygamy, and there are some hadiths that suggest that he may have considered women morally and intellectually inferior. However, there is also evidence that the three men displayed a progressive attitude to women relative to their historical context. Despite his hesitation, the Buddha's decision to admit nuns flew in the face of Brahmanic prejudice. Given that the Twelve symbolized the Israelite tribes that originated with the sons of Jacob, Jesus probably had no choice but to omit women from that particular group. Nevertheless, many of his closest friends were female, and he was willing to break traditional taboos in his general dealing with women, even risking considerable scandal by allowing an entourage of female disciples to travel around with him. The Qur'an allowed polygamy but set an upper limit of four wives and insisted on their equal treatment. Moreover, it banned female infanticide, created rules regarding the treatment of female prisoners of war, established a personal dowry for the wife and endorsed inheritance rights for female relatives.

Finally, there were problems concerning the succession of authority after the death of each founder. The Buddha's main deputies, Sariputta and Moggallana had died before him and he had declared the dhamma to be the true leader of the sangha – an idealistic claim but one that could not avert schism in the long run. There is also ambiguity in the case of Jesus who gave authority to the Twelve but who also invested Peter with some sort of special role, thus sowing the seeds of later ecclesiastical disputes about church leadership. Finally, while Sunnis accept the historical appointment of Abu Bakr as the first caliph, Shi'ites insist that Muhammad explicitly anointed Ali as his successor.

The comparative analysis has also revealed common areas shared by two of the founders while the third figure stands apart in contrast as the odd man out. These paired intersections form a more detailed map of the complex ways in which the Buddha, Jesus and Muhammad relate to each other. First, there are those narrative elements common to the Buddha and Jesus but not Muhammad. One example is the presence of a tempting spirit (Mara and Satan) in contrast to Muhammad whose chief initial obstacle was not the wiles of an external being but his own inner fears. Another is the confident, commanding manner in which the Buddha and Jesus recruited many of their first followers from the ranks of strangers in contrast to Muhammad's cautious, discreet approach that was initially confined to trustworthy family and friends. A third example is the proliferation of miracles in the stories of the Buddha and Jesus in contrast to the lack of miracles in the earliest traditions concerning Muhammad, including the Qur'an itself. But perhaps the two most striking instances of convergence between the Buddha and Jesus are the importance given to worldly renunciation and the explicit rejection of force.

A tradition that advocated the radical abandonment of material comfort and an itinerant celibate lifestyle was already present in the Indian shramanic movement and the wandering Cynic philosophers. In similar style, Siddhattha and Jesus opted for religious celibacy over family life. It was a painful choice for Siddhattha, who was already married with a son. It was a strange choice for Jesus given his Jewish background but one that made sense given the expectation of an imminent apocalypse. In contrast, there was no equivalent tradition in seventh-century CE Arabia and, not surprisingly, Muhammad saw no spiritual value in anyone deliberately remaining unmarried. He himself enjoyed a fruitful monogamous marriage with Khadija during the Meccan period and then wedded another 11 women for various reasons in the Medinan period. Three of these marriages have controversial aspects and attract some criticism today ('A'isha, Zaynab bint Jahsh and Safiyya), but Muhammad is also depicted as a caring husband to his wives and a loving father to his four daughters. The Buddha and Jesus were also itinerants with no established base and, with their fellow wanderer-disciples, relied heavily on the practical support of generous lay followers. Although Muhammad and his community were forced to abandon Mecca, losing much of their property and assets in the process, he adopted Medina as his new home-headquarters and remained there until his death.

The Buddha and Jesus also share an explicit rejection of political power as a means to further their cause. Although he was raised as heir to a local throne Siddhattha abandoned the path of world ruler (cakkavatti) and chose instead the path of spiritual leadership, overcoming the temptations of Mara and Bimbisara in the process. Jesus also declined Satan's offer of earthly kingship and similarly rejected the messianic title from enthusiastic crowds and disciples, declaring that his kingdom was not of this world. In avoiding political office, both also rejected military force, which stood in fundamental conflict with the Buddha's stress on nonviolence and with Jesus's principle that those who live by the sword will die in the same manner. Muhammad's troubled time in Mecca resonates with these positions, but his post-Hijra acceptance of political office in Medina and the accompanying Qur'anic endorsement of armed struggle changed everything. In the end, he saw no contradiction between the roles of divine spokesman and army commander, interpreting military success as heavenly blessing, using political power to establish God's reign on earth and aligning himself more with figures such as Moses and Joshua.

The second pairing concerns the common ground between Jesus and Muhammad in contrast to the Buddha. One example is the relatively low socioeconomic conditions of their childhood compared with the regal opulence of Siddhattha's upbringing. Despite claims that Jesus stemmed from royal Davidic pedigree and the fact that Muhammad was born into the powerful Quraysh tribe, their actual circumstances were modest at best, whereas Siddhattha was surrounded by the entire gamut of palatial pleasures as well as the extensive and comprehensive education program of a crown prince. Another example is the dearth of information and lack of interest concerning the early years of Jesus and Muhammad prior to their public careers in comparison with the unmistakeable focus in the classical biographies on Siddhattha's long quest for illumination and a corresponding lack of interest in the post-Enlightenment phase of his life. A third example is the considerable external political opposition that Jesus and Muhammad faced in contrast to the broad support or, at least, the laissez-faire attitude shown to the Buddha's movement by the rulers of the northern Indian kingdoms, such as Bimbisara and Pasenadi. The Buddha's main opposition arose from within his ranks in the form of Devadatta, and it included a rigorist schism and several assassination attempts. In contrast, Jesus faced serious enmity from religious and political groups, such as the Pharisees, the Jerusalem priesthood and, ultimately, the Roman prefect who saw him as a potential rebel leader. Similarly, Muhammad and his nascent community endured a decade of systematic persecution from the polytheistic Meccan authorities. Even after the Hijra, which provided safe haven, the first Muslims had to engage in three battles against the Meccans before the threat was removed and the tables were turned in dramatic fashion.

However, the most striking similarity between Jesus and Muhammad in contrast to the Buddha is the theological context in which they operated. On one hand, Jesus and Muhammad both hailed from the Middle East and professed Abrahamic monotheism with its linear view of human existence, bodily resurrection and divine judgment. On the other hand, the Buddha's provenance was the Upanishadic cyclic view that presumed multiple reincarnations determined by the law of karma, ending in final liberation from the wheel of samsara. Although Jesus's Jewish audience would have presumed the divine oneness, Muhammad had to combat entrenched Arabian polytheism. Nevertheless, both men professed a worldview in which humans live and die under the sovereignty of a single, just and merciful Creator God. It is a completely different paradigm for the Buddha, who taught that a person's ultimate liberation does not depend on the saving action of a divine being such as Shiva or Vishnu but on one's own dedicated application of the dhamma. Final liberation (nibbana), defined in negative terms as the extinguishing of the flames of ignorant desire, is notoriously difficult to pin down, but it is certainly not eternal communion with a Creator God. Even the miracles of the Buddha are the result of natural human powers unleashed by disciplined meditation rather than the unambiguous in-breaking of supernatural power as in the monotheistic tradition. Thus, the religions spawned by Jesus and Muhammad see themselves as members of the Abrahamic family, whereas Buddhism is paradoxically described as a nontheistic religion.

The third pairing involves areas of similarity between the Buddha and Muhammad in contrast to Jesus. One could point to the parallel economic trends in the societies of Siddhattha and Muhammad where a new merchant class threatened traditional social structures and allegiances. One could also note that both men lost their natural mother at a very young age, whereas Jesus's mother not only outlived him but was eventually acknowledged as a perfect model of discipleship and, in some branches of Christianity, elevated to quasi-divine status alongside her son. One could also cite the fact that both Siddhattha and Muhammad experienced married life and father-hood first-hand, whereas the evidence suggests that Jesus never married or sired children. However, the most striking difference between Jesus and the other two founders concerns the timing, manner and consequences of their deaths.

The Buddha and Muhammad both died of natural causes in their senior years after decades in the public forum and at the helm of their respective communities. Jesus, on the other hand, was killed by human design in his early thirties after a brief min-istry of two or three years. While the Buddha and Muhammad died peacefully sur-rounded by companions and loved ones, Jesus died a humiliating death abandoned by his closest followers and ostensibly by his heavenly Father as well. The numbers suggest that the Buddha and Muhammad had ample time to establish, develop and refine their communities in terms of fundamental principles, practical guidelines and organizational structures. By the time the Buddha passed away, his monastic sangha was able to draw on over 40 years of example and teaching from its leader. Similarly, Muhammad's Farewell Sermon indicates that the Qur'anic revelations had been completed, and the pillars of Islam were firmly in place. This is not to say that eve-rything was frozen from that point in time, but it does suggest that the Buddha and Muhammad had genuinely founded something by the time their lives came to an end. It is more challenging to recognize in detail the central beliefs and practices of early Christianity in Jesus's short-lived mission to Israel's lost sheep. For many, it is debatable whether what emerged as Christianity had been truly "founded" by the time of his premature death.

It is not just the timing of his death that sets Jesus apart from the other two founders. Claims about the fate of his corpse are also critical. While Muhammad lies buried in Medina, on the very spot where he died, and while the ashes of Siddhattha were allegedly shared among eight kingdoms, the Christian faith professes that Jesus's tomb was found empty and that he was seen in bodily form by many of his followers, leading to the conviction that he had been raised from the dead. Belief in the resurrection naturally led to a rethinking of both his death and his identity. The crucifixion was subsequently reinterpreted as the supreme sacrifice that brings salvation to the world, while the prophet-healer from Nazareth was acclaimed as the long-awaited Jewish Messiah (Christ) and, eventually, as the unique incarnation of God in history. Such a claim goes well beyond Islam's assessment of its founder as the Seal of the Prophets and even Buddhism's acknowledgement of Siddhattha as one Buddha among many.

In the end, one must conclude that the network of similarities and dissimilarities between the Buddha, Jesus and Muhammad is complex and nuanced. It is misleading to gloss over the very real differences that set them apart, but it is equally inaccurate to say glibly that they have absolutely nothing in common. Without doubt, each founder is a unique personality in his own right, with his own unrepeatable story, but that story also overlaps with one or both of the others in fascinating and distinctive ways. Hopefully mapping the topography of these commonalities and contrasts has not only deepened our appreciation of their cherished individuality, but also revealed the many points of contact between the former prince, carpenter and merchant and, indirectly, the three great religious traditions that their lives inspired.

FURTHER READING

1. Comparative Works

Ali, Maulana Muhammad (2007/first published 1921) *Muhammad and Christ*. Whitefish, MT: Kessinger.

Dods, Marcus (2008/first published 1877) *Mohammed, Buddha and Christ: Four Lectures on Natural and Revealed Religion*. Charleston, SC: BiblioBazaar.

George, Timothy (2002) *Is the Father of Jesus the God of Muhammad?* Grand Rapids, MI: Zondervan.

Jaspers, Karl (1962) *Socrates, Buddha, Confucius, Jesus. The Great Philosophers: Volume I*. Orlando: Harcourt Brace.

Robinson, Neal (1991) *Christ in Islam and Christianity. The Representation of Jesus in the Qur'an and the Classical Muslim Commentaries*. New York: State University of New York Press.

Sasson, Vanessa R. (2007) *The Birth of Moses and the Buddha: A Paradigm for the Comparative Study of Religions*. Sheffield: Phoenix.

Streeter, Burnett Hillman (2007/first published 1933) *The Buddha and the Christ: An Exploration of the Meaning of the Universe and the Purpose of Human Life*. Whitefish, MT: Kessinger.

2. Buddha

Auboyer, Jeannine (1983) *Buddha: A Pictorial History of his Life and Legacy*. New York: Crossroad.

Boisselier, Jean (1994) *The Wisdom of the Buddha*. London: Thames & Hudson.

Burland, C.A. (1972) *The Way of the Buddha*. Amersham: Hulton Educational.

Burtt, Edwin A. ed. (2000/first published 1955) *The Teachings of the Compassionate Buddha*. New York: Penguin.

Byles, Marie Beuzeville (1963) *The Lotus and the Spinning Wheel*. London: George Allen & Unwin.

Buddha, Jesus and Muhammad: A Comparative Study, First Edition. Paul Gwynne.
© 2014 John Wiley & Sons, Ltd. Published 2014 by John Wiley & Sons, Ltd.

Byles, Marie Beuzeville (1967) *Footprints of Gautama the Buddha.* London: Theosophical Publishing House.

Corless, Roger (1989) *The Vision of Buddhism: Space under the Tree.* New York: Paragon House.

Davidson, Ronald M. (2003) *Indian Esoteric Buddhism.* New York: Columbia University Press.

Edwardes, Michael (1976) *In the Blowing Out of a Flame: The World of the Buddha and the World of Man.* London: Allen & Unwin.

Gombrich, Richard (1988) *Theravada Buddhism: A Social History from Ancient Benares to Modern Colombo.* London: Routledge & Kegan Paul.

Gombrich, Richard (1996) *How Buddhism Began: The Conditioned Genesis of the Early Teachings.* London: Routledge.

Harvey, Peter (1990) *An Introduction to Buddhism. Teachings, History and Practice.* Cambridge: Cambridge University Press.

Herold, A. Ferdinand (2008/ first published 1954) *The Life of Buddha, According to the Legends of Ancient India.* Seattle, WA: CreateSpace.

Ikeda, Daisaku (2008) *The Living Buddha: An Interpretive Biography.* Santa Monica: Middleway.

Ling, Trevor (1973) *The Buddha: Buddhist Civilization in India and Ceylon.* London: Penguin.

Nanamoli, Bhikkhu (2001) *The Life of the Buddha according to the Pali Canon.* Onalaska, WA: Pariyatti.

Narada Maha Thera (1988) *The Buddha and His Teachings.* Kandy, Sri Lanka: Buddhist Publication Society.

Narayan, B. K. (2003) *The Immortal Buddha's Path to Liberation.* New Delhi: Har-Anand Publications.

Nelson, Walter Henry (1996) *Buddha: His Life and His Teaching.* New York: Tarcher.

Niwano, Nikkyo (1989) *Shakyamuni Buddha. A Narrative Biography.* Tokyo: Kosei.

Parrinder, Geoffrey (1977) *The Wisdom of the Early Buddhists.* New York: W.W. Norton.

Penner, Hans H. (2009) *Rediscovering the Buddha.* Oxford: Oxford University Press.

Percheron, Maurice (1984) *Buddha and Buddhism.* New York: Overlook.

Piyadassi, Thera (2009) *The Buddha's Ancient Path.* Delhi: Bharatiya Kala Prakashan.

Pye, Michael (1981) *The Buddha.* London: Duckworth.

Rockhill, William Woodville (2009/first published 1884) *The life of the Buddha and the early history of his order derived from Tibetan works in the Bkah-hgyur and Bstanhgyur.* Charleston, SC: BiblioBazaar.

Saddhatissa, Hammalawa (1976) *The Life of the Buddha.* London: Allen and Unwin.

Saddhatissa, Hammalawa (2000) *Before He Was Buddha. The Life of Siddhartha.* Berkeley: Seastone.

Schober, Juliane ed. (2002) *Sacred Biography in the Buddhist Traditions of South and Southeast Asia.* Delhi: Motilal Banarsidass.

Schumann, H.W. (2004) *The Historical Buddha. The Times, Life and Teachings of the Founder of Buddhism.* Delhi: Motilal Banarsidass.

Singh, I., Radhakrishnan, S. & Sharma, A. (2004) *The Buddhism Omnibus.* New York: Oxford University Press.

Thich Nhat Hanh (1991) *Old Path, White Clouds. Walking in the Footsteps of the Buddha.* Berkeley: Parallax Press.

Warder, A.K. (2002) *Indian Buddhism.* Delhi: Motilal Banarsidass.

Wickremesinghe, K.D.P. (1972) *The Biography of the Buddha.* Colombo: Gunaratana Press.

Wiltshire, Martin Gerald (1990) *Ascetic Figures Before and In Early Buddhism. The Emergence of Gautama as the Buddha.* New York: Mouton de Gruyter.

3. Jesus

Allen, Charlotte (1998) *The Human Christ. The Search for the Historical Jesus.* New York: The Free Press.

Allison, Dale (1998) *Jesus of Nazareth: Millenarian Prophet.* Minneapolis, MN: Fortress Press.

Banks, Robert (1975) *Jesus and the Law in the Synoptic Tradition.* Cambridge: Cambridge University Press.

Bauckham, Richard (2006) *Jesus and the Eyewitnesses. The Gospels as Eyewitness Testimony.* Grand Rapids, MI: W.B. Eerdmans.

Bowker, John (1973) *Jesus and the Pharisees.* Cambridge: Cambridge University Press.

Braun, Herbert (1979) *Jesus of Nazareth. The Man and His Time.* Philadelphia: Fortress.

Buchanan, George W. (1984) *Jesus: The King and His Kingdom.* Macon, GA: Mercer.

Charlesworth, James H. (1988) *Jesus Within Judaism. New Light from Exciting Archaeological Discoveries.* New York: Doubleday.

Charlesworth, James H. ed. (1991) *Jesus' Jewishness. Exploring the Place of Jesus in Early Judaism.* New York: Crossroad.

Charlesworth, James H. (1992) *Jesus and the Dead Sea Scrolls.* New York: Doubleday.

Charlesworth, James H. ed. (2006) *Jesus and Archaeology.* Grand Rapids, MI: W.B. Eerdmans.

Chilton, Bruce (2000) *Rabbi Jesus. An Intimate Biography.* New York: Image.

Cook, Michael L. (1981) *The Jesus of Faith.* New York: Paulist.

Crossan, John Dominic & Reed, Jonathan (2001) *Excavating Jesus. Beneath the Stones, Behind the Texts.* San Francisco: Harper.

Dawes, Gregory W. ed. (1999) *The Historical Jesus Quest. Landmarks in the Search for the Jesus of History.* Nashville: Westminster John Knox.

Dawes, Gregory W. ed. (2001) *The Historical Jesus Question. The Challenge of History to Religious Authority.* Nashville: Westminster John Knox.

Eddy, Paul Rhodes & Boyd, Gregory A. (2007) *The Jesus Legend. A Case for the Reliability of the Synoptic Jesus Tradition.* Grand Rapids, MI: Baker Academic.

Efroymson, David P. (1993) "Jesus: Opposition and Opponents", in Mary C. Boys et al. eds. *Within Context: Essays on Jews and Judaism in the New Testament.* Collegeville, MN: Liturgical Press, 85–103.

Ehrman, Bart D. (1999) *Jesus: Apocalyptic Prophet of the New Millennium.* New York: Oxford University Press.

Evans, C. Stephen (1996) *The Historical Christ and the Jesus of Faith. The Incarnational Narrative as History.* New York: Oxford University Press.

Evans, Craig A. (2001) *Jesus and His Contemporaries.* Leiden: Brill Academic.

Eve, Eric (2002) *The Jewish Context of Jesus' Miracles.* London: Sheffield Academic Press.

Fitzmyer, Joseph (1991) *A Christological Catechism: New Testament Answers.* New York: Paulist.

Fredriksen, Paula (1999) *Jesus of Nazareth, King of the Jews: A Jewish Life and the Emergence of Christianity.* New York: Vintage.

Freyne, Sean (1988) *Galilee, Jesus, and the Gospels.* Philadelphia: Fortress.

Freyne, Sean (2004) *Jesus, A Jewish Galilean: A New Reading of the Jesus Story.* New York: T&T Clark.

Funk, Robert W. (1997) *Honest to Jesus.* San Francisco: Harper.

Funk, Robert W. ed. (1997) *The Five Gospels: The Search for the Authentic Words of Jesus.* San Francisco: Harper.

Funk, Robert W. ed. (1998) *The Acts of Jesus: The Search for the Authentic Deeds of Jesus*. Salem, OR: Polebridge Press.

Goergen, Donald J. (1986) *Mission and Ministry of Jesus*. Wilmington, DE: Glazier.

Gowler, David (2007) *What Are They Saying About the Historical Jesus?* New York: Paulist.

Harvey, A. E. (1982) *Jesus and the Constraints of History*. London: Duckworth.

Horsley, Richard A. (1987) *Jesus and the Spiral of Violence. Popular Jewish Resistance in Roman Palestine*. New York: Harper.

Horsley, Richard A. (2002) *Jesus and Empire. The Kingdom of God and the New World Disorder*. Minneapolis, MN: Fortress.

Johnson, Luke Timothy (1995) *The Real Jesus. The Misguided Quest for the Historical Jesus and the Truth of the Traditional Gospels*. San Francisco: Harper.

Keck, Leander (2000) *Who Is Jesus? History in Perfect Tense*. Columbia: University of South Carolina Press.

Kee, Howard Clark (1995) *What Can We Know About Jesus?* Cambridge: Cambridge University Press.

Khalidi, Tarif (2003) *The Muslim Jesus. Sayings and Stories in Islamic Literature*. Cambridge, MA: Harvard University Press.

Levine, Amy-Jill (2006) *The Misunderstood Jew. The Church and the Scandal of the Jewish Jesus*. San Francisco: HarperOne.

Levine, A., Dale, C. & Crossan, J. eds. (2006) *The Historical Jesus in Context*. Princeton, NJ: Princeton University Press.

Malina, Bruce J. (2000) *The Social Gospel of Jesus. The Kingdom of God in Mediterranean Perspective*. Minneapolis, MN: Fortress.

Miller, Robert J. (1999) *The Jesus Seminar and Its Critics*. Salem, OR: Polebridge Press.

O'Collins, Gerald (1983) *Interpreting Jesus*. New York: Paulist.

Rivkin, Ellis (1984) *What Crucified Jesus?* London: SCM.

Stanton, Graham N. (1989) *The Gospels and Jesus*. New York: Oxford University Press.

Theissen, Gerd (1987) *The Shadow of the Galilean*. Philadelphia: Fortress.

Theissen, Gerd & Merz, Annette (1998) *The Historical Jesus. A Comprehensive Guide*. Minneapolis, MN: Augsburg Fortress.

Twelftree, Graham H. (1993) *Jesus the Exorcist. A Contribution to the Study of the Historical Jesus*. Peabody, MN: Hendrikson.

Van Voorst, Robert E. (2000) *Jesus Outside the New Testament. An Introduction to the Ancient Evidence*. Grand Rapids, MI: W.B. Eerdmans.

Witherington, Ben, III (1997) *The Jesus Quest. The Third Search for the Jew of Nazareth*. Downer's Grove, IL: Intervarsity Press.

Witherington, Ben, III (2000) *Jesus the Sage. The Pilgrimage of Wisdom*. Minneapolis, MN: Fortress.

Wright, N.T. (1992) *Who Was Jesus?* Grand Rapids, MI: W.B. Eerdmans.

Wright, N.T. (1997) *Jesus and the Victory of God*. Minneapolis, MN: Fortress.

Wright, N.T. (1999) *The Challenge of Jesus. Rediscovering Who Jesus Was and Is*. Downers' Grove, IL: Intervarsity Press.

4. Muhammad

Adil, Hajjah Amina (2002) *Muhammad: The Messenger of Islam*. Washington, DC: Islamic Supreme Council of America.

Asani, Ali Sultaan (1995) *Celebrating Muhammad. Images of the Prophet in Popular Muslim Poetry*. Columbia: University of South Carolina Press.

Azzam, Abd al-Rahman (1965) *The Eternal Message of Muhammad*. Los Angeles: New English Library.

Barakat, Ahmad (1979) *Muhammad and the Jews: A Re-Examination*. New Delhi: Vikas.

Berg, Herbert ed. (2003) *Method and Theory in the Study of Islamic Origins*. Boston: Brill.

Blachère, Régis (1952) *Le probleme de Mahomet. Essai de biographie critique du fondateur de l'Islam*. Paris: Presses Universitaires de France.

Brockopp, Jonathan E. ed. (2010) *The Cambridge Companion to Muhammad*. Cambridge: Cambridge University Press.

Cragg, Kenneth (1984) *Jesus and the Muslim: An Exploration*. London: Darton Longman &Todd.

Cragg, Kenneth (1984) *Muhammad and the Christian: A Question of Response*. London: Darton Longman and Todd.

Dashti, Ali (1994) *Twenty-Three Years: A Study of the Prophetic Career of Mohammad*. Costa Mesa, CN: Mazda.

Dermenghem, Emile (1983/first published 1930) *Muhammad and the Islamic tradition*. New York: Overlook.

Esposito, John (2010) *Islam. The Straight Path*. Oxford: Oxford University Press.

Gabrieli, Francesco (1968) *Muhammad and the Conquests of Islam*. Worthing, UK: Littlehampton.

Glubb, John Bagot (1970) *The Life and Times of Muhammad*. London: Hodder & Stoughton.

Hakim, Tawfiq (1985) *Muhammad*. Cairo: Al-Adab Press.

Hamidullah, Muhammad (1998) *The Life and Work of the Prophet of Islam*. Islamabad: Islamic Research Institute.

Gülen, M. Fethullah (2000) *Prophet Muhammad: Aspects of His Life*. Fairfax, VA: Fountain.

Ibn Kathir (trans. Trevor Le Gassick) (2000) *Life of the Prophet Muhammad*. Reading, UK: Ithaca.

Ibn Sa'd, Muhammad (1997) *The Women of Madina*. London: Ta-Ha Publishers.

Iyad ibn Musa al-Yahsubi (trans. A. A. Bewley) (1991) *Muhammad, Messenger of Allah. Ash-Shifa of Qadi Iyad*. Inverness: Madinah.

Jones, David H. (1988) *Muhammad and the spread of Islam*. Edinburgh: Holmes McDougall.

Kelen, Betty (2001) *Muhammad: The Messenger of God*. Montgomery, TX: Taylor.

Khan, Majid Ali (1998) *Muhammad: The Final Messenger*. New Delhi: Islamic Book Service.

Khan, Muhammad Zafrulla (1980) *Muhammad, Seal of the Prophets*. London: Routledge & Kegan Paul.

Lari, Mujtaba Musavi (2000) *The Seal of the Prophets and His Message*. Potomac, MD: Islamic Education Centre.

Malik, Ghulam (1996) *Muhammad: An Islamic Perspective*. Lanham, MD: University Press of America.

Motzki, Harald ed. (2000) *The Biography of Muhammad: The Issue of the Sources. Volume 32. Islamic History and Civilization: Studies and Texts*. Boston: Brill.

Muir, William (1988/ first published 1888) *The Life of Mahomet*. Ashland, OH: Biblio.

Nagel, Tilman (2000) *The History of Islamic Theology from Muhammad to the Present*. Princeton, NJ: Markus Weiner.

Nasr, Seyyed Hossein (1982) *Muhammad: Man of God*. London: Muhammadi Trust of Great Britain & Northern Ireland.

Newby, Gordon Darnell (2009) *The Making of the Last Prophet. A Reconstruction of the Earliest Biography of Muhammad*. Columbia: University of South Carolina Press.

Nursi, Bediuzzaman Said (2007) *The Letters. Epistles on Islamic Thought, Belief and Life*. Somerset, NJ: The Light.

O'Leary, De Lacy (1989) *History of Arabia before Muhammad*. Noida, India: Alliance.

Reeves, Minou (2003) *Muhammad in Europe. A Thousand Years of Western Myth-Making*. New York: New York University Press.

Rogerson, Barnaby (2003) *The Prophet Muhammad: A Biography*. Mahwah, NJ: Paulist.

Rubin, Uri (1995) *The Eye of the Beholder. The Life of Muhammad as Viewed by the Early Muslims*. Princeton, NJ: Darwin.

Rubin, Uri ed. (1998) *The Life of Muhammad*. Aldeshot, UK: Ashgate.

Safi, Omid (2009) *Memories of Muhammad. Why the Prophet Matters*. New York: Harper Collins.

Salahi, Adil (2002) *Muhammad: Man and Prophet*. London: Islamic Foundation.

Sells, Michael (2007) *Approaching the Qur'an: The Early Revelations*. Ashland, OR: White Cloud.

Stetkevych, Jaroslav (1996) *Muhammad and the Golden Bough: Reconstructing Arabian Myth*. Bloomington: Indiana University Press.

Stillman, Norman (1975) *The Jews of Arab Lands: A History and Source Book*. Philadelphia: Jewish Publication Society of America.

Zeitlin, Irving (2007) *The Historical Muhammad*. Oxford: Wiley Blackwell.

REFERENCES

Al-Tabari (trans. Ismail Poonawala) (1990) *The History of Al-Tabari. Volume IX. The Last Years of the Prophet*. New York: State University of New York.

Amer, Patrick (2008) *The Five Commandments of Jesus*. Bloomington, IN: iUniverse.

Amore, Roy C. (1978) *Two Masters, One Message. The Lives and Teachings of Gautama and Jesus*. Nashville, TN: Abingdon.

Andrae, Tor (2000) *Mohammed: The Man and His Faith*. Mineolo, NY: Dover.

Armstrong, Karen (1993) *Muhammad: A Biography of the Prophet*. San Francisco: Harper.

Armstrong, Karen (2000) *Buddha*. London: Weidenfeld & Nicolson.

Ashvaghosha (trans. Samuel Beal) (2010) *The Fo-Sho-Hing-Tsan-King. A Life of Buddha*. Oxford: Clarendon Press.

Blackburn, Barry L. (2011) "The Miracles of Jesus", in Graham H. Twelftree ed. *The Cambridge Companion to Miracles*. Cambridge: Cambridge University Press, 113–130.

Blomfield, Vishvapani (2011) *Gautama Buddha*. London: Quercus.

Borg, Marcus J. (1987) *Jesus: A New Vision*. New York: Harper Collins.

Borg, Marcus J. & Wright, N.T. (1999) *The Meaning of Jesus: Two Visions*. San Francisco: Harper.

Braden, Charles (1957) *Jesus Compared: A Study of Jesus and Other Great Founders of Religions*. Upper Saddle River, NJ: Prentice-Hall.

Breckenridge, Ian (2010) *Reclaiming Jesus*. London: CPI Antony Rowe.

Brown, Raymond (1999) *The Birth of the Messiah. A Commentary on the Infancy Narratives in Matthew and Luke*. New York: Doubleday.

Carmody, Denise & Carmody, John (1996) *In the Path of the Masters: Understanding the Spirituality of Buddha, Confucius, Jesus and Muhammad*. Armonk, NY: M.E. Sharpe.

Carpenter, Humphrey (1984) *Jesus*. Oxford: Oxford University Press.

Carrithers, Michael (1983) *The Buddha*. New York: Oxford University Press.

Cohen, Richard S. (2000) "Shakyamuni: Buddhism's Founder in Ten Acts", in David Freedman & Michael McClymond eds. *The Rivers of Paradise: Moses, Buddha, Confucius, Jesus and Muhammad as Religious Founders*. Grand Rapids, MI: W.B. Eerdmans, 121–232.

Cook, Michael (1983) *Muhammad*. Oxford: Oxford University Press.

Cook, Michael (2000) *The Koran. A Very Short Introduction*. Oxford: Oxford University Press.

Buddha, Jesus and Muhammad: A Comparative Study, First Edition. Paul Gwynne.
© 2014 John Wiley & Sons, Ltd. Published 2014 by John Wiley & Sons, Ltd.

Crone, Patricia (2004) *Meccan Trade and the Rise of Islam*. Piscataway, NJ: Gorgias.

Crone, Patricia & Cook, Michael (1977) *Hagarism: The Making of the Islamic World*. Cambridge: Cambridge University Press.

Crossan, John Dominic (1991) *The Historical Jesus. The Life of a Mediterranean Jewish Peasant*. New York: Harper Collins.

Dhammika, Shravasti (1992) *Middle Land, Middle Way*. Colombo: Buddhist Publication Society.

Drummond, Richard Henry (1995) *A Broader Vision: Perspectives on the Buddha and the Christ*. Virginia Beach, VA: A.R.E. Press.

Emerick, Yahiya (2002) *Muhammad*. Indianapolis, IN: Alpha.

Foucaux, Philippe Edouard trans. (1860) *Histoire du Bouddha Sakya Mouni (The Lalitavistara)* Paris: Benjamin Duprat.

Foucher, Alfred (1963) *The life of the Buddha, according to the ancient texts and monuments of India*. Middleton, CT: Wesleyan University Press.

Freedman, David & McClymond, Michael eds. (2000) *The Rivers of Paradise: Moses, Buddha, Confucius, Jesus and Muhammad as Religious Founders*. Grand Rapids, MI: W.B. Eerdmans.

Gabriel, Mark (2004) *Jesus and Muhammad: Profound Differences and Surprising Similarities*. Lake Mary, FL: Charisma House.

Garland, R. (2011) "Miracles in the Greek and Roman World", in Graham H. Twelftree ed. *The Cambridge Companion to Miracles*. Cambridge: Cambridge University Press, 75–94.

Gokhale, Balkrishna Govind (1995) *Ancient India: History and Culture*. Columbia, MO: South Asia Books.

Gombrich, Richard (2009) *What the Buddha Thought*. London: Equinox.

Green, Joey ed. (2002) *Jesus and Muhammad: The Parallel Sayings*. Berkeley, CA: Ulysses.

Guang Xing (2005) *The Concept of the Buddha*. London: Routledge.

Hassan, Riaz (2013) *Islam and Society: Sociological Explorations*. Melbourne: Melbourne University Press.

Haykal, Muhammad Husayn (2005) *The Life of Muhammad*. Oak Brook, IL: American Trust Publications.

Hilliard, F.H. (1956) *The Buddha, the Prophet and the Christ*. New York: MacMillan.

Horsley, Richard A. (1995) *Galilee: History, Politics and People*. London: Continuum.

Ibn Ishaq (trans. A. Guillaume) (1967) *The Life of Muhammad. A Translation of Ibn Ishaq's Sirat Rasul Allah*. Oxford: Oxford University Press.

Jeremias, Joachim (2002) *Jesus and the Message of the New Testament*. Minneapolis, MN: Fortress.

Johnson, Elisabeth (2003) *Truly Our Sister*. Sydney: Bloomsbury.

Jones, J.J. trans. (1952) *The Mahavastu. Volume II*. London: Luzac & Co.

Keown, Damien (1996) *Buddhism. A Very Short Introduction*. Oxford: Oxford University Press.

Lings, Martin (1983) *Muhammad. His Life Based on the Earliest Sources*. London: Allen & Unwin.

Madelung, Wilferd (1997) *The succession to Muhammad: A study of the early Caliphate*. Cambridge: Cambridge University Press.

Margoliouth, David (1905) *Mohammed and the Rise of Islam*. New York: Putnam.

McClymond, Michael J. (2000) "Jesus", in David Freedman & Michael McClymond eds. *The Rivers of Paradise: Moses, Buddha, Confucius, Jesus and Muhammad as Religious Founders*. Grand Rapids, MI: W.B. Eerdmans, 309–456.

Meier, John P. (1991) *A Marginal Jew: Rethinking the Historical Jesus. Volume 1: The Roots of the Problem and the Person*. New York: Doubleday.

Meier, John P. (1994) *A Marginal Jew: Rethinking the Historical Jesus. Volume 2: Mentor, Message, Miracles.* New York: Doubleday.

Meier, John P. (2001) *A Marginal Jew: Rethinking the Historical Jesus. Volume 3: Companions and Competitors.* New York: Doubleday.

Meier, John P. (2009) *A Marginal Jew: Rethinking the Historical Jesus. Volume 4: Law and Love.* New York: Doubleday.

Mizuno, Kögen (1980) *The Beginnings of Buddhism.* Tokyo: Kosei.

Murcott, Susan (1991) *First Buddhist Women. Poems and Stories of Awakening.* Berkeley, CA: Parallax.

Nakamura, Hajime (2001/2005) *Gotama Buddha. A Biography Based on the Most Reliable Texts. Volumes I and II.* Tokyo: Kosei.

Nigosian, Solomon A. (2004) *Islam: Its History, Teaching, and Practices.* Bloomington: Indiana University Press.

Novakovic, L. (2011) "Miracles in Second Temple and Early Rabbinic Judaism", in Graham H. Twelftree ed. *The Cambridge Companion to Miracles.* Cambridge: Cambridge University Press, 95–112.

Oldenberg, Hermann (2010/first published 1881) *Buddha: His Life, His Doctrine, His Order.* Whitefish, MT: Kessinger.

Panikkar, Raimundo (1989) *The Silence of God: The Answer of the Buddha.* London: Orbis.

Perrin, Norman (1976) *Jesus and the Language of the Kingdom.* Minneapolis, MN: Fortress.

Peters, F.E. (1994) *Muhammad and the Origins of Islam.* Albany: State University of New York Press.

Peters, F.E. (1995) *The Hajj. The Muslim Pilgrimage to Mecca and the Holy Places.* Princeton, NJ: Princeton University Press.

Peters, F.E. (2011) *Jesus and Muhammad. Parallel Tracks, Parallel Lives.* New York: Oxford University Press.

Peterson, Daniel C. (2001) *Muhammad, Prophet of God.* Grand Rapids, MI: W.B. Eerdmans.

Phipps, William E. (1999) *Muhammad and Jesus: A Comparison of the Prophets and Their Teachings.* London: Continuum.

Rahman, Fazlur (2009) *Major Themes of the Qur'an.* Chicago: University of Chicago Press.

Rahula, Walpola (1974) *What the Buddha Taught.* New York: Grove.

Ramadan, Tariq (2007) *The Messenger. The Meanings of the Life of Muhammad.* London: Allen Lane.

Rodinson, Maxime (2002) *Muhammad.* London: Penguin.

Safrai, Ze'ev (1994) *The Economy of Roman Palestine.* New York: Routledge.

Sanders, E.P. (1985) *Jesus and Judaism.* Philadelphia: Fortress.

Sanders, E.P. (1993) *The Historical Figure of Jesus.* New York: Penguin.

Sartre, Maurice (2005) *The Middle East Under Rome.* Harvard, MA: Belknap Press.

Schimmel, Annemarie (1985) *And Muhammad is His Messenger: The Veneration of the Prophet in Islamic Piety.* Chapel Hill: University of North Carolina Press.

Stein, Burton (1998) *A History of India.* Oxford: Blackwell.

Strong, John (2001) *The Buddha: A Short Biography.* Oxford: Oneworld.

Thapar, Romila (2004) *Early India: From the Origins to AD 1300.* Berkeley, CA: University of California Press.

Thomas, David (2011) "Miracles in Islam", in Graham H. Twelftree ed. *The Cambridge Companion to Miracles.* Cambridge: Cambridge University Press, 199–215.

Thomas, Edward Joseph (1969/first published 1927) *The Life of Buddha as Legend and History.* London: Routledge & Kegan Paul.

Thundy, Zacharias P. (1993) *Buddha and Christ: Nativity Stories and Indian Traditions.* Boston: Brill.

Twelftree, Graham H. ed. (2011) *The Cambridge Companion to Miracles*. Cambridge: Cambridge University Press.

Vermes, Geza (1973) *Jesus the Jew*. London: Collins.

Vermes, Geza (2001) *The Changing Faces of Jesus*. New York: Penguin.

Von Grunebaum, G.E. (1970) *Classical Islam. A History 600AD to 1258AD*. New York: Aldine.

Von Pochhammer, William (2005) *India's Road to Nationhood*. Mumbai: Allied Publishers.

Watt, William Montgomery (1953) *Muhammad at Mecca*. Oxford: Oxford University Press.

Watt, William Montgomery (1956) *Muhammad at Medina*. Oxford: Oxford University Press.

Watt, William Montgomery (1961) *Muhammad: Prophet and Statesman*. Oxford: Oxford University Press.

Weddle, David (2010) *Miracles. Wonder and Meaning in World Religions*. New York: New York University Press.

Welch, A.T. (1993) "Muhammad" in C.E. Bosworth et alia eds. *Encyclopedia of Islam* (2nd ed.). New York: E.J. Brill, Volume VII, 360–376.

Wilson, A.N. (1992) *Jesus*. New York: Norton.

Zwettler, Michael (1990) "A Mantic Manifesto", in James Kugel ed. *Poetry and Prophecy: The Beginnings of a Literary Tradition*. Ithaca, NY: Cornell University Press, 75–119.

INDEX

Buddha, Jesus and Muhammad: A Comparative Study, First Edition. Paul Gwynne.
© 2014 John Wiley & Sons, Ltd. Published 2014 by John Wiley & Sons, Ltd.